For Martha, Josh, and Nathaniel,
with affection.

The
American
Political
System

Little, Brown and Company

Boston   Toronto

The
American
Political
System

A Radical Approach

Fourth Edition

Edward S. Greenberg
University of Colorado

Library of Congress Cataloging-in-Publication Data

Greenberg, Edward S., 1942-
   The American political system.

   Includes bibliographies and index.
   1. Business and politics--United States.
2. Marxian economics. 3. United States--Politics and
government--1945-   4. United States--Economic
conditions--1945-   I. Title.
JK467.G69 1986   320.973   85-25624
ISBN 0-316-32685-2

Library of Congress Catalog Card No. 85-25624

ISBN 0-316-32685-2

9   8   7   6   5   4   3   2   1

HAL

Published simultaneously in Canada
by Little, Brown & Company (Canada) Limited

Printed in the United States of America

The author gratefully acknowledges
permission to use the following material:

Text: Pages 4–5: © 1968 by The New York Times Company. Reprinted by permission. Page 95:
© 1984 by The New York Times Company. Reprinted by permission. Pages 206–207: Abridged from
pp. 81, 87–88 in "Letter from Birmingham Jail—April 16, 1963" from *Why We Can't Wait* by Martin
Luther King, Jr. Copyright © 1963 by Martin Luther King, Jr. Reprinted by permission of Harper &
Row, Publishers, Inc.
Illustrations: opposite page 1, United Mine Workers of America; page 7, Earl Dotter/American
Labor; page 21, BBC, Hulton Picture Library; page 26, © Bob Adelman, 1979/Magnum Photos; page
34, Bruce Davidson, © 1970/Magnum Photos; page 39, BBC, Hulton Picture Library; page 47, Bill
Owens, Photographer; page 58, The National Archives; page 64, The Supreme Court Historical Society;
page 84, The Museum of Modern Art/Film Stills Archive; page 91, © Dennis Brack, 1979/Black Star;
page 96, Cary Wolinsky/Stock, Boston; page 104, John Launois/Black Star; page 112, Ellis Her-
wig/Stock Boston; page 121, M. E. Warre/Photo Researchers; page 130, AP/Wide World Photos; page
136, Pete Souza/The White House; page 153, © Mark Pokempner, 1982/Black Star; page 171, Library
of Congress; page 172, Reprinted by permission of Newspaper Enterprise Association; page 177, J. L.
Atlan/Sygma; page 199, UPI/Bettman Newsphotos; page 206, © James H. Karales; page 218, Owen
Franken/Sygma; page 224, AP/Wide World Photos; page 233, UPI/Bettman Newsphotos; page 240,
AP/Wide World Photos; page 253, UPI/Bettman Newsphotos; page 286, United States Air Force
Photo; page 297, Library of Congress; page 304, UPI/Bettman Newsphotos; page 316, UPI/Bettman
Newsphotos; page 318, Melvin Grier; page 336, © Charles Harbutt/Archive Pictures; page 344, J. P.
Laffont/Sygma; page 347, © Burk Uzzle, 1969/Magnum Photos.

Preface

This edition has been revised to lend greater coherence to its main line of argument and to incorporate the most important implications of what some have called the Reagan Revolution. I have cut material from previous editions that is tangential to my main point of view, and I have woven the thread of the argument throughout each of the chapters. I have done this by continuously addressing the interrelationships of American politics, American capitalism, social justice, and democracy. In each section of the text, I have also tried to incorporate the Reagan phenomenon, assessing its impact on American culture, the shape of the economy, the conduct of politics, and the content of public policy.

Table
of Contents

    The Giant Corporations   111

    What Is a Corporation?   112
    Some Implications of Corporate Economic Power   119
    Corporate Power and Democratic Control   122
    Concluding Remarks   126
    Notes   127
    Suggestions for Further Reading   128

PART III: THE POLITICAL PROCESS   131

8   The Group Process and
    the Politics of Unequal Power   132

    The Group Process   133
    The Background of Political Decision Makers   135
    The Politics of Corporate Power   142
    The Myth of Labor Union Power   152
    Concluding Remarks   156
    Notes   157
    Suggestions for Further Reading   159

9   Elections Amidst Inequality   160

    Money in American Electoral Politics   161
    Problems of Political Accountability   168
    The Meaning of Elections   182
    Concluding Remarks   186
    Notes   187
    Suggestions for Further Reading   189

10 Protest and Disruption:
    The Politics of Outsiders   191

    Politics as Bargaining   192
    Disruption as Bargaining   193
    The Vote in the History of Black Americans   194
    Beyond the Ballot   204
    The Prospects and Limits of the Politics of Disruption   211
    Concluding Remarks   215

The
American
Political
System

Letter written by Jacob L. Vowel shortly before he died of suffocation in the 1902 Fraterville, Tennessee, mine disaster.

Ellen, darling, goodbye for us both. Elbert said the Lord has saved him. We are all praying for air to support us, but it is getting so bad without any air.

Ellen I want you to live right and come to heaven. Raise the children the best you can. Oh how I wish to be with you, goodbye. Bury me and Elbert in the same grave by little Eddy. Goodbye Ellen, goodbye Lily, goodbye Jemmie goodbye Horace. We are together. Is 25 minutes after two. There is a few of us alive yet.

Jake and Elbert

Oh God for one more breath. Ellen remember me as long as you live. Goodbye darling

Part

I

Overview and

Analytic Approach

In this section, the reader is introduced to the principal themes of the text and to the theoretical materials that will serve as guideposts in our trek through the sometimes confusing landscape of American political, economic, and social life.

1

Capitalism
and American Politics:
An Introduction to
Central Themes

AN INTRODUCTION:
DEATH, MAYHEM, AND PUBLIC POLICY

□ Of the butchers and floorsmen, the beef boners and trimmers, and all those who used knives, you could scarcely find a person who had the use of his thumb; time and time again the base of it had been slashed, till it was a mere lump of flesh against which the man pressed the knife to hold it. The hands of these men would be criss-crossed with cuts, until you could no longer pretend to count them or to trace them. They would have no nails—they had worn them off pulling hides; their knuckles were swollen so that their fingers spread out like a fan. There were men who worked in the cooking rooms, in the midst of steam and sickening odors, by artificial light; in these rooms the germs of tuberculosis might live for two years, but the supply was renewed every hour. There were the beef-luggers, who carried two-hundred-pound quarters into the refrigerator-cars; a fearful kind of work, that began at four o'clock in the morning, and that wore out the most powerful men in a few years. There were those who worked in the chilling rooms, and whose special disease was rheumatism; the time limit that a man could work in the chilling rooms was said to be five years. There were the wool-pluckers, whose hands went to pieces even sooner than the hands of the pickle men; for the pelts of the sheep had to be painted with acid to loosen the wool, and then the pluckers had to pull out this wool with their bare hands, till the acid had eaten their fingers off. There were those who made the tins for the canned meat; and their hands, too, were a maze of cuts, and each cut represented a chance for

2

blood poisoning. Some worked at the stamping machines, and it was very seldom that one could work long there at the pace that was set, and not give out and forget himself, and have a part of his hand chopped off. There were the "hoisters," as they were called, whose task it was to press the lever which lifted the dead cattle off the floor. They ran along upon a rafter, peering down through the damp and the steam; and as old Durham's architects had not built the killing room for the convenience of the hoisters, at every few feet they would have to stoop under a beam, say four feet above the one they ran on; which got them into the habit of stooping, so that in a few years they would be walking like chimpanzees. Worst of any, however, were the fertilizer men, and those who served in the cooking rooms. These people could not be shown to the visitor—for the odor of a fertilizer man would scare any ordinary visitor at a hundred yards, and as for the other men, who worked in tank rooms full of steam, and in some of which there were open vats near the level of the floor, their peculiar trouble was that they fell into the vats; and when they were fished out, there was never enough of them left to be worth exhibiting—sometimes they would be overlooked for days, till all but the bones of them had gone out to the world as Durham's Pure Leaf Lard![1]

☐ You may wonder why asbestos workers walk backwards. They don't always walk backwards. It is only going upstairs. They are so short of breath that after two steps they have to sit down. It is easier to go up a flight of stairs backwards than walking up. It is a terrible way to die.[2]

☐ REPRESENTATIVE DANIELS: Why did these people who work on the farm become sick?

MRS. OLIVERAS: Because the day before, they spray the field. The next morning they put the people in the field and they took about six of these workers to the doctor and the doctor talked to the people. He said they get sunstroke. The people are going to get sunstroke by seven o'clock in the morning?[3]

☐ A young sprayer was found dead in the field in the tractor which had been pulling his spray-rig. He had been pouring and mixing parathion concentrate into the spray-rig tank. Parathion has an estimated fatal dose of about nine drops orally and thirty-two drops dermally. In the process of mixing the concentrate, the worker contaminated his gloves inside and out. He rested his gloved hands on his trousers as he pulled the rig to apply the spray. Parathion was absorbed through the skin of his hand and thighs. He began to vomit, an early symptom of parathion poisoning. He could not remove his respirator and he aspirated the vomitus. The diagnosis of poisoning was confirmed by postmortem cholinesterase tests.[4]

☐ When I went to work, I was in good health, I thought, as a boy of that age. I could get out and run and play and wasn't bothered any. So I went to work in the carding department. . . .

The mill then was much more open than today. But I began to notice when I would play I couldn't breathe as good as I could before I went to work. Being young and not thinking much about it, I kept on going at it, and finally I married and then I was hooked to keep on working.

So I kept on working and my breathing kept on getting worse. I went along, and I got to the point where I would just cough and sometimes hang over a can and cough and become nauseated in my stomach, and I began to be bothered about my condition.

I decided that maybe this dust was doing that. I started taking a little bit closer watch on that and taking a little closer check on it. I have seen three-hundred-watt electric bulbs in the plant that I worked in where the ceiling was high, and they looked like they were red and not much more than a twenty-five watt bulb. When the mill would run two or three days, you could look up and see the light bulbs and they looked like they were red. You could get over by the window where the sun was shining through, and the dust particles were so thick when you looked into that sunshine that it looked like you could just reach out and grab a handful of it. . . .

Apparently, people would look at me and say that I am in very good physical shape. All of my life I have been very active, but now I am short of breath, and I can't do anything. I get so short of breath and so weak, I can hardly go.

As far as I see things, and as far as the doctor says, I will be like this as long as I live.[5]

☐ He often had to clean out large tanks that had been used to store toxic chemicals. He sometimes got dizzy and groggy at work. Like a good soldier, he would continue to work and not complain. Then one day he blacked out at home. He began to spit blood. . . . Jim began to develop skin lesions all over his body.

Jim took off time from work during the worst onslaughts of dizziness, but he went back as soon as he possibly could. He had a family to support. At work one day, the foreman told him to climb inside a particularly noxious chemical tank and clean it out. Jim refused, saying that there wasn't enough breathable air in it. The foreman told Jim that if he didn't do what he was told he'd be laid off for ten days. This was not a union ship and Jim had absolutely no recourse. "I got a family and the rent to pay and my phone and light and my transportation to and from work. So I went ahead and cleaned the tank because I couldn't afford to be off. I had four kids at home then." His only protection was a mask that didn't really stop any of the toxic fumes.

By late 1979 Jim was unable to work any longer. He just couldn't breathe if he was on his feet for any length of time. Schwinn fired him since he wouldn't work. Jim's medical insurance was dependent on his working at Schwinn. He lost the insurance when he lost the job.[6]

☐ On November 20, 1968, at 5:25 A.M., a massive explosion at Consolidation Coal Company's No. 9 mine at Farmington, West Virginia, snuffed out the lives of seventy-eight miners. According to the experts, the explosion was detonated by a lethal combination of methane gas (the mine, strangely enough, was situated above a massive natural gas field) and high concentrations of coal dust caused by inadequate safety procedures on the part of Consolidation Coal. The No. 9 mine had been found in violation of government rock dusting requirements in every inspection made in the five years previous to the disaster at Farmington.[7] One federal mine inspector reported that during his inspection of the mine the previous August, he had reported four serious violations of federal safety laws.[8] Yet, in the immediate aftermath of the disaster, public and private officials rushed to Farmington to absolve Consolidation Coal and its parent company, Continental Oil, from any moral responsibility or legal culpability.

"We must remember that this is a hazardous business and that what has occurred here is one of the hazards of being a miner."

—Gov. Hulett C. Smith of West Virginia

"Unfortunately—we don't understand why these things happen—but they do happen. . . . The company here has done all in its power to make this a safe mine."

—J. Cordell Moore, Assistant Secretary of the Interior

"If the mine was unsafe, we would have stopped operations and that's all there is to it."

—William Parks, Bureau of Mines, Department of the Interior

"I share the grief. I've lost relatives in a mine explosion. . . . This happens to be one of the better companies, as far as cooperation with our union and safety is concerned."

—Tony Boyle, President, United Mine Workers

"Whatever is our fate, may we accept it."

—The Rev. John Barnes, Farmington, West Virginia

Working miners, on the other hand, were under no illusions about the cause of the disaster:

"It's been filled with gas . . . something was bound to happen."[9]

—Ora Haught, miner for twenty-seven years

BUSINESS, GOVERNMENT, AND THE WORKPLACE

Work, it seems, is hazardous to one's health. The overall figures on the scope of the hazard in the United States are staggering in their dimensions. On the average, over 5 million Americans are injured on the job annually, over 400,000 contract *new* cases of disabling occupational disease, more than 100,000 die from such diseases, and 14,000 die in accidents. This level of carnage must strike even the most casual observer as the equivalent of full-scale warfare in its effects. More Americans died from job accidents or from work-related diseases annually, in fact, than were killed in combat action during the same years in Korea or Vietnam.[10]

Mining is particularly dangerous, especially in the United States which has by far the *worst* safety and health record in the industrialized western world. The United States' violent death rate in mining, for instance, is almost four times greater than that of Great Britain, and six times that of the Netherlands. Indeed only Zimbabwe, Namibia, and South Africa have worse records, despite the fact that American mines enjoy uniquely favorable conditions—"seams which are thicker, more horizontal, closer to the surface, and less gaseous"[11] than those found in most other parts of the world. Farmington was but a dramatic instance of the generally bloody history of the mining industry. Though records are not entirely accurate, one student of mining history estimates that "in the 100 years that partial records of fatal mine accidents have been kept . . . more than 120,000 men have died violently in coal mines, an average of 100 every month for a century."[12] By all estimates, mining is the most dangerous occupation in the United States, with an injury rate four times greater than the industrial average. Mining leads in both *severity* of injuries and in total number of injured persons. Furthermore, miners lead workers in all other occupations in the incidence of what might be called slow death. Among miners aged sixty to sixty-four, the "natural" death rate is eight times that of workers in any other industrial occupation.[13] This slow and painful death derives from years of breathing coal dust, which eventually leads to the condition known as pneumoconiosis, or "black lung." Well over 100,000 today suffer its effects. And it is not a pretty way to live or die:

> I was a coal miner for thirty-nine years. I went to work in the coal mine when I was thirteen years old. Out of the thirty-nine years, I served five years in the armed forces in World War II. I had to quit work on account of pneumoconiosis, or black lung, whichever you want to call it, and I was advised by ten different doctors to quit work, that I am not supposed even to drive my car. I am not supposed to go fishing. I am not supposed to do anything according to the depositions from the doctors. I have, and I am supposed to fall dead any time. I never sleep at night. I stay awake and sleep on the average about two and one-half hours a day, and most of that is sitting in a chair. I never had any pleasure out of life at all since I had to quit the mine. On eight different occasions I was hauled out of the mine because I was passing out because I could not get enough air to breathe.[14]

Despite the hue and cry raised against the supposed perfidies and absurdities of OSHA (Occupational Safety and Health Administration) in recent years by business corporations and their spokespersons, the history of government involvement in questions of job safety has been one of general neglect and indifferent enforcement of the law. Concerned about the prerogatives of business and sensitive to the need for corporate profitability, political leaders have turned their attention to the hazards of the workplace with the greatest reluctance and only after years of pressure from workers, unions, and reformers.

Take mine safety as an example. Government has not been of much assistance to working miners because industry-government relations have generally been collusive and cooperative rather than antagonistic. In West Virginia, in eastern Kentucky, and in eastern Tennessee, where most deep mining is done, the coal companies have literally *been* the government for at least three generations. In the early days of the industry, most miners lived in company towns owned, organized, and closely managed by the coal companies. In more modern times, coal company power and money—particularly with local populations largely immobilized by exhaustion, poverty, and fear—have been the guiding forces in select-

Slow death: a black lung victim

ing both elected and appointed officials, particularly county judges, sheriffs, and tax commissioners (to say nothing of senators, representatives, and governors).[15] Selection of sheriffs and tax commissioners is particularly important to mine corporations; sheriffs police the often unruly miners, and tax commissioners keep coal company taxes at a minimum. Needless to say, such officials have not been overly eager to either propose or execute safety legislation.

The record of the federal government is not much better. To be sure, a number of mine safety laws dot the statute books, but these laws have not eliminated the mayhem in American mines. Federal mine safety legislation usually follows a predictable sequence of events: a major mining tragedy rouses public opinion; mine safety legislation is pushed through Congress. Characteristically, this legislation is rife with loopholes and industry-favoring compromises, or it is unenforceable, or simply unenforced. For instance, one act passed in 1941 gave the Bureau of Mines power to designate equipment as "permissible" or "nonpermissible," but no power to control the use of such equipment. Between 1941 and 1952, when the legislation was amended, at least half of all mine explosions, resulting in 835 deaths, were caused by the electric arcs of "nonpermissible" equipment.[16] The amended mine safety legislation of 1952 included a "grandfather'' clause by which companies could continue to use nonpermissible equipment already in place or on order. Much of this equipment, now rebuilt two or three times, is still in use. The 1952 act also exempted deaths and injury not related to major disasters from federal jurisdiction. Most accidents and deaths result from roof collapses at the working face of the mine and involve but a handful of miners at any one time.

The public outcry over the Farmington disaster caused mine safety legislation to be strengthened considerably. Yet, though the safety performance of the industry greatly improved during the 1970s, American deep-pit coal mining remained the most dangerous in the industrialized western world. This was not so much because of deficiencies in the Mine Safety Act of 1969 but because of deficiencies in its use and enforcement, which are listed as follows.

1. There were not enough federal mine inspectors to accomplish the safety goals specified in the law, especially after President Carter froze the budget for hiring inspectors in 1978.
2. Inspections of mines were usually announced in advance, giving mine companies time to temporarily fix or to disguise unsafe practices.
3. Inspectors rarely imposed solutions to unsafe conditions, typically negotiating compromise settlements with mining corporations instead.
4. Maximum fines allowable under the law are almost never imposed. Consolidation Coal was assessed $2,872,317 for 14,090 violations of the Mine Safety Act of 1969 between 1969 and 1972, but paid only $896,355.[17]
5. Although they have the legal power to do so, federal mine inspectors rarely shut down an operation, even when faced with flagrant, repeated, and demonstrably dangerous violations.

Given these shortcomings in the 1969 Coal Mine Health and Safety Act and its enforcement, disasters such as the one at Farmington have remained an unwelcome yet persistent factor in the mining industry. On March 9, 1976, twenty-six miners were killed in an explosion at the Scotia Coal Company mine in Oven Fork, Kentucky. The explosion was triggered by the electric arc of an archaic locomotive operating in a shaft in which illegal ventilation practices had caused lethal concentrations of methane gas. Investigators also noted a consistent failure to comply with monitoring and inspection requirements. Between 1970 and the time of the explosion, Scotia had been cited for 855 violations of federal standards. Yet in the face of this history of violations of the law and in the wake of the disaster, the chief of the Division of Safety for the Mine Enforcement and Safety Administration was moved to say that "Scotia stands tall in the industry" in matters of mine safety. Is it any wonder that between the Farmington and Scotia disasters over one thousand miners lost their lives despite the existence of the Mine Safety Act?[18]

Apparently, even these less than perfect efforts by the federal government to ensure the safety of coal miners was too much for the Reagan administration. In an attempt to end what Mine Safety and Health Administration director Ford B.

Ford has termed the "traditional adversarial relationship" between government and the coal operators, the Reagan administration further decimated the enforcement of the mine safety laws: the enforcement budget was drastically cut, the size of the inspection staff was reduced, fewer inspections were carried out, the number of citations dwindled, and the average amount of fines for safety violations shrank steadily. Director Ford is even reported to have promoted a scheme whereby the coal companies would police themselves and certify on their own that their operations were safe. This war on business regulation had the effect of seriously eroding working conditions for American coal miners. By the end of Reagan's first term, deaths in the mine were at their highest level since the early 1970s.[19] At the end of 1984, just before Christmas, twenty-seven miners died in a fire at the Wilberg Mine in Utah.

Much the same story can be told of the Occupational Safety and Health Act signed into law by President Nixon on December 29, 1970. Passed amid high hopes and florid rhetoric, the legislation was, in fact, less than it seemed. It represented an important step toward the protection of employees in the workplace, to the extent that it mandated "the greatest possible protection of the safety and health of the affected employee," required employers to provide a workplace "free from recognized hazards," gave individual workers and union locals a role in setting and enforcing standards, and granted OSHA the authority to inspect, issue citations for violations, and propose penalties; but business recalcitrance, legislative loopholes, and inconsistent enforcement have served to disappoint expectations in this seemingly revolutionary legislation.

The inclination of the Nixon administration was to depend on voluntary compliance with the legislation and soft persuasion, and to that end it appointed businessmen to head OSHA and its major divisions. Furthermore, OSHA based its inspections in its first years on safety standards formulated by the various industry trade associations, organizations that one would expect would be solicitous of employee concerns. Given the paucity of inspectors, only a tiny fraction of workplaces were visited by OSHA every year, and in those cases where violations were noted, fines were generally so small that most companies simply absorbed them as a minor cost of production. Between 1971 and 1975, in fact, the *average* penalty imposed by OSHA came to a mere $25. Business enterprises also became quite adept at contesting and delaying the process of inspection, citation, and penalty, and thus at minimizing the need to rectify hazardous conditions, through an elaborate appeals process. Many companies simply refused to comply and forced OSHA and complaining employees to seek redress in lengthy and costly court procedures. Workers thus found themselves at a great disadvantage, standing virtually alone against a battery of corporate lawyers. Without the desire or the ability to tackle the major violators of health and safety, OSHA was mainly reduced to writing "nitpicking" standards like the infamous ones mandating the design and use of toilet facilities.

During the administration of Jimmy Carter, who, it seems, owed his election to the labor union vote, and under the leadership of Eula Bingham, OSHA entered a brief period in which it enforced more rigorously than before the letter and the spirit of the law by issuing more stringent standards, increasing the rate of inspections, and slightly stiffening penalties. The result was a small yet significant improvement in the wholesomeness of the American work environment. Needless to say, the increased cost and inconvenience encouraged business leaders and their allies to launch a concerted and highly effective campaign to gut OSHA. The attack came from many directions. Corporate spokespersons complained about economic inefficiencies and costs[20] to their enterprises caused by OSHA requirements and bureaucratic bungling, and with their considerable resources were soon able to dominate the debate on the nation's airwaves and in its corridors of government power. To these public relations activities were joined the not-so-subtle threats by some corporations to move their production facilities to Third World nations less concerned about the safety of their workforce. Hand in hand with these attacks came the widespread practice of noncooperation (in terms of reporting data, opening enterprises to inspection, complying with directives), as well as a series of successful court challenges to the right of OSHA safety inspectors to enter the workplace unannounced.

In a very short period of time, the ground under the work safety movement had shifted dramatically. By the end of the Carter administration, OSHA officials had begun to retreat before the counterattack of the business community and to speak in terms of relying more on market forces and less on government coercion as a means to encourage healthy workplaces. By 1980, a series of measures with broad bipartisan support were introduced in the Congress designed to restrict the standard-setting, inspection, and enforcement machinery of the Occupational Safety and Health Administration. Under the openly pro-business regime of Ronald Reagan, the retreat within OSHA was given further impetus by severe cuts in the OSHA budget, by the new requirement that all regulations be subjected to "cost-benefit" analysis (initiated under President Carter), by a slowdown in the process of setting safety standards, and by appointment of agency leadership hostile to the agency's mission. Reagan's OSHA director Thorne Auchter, for instance, was a Florida construction company executive whose company had been repeatedly cited for safety violations by OSHA. He gained immediate fame by ordering the destruction of 100,000 copies of an OSHA booklet on "brown lung" which he found to be offensive and biased in favor of labor.

In short order, then, OSHA had been tamed, confined to activities that could, without too much exaggeration, be termed cosmetic. Leon Kruchten, for one, an electrician at the Oscar Mayer plant in Madison, Wisconsin, can attest to the change of OSHA into a "cooperative regulator" (Auchter's apt term). Sustaining major injuries while working at the Oscar Mayer plant because of a surge of 13,000 volts through his body, Kruchten received some satisfaction from an initial OSHA ruling in 1983 that Oscar Mayer's unsafe working conditions warranted a citation for a "serious" violation and a fine of $640. After consulting with company and union representatives, the citation was changed to "nonserious" and the fine was rescinded.[21] The thinking of the new OSHA was captured in a memo written by the chief attorney of the Department of Labor advising Auchter to loosen enforcement of the safety laws: "The relatively low profile of enforcement activities allows greater flexibility and avoids adverse public reaction. . . . ''[22]

THE ORIENTATION OF THE TEXT

You may be wondering by now what this extended discussion of occupational death, disease, and injury has to do with a textbook on American government and politics. To put it simply, it has *everything* to do with American government and politics; in its many tragic details may be found the essence of our political life, broadly and properly understood. In it we may discern the reality of business control of the workplace and of the conditions of daily existence of most Americans; the treatment of citizens of a democratic country as mere factors of production; the vast extent of the economic, political, and social role of concentrated private economic power; the close collaboration of business and governments at all levels in the United States; the pro-corporate bias in the letter and the administration of the law; the public policy continuities between Democratic and Republican administrations through the years; and the unequal distribution of political power. The various stories of death and injury on the job and the government response to these problems set out at the beginning of this chapter are, then, paradigmatic of the American system and a particularly dramatic way to introduce you to the central concerns and viewpoints of this book. The remainder of the book is, in some respects, merely a generalization from these examples to other aspects of American life. They graphically indicate the themes and concepts that will recur with some frequency in these pages: the nature of business enterprise, the relationship of business to government, the distribution of power and privilege in America, and the living conditions of working Americans. They open the way as well to a consideration of broader questions: What is capitalism and what are its implications for social and political life? How do the major institutions of economic and political life relate to each other? How do economic factors limit possibilities of political choice? How do political decisions affect economic organization and performance? What is the nature of democratic citizenship in a modern society where political, economic, and social power and influence are unevenly distributed?

What is unusual about the analysis in this book is that I do not consider political and governmental processes in spendid isolation but only as they are imbedded in and interact with an identifiable social structure and a particular kind of economic system. In fact, social structure and economy are treated prior to government and politics in this book because of my belief that together they determine the nature of the social problems with which government must deal, the range of permissible options for government policy makers, and the distribution of political power and influence. In other words, I approach the understanding of normal politics (elections, representation, public opinion, and the like) only after I grapple with the problem of understanding the structure, operation, and implications of American capitalism.

At a more concrete level, I am interested in this text in the general patterns of distribution of *social rewards and decision-making power* in American life, and in *the role that government and politics play in determining the shape of these distributions.* The text is mainly organized around the question raised by political scientist Harold Lasswell many years ago: "Who Gets What, When, and How?" In the attempt to answer this general question, the analysis in this text will focus on the following questions:

The distribution of social rewards and burdens:
1. How are wealth, income, shelter, health, security, legal justice, political rights, and the like distributed in American life?
2. What is the role of the capitalist economy in determining these patterns of distribution?
3. What is the role of government and politics in determining these distributions? What are the distributional implications of the vast and varied activities of government in the United States?

The distribution of social decision-making power:
1. Who or what decides the agenda of American politics and government?
2. Who or what determines the main directions of economic development?
3. Who or what shapes the cultural environment?
4. Who or what determines the contours of the material environment?
5. Do some social groups dominate decision-making in all or several of these sectors?
6. In which sectors is government decisive?
7. Why does government act as it does?

This book is concerned with the overall impact of government activity in an environment of corporate capitalism. It focuses less on institutions than on public policy and its impact on society. It seeks to understand why government does what it does with its vast resources and manpower, how it came to act in the way it does, and with what consequences it carries out its functions.

Political life also comprises values, ethics, the search for the good life; it is concerned with issues about which people feel strongly. The political analyst is invariably caught up in the issues and problems that wrack political life, and that give it its energy and color. The analyst cannot stand completely aloof in scientific objectivity, but imposes personal values on his or her work. Rather than deplore this situation, which is natural and inevitable, we ought to accept it and proceed with our analysis on that basis. If we are self-conscious, aware of our values, our predispositions, and our special points of view, we can use them as standards by which to judge the worth of political processes and outcomes. I shall attempt to do that here. I shall not only *describe* the American system, but ask about its worth, its utility, and its moral standing. In addition to describing, in short, I want to *evaluate*. To evaluate, one must construct clear, precise, and consistent standards against which to judge the American system. The two standards that seem to arise naturally from descriptions of the distributions of social rewards and decision-making power are *social justice* and *democracy.* Chapter 2 will defend these choices and discuss their various meanings.

NOTES

1. Upton Sinclair, *The Jungle* (New York: Harper & Row, 1951), pp. 98–99.
2. Testimony of Dr. Irving J. Selikoff before the Senate Subcommittee on Labor, May 5, 1970.
3. Testimony of Lupe Oliveras, member United Farm Workers Organizing Committee, before the House Select Subcommittee on Labor, November 21, 1969.
4. Steve Wodka, "Pesticides Since Silent Spring," in Garrett de Bell, ed., *Environmental Handbook* (New York: Ballantine, 1970), p. 85.
5. Testimony of Lacy Wright before the Senate Subcommittee on Labor, April 28, 1970.
6. Lawrence White, *Human Debris: The Injured Worker in America* (New York: Seaview/Putnam, 1983), p. 50.
7. *The New York Times,* November 22, 1968.
8. Ibid.
9. All of the above quotes are from *The New York Times,* November 22, 1968.
10. For these and related statistics, see Daniel M. Berman, *Death on the Job* (New York: Monthly Review Press, 1978); and White, *Human Debris.* Berman makes a convincing case that official statistics systematically understate the problem.
11. Paul Nyden, "An Internal Colony: Labor Conflict and Capitalism in Appalachian Coal," *The Insurgent Sociologist* 8:4 (Winter, 1979), p. 34.
12. Ben Franklin, "The Scandal of Death and Injury in the Mines," *New York Times Magazine,* March 30, 1967, p. 122.
13. Ibid.
14. *President's Report on Occupational Safety and Health,* Commerce Department Clearing House, May 22, 1972, p. 111.
15. Governor Aretas Brooks Fleming remained on retainer to major energy companies during his entire term of office. For penetrating analyses of the economics and politics of the Appalachian region see: Harry Caudill, *Night Comes to the Cumberlands* (Boston: Little, Brown, 1962); Harry Caudill, *Theirs Be the Power: The Moguls of Eastern Kentucky* (Urbana, Illinois: University of Illinois Press, 1983); and John Gaventa, *Power and Powerlessness: Quiescence and Rebellion in an Appalachian Valley* (Urbana: University of Illinois Press, 1980).
16. Franklin, "The Scandal of Death and Injury in the Mines," p. 124.
17. *United Mine Workers Journal,* July 1–15, 1974, p. 9.
18. Harry M. Caudill, "Manslaughter in a Coal Mine," *The Nation,* April 23, 1977, p. 496.
19. Jerry DeMuth, "The Deadly Results of Coal Deregulations," *America,* January 8, 1983, pp. 8–10.

20. Most studies have, in fact, demonstrated that the costs of safety compliance are no-where near as burdensome as business interests claim. See James Crawford, "The Dis-mantling of OSHA," *The Nation,* September 12, 1981, pp. 205–207.
21. Philip Simon and Kathleen Hughes, "OSHA, Industry's New Friend," *New York Times,* September 5, 1983, p. 17.
22. Cited in White, *Human Debris,* p. 149.

2

Evaluating the
American System:
Justice and Democracy

The aim of this book is to help readers understand the political arrangements and institutions characteristic of their society; to grapple with the implications of these political phenomena for their lives; and to compare the political life of their society to that of others. Understanding social systems and institutions always involves a twofold process: first, a factual understanding of the principal relationships under consideration, and second, a capacity for making judgments about the ultimate worth of such relationships. Most of this text will be devoted to a detailed description of the empirical or factual processes involved in the complex world of American politics. The purpose of this chapter is to demonstrate how one might make informed judgments about the worth of American political arrangements.

Most of the time, we tend to evaluate political, social, and economic practices carelessly, working from a base of common sense and unexamined prejudices. Informed evaluation, on the other hand, requires a clearly articulated and consistently applied set of standards against which to compare these practices. There are, of course, many possible standards for evaluating American political life, ranging from efficiency to equity. Since we are uniting description and evaluation as two parts of the process of understanding in this text, however, we shall use the evaluative standards that most reasonably evolve out of the empirical analysis.

Our first concern is with the general distribution of goods, benefits, services, and burdens in American society. The following questions immediately arise when one observes such distributions: "Is it right?" "Is it fair?" "Is it just?" These questions can be subsumed under a category customarily termed *social justice*.

Our second general concern is with the distribution of decision-making power in American society. The questions that immediately suggest themselves have to do with the relative balance between elites and masses in the decision process, and the relative influence of ordinary citizens versus representatives of wealth and property. Such considerations ultimately lead to the issue of *democracy*.

Is America just? Is America democratic? These two questions will be raised continually throughout the remainder of the book. The questions seem appropriate not only because of their logical connection to the factual materials we shall be examining, but because they are questions about which Americans have been deeply concerned since the founding of the Republic.

SOCIAL JUSTICE

Is America a just society? The problem we face in trying to answer this question is that no generally agreed upon definition of justice exists. Indeed, *justice* has been used in such a wide variety of ways that one is tempted to consider the word meaningless. What lies at the heart of the confusion about justice is that all such definitions are based upon personal moral and ethical positions. In any consideration of justice, one cannot avoid making some hard moral choices; there is no neutral, scientific procedure for arriving at a universally acceptable definition. Since the term "justice" has been used so ambiguously and since people differ widely in their ethical choices, it is likely that any two people, if asked, would give different definitions. How then can we construct a standard of justice against which to measure the American system?

In fact, we cannot arrive at a single, unified definition of social justice about which all Americans might agree. It is possible, however, to identify a handful of enduring positions to which political philosophers, political practitioners, and the public have gravitated over the centuries. The following discussion examines these positions. Particular attention is paid to the assumptions made by each theory of justice, the institutional arrangements considered appropriate to each, and the expected relative inequality in benefit distribution. As you attempt to answer the question "Is America just?" by examining the empirical materials that come later in this text, you should keep these various formulations of justice in mind.

Classical Conservatism and Social Justice

To avoid confusion, the conservatism I refer to in this section has little to do with what we call conservatism in the United States today, the conservatism of Barry Goldwater, William F. Buckley, Milton Friedman, Richard Vigurie, George Gilder, or Ronald Reagan. As strange as it may seem, the position of these individuals is, in an historical sense, a form of *liberal* theory. Historically understood, classical conservatism is a system of thought that arises primarily out of feudal and aristocratic societies characteristic of Europe, and is virtually nonexistent in the United States. Opposed to such traditional American values as progress, change, mobility, open opportunity, and equality of rights, classical conservatism poses the necessity and desirability of stability, order, harmony, social *in*equality, and leadership by a natural aristrocracy.

Plato is the best-known proponent of the classical conservative position. His *Republic* sketches the outlines of an ideal society characterized by perfect justice, which he defines as harmony and order. Much as in the healthy human body each organ plays a particular and restricted function, so also in society harmony exists when all individuals perform functions appropriate to their innate abilities. The just society is one in which such attributes can be identified in people, where people can be assigned appropriate roles, and where they can be convinced to remain happily at their assigned functions.

To Plato, people have neither comparable abilities nor potentialities. In his view, most people are fit only for various forms of productive labor, primarily small-scale farming. Another and smaller group of people is fit, by virtue of temperament and physical ability, for fighting and soldiering. Finally, an extremely small group, because of its intellect and philosophic training, is capable of true knowledge and is therefore fit to govern society. A just society is one in which each class of people plays its assigned function. To Plato, such an arrangement serves both the requirements of society (which must produce the means of subsistence, and be protected and governed) and the requirements of citizens, who are happiest when doing that for which they are most suited. This mode of thinking remains the basis for all forms of classical conservatism to the present day.[1]

Feudal Europe and the medieval Catholic church also held a basically conservative world view, one stressing order, loyalty, harmony, and place. The justification for such a social order was based not upon a Socratic form of reasoning, as was true for Plato, but upon natural law known through divine revelation. Despite these differences in method of deduction, Plato and the church fathers agreed about the static nature of human society, the fixed places of various classes of people, the harmony that is possible only through loyalty, obedience, and narrowly restricted personal initiative, and the necessity and appropriateness of governance by a naturally superior class of people.

In the late eighteenth century English parliamentarian Edmund Burke formulated his version of classical conservative doctrine in the course of attacking the virus of the French Revolution. Even in its moderate stage, the French Revolution posed a series of dangers in Burke's mind, for it spread ideas of progress, change, social contract, and personal initiative. Such an upheaval could only cause anguish to a man who argued that society was not something created by a contract among men (and thus revocable by men), but was rather a holy, organic thing, created both by divine guidance and by the historical experience of the human race. A revolution that destroyed at a stroke the French *ancien régime* could only cause horror to one who conceived a naturally static society in which each class had a fixed place, and in which a natural aristocracy, because of convention, tradition, and its own ability, was alone fit to provide society with cultural, social, spiritual, and political guidance. To Burke, inequality in all things was not only inescapable, but necessary in a harmonious and just society.

The conservative position is sharply distinguished from the other positions we shall discuss in its frank admission of the necessity, inevitability, and desirability of inequality in all sectors of social life, from access to rights and privileges to the distribution of material benefits. Other positions assume that equality is an unarguable, axiomatic value, that unequal treatment of some members of society relative to others, while permissible, needs convincing justification.

Classical conservatism never found a home in America, given the absence of a feudal past with its characteristic landed aristocracy, the weakness in the early Republic of the Catholic church, and the presence of an open frontier society where status differences were difficult to sustain. This is not to say, of course, that no such conservative seedlings were planted in American soil—note especially John C. Calhoun, George Fitzhugh, and their defense of slavery—but we can say that the soil proved most inhospitable.

Classical Liberalism and Social Justice

The liberal theory of justice is the position most familiar to Americans, as it is the bedrock of the American culture. (This will be further discussed in Chapter 3.) It is a system of thought derived from the experience of early market society and from reflections on such societies by such philosophers as Adam Smith, David Ricardo, and John Locke. The starting point for this formulation of justice is a belief in the self-regulating nature of the free market and in the naturally acquisitive, competitive character of human beings. Justice, in this view, is what happens in an ideal free market where each individual is free to pursue his or her self-interest and to acquire property.

Rather than review all of the many varieties of liberal thought, let us turn to what is perhaps the most widely acclaimed modern statement of the liberal theory of justice, Robert Nozick's *Anarchy, State and Utopia*.[2] Nozick's starting point is the claim that "individuals have rights, and there are things no person or group may do to them [without violating their rights]" (p. ix). Of all these rights, however, there is one that stands out in importance: the right to accumulate, enjoy, and transfer property. From this premise, Nozick proceeds to construct a defense for the accumulation of unequal wealth in a just society.

To what possessions is a person entitled? Nozick's response is that a person is entitled to those things acquired through a just process. A just process of acquisition, following the lead of philosopher John Locke, is the accumulation of property holdings through the exercise of one's talents and labors in such a way that no other person is worse off by not having available that which was accumulated. Individuals have the right, after accumulating property holdings, to do with their possessions anything that does not intrude upon the province of others, including transferring those possessions to others through gifts and inheritances. To Nozick, justice is about a process, a right way of doing things and not about results. There is no a priori method to judge the justice of any final distribution of material things. The existence of significant inequalities in income, wealth, housing, health care, and so on, tells us nothing about the justice or injustice of a society. The determination of justice is tied exclusively to a determination of whether individuals are *entitled* to the possessions they have under the distribution. The proper procedure to determine this is to inquire into the justice of the original acquisition of possessions and their transfer to others.

To define justice as anything other than a process, according to Nozick, cannot help but interfere with the rights of some individuals. People, in their infinite variety and complexity, will voluntarily choose to do diverse things with their possessions. Any distribution based on some value requires that some people be forcibly separated from their possessions whether it be in the name of merit, morality, equality, or some other value. Any such distribution, in Nozick's view, is not only arbitrary but unjust, because it interferes with the right of individuals to use their possessions as they see fit.

In short, a just distribution is *any* distribution that results from a just process. This just process entails a marketplace characterized by voluntary participation and free competition. Justice is, therefore, equality of rights and equality of opportunity. Justice is silent about the final form of benefit distributions. In the real world, this understanding of the concept of justice can be and has been used to justify rather severe inequalities in material conditions.

Twentieth-Century Liberalism. Nozick follows a long line of laissez-faire liberal theorists stretching from Adam Smith and John Locke to Milton Friedman and George Gilder. These theorists believe the just society to be immanent in the free operations of the marketplace. Most liberals in the twentieth century, however, while continuing to give primacy to the institutions of private property and the marketplace, have felt terribly uncomfortable with the severe inequalities allowed—indeed, required—by the free market position. These liberals have made various attempts to incorporate some measure of equality into liberalism. Modern liberals, among them Presidents Wilson, Roosevelt, Truman, Kennedy, and Johnson, while retaining a belief in the marketplace and in the need to protect property, have also believed that government is obliged to intervene in economic and social life in order to dampen the sharp inequalities that are a natural byproduct of the free market.[3] Government must at least minimally care for some of the wreckage wrought by its operations: poverty, unemployment, pollution, and the like. Because they believe in the primacy of private property, however, liberal political leaders have not found it possible to attack the main institution that generates inequality. While the modern liberal's heart tugs toward greater equality, the commitment to the primacy of free-enterprise capitalism traps him forever in the mire of inequality.[4]

Socialism and Social Justice

While classical conservatism celebrates inequality, and classical liberalism allows for stark inequalities of distribution in practice, socialism has always been committed to substantial equality as a basic element of a just society. To be sure, some inequalities in the distribution of benefits and burdens have appeared in societies that call themselves socialist (though to a far lesser degree than in capitalist so-cieties).[5] Some socialist thinkers have not even made the question of equality the first priority: Marx, for instance, was more interested in questions of exploitation and alienation. Yet the belief that the good society is one in which equality is the operative rule of social organization pervades the history of socialist thought. Though pre- and post-Marx socialists have often disagreed about the means of social change, the role of the vanguard party, or the function of the state, post-revolutionary, postcapitalist society is conceived as one composed of freely asso-ciated, equal producers who shape their group life through voluntary cooperation.[6]

The socialist position has always been that by virtue of their common hu-manity, people are equal in rights, claims, and potential. To allow substantial inequality is to reject this common humanity: hence, the urgent needs of all must be met before the private claims of the few. Inequality represents an attack on the human essence: it denies most people the opportunity to participate fully as citizens in the political life of the community, and it denies them the right to determine the directions of their creative and productive life. From this perspec-tive, exploitation, alienation, and material inequality merge into a single problem for socialists.

To socialist thinkers, equality is one of the central standards by which both capitalist and socialist societies may be judged. In Marx's words (in *The German Manifesto*), ''one of the most vital principles of communism . . . is its view . . . that differences of brain, of intellectual capacity, do not imply any differences whatsoever in the nature of the stomach, and of physical needs; therefore, the false tenet . . . 'to each according to his capacity,' must be changed . . . into the tenet 'to each according to his need.''' Or more simply, socialism is only assured when distribution of all benefits and burdens follows the maxim (from *The Com-munist Manifesto*), ''from each according to his ability; to each according to his need.''

Socialists also argue that the traditionally perceived opposition between lib-erty and equality, the claim that freedom and equality are contradictory concepts, is false, since inequalities in material condition block the free exercise of liberties. Equality, in this view, is the precondition for the expression of human individ-uality. Only with an end to the exploitation of the many by the few, and the strengthening of common humanity through material, social, and political equal-ity, will humankind have constructed the base upon which true diversity of human abilities, interests, and needs can freely develop. It is only after individuals de-velop their uniquely human capacities that fellowship and fraternity become pos-sible.

Social Justice as Evaluative Standard

The discussion of justice may seem to some readers a confusing trip through the philosophic bramble bushes, while to others it might appear to be an oversim-plification of a most complex subject. Granted the danger of offending both sets of readers, it would probably be useful to summarize the analysis thus far. I would

Karl Marx: the giant of the socialist tradition

suggest that discussions of social justice have organized themselves around three primary nodes:

- ☐ *Classical Conservatism:* the belief that inequality of status and condition is not only inevitable and natural, but basic to the operations of the good society. This is considered true particularly to the extent that the naturally superior are better able to guide society.
- ☐ *Classical Liberalism:* the belief that the just society is one in which people have equal opportunity to practice civil and political freedoms, and to pursue their self-interest in the marketplace. Inequality, while not celebrated, is interpreted as a natural byproduct of a free society. Moreover, the effort to eliminate inequality is seen as potentially dangerous to the free society itself.
- ☐ *Socialism:* the belief that the good society is one composed of social, political, and economic equals.

It is evident, then, that no single definition of social justice is available to us, although we have narrowed the perhaps hundreds of conflicting positions down to three. To the question "Is America just?" we now have three clearly articulated positions from which to choose. These positions can act as standards against which to measure the real-world activities and practices of American society.

This book will demonstrate that *the United States is not a just society* by whatever standard one chooses to use. It is certainly not surprising that the United States meets neither the classical conservative test, that being a historically archaic position never very popular in this country, nor the stringent socialist test of equality. What is striking is the degree to which it fails to meet the rather minimal classical liberal tests of equality of rights, freedoms, and opportunities. Such a failure is not merely accidental, but is inherent (as we shall see in subsequent chapters) in the very economic organization of liberal society: capitalism.

DEMOCRACY

As was true for the concept of justice, it is impossible to locate a single, mutually agreed upon definition for the concept of democracy. While it might seem quite simple and uncomplicated on its face, the term *democracy* has been used in many contradictory ways. The problem with the concept is its great popularity. The word *democracy* has gained such esteem around the globe that virtually all political regimes attempt to envelop their rule in democracy's nimbus. We thus hear of *people's democracies, stockholder democracy, union democracy, pluralist democracy, interest group democracy, socialist democracy* and so on. Confusion and ambiguity have invariably followed in the wake of this popularity. To most Americans, democracy is essentially a system of political organization in which certain rights and liberties exist. By so defining democracy, they miss other, perhaps richer ways of thinking about and practicing democracy.[7]

As we did with social justice, we shall examine three primary ways in which democracy has been defined. We shall attempt to demonstrate that no single democratic theory exists, and that there are competing notions, each of which implies different citizen behavior, different expectations of human capacities, and different institutional arrangements.

Participatory Democracy

Most Americans associate democracy with elections, representation, and civil liberties. Yet until recent times the core meaning of democracy has been the organization of political society so that *direct, face-to-face* participation by ordinary people in their own governance is assured.[8] In its original meaning, democracy simply meant government by and for the common people. It was understood as a system of governance and a way of life in which the great mass of ordinary people acted publicly to affect the directions of collective life. One immediately thinks of the New England town meeting and the Israeli kibbutz as modern examples of this ancient form of democracy.

Central to this notion of democracy is a belief in direct, face-to-face partic-ipation in community decision making. To the Greeks, the meaning of the term *citizen* was inseparable from this notion of continuous involvement in the public life of the community. To be a passive observer, to be unconnected to the decision processes that established the overall direction of community affairs, was to be a noncitizen. To the Greeks, citizenship did not entail a set of *rights* and *freedoms* opposed to the interests of the community—that is, it was not a "negative" con-cept involving freedom from interference by others, including government (as in our Bill of Rights)—but a set of obligations and opportunities to participate in governance. One might even go further and say that to the Greek mind, people were only human to the extent that they were part of and involved in the life of human community, and to the extent that they interacted with other human beings in the public arena. In such a public space, through public discussion, deliberation, and argument, it was believed that the distance between ruler and ruled would be obliterated, as would the distance between amateur and profes-sional politician, making for a situation of political equality and mutual respect (see Figure 2.1).[9]

Involvement in public deliberations whereby community life is directed is thus at the heart of this conception of democracy. Taking the reverse side of this democratic coin, theorists of direct participatory democracy have often defined "tyranny" not so much as the transgression of rights and freedoms by a ruler, but as the interference by the ruler in the legitimate participatory role of the citizen. As Hannah Arendt has stated:

> Tyranny . . . was a form of government in which the ruler, even though he ruled according to the laws of the realm, had monopolized for himself the right of action, banished the citizens from the public realm into the privacy of their households, and demanded of them that they mind their own, private business.

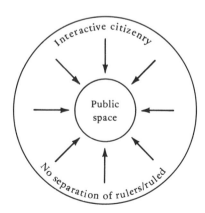

FIGURE 2.1 Classical participatory democracy

Tyranny, in other words, deprived the public of happiness, though not necessarily of private well-being, while a republic granted to every citizen the right to become "a participator in the government of affairs," the right to be seen in action.[10]

The conception of democracy as "direct," "face-to-face," and "participatory" (that is, not mediated through other persons or institutions) represents an important deviation from historic conceptions of the proper organization and operation of the political community. Social and political thought through the ages has tended toward autocratic, aristocratic, or elitist notions of governance. To most political practitioners and thinkers, governance was a difficult art requiring the greatest sophistication, intelligence, character, and training. It was not something to be left to the whims and devices of ordinary people. Whether one finally settled on a superior social class, a king, a philosopher, or a religious elect as the proper ruler, most political philosophers and practitioners imposed formidable barriers to the participation of the common person in government.

When seen against centuries of such thinking, it is clear that democratic theory, defined as self-governance by ordinary people, represented an important departure. Most of the thinkers acknowledged today as the progenitors of democracy believed that everyone has deliberative and moral potential; that, given the proper education and environment, ordinary people could be responsible and reflective. At the heart of classical democratic theory is this faith in the capacity of ordinary human beings to govern themselves wisely.

> The foundation of democracy is faith in the capacities of human nature; faith in human intelligence and in the power of pooled and cooperative experience. It is not belief that these things are complete but that if given a show they will grow and be able to generate progressively the knowledge and wisdom needed to guide collective action.[11]

Liberal-Representative Democracy

Central to direct democracy is the notion that government and the governed are identical, that no distance exists between ruler and ruled; or, more basically, that within the boundaries of the political community, ruler and ruled are identical: *citizens*. In a principal competing model of democracy, *representative democracy*, government and the governed are separate and distinct, and politics becomes not a process of deliberation but of forging instruments by which citizens may exercise some control over and protection against government leaders (see Figure 2.2). In this conception, the people rule indirectly, through representatives authorized to make policy decisions in the name of those who elected them. While citizen participation remains an important constituent element, it is limited to the periodic election of persons who act as representatives, and to the occasional transmission of instructions to them.

Why representative democracy rather than the inherently more appealing "direct" variety? Why substitute an essentially two-step process of participation

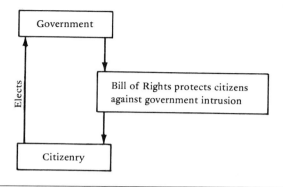

FIGURE 2.2   Liberal-representative democracy

for the more unitary one? Most central to these questions, in the view of political scientist Robert Dahl, are problems of size and time.[12] First, there is an upper limit to the size of a group that can meet and deliberate face to face. Once a certain maximum size is surpassed, it is not feasible to allow everyone to express a view or opinion about whatever matter is under consideration. Second, a general meeting of the political community cannot be in continuous session, since all members of that community have other concerns to which they must attend, including those of family and livelihood.

While representative forms of democracy can compensate for certain inherent problems in the "direct," participatory variant, it is itself prone to serious difficulties relating to the distance between citizen, representative, and government. First, to reiterate a point already made, participation in such a system is only intermittent, revolving mainly around the election of representatives and the occasional conveyance of demands or expressions of concern to those representatives. Such a limited involvement potentially destroys the capacity of self-governance to be educative and broadening in its effect. Second, representative democratic systems have a strong tendency to create a professional political class—a group of people who make life as a representative a full-time occupation, while the ordinary citizen assumes amateur status. The possibility that this professional class will go its own way, evolving policy in directions inconsistent with popular desires, is obvious. Finally, as the distance between government and governed becomes pronounced, a central concern of the governed becomes that of defining and protecting a private space into which a potentially threatening government might intrude unless limited and constrained. It is with respect to this recurrent problem that questions of rights and liberties come center stage, and the conception of active self-governance recedes to the wings. The sacred core of political life becomes the protection of the people against government interference with the exercise of their liberties. For most Americans, the essence of democracy has come to mean a system in which individual freedoms exist (freedom of speech, asso-

Indirect democracy: voting for representatives

ciation, religion, and so on); in which certain judicial rights are available (such as due process of law, trial by jury, freedom from self-incrimination); and in which people have the right to freely elect representatives.

Pluralist Democracy

Modern political science has formulated yet another conception of democracy: pluralism, or pluralist democracy. This formulation, rooted in the writings of James Madison (especially in his justly famous #10 of *The Federalist*) and given modern form by political scientists Robert Dahl, Charles Lindblom, and David Truman (among others) in the 1950s, represents a rejection of direct, participatory democracy and an extension of representative democracy. Participatory democracy is rejected because of its proported "utopian" qualities, that is to say, the impossibility of its functioning in a modern, populous, industrial society. Representative democracy is seen in the pluralist view as correct yet limited in the sense that it fails to capture the richness and complexity of the functioning modern democracies like the United States.[13]

Pluralism starts from two basic assumptions:

1. *That citizens of the United States do not measure up to the standards set by theorists of democracy.* Theorists of direct democracy such as J. S. Mill and Rousseau talked about a democratic citizen who was essentially *rational, informed,* and *interested* in political life. Such a description, say the pluralists, sets much too great a demand on the limited capacity of ordinary people. This is demonstrated by social science research that clearly demonstrates that most Americans are uninformed about politics and are neither overly interested nor particularly sophisticated about political events.

2. *That the system works.* Pluralists argue that while the distance between pluralism and the classical, participatory conception is enormous, the American system works, and often with distinction. It not only provides for the peaceful transfer of power between ruling groups but for a method whereby the voices of all groups with interests in government policy are heard and considered.

In juxtaposing research evidence about the shortcomings of American citizens with their own belief in the democratic character of the United States, political

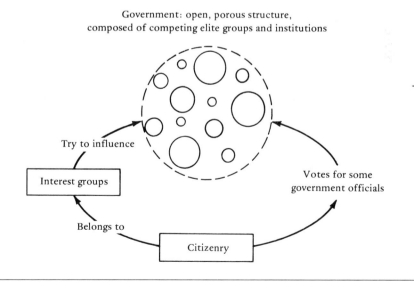

FIGURE 2.3   Pluralist democracy

scientists go on to claim that it is the prevailing theory of democracy that is wrong, not the operating system, and that democratic theory must, as a result, be reformulated. What does this theory look like?

The Functional Necessity of Apathy. Since most citizens are uninformed, uninterested, and often irrational in political areas, it is best that they should remain apathetic, especially since the system works so well. Indeed, since the system works the way it does without widespread popular involvement, it must follow that there is something necessary or functional about apathy.

Apathy is not evenly distributed through the population, but is correlated very strongly with the stratification system. Those near the top of the social strata are more likely to be participants than those near the bottom. We should be thankful for this, because it is primarily among the masses that we find, according to sociologist Seymour Martin Lipset, extremist-millennial religious movements (implying rigid fundamentalism and dogmatism), irrationality and prejudice, insecurity and instability, simplistic views and personal concerns, and anti-intellectualism and authoritarianism.

In light of this picture of the uninvolved yet potentially dangerous mass, we should not regret noninvolvement (as do "get out the vote" groups), but heave a sigh of relief that things are as they are. If this untapped pool were mobilized, it would be a source of extreme danger and instability for the democratic system of the United States, according to this view.

If we cannot depend on the mass population for support of democratic principles and practice, to whom can we turn? How does the system continue to operate as well as it does?

Democracy and Elites. From Jefferson's profound skepticism about elites, most contemporary political scientists have come to believe that the very survival of democratic systems depends on elites who are the repository for democratic values. Thus political scientist V. O. Key, after reviewing evidence from public opinion studies that seemingly demonstrate that persons from the upper reaches of society are more likely than the lower to hold to democratic norms (tolerance, belief in free speech, openness to public opinion, playing by the rules, rejection of "total politics," and so on), argues that *"the critical element for the health of a democratic order consists in the beliefs, standards, and competence of those who constitute the influentials, the opinion-leaders, the political activists in the order."*[14]

This is closely related to the concept of functional apathy. Since elites are supportive of a democratic system, and since the masses have serious antidemocratic tendencies, it is fortunate that politics is primarily the domain of elites. This phenomenon has been praised as the *division of political labor,* allowing elites the elbow room they need for action in a world of great complexity and danger. Interference from ordinary citizens brings emotionalism, irrationality, and delay into the deliberations of policy makers.

It is not at all apparent how a system based on elite policy making and mass noninvolvement can legitimately be called democracy. How do pluralists deal with this thorny problem? They do so by means of two methods for transmitting mass wants, aspirations, and demands to government officials: elite competition and interest groups.

Elite Competition. We have seen that those who are economically, socially, and educationally "better off" are the major actors in politics. It is the less well off who make up the bulk of the apathetic. We have also heard the claim that such a state of affairs is fortunate, given the democratic proclivities of the elites and the antidemocratic proclivities of the masses. *What keeps this division of labor from evolving into a rigid oligarchy is the intense competition among groups of elites.* The elite stratum is united only on the "rules of the game"; beyond that, it is riven by deep divisions of interest and inclination. *Moreover, it is primarily by means of this competition that elites remain open and responsive to pressure from the mass public.* Thus elite competition, whether taking place through elections or through interest group conflict and bargaining, serves democratic values. As Dahl says, "Democratic theory is concerned with processes by which ordinary citizens exert a relatively high degree of control over leaders."[15] Perhaps the purest statement of the relationship between elite competition and the body of citizens was made by Joseph Schumpeter in *Capitalism, Socialism and Democracy.* His claim is that the democratic process involves nothing more than a method by which potential leaders compete for the vote, and where the role of the citizen is to help produce a government, to choose leaders, and then to withdraw from participation. Government, in a nice reversal of Lincoln, is not government *by* the people but one occasionally *approved* by the people.

Interest Groups. Pluralists understand society to be composed of a complex set of groups, each with a distinct set of interests and goals. Pluralists also assume that most Americans belong to a variety of groups and seek through such groups, ranging from the American Medical Association to the NAACP and the American Automobile Association, to advance their own interests and aspirations. It is the competition and bargaining among and between these many groups that is the essence of the political process. The role of government, in the pluralist view, is that of umpire (setting and enforcing the "rules of the game") and score-keeper. Government is the score-keeper in the sense that the public policies it produces (laws, regulations, and so on) are simply the formal outcomes of the various contests between and the bargains struck among the many interest groups in American society.

This interest group system, in the pluralist view, is democratic in two fundamental ways. First, groups are so easy to form that ordinary Americans may choose to form one whenever they feel the need to advance their interests and aspirations in the political process. Second, government in the United States is so permeable and accessible—through elections, the courts, lobbying, and the like—that any and all groups in society can have their views heard and considered at some point in the policy-making process. To the pluralists, while democracy is quite indirect in this conception, it is truer to the ways in which actual democracies work in places like the United States and Great Britain.

Democracy as Evaluative Standard

In attempting to answer the question "Is America democratic?" we now have available three distinct models of democracy that can be used to evaluate the everyday operations of the American system. Each one asks us to look at different aspects of that system. The participatory model compels us to look at the civic lives of Americans, and to ask whether they are active participants in the processes by which public policies are decided. Liberal-representative democracy compels us to look at the state of civil liberties in the United States, the availability of juridical rights, and the quality of the relationship between elected representatives and the electorate. Pluralism asks us to look at elites in American society with an eye toward determining the extent to which they are competitive, open, and responsive to mass aspirations and at the vitality and competitiveness of the interest group system. I shall take the perhaps surprising position in this book that *the United States does not fulfill the expectations of any of the democratic models,* though, to be sure, it comes closer to fitting some (liberal-representative) than others (participatory). You are urged, of course, to reach your own conclusions, comparing the factual materials to the models in the pages that follow.

CONCLUDING REMARKS

This chapter has developed several ways to evaluate the American system, to answer the questions "Is America just?" and "Is America democratic?" There are, to be sure, any number of other ways to evaluate the American system. Nevertheless, *social justice* and *democracy* remain the most important standards of evaluation in this book, not only because of their obvious connections to the descriptive materials we will encounter in the chapters that follow, but also because of the great concern for social justice and democracy that Americans have demonstrated throughout their history.

This discussion of the forms of justice and democracy should serve other important functions as well. It should demonstrate that most political language is value-laden and imprecise (when people use words such as *justice, democracy, community,* and *freedom,* one ought to ask what is meant by them); that modern social science comes perilously close to traditional conservative and aristocratic views without openly admitting so; and most importantly, that other possibilities exist in the world, that alternative forms of social and political organization are available, and that political systems are open to and capable of change. Finally, the discussions of justice and democracy should have demonstrated to you the necessity of stepping outside the boundaries of your own system to make evaluations and to develop standards of judgment independent of particular systems.

NOTES

1. Plato, however, unlike all other conservative thinkers, did not equate the right to rule with the right to hold disproportionate riches.
2. Robert Nozick, *Anarchy, State and Utopia* (New York: Basic Books, 1974).
3. For a discussion of twentieth-century government policy and its connection to liberal reform, see Edward S. Greenberg, *Capitalism and the American Political Ideal* (Armonk, N.Y.: M. E. Sharpe, 1985); and Alan Wolfe, *The Limits of Legitimacy* (New York: The Free Press, 1977).
4. The processes by which property generates inequality will be extensively examined in later chapters. For a provocative attempt to tie liberalism to equality see John Rawls, *A Theory of Justice* (Cambridge, Mass.: Harvard University Press, 1971).
5. For a comparison between capitalist and socialist inequalities see Branko Horvat, *The Political Economy of Socialism* (Armonk, N.Y.: M. E. Sharpe, 1982), and Frank Parkin, *Class Inequality and Political Order* (New York: Praeger, 1971); see also Branko Horvat, "Welfare of the Common Man in Various Countries," *World Development* 2:7 (July 1974); and Jay Mandle, "Basic Needs and Economic Systems," *Review of Social Economics* 38:2 (October 1980), pp. 179–189.
6. R. H. Tawney poses the appropriate response to those who oppose equality on practical grounds. "To say that since men can never have complete equality they should not try to do it, is like using the impossibility of absolute cleanliness as a pretext for rolling in a manure heap." From R. H. Tawney, *Equality* (London: Allen and Unwin, 1952).
7. For a brilliant discussion of the many meanings of democracy, see C. B. MacPherson, *The Real World of Democracy* (Oxford: Clarendon Press, 1965).
8. This form is called "unitary democracy" by Jane Mansbridge in her book *Beyond Adversary Democracy* (New York: Basic Books, 1980).
9. It is important to add that the Greeks held to a narrowly construed concept of the eligibility pool. The slave class, for instance, was not admitted to citizenship in the polity.
10. Hannah Arendt, *On Revolution* (New York: Viking, 1965), p. 127.
11. John Dewey, *The Public and Its Problems* (New York: Holt, 1927), p. 211.
12. Robert Dahl, *After the Revolution* (New Haven: Yale University Press, 1970).
13. The following discussion of pluralism is based upon a synthesis of the major works on this topic. While the synthesis may not be perfectly representative of any single work, my hope is that the general description I present is true to the basic intent of each. The seminal works on pluralism are the following: Bernard Berelson, "Democratic Theory and Public Opinion," *Public Opinion Quarterly* 16 (Fall, 1952) pp. 313–330; Bernard Berelson, Paul Lazarsfeld, and William McPhee, *Voting* (Chicago: University of Chicago Press, 1954); Robert Dahl, *A Preface to Democratic Theory* (Chicago: University of Chicago Press, 1956); Robert Dahl, *Who Governs?* (New Haven: Yale University Press, 1961); Robert Dahl and Charles E. Lindblom, *Politics, Economics and Welfare* (New York: Harper & Row, 1963); V. O. Key, *Public Opinion and American Democracy* (New York: Alfred H. Knopf, 1961); Seymour Martin Lipset, *Political Man* (New York: Doubleday, 1963); Giovanni Sartori, *Democratic Theory* (Detroit: Wayne State University Press, 1962); and Joseph A Schumpeter, *Capitalism, Socialism and Democracy* (New York: Harper & Row, 1950). For some fascinating second thoughts about the nature of pluralism, see Charles Lindblom, *Politics and Markets* (New York: Basic Books, 1977).

14. Key, *Public Opinion and American Democracy*, p. 537.
15. Dahl, *A Preface to Democratic Theory*, p. 3.

SUGGESTIONS FOR FURTHER READING

Robert A. Dahl. A PREFACE TO DEMOCRATIC THEORY. *Chicago: University of Chicago Press, 1956.* A concise statement of the pluralist theory of democracy.

Charles Lindblom. POLITICS AND MARKETS. *New York: Basic Books, 1977.* A stimulating reexamination of pluralist democracy with particular emphasis on the incompatability of the giant corporation and genuine democratic politics.

C. B. MacPherson. A REAL WORLD OF DEMOCRACY. *Oxford: Clarendon Press, 1965.* A stimulating tour of the several meanings of democracy.

Jane Mansbridge. BEYOND ADVERSARY DEMOCRACY. *New York: Basic Books, 1980.* A highly influential empirical study of the tension in organizations between unitary and adversary democracy.

John Stuart Mill. ON REPRESENTATIVE GOVERNMENT. *London: Everyman edition, 1910.* The classic formulation and defense of representative democracy.

Robert Nozick. ANARCHY, STATE AND UTOPIA. *New York: Basic Books, 1974.* Award-winning exposition of the classical liberal position on distributive justice.

Carole Pateman. PARTICIPATION AND DEMOCRATIC THEORY. *London: Cambridge University Press, 1970.* A careful analysis of the contending democratic traditions and a spirited defense of the participatory form.

John Rawls. A THEORY OF JUSTICE. *Cambridge: Harvard University Press, 1971.* A widely discussed philosophic attempt to infuse the liberal theory of justice with equality.

R. H. Tawney. EQUALITY. *London: Allen and Unwin, 1952.* A classic statement of the socialist commitment to equality.

Part

II

The Context
and Basis of
American Politics

This section of the book argues that to understand American life in general and American political life in particular one must first understand capitalism—its defining characteristics, its typical means of operation, its principal supporting ideas and ideologies, and its implications for the everyday lives of the American people.

3

The Cultural Milieu:
Liberalism

AMERICA AS A LIBERAL CULTURE

Every stable society is tied together and sustained by widely disseminated sets of ideas about what is right and proper in political, economic, and social life. The United States is no exception to this general rule, for it is shaped and significantly directed by an elaborate and coherent system generally labelled *liberalism*. One cannot possibly understand American politics without first coming to grips with liberalism, for its ideas, values, and assumptions pervade every nook and cranny of our society and leave their mark on virtually every social, economic, and political decision we make individually or collectively. Liberalism is, in the words of one scholar, *the* American ideology."[1] To another writer, liberalism is "the whole of [American] history."[2] From the viewpoint of eminent historian Louis Hartz, America has always been "a liberal civilization."[3] By this he means one in which notions of individualism, private property, the self-regulating market, and limited government hold center stage. An understanding of liberalism is vital in any effort to understand the American system; to a great extent, it is the basis for our major ideas about politics, about economic life, and, ultimately, about ourselves. Liberalism has no serious rival as a system of ideas in America.

Liberalism, like many other concepts used in this book, is not unambiguous in meaning. The ideas that together comprise liberalism are so familiar and pervasive, so much a part of our lives, that they seem obvious, commonsensical, even universal in their applicability. They have become the unexamined and unques-

36

tioned premises of the American people; since they are so familiar, we rarely think carefully about them, or, more important, about how commitment to such values affects our lives.

There is also the persistent problem of ambiguous terminology. Both modern liberals (stretching from Franklin Delano Roosevelt to Tip O'Neill and Ted Kennedy) *and* modern conservatives (stretching from Robert Taft and Barry Goldwater to Ronald Reagan and William F. Buckley) are liberal in the traditional meaning of that term. Modern liberals and modern conservatives are but two currents within the general classical liberal tradition (see Figure 3.1). While members of these two modern currents of the liberal tradition are constantly bickering about the proper scale of government activity and responsibility, they jointly hold to the values of private property, the market, and individualism. Modern conservatives do not, for instance, call for reconstructing American life around the traditional European feudal model of conservatism (a society organized around the values of hierarchy, order, status, religion, duty, service, and the like, discussed in Chapter 2). Nor do modern liberals propose eliminating market capitalism. While disagreeing about how to accomplish the traditional ends of liberalism, both are united in their common commitment to such ends.

WHAT IS LIBERALISM?

The above introduction has attempted to give the reader some notion of the centrality of liberal culture to American life, and to clear up some of the ambiguity attached to the term *liberalism*. We now examine more closely the component elements of liberal culture.

Competitive Individualism

At the heart of liberal culture is a belief that human nature is selfish, individualistic, and competitive. Many scholars, writers, and travelers to the United States

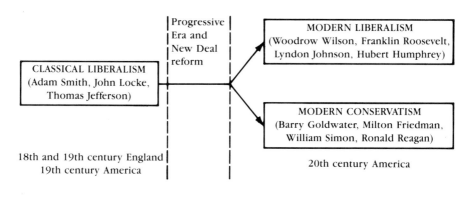

FIGURE 3.1   Modern liberalism and conservatism

have been struck by the tenacity of the competitive individualism found here. The brilliant French observer of the early republic, Alexis de Tocqueville, described how Americans thought of themselves in the following terms:

> They owe nothing to any man, they expect nothing from any man; they acquire the habit of always considering themselves as standing alone, and they are apt to imagine that their whole destiny is in their own hands.[4]

De Tocqueville's short description rings true; it is entirely familiar to us. The cultural makeup of the average American (whoever that elusive creature might be) includes a belief that people are meant to stand on their own two feet; that other people owe them nothing; nor do they, in turn, owe anything to others. (This standard refrain is heard in a variety of contexts, but never more clearly than in the recurrent complaints about people on welfare or food stamps.) It is of more than passing interest to note that the archetypical American hero has always been the "loner," whether we encounter that hero in the traditional Western myth (Gary Cooper in *High Noon* and John Wayne in any number of films), as a private eye (Bogart in *The Maltese Falcon*), as the tough but incorruptible cop (Clint Eastwood), or as the vigilante (Charles Bronson).

Closely tied to this image of the individual standing alone is the common belief that people are naturally competitive, that they are always striving to better themselves in relation to others. Their aim is not only to keep up with the Joneses, but to pass them by. An abundance of popular nonfiction literature in America has always conveyed this theme. In recent years, the "best seller" list has featured such titles as *Power and How to Get It, Looking Out for Number 1, Dress for Success* and *Winning Through Intimidation*, as well as other similar manuals of competitive advancement. Horatio Alger and Dale Carnegie, while outfitted in various forms of dress to suit the times, are always there to remind Americans of their basic nature.

Through the ages, many philosophers have contributed to this conception of human nature, with Thomas Hobbes and John Locke foremost among them. To Hobbes, in particular, man is an aggressive, competitive, ever-striving being, moved by the compulsion to fill his unlimited appetites, engaged in an ongoing "war of all against all."

> I put for a general inclination of all mankind, a perpetual and restless desire of power after power, that ceaseth only in death. And the cause of this, is not always that a man hopes for a more intensive delight, than he has already attained to; or that he cannot be content with a more moderate power: but because he cannot assure the power and means to live well, which he hath present, without the acquisition of more.[5]

The Right to Private Property

Another important element in the traditional liberal belief system is the idea that human beings have a natural right to accumulate, enjoy, and transfer private property. It is mainly to seventeenth-century philosopher John Locke that we owe

John Locke: theorist of private property and limited government

most of our present ideas on the subject. Locke argued that while God gave the earth and its resources to humankind in common (to be enjoyed by all), he also gave human beings a set of capacities like industry and creativity which they had a right and obligation to exercise, and by so doing, they transformed the commons to private property. Individuals, that is to say, by mixing their labor with the naturally occurring abundance of the earth (the land, forests, rivers, and so on), were justified in taking the products of that effort for their own as private property. Since people always bring different abilities and inclinations to labor to this encounter with nature, private property taken out of the commons will always be disproportionately distributed. Out of the commons, out of the land and its resources held equally by all, naturally and through no act of coercion or theft, comes the unequal ownership of private property.

To Locke, as well as to many of his contemporaries, the right to accumulate private property and to freely enjoy the fruits of one's labor was an inalienable right, derived from God's natural law. The link to natural law is crucial, for it confers a sacred and transcendent quality upon the ordinary business activities of the new class of traders and merchants of Locke's time who were beginning to build vast fortunes. Being sacred and natural, property rights become fundamental to all other rights, or, more accurately, they come before other rights. According to Locke, individuals have an inviolable right to appropriate whatever they can through their labor, and this right takes precedence over the claims of society or government. Individuals require the consent of no institution or person to carry out their acts of appropriation or to enjoy what they manage to accumulate. Property rights become fundamental, since such rights are inseparable from what it means to be a human being.

It follows that if property rights precede all other claims, including those of society in general, then no other person is justified in taking away any property legally acquired through one's own labor. In fact, Locke argues, it is to prevent just such an occurrence that people voluntarily come together and agree to form governments.

> The great and chief end of Men's uniting into Commonwealths, and putting themselves under government, is the Preservation of their Property.[6]

Limited Government

Derived mainly from Locke, and deeply imbedded in liberal culture, is the theory of limited government. Notice that in Locke the purposes of government are strictly limited to the protection of natural rights—and in particular, the set of rights connected to property. Under the original agreement by which it was instituted, government has no mandate to go beyond the protection of rights, for to do so would inevitably infringe upon the basic rights of some persons. If, in fact, governments do trespass these bounds, people have the right to dissolve their original compact and to form a new government. Our own Declaration of Independence, with its substance drawn almost directly from Locke, expresses this sentiment in words very familiar to Americans:

> We hold these truths to be self-evident, that all men are created equal, that they are endowed by their Creator with certain unalienable Rights, that among these are Life, Liberty and the pursuit of Happiness.[7] That to secure these rights, Governments are instituted among Men, deriving their just powers from the consent of the governed. . . . That whenever any Form of Government becomes destructive of these ends, it is the Right of the People to alter or to abolish it, and to institute new Government, laying its foundation on such principles and organizing its powers in such form, as to them shall seem most likely to effect their Safety and Happiness.

The notion of limited government is vital to the American political culture. Even while government in the United States grew vast, active, and interventionist during the twentieth century, political leaders felt duty-bound to pay homage to the liberal tradition by claiming that they had been forced by circumstances to institute some program, or that the latest government measure was only temporary. It has always been safe, and has today become mandatory, for a candidate to campaign against "big government." In recent times popular reaction against government has taken such forms as California's antitax Proposition 13, the Kemp-

Roth (Reagan) tax cut, state constitutional amendments mandating balanced budgets, and the like. The Reagan administration, with its deep slashes in income taxes and in domestic spending programs, has made this commonly articulated sentiment the very centerpiece of public policy in the United States.

Since government is limited in purpose—namely, to protect property—how is it that economic and social life are able to function? How is it that economic and social life do not degenerate into the basest sort of anarchism?

The Free Market

If left alone to operate in its natural fashion, it is argued, the market acts as the main coordinating mechanism of social, economic, and political life. It is mainly to Adam Smith that we owe this insight, though it has been a standard part of the intellectual equipment of all liberal thinkers since the seventeenth century. Smith proposed the existence of a natural law of economic life by which the social good is served only when individuals are free to pursue their own interest in the marketplace. The breakthrough made by Smith is twofold. First, if market relations are considered part of natural law, then any government intervention in economic life constitutes interference with nature itself. In this sense, Smith is also an important contributor to ideas about limited government. Second, he links individual selfishness to the general advance and betterment of society, thereby reversing the entire history of values, at a stroke rendering selfishness not only palatable, but admirable.

> [Each person] is led by an invisible hand to promote an end [the common good] which was not part of his intention.[8]

The link betwen individual greed and social good—the instrument of the "invisible hand"—is the market.

Americans have generally believed in the efficiency and utility of the market, both for the individual and for society. In economic life, the market is seen as a place where scarce goods and services are allocated in the best possible fashion, where goods are produced that people will want to buy at prices they are willing to pay. The market is also seen as a place where people test their skills, their abilities, and their mettle against others. Through the competitive struggle, society is well served, for such a struggle produces better people (toughened, hardened, tested) and better products. It has been traditional American belief, for instance, that interference with the market mechanism produces both inefficiencies (think of the never-ending jokes about the Postal Service) and people of deficient and warped character (people "on the dole," "welfare chiselers," and so on).

THE SOCIAL RAMIFICATIONS OF LIBERALISM

Americans are immersed in liberal culture, in a set of ideas, values, and assumptions that seem natural, inevitable, the very pinnacle of common sense. Liberal culture is the milieu, the growth medium within which all Americans find themselves. As such, it largely determines how Americans think about themselves, about other persons, and about the society around them. Liberal culture translates into the concrete, everyday life of the American people. In so doing, it takes on a variety of observable forms.

Take, for instance, the place of "success." Observers of the American character, going as far back as de Tocqueville in the 1830s, have noted the primacy and tenacity of the "success ethic,"—the belief in "getting ahead," "making it," striving, achieving. The "self-made man," the Horatio Alger character, is in fact a peculiarly American hero and his myth is remarkably appealing to many, who are inspired to revise their own history in his image. Among the wealthy in America one often hears the plaint that they have earned their position through hard work, intelligence, skill, daring, and so on, and that nothing was handed to them on a "silver platter." Whether such talk is self-delusion or mere camouflage is beside the point. The power of liberal culture requires that the wealthy make such protestations.

Observers have also noted the strong emphasis on materialism in American life. This is a natural outgrowth of the individual success ethic, for how else is one to measure one's worth relative to others? Money especially is the measure and symbol of success. The self-made individual in a success-oriented society has no other standard by which to measure success. Consider the relationship between money and success in the life of Richard Nixon, for example. Garry Wills, in his stimulating examination of Nixon and of liberalism, *Nixon Agonistes*, points out:

> He had risen, politically, from the dead. And he had done it by the route these men respected—by making money. Nixon had been a candidate before . . . but only after his 1962 defeat did he become a wealthy man. . . . Only when he became a Wall Street lawyer, with $200,000 a year from his practice, and with Bebe Rebozo to help him invest in Florida land, could he look his fellow Republicans straight in the eye at last. A campaign coordinator who worked with Nixon through the years put it this way: "Dick could not have made it to first base in nineteen sixty-eight without a substantial personal income. Republicans, especially those who finance the party, respect only one thing, success, and they have only one way of measuring success, money. Dick never had any money before now. He could not talk to these people as an equal, even when he was Vice-President. The thing that would have killed him with them was any suspicion that he simply needed a job. Now they knew he'd be giving up a damn good job, and good money."[9]

Others have pointed out the peculiar loneliness of liberal culture, arguing that a society that stresses aggressive, individualistic competition is likely to be deficient in fellowship and community. Philip Slater argues that liberal society is essentially a frantic place, a Hobbesian world where the success of one race is challenged almost immediately by the next race, and where the natural human longing for fellowship is frustrated by the need to prevail over one's competitiors.

> It is easy to produce examples of the many ways in which Americans attempt to minimize, circumvent, or deny the interdependence upon which all human so-

cieties are based. . . . An enormous technology seems to have set itself the task of making it unnecessary for one human being ever to ask anything of another in the course of going about his daily business. Even within the family Americans are unique in their feeling that each member should have a separate room, and even a separate telephone, television, and car, when economically possible. We seek more and more privacy, and feel more and more alienated and lonely when we get it.[10]

To make matters worse, there is a tendency to deal with alienation and loneliness in individualist ways that run the gamut from organizations like est and Esalen, to popular books like *How to Be Your Own Best Friend*, to magazines like *Self* and *Psychology Today*. All of these privatized efforts to "get in touch with yourself" simply further the processes of isolation and increase the market for additional "self-help" remedies. Is it any wonder that the United States suffers the highest combined rates of alcoholism, drug use, suicide, and interpersonal violence in the world?

As one might suspect, a culture that strongly believes in self-reliance, aggressiveness, and competition is unlikely to be friendly to those social groups that profess and live by other values, or that fail to live up to the expected standards. Several scholars have pointed out that social groups that live cooperatively and communally, either because they stand as living rejections of the dominant culture or because of the envy that such a "childlike," "pristine" existence seems to evoke, have been dealt with quite harshly by other Americans. The case of the native Americans is the most notable and horrible.[11]

Or take the poor, a group that by its very material failure proves its unworthiness to other Americans. Poverty has always been a problem for those who find themselves in that sorry state. To be poor in a society that stresses success, achievement, and opportunity is an unmitigated disaster. Such a situation subjects one's self-esteem to continuous assault by other members of society. Since Americans generally believe that success or failure depends entirely upon a person's willingness to strive and to work, the poor are generally judged by others to entirely deserve their position. They are failures, it is believed, because of some basic defect in their characters. People on welfare, for instance, are generally believed to be lazy, immersed in drugs, or tied to hoards of babies, produced, so it is assumed, to increase the size of the welfare check. Drawing on these sentiments, and making clever distinctions between the "deserving" and "undeserving," the Reagan administration emasculated programs for the poor and near-poor with nary a whimper of protest from other Americans.

LIBERAL CULTURE
AND THE AMERICAN EXPERIENCE

Although liberal thought originated in western Europe and England, it took root most deeply in the soil of the United States. In fact, only in the United States does liberalism form the bedrock of the entire culture. In no other society is such homage paid to individualism, to the sacrosanctity of private property, and to the imperative of striving toward success. Nowehere else is "private enterprise" so venerated a term. Nowhere else (with the possible exceptions of South Africa, Brazil, or Chile) does the word "socialism" elicit such fear and loathing—not even in England, the society in which liberal thought was for the most part created (Smith, Ricardo, Hobbes, and Locke were all English), and where the first full-blown capitalist society developed.

Why is this so? What special affinity does the United States have with liberalism? Why is it, in the words of historian Louis Hartz, that "the American way of life" is "the national articulation of the thoughts of John Locke?"[12] Though any answer or set of answers to these questions is bound to be incomplete, some possible reasons follow.

The Protestant Base of the Early American Settlements. A close affinity exists between liberalism and the Protestant Reformation, particularly in their mutual focus on individualism. In America, the liberation from certain religious ties, loyalties, and claims carried over into all of economic and social life. The early settlers of the New World were largely, if not exclusively, Protestant, and in many cases extreme libertarian Protestants.

The Existence of a Lockean Wilderness. Locke based his theoretical work on a hypothetical *state of nature* in which people exercised their labor and ingenuity upon a virgin land provided by God. Since this God-given land was a "commons" available to all, all were entitled to whatever they could individually produce, and in so doing no one would disadvantage or harm anyone else. No such virgin wilderness existed in the world familiar to Locke; Europe and England were characterized either by private ownership of land or by feudal patterns of landholding. In America, however, once the native population had been tricked, expelled, or exterminated, the Lockean wilderness was a reality. The early settlers not only carried the liberal seeds of Protestantism, but they had available to them the raw material upon which to practice that individualism.

The Widespread Ownership of Property in the Early Republic. America was populated with individualistic seekers of private gain, who had available to them virtually untouched natural wealth and plentiful, productive land. It is no wonder that within a century and a half of its discovery, North America was a land of yeoman farmers, free artisans, small businesspeople, and a great many property owners. To be sure, neither women nor slaves were offered such opportunities. The society that was to become the United States looked remarkably similar to Locke's imagined state of nature.

The Absence of Competing Political, Social, and Economic Traditions. In Europe, both capitalism and liberalism were forced to fight their way through and against other traditions. Capitalism, for instance, ran contrary both to feudal agricultural organization and to the dominant mercantilist form of international trade. Moreover, capitalism encouraged forms of business behavior (lending money at interest, for example) that ran counter to the ethical teachings of the medieval Catholic church as well as of the early Protestant churches. Liberal ideas, in general, were contrary to prevailing notions of human nature and to the purposes of government. As a result, while capitalism eventually came to hold sway in western Europe, liberal ideas and values were never totally triumphant there, for liberalism never entirely replaced older modes of thought and behavior. One practical result is that European elites, because of their aristocratic tradition of *noblesse oblige* (a sense of obligation felt by the upper class toward the lower classes), have always been more amenable to social welfare programs than have American elites.

In the European setting, then, both capitalism and liberalism were forced to strike many compromises and were thus diluted from the pure form. In the United States, neither capitalism nor liberalism was faced with any countertraditions or set of institutions that would soften their influence; they quickly monopolized the American social world view.

LIBERAL CULTURE AND CAPITALIST SOCIETY

One of the curious things about liberalism is the evolving divergence between its original theory and actual social reality. The contemporary United States hardly conforms to the Lockean world of small property holders, limited government, and open opportunity. On the contrary, it is a society of giant corporations, bureaucratized and centralized government, wage and salary earners, and limited social mobility. The correspondence between the dominant set of ideas and social reality seems increasingly tenuous.

The question then arises: if liberalism no longer helps citizens make sense of their world, why does it remain the repository for the dominant ideas in our political culture? While some would probably suggest *cultural lag* as an answer—that is, the long lead time required for ideas to change—I would suggest another: liberal ideas are consciously taught and reinforced, through the institutions of socialization, because liberal ideas support and sustain capitalism and those who control and most benefit from it.

In every society, except during times of turmoil and rapid social change, a rough equilibrium exists between the culture and the principal institutional arrangements of society. In capitalist society, individualist values are dominant, not communal ones. Likewise, in contemporary socialist societies, individualistic values rank lower than collective ones. This fusion of culture and social structure is never left to chance. The dominant class or group in every society attempts to ensure that appropriate values, norms, and behaviors are taught to the population in general. In most societies, this is done through the main institutions of socialization—religion, education, and communications. The United States is no exception, for schools, churches, and the mass media continually bombard the American people with the tenets of liberal culture. Seen in this light, liberalism is neither "natural" nor "inevitable." It is carefully nurtured.

It is not enough to realize that liberal values remain dominant in American political culture because the principal institutions of socialization continue to teach them. We want to know *why* these institutions do so. If we remind ourselves that institutions of socialization are normally tied to the purposes of the dominant groups or class in any society, this would lead us, in the case of the United States, to look to the capitalist class, and to ask how the diffusion of liberal values throughout society serves its interests. I would suggest that liberalism constitutes a major prop of the modern capitalist order.

Liberalism and Private Business

Liberalism helps to maintain the legitimacy of private business decision making. Contemporary capitalism is a system in which a handful of people occupying positions of industrial and financial power in the nation's corporations make decisions producing effects far beyond the walls of their particular enterprises. To the extent that liberalism encourages a respect for private property and a general hostility to government intervention in the affairs of private enterprise, it leaves the leaders of these dominant economic institutions free to act in their own interest. Even though the modern corporation looks nothing at all like the enterprises characteristic of the time of Adam Smith or John Locke, modern business leaders appropriate the language and rhetoric of liberalism to protect themselves from unwanted public intrusions. The most important function that liberalism serves here is to establish an artificial separation between politics and economics, to buttress the claim that government has no business in economics (except when it can be of use to the corporation).

Liberalism and Mass Consumption

Capitalism cannot survive without selling an ever-expanding volume of goods and services. It must expand or wither: there are no alternatives. A steady-state, no-growth capitalism is an entity that no one has yet seen and from which no credible theory has been advanced. No growth or diminishing rates of growth in the economy are always occasions for public expressions of worry by political leaders and government economists. The same situation in the private firm causes serious consideration of a change in the management team. For the economy as a whole, no growth means unemployment and underutilization of capacity. For the individual firm, no growth means declining profits, declining market share, and diminishing stock value.

Overall economic growth depends on an ever-expanding consumption of goods and services, either by the government or by the public. The main problem with consumption by the public (unless population is rapidly expanding) is that people are always in danger of becoming satiated, or of becoming satisfied with what they have. Worrying about what would happen if the consumer became satisfied, one prominent investment banker made the following observation:

> Clothing would be purchased for its utility value; food would be bought on the basis of economy and nutritional value; automobiles would be stripped to essentials and held by the same owners for the full ten to fifteen years of their useful lives; homes would be built and maintained for their characteristics of shelter, without regard to style, or neighborhood. And what would happen to a market dependent upon new models, new styles, new ideas?[13]

It is with respect to this recurrent problem of capitalist production that liberalism plays its supportive role. Liberalism, let us recall, emphasizes the values of individualism, competition, and striving toward success. At one time, these values helped a vigorous people tame a vast continent. In the modern era, however, in a world of giant bureaucratic organization, economic power concentrated in corporations, and the disappearance of cheap and plentiful land, liberal values can find few such outlets for their expression. The United States is no longer a place in which every person can aspire to be rich or to be president (if that were ever the case). But one place remaining for Americans to express their individuality, their desire to better themselves and to prevail over their fellows, is in the realm of consumption. The individualistic energy of liberal society which once expressed itself in entrepreneurship is now redirected into the prodigious con-

Self-fulfillment: the accumulation of material possessions

sumption of goods and services. This inclination is nurtured and directed by the advertising that assaults Americans at every turn. Advertising directs these individualistic energies by focusing its message not on the intrinsic worth of products, but on how their possession can make one the envy of one's neighbor.

Liberal values and capitalist requirements thus join forces in militating against satisfaction with what exists. Liberalism, given its emphasis on competitive individualism, constantly undermines any and all resting points at which people might say "enough is enough," and sends them hurtling into their next binge of consumption. It is precisely because capitalism requires such spending binges that liberalism is of incalculable value in maintaining the present system of production.

Liberalism and Collectivism

Liberalism undermines, in advance, collective definitions of problems and their collective solution by the American people. Although it may be reasonably argued that people are poor because they happen to have the wrong skill, or live in the wrong area, or to have been born the wrong sex or race, by and large people become unemployed because of the uncertainties of private investment and resultant fluctuations in the business cycle. Most economic problems that people suffer lie outside themselves. There is not much they personally can do about them. The most powerful function that liberalism performs for capitalism is to prevent people from realizing this. A people imbued with liberal values will not as a rule see their own situation as derived from the operations of the economy as a whole; rather, they will blame themselves. Such an outcome is useful for the overall system, since it shifts analysis of problems from criticism of dominant groups and institutions to criticism of self.

> I could have been a lot better off but through my own foolishness, I'm not. . . . When I came out of the service, my wife had saved a few dollars and I had a few bucks. I wanted to have a good time. I'm throwing my money away like water. . . . I don't feel sorry for myself—what happened, happened, you know. Of course you pay for it.[14]

> You just seem to reach a certain point, and if you don't have it . . . you don't make the grade. I've found that to be true. I always seem to be one step away from a good spot. And it's no one's fault—it's my fault.[15]

CONCLUDING REMARKS

We have covered a great deal of ground in this chapter, including a consideration of the meaning of liberalism, its origins, its social ramifications, and its ties to capitalism. We have done so not to pursue some arcane and irrelevant academic issue, but to go directly to the heart of the defining values of the American political culture, and to demonstrate how such values help shape the behavior of the American people and their institutions. Most important, the discussion has demonstrated how liberalism serves as a major prop and support of the capitalist system.

Given the pre-eminence of classical liberal ideas and values, moreover, it is inescapably the case that certain understandings of social justice and democracy have come to prevail in the United States. Liberalism, that is to say, provides an environment that is compatible with certain forms of justice and democracy and incompatible with others. In a society where individual success, striving, self-reliance, and competition are honored, for instance, it is hardly surprising that neither the socialist conception of justice, with its emphasis on substantive equality, nor the classical conservative conception, with its celebration of fixed social places and reward, have much of a chance. Given a society where values of individualism prevail over values of community, and where private interests take precedence over the public interest, moreover, it is hardly surprising that the direct, participatory form of democracy is not much in evidence. Such a culture strongly favors the indirect, representative form, where the ordinary citizen need not take undue time and attention from private pursuits in order to participate in the political process, as well as the pluralist form, where private interests are advanced in the formation of public policy through the conflict, bargaining, and agreements of interest groups.

NOTES

1. Richard P. Young, "Liberalism: The American Creed," in Edward S. Greenberg and Richard P. Young, eds., *American Politics Reconsidered* (Belmont, California: Wadsworth Publishing Co., 1973), p. 18.
2. Bruce C. Johnson, "The Democratic Mirage," in Herbert Reid, ed., *Up the Mainstream: A Critique of Ideology in American Politics and Everyday Life* (New York: David McKay, 1974), p. 185.
3. Louis Hartz, *The Liberal Tradition in America* (New York: Harcourt, Brace & World, 1955), p. 2.
4. Alexis de Tocqueville, *Democracy in America* (New York: Langley Press, 1845), Vol. 2, p. 107.
5. From *The Leviathan* (1651), ch. 11.
6. John Locke, *Two Treatises of Government* (New York: Mentor, 1965), p. 396.
7. Jefferson substituted "the pursuit of Happiness" for Locke's "property."
8. From Smith's *An Inquiry into the Nature and Causes of the Wealth of Nations* (1776).
9. Garry Wills, *Nixon Agonistes: The Crisis of the Self-Made Man* (New York: New American Library, 1970), p. 283.
10. Philip Slater, *The Pursuit of Loneliness* (Boston: Beacon Press, 1970), p. 8.
11. See Michael Rogin, "Liberal Society and the Indian Question," *Politics and Society* 3 (May 1971), pp. 269–312.
12. Hartz, *The Liberal Tradition in America*, p. 11.
13. Paul Mazur, *The Standards We Raise* (New York: Harper & Row, 1953), p. 32, quoted in Paul Baran and Paul Sweezy, *Monopoly Capital* (New York: Monthly Review Press, 1966), p. 124.

14. Quoted in Robert E. Lane, *Political Ideology: Why the American Common Man Believes What He Does* (New York: Free Press, 1962), p. 69.

15. Ibid., p. 70.

SUGGESTIONS FOR FURTHER READING

Robert N. Bellah, et al. HABITS OF THE HEART: INDIVIDUALISM AND CONTENTMENT IN AMERICAN LIFE. *Berkeley: University of California Press, 1985.* An award-winning, in-depth analysis of individualism as the American world view.

Louis Hartz. THE LIBERAL TRADITION IN AMERICA. *New York: Harcourt, Brace and World, 1955.* A view of American history as an unfolding of the liberal tradition.

John Locke. TWO TREATISES OF GOVERNMENT (many editions). The classic statement of the liberal theory of limited government.

C. B. MacPherson. THE POLITICAL THEORY OF POSSESSIVE INDIVIDUALISM. *Oxford: Clarendon Press, 1962.* The classic description of the linkages between early liberal thought and the rise of market capitalism.

Philip Slater. THE PURSUIT OF LONELINESS. *Boston: Beacon Press, 1970.* A powerful critique of liberal society, its heightened loneliness, and absence of community.

Garry Wills. NIXON AGONISTES. *New York: New American Library, 1970.* A biography of Richard Nixon written with the view of Nixon as the prototypical liberal product.

4

Law and
the Constitution

THE MYSTIQUE AND BIAS OF THE LAW

This chapter addresses a subject that is so obscured by mythology, wishful thinking, and patent distortion of the facts that the reader is likely to resist efforts to shed some light on a little-understood aspect of American life: the nature of the Constitution and the basic law of the land. Most Americans seem to share the view that no matter what else might be amiss in our country, no matter how unequal the distribution of benefits and burdens in other areas of social, economic, and political life, we remain a society subject to a body of law and a set of legal procedures that are just, fair, and impartial in the long run. In that perpetual process by which Americans judge themselves either superior to or more fortunate than other nations past or present, the themes which are most often encountered are those that stress the wide availability of civil liberties (the freedom of speech, assembly, religion, and so on), the equality of all persons before the law irrespective of rank or material situation, and the availability of judicial remedies to abuses in the administration of justice. These qualities, particularly as they are embodied in the actions of the nation's courts, set the United States apart as a unique and superior system in most people's minds. An uncritical, even reverential regard for the legal order exists among the American people, and this regard serves as one of the strongest props of the American system in an era when respect for other political and governmental institutions has seriously eroded. The mystery and symbolism that surround the law make it appear above faction or interest, the embodiment of the will and ideals of the community. Indeed, the law and those institutions attached to it are granted dignity and respect attached to no other governmental institution.

> Courtrooms are built to resemble temples; they tend to be dark, richly paneled, and high ceilinged—violating most precepts of the functional design that pervades so many other public structures. The courtroom is built so that attention is focused on the judge who sits on a pedestal above the other participants. No visitor's gallery rises above him; those who work in the courtroom are not allowed to sit or stand at his level; everyone else operates below him. He is the only official in the courtroom who wears a special costume—a robe. Everyone must rise when he enters or leaves the courtroom. He is addressed as "Your Honor" even though individual attorneys may despise him as a person. Attorneys are considered officers of the court and subject to his discipline; ordinary citizens who come to court for redress of grievances are labeled "petitioners," or if they stand accused of a crime or civil offense, "defendants." Thus architecture, dress, behavior, and language reinforce respect for the law and for the courts.[1]

The Law and Social Classes

To most Americans, law is the glue distilled from generations of human history that holds civilized society together and frees it from the terrors of both arbitrary tyranny and fearful anarchy. What is all too often forgotten is that the law is a human invention, fashioned out of the perceived needs, interests, and actions of particular groups of individuals. Almost invariably, these groups are the very same ones that dominate society in most of its other aspects. Law, that is to say, is a reflection of the domination of society by certain powerful groups, the simple codification of the characteristic power relationships that prevail in any particular society. The law is an instrument for placing the power of government behind the unequal rules and practices of everyday life. In feudal society, for instance, lord and serf faced each other as highly unequal persons, and over time worked out habitual and customary ways of relating to each other economically, socially, politically, and religiously. In time, these relationships came to be codified in laws specifying the relationships, and spelling out the rights, duties, and obligations of each of the parties. Similarly in capitalist society, the law comes to embody, protect, and legitimate the domination of the most powerful economic class.

There should be no mystery about all of this. The law was not handed down from Sinai. Law in the United States is the product of the actions of government institutions (legislatures, executives, courts), all of which are significantly influenced by the actions of the most powerful economic groups in the nation and solicitous of their interests. Nor is this view a particularly radical one, for it has long been recognized by theorists friendly to market society. Adam Smith once pointed out that "till there be property there can be no government, the very end of which is to secure wealth, and to defend the rich from the poor." Or as Jeremy Bentham expressed it many years later, "Property and law are born together and must die together. Before the laws there was no property; take away the laws, all property ceases.''

Law is thus one of the ways by which those groups who predominate in society, the economy, and government come to legitimate and solidify their position, and make it seem right and proper to the remainder of the population. One can see this manifested in many places within the Anglo-Saxon legal tradition. In that tradition, private property holds an almost sacred place, with many legal protections surrounding its accumulation and use.[2] Roadblocks are placed in the way of both private and public threats to its autonomy. Closely connected to the privileged position of private property in the Anglo-Saxon legal tradition is the sanctity and inviolateness of contract, and of the natural liberty to pursue economic self-interest. The invocation of ''the general welfare'' or the ''public interest'' against this array of legal protections for the economically powerful has rarely been successful in the United States, and has been so only under unusual sets of circumstances.

THE CONSTITUTION AND PROPERTY

''In the beginning was the Constitution; and the Constitution was with the Founding Fathers; and the Constitution was the Founding Fathers.'' This, without much exaggeration . . . describes the relationship between the American attitudes toward history and toward the Constitution.[3]

Probably no single institution of American life is as venerated as the Constitution, the founding document of the American Republic. Indeed, we have been virtual ''Constitution-worshipers'' throughout our entire history as a nation, seeing in the Constitution not only the firm design for our political life and our universally admired government institutions, but also for the legal structure that guarantees a life of equality and liberty for all Americans. The Supreme Court once affirmed this belief in the following grandiloquent terms:

The Constitution is a law for rulers and people, equally in war and in peace, and covers with the shield of its protection all classes of men at all times and under all circumstances (*Ex Parte Milligan*, 1866).

It has never been fashionable to criticize the document in either professional or lay circles. Tampering with it has been almost unheard of during the entire course of our history.[4] Spokespersons for every conceivable political position invoke its name. To denounce one's opponents as acting contrary to the letter or the spirit of the Constitution, or to interpret their proposals as unconstitutional, has been a tempting tactic for adversaries of every persuasion.

The Constitution must be seen in another light if we are to make sense of it. I would suggest that we look at the Constitution as the foundation for a system of government appropriate to a capitalist economy and to the protection of the highly unequal class structure which prevails in such an economy. It was not intended at its creation nor is it today the foundation for a genuinely democratic political life; it is, rather, the basis for a system in which those who own the main economic and productive assets of society are secure in their control, use, and enjoyment of such assets. The Constitution helps shape a government and a political system in which those with predominant economic power are free, in Adam Smith's words, to "truck, barter, and exchange." The claim I am making is surely a strong and controversial one, yet I believe it is a claim that is borne out by the language of the Constitution, the substance of its provisions, and its historical usage as defined by the courts and other government bodies. Much of the remainder of this chapter takes up the details of this story.

The Movement for a Constitutional Convention

People of wealth and property, mainly merchants, financiers, and planters afraid of the radical democratic tendencies unleashed during the American Revolution, initiated the movement to revise the Articles of Confederation and to substitute a document that emphasized a strong, property-respecting, centralized government. To be sure, the Articles of Confederation were deeply flawed as the basis for the formal organization of a new nation-state. Under their terms, the central government was devoid of the power to levy taxes, to regulate economic relations among the states, or to raise an army. They made no provision for any executive authority to carry out the few mandates passed by Congress, depending instead on the voluntary cooperation of the states. Nevertheless, what was most central to the fear of privileged classes in post-Revolutionary America was the responsiveness of state government to the rising tide of democracy and the possibility that they might eventually turn against economic privilege and demand greater equalization.

Their worst fears were confirmed by the activities of the government of Rhode Island, which, being favorable to the interests of debtors, began to print cheap paper money for the payment of debts. Creditors were not happy with this turn of events. The ratification of the constitution of Pennsylvania, a document with "leveling tendencies" so strong that it has been characterized by historian Samuel Eliot Morison as "the nearest thing to a dictatorship of the proletariat that we have had in North America,"[5] also provoked great alarm among property holders. The triumph of this extremely democratic constitution represented the annihilation of the political power of the old established families, merchants, and landholders of the Philadelphia area, and the rise to political power of the debt-ridden western agrarians. The future Federalist Benjamin Rush felt that the new constitution was "too much upon the democratic order."[6] The possibility that some of the democratic devices of this constitution might spread to other state constitutions further worried the privileged.

Even more dramatic was the fear that struck the wealthy upon the outbreak of populist-style rebellions, particularly Shays's Rebellion. This revolt was a response by small farmers of western Massachusetts who acted after years of peaceful protest and petition against the heavy taxes imposed by eastern merchants and financial interests. These were designed to pay off the state debt (the notes for which were held by the wealthy). The rebellion struck fear into the hearts of people of property throughout the colonies.

> It was Shays's Rebellion, that militant outbreak of populism that set all Western Massachusetts in uproar, and spread to the very outskirts of Boston, which crystallized the antidemocratic sentiment, and aroused the commercial group to decisive action. With its armed attack upon lawyers and courts, its intimidation of legislators, its appeal for the repudiation of debts, it provided the object lesson in democratic anarchy which the friends of law and order greatly needed. The revolt was put down, but the fear of democracy remained and called aloud for stronger government.[7]

Shays's Rebellion and others like it worried men of great wealth in the new nation. John Jay wrote of his uneasiness to George Washington: "Our affairs seem to lead to some crisis, some revolution—something I cannot foresee or conjecture. I am uneasy and apprehensive; more so than during the war." For his part, George Washington wrote to James Madison of his concerns: "If government cannot check these disorders, what security has a man for life, liberty, or property?" Jay and Washington spoke for considerable numbers of their class, because the spread of the news of Shays's Rebellion had the effect of solidifying men of property in all of the colonies in their fear of democratization. Out of this fear arose a desire for a strong national government, complete with a standing army capable of controlling the excesses of the states and random mobs. It is within this context, within this framework of discontent and fear among the well-to-do, that the movement for revision of the Articles swept forward.

The Constitutional Convention

It is clear that the move toward revision and then replacement of the Articles of Confederation was on behalf of those men of considerable property who opposed the further democratization of American society. Let us look at the Constitutional Convention itself—in particular, the composition and views of its membership—and demonstrate that it represented an attempt by the well-to-do to dam the tides of participation unleashed by the widespread dissemination of democratic ideas. A great deal has been written about the Constitutional Convention, especially in response to Charles Beard's *Economic Interpretation of the Constitution*,[8] which first and most emphatically proposed the class nature of the proceedings. Despite numerous counterattacks by established historians, the weight of evidence still lies with the essence of Beard's arguments (though not necessarily the particulars). The most telling evidence concerning the class nature of the convention is the composition of the delegates and how the delegates interpreted their own roles and objectives.

The men who gathered in Philadelphia to put a lid on democratic excesses were of a particular sort. While they came from different regions of the new nation, spoke with distinctly different accents, and made their living from different lines of work, they were all men of considerable wealth and standing. Nowhere to be found in this august gathering were ordinary mechanics, farmers, and workers; certainly there were no indentured servants or women. Only wealthy merchants, financiers, and planters were there; what they shared was a belief in the Lockean dictum that "the great and chief end of men's uniting into commonwealths, and putting themselves under government, is the preservation of their property."

The delegates knew, furthermore, why they had gathered in Philadelphia; the issues were transparent for all to see. While much of the time was taken up with the question of the relative powers of state and national governments, the essence of the debate actually lay elsewhere for the participants. The Anti-Federalists (those opposed to the new Constitution) favored only minor changes in the Articles of Confederation, for they saw the states as increasingly democratized and amenable to debtor and small farmer interests. They correctly perceived, and the proponents of the Constitution admitted, that the move to enhance national power was designed to protect the interests of the property-owning class. Thus the state-national, and the Articles-Constitution debates reflected class factors. One of the landed participants put the case clearly: "The more we abridge the states of their sovereignty, . . . the more safety, liberty and prosperity will be enjoyed by each of the states." Such a national government "could then be freed from popular control, for were all power held by the people, disorder and tyranny must ensue."

While contemporary historians continue to debate the ideological and class factors dominant among the designers of the Constitution, to the participants themselves there was no question why they had gathered.[9] They had done so to halt what they considered to be the excesses of democracy, and to reestablish a stable climate for business activity and elite governance. One of the participants, a clergyman named Jeremy Belknap, put the issue for his fellows: "Let it stand as a principle that government originates from the people; but let the people be taught . . . that they are not able to govern themselves." The business of the Constitution became that of working out the machinery embodying Belknap's observation.

There is no doubt that most of the participants at the Convention shared Belknap's sentiments. The eminent historian Richard Hofstadter observes that the main theme of the convention was the profound distrust of the common person, and logically, of democratic rule.[10] Historian Vernon Parrington observes that of all the philosophers discussed during the debates, only a handful were democrats. The majority were either aristocratic republicans (who favored a republic ruled by aristocratic elements) or constitutional monarchists.

Historians are also agreed about the other major themes of the debates, in particular the need for a national government with sufficient strength to regulate commerce, halt currency inflation, check the excesses of rebellion and anarchy, and protect against the "leveling" tendencies so feared by Madison. All of these desires put them in conflict with small property-owning farmers (who, it ought to be stressed, comprised the majority of the free population), who enjoyed their greatest influence at the state level. As Parrington suggests, the need for a strong national state was the basic underlying assumption, along with antidemocratic sentiments, of the Constitutional Convention.

From Philosophy
to Constitutional Provisions

The logical consequence of these antidemocratic sentiments and of the desire for a strong national government was a search for methods to check majorities and protect the interests of minority property holders. As John Jay so bluntly put it, "The people who *own* the country *ought to govern it.*" While it is the fashion today to interpret minority protection in the Constitution as a means to aid helpless minorities, to the Founders the minorities to be protected were clearly the *propertied* and the *wealthy*. James Madison, rightly called the father of the Constitution, saw the issues in these terms in *The Federalist*:

> In all civilized countries the people fall into different classes having a real or supposed difference of interests. There will be creditors and debtors, farmers, merchants and manufacturers. There will be particularly the distinction of rich and poor.

Given this division, he suggested that the role of government was to check the majority and to protect against "leveling" tendencies that might lead to an "agrarian law." "Wherever the real power in a government lies, there is the danger of oppression. In our government the real power lies in the majority of the community." As Richard Hofstadter has argued, the goal of the Founders was not to extend liberty to slaves and indentured servants, or to protect the civil liberties of the common person. To the framers of the Constitution, *liberty* was linked to property, not to democracy.[11]

> The Convention was a fraternity of types of absentee ownership. All property should be permitted to have its proportionate voice in government. Individual property interests might have to be sacrificed at times, but only for the community of propertied interests. Freedom for property would result in liberty for men—perhaps not for all men, but at least for all worthy men. . . . To protect property is only to protect men in the exercise of their natural faculties. Among the many liberties, therefore, freedom to hold and dispose property is paramount. Democracy, unchecked rule by the masses, is sure to bring arbitrary redistribution of property, destroying the very essence of democracy.[12]

THE STRUCTURE
OF THE CONSTITUTION

Given a state of affairs where common people were despised, democracy was feared, and property felt itself under attack in the various states, the convention formulated a constitutional structure which, while providing some safeguards for dissenters and various minority groups, formed a stable legal and governmental base for the development of American capitalism. Let us review some of the major features of that document.

The Creation of a Strong Central Government. The convention was charged by Congress with the task of amending the Articles of Confederation to solve some of their recurrent problems; but it instead reached the momentous decision to substitute an entirely new document establishing a more powerful national government. Given its legal charge from Congress, the national power articulated in the document is truly impressive, even audacious in the scope of its claims.[13]

PREAMBLE:

We the People of the United States in Order to form a more perfect Union, establish Justice, insure domestic Tranquility, provide for the common defence, promote the general Welfare, and secure the Blessings of Liberty to ourselves and our Posterity, do ordain and establish this Constitution for the United States of America.

The Constitution of the United States

FROM ARTICLE VI:

This Constitution, and the Laws of the United States which shall be made in Pursuance thereof; and all Treaties made, or which shall be made, under the Authority of the United States, shall be the supreme Law of the Land; and the Judges in every State shall be bound thereby, any Thing in the Constitution or Laws of any State to the Contrary notwithstanding.

Safeguards for Private Property and a Market Economy. Above all else, the purpose of the convention was to provide a framework for the acquisition, use, and transfer of private property, free from the fears of both populist-style intrusions and an unreliable financial and economic environment. A number of provisions speak directly to these needs, some of which provide for domestic order, some of which provide for a stable currency and business environment.

ARTICLE I, SECTION 8:

The Congress shall have power . . . to regulate Commerce with foreign nations, and among the several states and with the Indian tribes; To establish . . . uniform laws on the subject of bankruptcies throughout the United States;
To raise and support armies . . .
To coin money . . .
To provide for organizing, arming, and disciplining the militia. . . .

ARTICLE IV, SECTION 1:

Full faith and credit shall be given in each state to the public Acts, Records, and Judicial Proceedings of every other State. . . .

The latter provision represents not only a powerful statement of the unification of the states into a single nation, but also a defense of the notion of the inviolability of contract, one of the basic building blocks of a national market economy. The Constitution also provides numerous defenses of property against tampering by any level of government. Note, in particular (though it is hidden in rather elaborate language), the protection of property in slaves.

ARTICLE IV, SECTION 2:

No person held to Service or Labour in one State, under the Laws thereof, escaping into another, shall, in Consequence of any Law or Regulation therein, be discharged from such Service or Labour, but shall be delivered up on Claim of the Party to whom such Service or Labour may be due.[14]

Safeguards Against Majority Rule. It has often been pointed out that the genius of the American Constitution rests in its elaborate provisions for the separation of powers and for checks and balances among government institutions. Any judgment as to its genius depends, of course, on an evaluation of the uses to which government has been put. Nevertheless, recall that the overriding concern at the convention was to ensure that the passions of the population would not be permitted to overwhelm the government and move it in possibly dangerous directions. Believing that tyranny results when a majority imposes its will on a minority (property holders), the Founders formulated a series of provisions to ensure that no such majority could easily capture the policy-making machinery of the various branches of government. Such provisions pervade the Constitution and are too numerous to be listed here. Most important, perhaps, the national government is split into three separate branches—the judicial, the executive, and the legislative—each with a distinctly different method for filling its offices, and each with some check on the activity of the others.[15] The president may veto congressional legislation, for instance; while Congress must appropriate funds for presidential activities, approve many executive appointments, and formally approve treaties (in the Senate). Congress depends on the president to carry out its legislative mandates. The judicial branch may judge the legality of executive and legislative activities, yet is itself dependent upon the particulars of its formal organization, upon funding from Congress, and upon the president to enforce its decisions. With such an elaborate intermixing yet separation of the branches, no single branch, it was believed, could act tyrannically. Separated as they were, no popular majority could capture them simultaneously. And since the branches were interdependent, no branch could unilaterally impose its will on the nation.

The Constitution is filled with additional provisions designed to check the unbridled intrusions of a government moved by passionate majority sentiment. The most popular branch, Congress, is itself divided into two houses in order to check hasty and ill-considered legislation, or, to put another face on the issue, to considerably slow down the legislative process. The Senate elects but one-third of its membership at each congressional election, further protecting Congress from tides of popular sentiment.[16] Note also the very difficult process by which the Constitution itself is amended;[17] strong democrats such as Thomas Paine, Thomas Jefferson, and Samuel Adams believed that the fundamental law ought to be easily amended at any time by a majority of citizens. The document, moreover, arranged for the election of the president not through a direct popular vote but through intermediaries (electors), whom the Founders hoped would be the ''social betters'' in the community.[18]

Other Constitutional Features. The Philadelphia conferees formulated a constitutional document whose aim was to create a framework for a strong national government; for a stable, nonthreatening environment protective of property in which a market economy might operate; and finally, for a national government insulated against popular majorities. To a great extent, the Founders succeeded in their efforts, although several of their designs did not work out as intended. Despite the electoral system, for instance, the presidency has emerged as a genuinely popular institution. Through the amendment process, the provision for the indirect election of senators was altered, as was the protection of property in slaves. What is most impressive about the Constitution, in fact, as many scholars and commentators have pointed out, is its historic flexibility, its ability to serve as the foundation of American governmental and political life during radically different times. In the main, its very simplicity and brevity have made it amenable to reinterpretation as the times have demanded it.

The creation of a strong national government, protective of property and insulated against popular majorities, is the heart of the constitutional framework, but does not exhaust all of its features. Two others are particularly worthy of attention: federalism and the Bill of Rights. The Constitution represented a compromise solution at the Convention between those who advocated a centralized government (some even proposed a constitutional monarchy), and those who feared any diminution of power in the state governments. The Constitution effected this compromise by reserving some powers exclusively to the states (such as the specification of electoral qualifications[19], the conduct of elections, the ratification of the Constitution and its amendment); by reserving certain powers exclusively to the national government (such as the provision of a currency, the regulation of commerce, and the conduct of foreign relations); and by lodging all residual powers in the states (Amendment X: "The powers not delegated to the United States by the Constitution, nor prohibited by it to the States, are reserved to the States respectively, or to the people"). While the relative weight of power has shifted to the national government during our history, particularly during the twentieth century, the United States remains a system in which the powers and responsibilities of government are divided and shared between government levels.

It is also important to mention the Bill of Rights, that section of the Constitution considered its very heart by most Americans, the foundation stone of American liberties. Strangely enough, the Bill of Rights was not a part of the original document as written in Philadelphia at the Convention and transmitted to the states for ratification. Indeed, it was not until the ratification of the Constitution came to be in doubt that its supporters promised to introduce a set of amendments specifying the rights and liberties of Americans at the first Congress, a promise that was kept with the passage of Amendments I through X (ratified December 15, 1791). Much more will be said about the practice and protection of these rights and liberties in a later section.

Ratifying the Constitution

An important question remains: "If the Founders were engaged in an antidemocratic counterrevolution, how did it happen that the Constitution was approved by eleven states within the following year?"[20] In the most extensive analysis yet made of the fight over the ratification, it has been convincingly demonstrated that *sentiment in the majority of states was against ratification of the Constitution*.[21] The answer is really quite simple: the ratification process was itself highly undemocratic, largely controlled by the same people and groups responsible for writing the document. Eminent historian Jackson Turner Main shows that seven states were certainly *against* ratification, three were strongly for it, and three were uncertain. The obvious question is how the Constitution came to be ratified. Main shows that ratification was primarily the product of the superior economic position of the Federalists. The control of wealth allowed them to control most newspapers and thus to play down Anti-Federalist arguments, feature pro-Constitution writers, and distort the news. False reports were constantly given, for instance, on Federalist strength, the inevitability of Federalist victory, and the support for the Constitution by prominent people (such as Patrick Henry, who was, in fact, a passionate opponent). Wealth also enabled the Federalists to create superior organization, to locate and mobilize their supporters, and to discourage opponents. In almost every state, the Anti-Federalists gathered too little, too late. Superior wealth also allowed proponents of the Constitution in many cases to resort to economic pressure and intimidation against their opponents. Jackson Turner Main documents innumerable cases of advertiser pressure against Anti-Federalist newspapers, the bribing of prominent opponents in the states, and the calling-in of notes of Anti-Federalist debtors. In an interesting preview of contemporary politics, furthermore, voter turnout in the states was extremely low, enabling economically powerful and well-organized groups to wield influence far beyond their numbers. It is useful to remember, finally, that the new Constitution was never ratified by popular vote. Instead, ratification was by state conventions in which the election of delegates was by very limited franchise based on property qualifications. The common people of the time were largely excluded from a ratification process controlled, in the end, by their economic and social superiors.

It is important to note that these observations are not merely the charges of disappointed losers in the struggle, but were affirmed by many Federalists who found the proceedings a bit distasteful, though necessary. A prominent Massachusetts supporter of the Constitution, George Richards Minot, observed that the Federalists were obliged "to pack a Convention whose sense would be different from that of the people." Indeed, Minot titled a long list of Federalist trickery and unethical tactics "bad measures in a good cause."

THE CLASS INTERPRETATION OF THE CONSTITUTION

Those who, like Charles Beard and Vernon Parrington, argue for a so-called "economic interpretation" of the Constitution (what I would call a "class interpretation") must answer those critics who suggest that while the Founders were surely a very narrow and exceedingly privileged sector of the American population, they were, nevertheless, men of vision, guided by more than their own class interests. Their intent, it has been claimed by their defenders, was to create a governmental system for the ages, broadly democratic yet prudent, and in the end, sensitive to the needs of all classes and social groups. Other than "Fourth of July" rhetoric and unsupported claims of this sort, however, the evidence that is usually marshalled in defense of this position are various demonstrations that the individual members of the convention did not enjoy immediate economic gains from the specific proposals upon which they voted. These demonstrations are, in the end, but attacks on a "strawman." What is at issue here is not a direct one-to-one relationship between immediate economic interests and elite behavior but an entire structure of relations in which certain dominant groups benefit. As historian Staughton Lynd has so nicely put the issue, "What was at stake for [the Founders] was more than speculative windfalls in securities; it was the question, what kind of society would emerge from the revolution when the dust had settled, and on which class the political center of gravity would come to rest."[22] To the members of the Convention, their purpose was clear. While they disagreed among themselves, often passionately, about how they might achieve their objective, they were nearly unanimous in their desire to protect against "leveling" tendencies and to ensure that "the people who own the country . . . govern it."

It may also be objected that the Constitution, while written with such intentions in mind, nevertheless has become more democratic over the years. To a great extent, this objection is valid; the governmental and political systems have become far more democratic than the Founders could have wanted or imagined. We now elect senators by direct popular vote; the franchise has been expanded by the elimination of property qualifications and the loosening of residency requirements; women and black Americans have been added to the electorate; while the presidency has largely transcended the limitations of the electoral college and become a genuinely popular institution. Nevertheless, it remains the case that our governmental system remains greatly resistant to popular majorities and prone to excruciating periods of stasis and deadlock. The Founders quite consciously created a system of government in which the formulation of coherent national policy would be difficult to achieve, for they feared that such policy, if controlled by popular majorities, would be directed at them and their holdings. We remain saddled by their creation to the present day. That creation, as political scientist Ted Lowi puts it, is "uniquely designed for maintenance." In the main, the only forces that are generally capable of moving the system out of deadlock are severe crises (as in the Civil War, the Great Depression, and so on) and massive, disruptive social movements.

THE SUPREME COURT, THE CONSTITUTION, AND THE RISE OF CAPITALISM

There is no denying that the Constitution has played an important role in the protection of the liberty of the American people. Nevertheless, and equally important, the Constitution has provided a protective environment for the development of capitalism, which, as we shall see, has had serious adverse consequences for the health, safety, and freedom of the American people. The Supreme Court, as the primary interpreter of the Constitution, has further solidified it over the years as an instrument for the use and protection of the most powerful economic forces in the nation. Some of the most important and lasting contributions to this tradition were made by the Marshall Court in the first three decades of the nineteenth century, which, through a series of landmark decisions, advanced the intentions of the writers of the Constitution and served to shape all later constitutional history.

The Marshall Court. Chief Justice John Marshall was a follower of the doctrines of Alexander Hamilton, who had proposed that the future greatness of the United States must be built on an alliance of a powerful central government and big business. Marshall's aim was to free business from the restraints of state and local governments, to enhance the federal role in interstate commerce, and to thereby help construct an open, vital, national economy. In *McCulloch* v. *Maryland* (1819) the Court affirmed the supremacy of the federal government over state governments by forbidding the state of Maryland to tax a federally chartered United States bank, claiming that "the power to tax is the power to destroy." Of even more interest in that case, the Court decided that Congress had acted properly in creating an institution not mentioned in the body of the Constitution, citing Congress's power "to make all laws necessary and proper for carrying into execution" its other duties and powers (Article I, Section 8). In *Gibbons* v. *Ogden* (1824), the Court futher enhanced the powers of the federal government by affirming and clarifying its domination in the regulation of commerce between the states. In *Trustees of Dartmouth College* v. *Woodward* (1819), the Marshall Court held that a corporation was equivalent to a person in the eyes of the law, and was a holder of rights against society and thus protected by the Constitution. For any government to impose social obligations upon the operations of a corporation, to regulate it in the public interest, necessarily intrudes upon its rights as a person who had entered into a valid contract. While Dartmouth College was not a business enterprise, this decision opened the gates to untrammeled and unrestricted

The Supreme Court of the United States

free enterprise under corporate auspices later in the nineteenth century. Perhaps the most famous case of the Marshall Court was *Marbury* v. *Madison* (1803), in which the principle was first articulated that the Supreme Court may declare a law passed by Congress or by the states unconstitutional and thus void. In the process, the Court established in law the federalist principle of judicial review, a principle seen at the time as a bastion against the passions of popularly elected legislators. Through this series of landmark cases, the Marshall Court built the legal structure for the supremacy of the national government, the protection of property rights, and the free operations of a capitalist economy.

The Supreme Court and Emerging Capitalism. In the second half of the nineteenth century, the Supreme Court became the virtual handmaiden of the newly emerging industrial corporations. It rendered a series of decisions that reaffirmed their status as persons and holders of rights to be left free from interference in their operations. Moreover, the Court interpreted the *due process* clause ("No state shall make or enforce any law which shall abridge the privileges or immunities of citizens of the United States; nor shall any state deprive any person of life, liberty, or property, without due process of law. . . .") of the Fourteenth Amendment, which was originally placed in the Constitution to protect newly enfranchised black citizens in the wake of the Civil War, as a prohibition against state regulation of business corporations and efforts by working people to form unions.

The Court also interpreted the Sherman Anti-Trust Act, originally directed toward the problem of monopoly, as a law prohibiting the unionization of workers, for unionization would interfere with the freedom of contract between two persons—the business corporation and the worker. Finally, in *Pollock* v. *Farmer's Loan and Trust Co.* (1895), the Court invalidated a law in which Congress imposed a tax upon individual incomes. The identification of the Court with national economic interests was so close, in fact, that one New York bank president was moved to toast the court to an audience of businessmen in 1895 in the following euphoric terms: "I give you, gentlemen, the Supreme Court of the United States—guardian of the dollar, defender of private property, enemy of spoliation, sheer anchor of the Republic!"[23]

The Court and the Depression Watershed. For most of its history, from the era of John Marshall through the 1920s, the Court substantially agreed with the interests and needs of the leading national economic institutions. In the last decades of this era, the Court was particularly active in protecting the corporation from the dual threats of regulation by state governments and a unionized work force. This happy relationship was torn asunder by the events that surrounded the collapse of American capitalism in 1929. The crisis of capitalism was reflected in a crisis for the Supreme Court itself. In response to the Great Depression, the leaders of the most advanced sectors of the business community as well as national political leaders moved in directions sharply at odds with prevailing notions on the Court. While members of the Court remained tied to fairly strict *laissez-faire* notions, corporate and political leaders were becoming sensitive to the necessity of constructing a form of cooperative, corporate capitalism in which the national government would be actively involved in the protection, coordination, and stabilization of the entire economy. When the Roosevelt administration moved in a vigorous way to translate its interpretation into legislation, the Court responded by rejecting many of the landmark programs of the New Deal, the most important ones being minimum wage legislation, the National Industrial Recovery Act, and the Agricultural Adjustment Act. Despite the loud public debate about the "nine old men" of the Supreme Court, the constitutional crisis was short-lived. The Court has never for long been out of step with other national elites. It is impossible to determine the exact causes, but it is striking that with little change in personnel, the Court began to find New Deal legislation perfectly constitutional after 1937, including its new conceptions of governmental activism. Whether this transformation was influenced most centrally by the power of public opinion as reflected in FDR's smashing 1936 electoral victory, by the fear elicited among justices by Roosevelt's ill-fated plan to expand and "pack" the Court with friendly jurists (he was fond of saying that he "lost the battle but won the war"), or by pressures from corporate and financial leaders, is largely immaterial. It remains an inescapable fact that after 1937, the Court returned to the elite fold. From that date through the present day, the Court has given the national government a virtual free hand in regulating and coordinating corporate capitalism.

The Court and Antiproperty Dissidents. The Court has made another important contribution in linking the Constitution to the interests of private property. Despite a seemingly clear and unambiguous prohibition in the Constitution against any limitation on the exercise of free speech ("Congress shall make no law . . . abridging the freedom of speech . . . "), the Court has been willing throughout its history to allow government a very wide latitude in suppressing the political activities of dissident groups and individuals as well as the free expression of antiproperty ideas. Indeed, from the passage of the Alien and Sedition Acts during the administration of John Adams, up to the present, *the Supreme Court has never declared unconstitutional any act of Congress designed to limit the speech of dissidents*.[24] Nor has it been particularly tough on governmental authorities in their use of police, investigative, and administrative powers against those bold enough to express antisystem points of view. I shall have much more to say about this aspect of the behavior of the Court.[25]

LIBERTY AND DISSENT

The discussion of the Constitution and the role of the Supreme Court in the regulation of dissent and the expression of unpopular views leads us to consider the larger question of civil liberties and their exercise in the United States. To most Americans, what distinguishes the United States from all other societies is that it is a "free society," one in which every individual has the right and the opportunity to hold whatever beliefs he or she chooses, to criticize the government, to publish and to read all manner of opinion on public issues, to associate with others of like mind for the purpose of petitioning the government (or to turn it out in an election), to practice the religion of one's choice, and so on. Our "free society" is constantly and favorably compared (rightly so) to repressive and totalitarian societies like the Soviet Union. Every time a political dissident is jailed or expelled from that country—the cases of author Alexander Solzhenitsyn and physicist Andre Sakahrov being the most prominent—editorialists around the country, from big city to rural village, write in almost rhapsodic terms about American freedom. The average American, continually exercising the right to complain, to vote, to move, to worship, and so on, sees the theory of the free society reflected in the reality of his or her life, thus strongly reaffirming the belief in America's special place in the world and in history.

I will not claim in this discussion that the above assertions are simple myths. Civil liberties have been practiced and defended, often quite vigorously, at many times and places in American history. Nor will I belittle the importance of civil liberties, for any decent society must be concerned with the rights and liberties of the individual. Rather, we shall see that the history of the exercise and the protection of civil liberties in the Unites States is not what it has been cracked up to be. The history of civil liberties in the United States is, in fact, a rather spotty one, fluctuating with changes in the political, social, and economic climate.

This is a most important point, for many political commentators acknowledge the many examples of government interference with and suspension of civil liberties to be discussed here. Many will even acknowledge the existence of periods of repression in American history. Nevertheless, most historians and political scientists tend to see such periods as random events, recurrent, yet aberrant and atypical. The "Red Raids" of 1919, for instance, are seen as the product of an attorney general who was an antiradical zealot. McCarthyism is seen as a lamentable but unpredictable accident, the product of a particularly opportunistic senator from Wisconsin. I shall take a diametrically opposed position, one that argues that the history of civil liberties in the United States is *patterned*: that government *allows* their exercise when no threat to dominant power relations is involved, but severely *limits* their exercise when groups or persons seriously threaten the capitalist status quo. Repression—public and private efforts to limit or deny the free exercise of constitutional liberties—while brought to bear only intermittently, stands ready at all times for use during periods of disorder and discontent, against persons or groups offering a fundamental challenge to the capitalist order.

The Long History of Limitations on Liberty[26]

No sooner had the Founders written the Constitution and attached the Bill of Rights than some of them turned to the task of denying freedom of speech to their opponents. Frightened by the radical ideas set loose by the French Revolution, Federalist leaders at the local, state, and national level used first the courts and then Congress to silence their critics and maintain social stability. Using the common-law concept of seditious libel in which criticism of sovereign government was considered to be a criminal act, Federalist officials hauled their Republican opponents before the bar and managed to fine and imprison a significant number of them. Not satisfied with the results, the Federalist-dominated Congress passed the Sedition Act in 1798 which made it illegal to:

> . . . write, print, utter, or publish . . . any false, scandalous and malicious writings against the government of the United States, or either House of Congress . . . or the President with intent to defame . . . or to bring them into contempt or disrepute. . . .

While the Sedition Act proved to be extremely unpopular and contributed to the defeat of the Federalist Party in 1800 and its subsequent decline and collapse, the Supreme Court never rejected the statute or the common-law convictions. Indeed, several of the antifree-speech concepts from the common-law tradition—the "bad tendency" doctrine that allowed prosecution for speech or writing that might lead to disorder at some future time; and the "constructive-intent" doctrine that allowed prosecutors to ascribe intent to writers or speakers who might contribute to later illegal activities by others—continued to be used by the courts until well into the twentieth century.

For much of our history, this attitude and such precedents guided the activities of local, state, and national officials. Dissenters and minorities have been fair game. In many states, during our first century, Masons and Jews were barred from public office, juries, and certain professions. Irish Catholics were discriminated against by almost every state, as were members of the Church of Latter Day Saints (Mormons). Laws in various states prohibited any utterances against the institution of slavery or favorable to women's suffrage. Peaceful assemblies by working people to form labor unions in the late nineteenth century were regularly broken up by local and state authorities with the full concurrence of the courts. The same was true for those brave enough to advocate anarchist or socialist ideas in the land of private property and free enterprise. The point of this brief review is to argue that civil liberties in the United States, right from the very moment of our founding as a republic, have been honored more in theory than in practice and that the courts have not been, until very recent times, consistent advocates and protectors of the rights of free speech and assembly. What we shall learn, in fact, is that the expansion of the practice of liberty in the United States came not from the magnanimity of political and economic elites but from democratic pressures from below.

The Many Forms of Repression

Efforts to prevent dissident individuals and groups from freely exercising their liberties have taken a wide variety of forms in American history, from the crudest sorts of vigilante violence to orderly processes in courts of law. The subject of repression in the United States is especially difficult to discuss because it is located in no single, identifiable place. There is no KGB or its equivalent. Repression in the United States is marked by its complex instruments and the decentralized control of these instruments, scattered as they are among various branches of federal, state, and local governments, as well as among private individuals and groups. Let us examine some of the many forms that repression takes in American life.

Violent Repression. Threats to the status quo have almost always, at some point, been answered by violence from its self-proclaimed or official protectors. When the labor movement was in its infant stages in the late nineteenth century, efforts to organize were almost invariably met by vigilante violence customarily organized by local businessmen. Given their radical political stance, the Industrial Workers of the World (IWW) were particularly subject to such privately organized violence, especially where they generated large followings. In Bisbee, Arizona, for instance, vigilante mobs forceably deported striking miners and refused to allow them to return. In Butte, Montana, labor organizer Frank Little was lynched by a businessmen's group in 1918. Working people who try to unionize have also been forced to deal with the private police forces of employers (Henry Ford had a particularly tough, brutal, and justly infamous police force for his auto plants), antiunion detective and security agencies such as the Pinkertons, and occasional hired thugs. In their study of violence in American life, Hugh Graham and Ted Gurr point out:

> Most labor violence in American history was not a deliberate tactic of working class organization but a result of forceful employer resistance to worker organization and demands. Companies repeatedly resorted to coercive and sometimes terroristic activities against union organizers and to violent strike-breaking tactics. The violence of employers often provided both model and impetus to counter-violence by workers, leading in many situations to an escalating spiral of violent conflict to the point of military intervention.[27]

Private violence, while often successful in the short run, tends to be distasteful to most Americans, and its overuse very often leads to a growth in sympathy for the victims. Much more acceptable, because it wears the mantle and the trappings of the law, is violent repression practiced by government. Military force has often been used to resolve domestic conflicts in the United States, particularly those conflicts involving labor and business. Almost without exception, such force has been exercised in the interests of property and of corporate management. From the massacre of striking miners and their families at Ludlow, Colorado, in 1914 by state militia, to the violent repression of the American Railroad Union by federal troops in the relatively peaceful Pullman strike of 1894, to the numerous National Guard interventions against the CIO in the 1930s, the biases in the use of military force have been unambiguous. This pattern found later expression in the use of the National Guard against urban black populations and antiwar demonstrators during the turmoil of the 1960s.

Much more important than federal troops in the violent repression of dissi-

dent and discontented groups in the United States are the police forces of the
various states and local communities. The Texas Rangers, for instance, have traditionally been used as an antiunion, antistrike force in that state. Local and state
police forces were used extensively against civil rights organizers in the south during the 1960s. On several occasions they were directly implicated in the murder
of civil rights workers, as in Philadelphia, Mississippi. The police were also among
the major weapons in the violent suppression of the Black Panther Party. Not only
were members of that party subjected to continual harassment (arrest for minor
infractions such as loitering, curfew violations, profanity, jay-walking, malicious
behavior, defacing a monument, and so on), but they often faced violent police
assault on their homes and meeting places. Between 1967 and 1969, police departments around the country were involved in twenty-one raids and gunfights
with members of the party.[28] The most notorious case involved Chicago Black
Panther leader Fred Hampton, who was killed in his bed during a police raid in
December 1969, a raid purportedly designed to search for illegal weapons. To this
date, there is no evidence showing that any shots were fired at the police by
Hampton or any of his people.[29] Finally, at least 200 police "Red Squads" operated in American cities during the early and mid-1970s, tied together by the
federally funded Law Enforcement Intelligence Unit, whose function seems to
have been the disruption of dissident organizations through surveillance, harassment, intimidation, and even violence. The San Diego Red Squad, for instance,
financed the violent antiradical activities of various right-wing groups in that city.

Repression Through Government Harassment. The ways in which government
can harass and disrupt the activities of dissident groups and organizations while
remaining within the letter of the law are seemingly limited only by the ingenuity
and imagination of officials. During the period of antiradical hysteria immediately following World War I, guided and justified by a Supreme Court decision
defining deportation proceedings as administrative in nature and not punitive,
the government used the Immigration and Naturalization Service as an instrument for the mass purge of the leadership of the Socialist Party and of the IWW.
During the early 1950s, the period of so-called "McCarthyism," congressional
committees ran roughshod over the liberties of many Americans, denying them
their rights to free expression, privacy, and due process. Indeed, in only one case
during this period (*Watkins* v. *United States*, 1957) did the Supreme Court find
these "witch hunts" constitutionally intolerable.[30]

The FBI and J. Edgar Hoover were also very busy during the McCarthyite
hysteria. Besides spying on legal groups, planting false information, and otherwise
disrupting the political activities of groups and individuals exercising their First
Amendment freedoms, Hoover encouraged the American people to report any
suspicious acts of their friends and neighbors to the FBI so that the "communist
germs" might be eliminated from the American bloodstream. Reflecting on this
FBI program, journalist David Caute has observed that:

The results in terms of public attitudes, were highly satisfactory. Asked in 1954 whether people should report to the FBI those neighbors or acquaintances they suspected of being Communists, 72 percent of a national cross section replied in the affirmative.[31]

During the civil rights demonstrations of the 1960s, officials regularly, arbitrarily, and without due process terminated the benefits of welfare recipients exercising their First Amendment rights in peaceful demonstrations. Occupants of public housing who were similarly involved often found themselves without shelter.[32] Antiwar activists, even those who had broken no law, were occasionally denied government-funded student loans during the Vietnam War. Police, as already pointed out in the case of the Panthers, exercise wide discretion out on the street, and have a variety of weapons with which to harass dissidents. Their most effective weapon has been the overenforcement of minor laws as a way to prevent gatherings (freedom of association) or the dissemination of leaflets (freedom of speech), usually citing obstructions to traffic, loitering, creating a public nuisance, and so on, to support their action. In the interests of public order, police officials regularly deny parade permits to dissident groups, though "patriotic" and civic groups do not seem to have similar problems. Agencies ranging from the local police to the Central Intelligence Agency regularly and as a matter of policy infiltrate, disrupt, and undertake wide-scale surveillance of dissident organizations, practices that most certainly destabilize legal political organizations, and undermine public support for them because of their "chilling effects."

In recent years, the Reagan administration has been especially alert to the possible contagious effects of information and ideas and has made a major effort to stop the virus before it gets out of control. Without congressional approval and with the full concurrence of the nation's highest courts, it has attempted to cut off the flow of information from the government, deny America the opportunity to hear critical points of view from foreign visitors, and ensure that American travelers are inoculated against contact with dangerous ideas. Among Attorney General William French Smith's very first official actions upon coming to office in 1981 was to inform all federal agencies that they should be less cooperative and generous in responding to requests for information under the Freedom of Information Act. In 1983, President Reagan issued an executive order establishing a life-time censorship system for over 100,000 federal employees in touch with sensitive or embarrassing information. Under terms of the "ideological exclusionary" clauses of the McCarran-Walter Act (1952), visas to visit the United States were denied to such luminaries as Columbian novelist and Nobel Laureate Gabriel García Marquez (*One Hundred Years of Solitude*), Mexican novelist Carlos Fuentes, apartheid critic Dennis Brutus, Hortensia Allende, widow of slain Chilean President Salvador Allende, philosophers Leszek Kolakowski, Michael Foucault, and Regis Debray, and Italian playwright Dario Fo.[33] Finally, the President issued an executive order banning travel to Cuba for all Americans except journalists, professionals, and scholars (upheld by the Supreme Court in *Regan* v. *Wald*) and conducted highly publicized investigations of groups permitted to travel to Cuba as well as travel agencies arranging such visits.

The list could be extended, and probably most readers have seen evidence of such official harassment in their own communities in the face of dissent. It is all too painfully obvious that the liberties spelled out in the First Amendment have a difficult time away from the rarefied chambers of the Supreme Court, even in those rare instances when the Court has acted to support the right of dissent.

Private Sector Harassment. Violent repression, whether by public officials or by private individuals, is a blunt instrument, very often creating sympathy for the victims, and providing those same victims with a concrete and readily identifiable target. Official harassment also tends, in the long run, to smack of injustice. Far more effective are those tools of repression in American life that are decentralized and obscure, tools that are seemingly accidental, random, and impersonal, leaving no group or institution accountable or responsible. One of the most effective instruments relates to the precarious employment possibilities of social critics. During the early struggles of working people to organize into unions, labor leaders were regularly *blacklisted*—named on lists compiled by and for employers so that they might better guard against accidentally hiring "troublemakers." During the McCarthy era, many actors, directors, and writers were blacklisted from employment in the film industry. During periods as disparate as the Red Scare of 1919, the McCarthy period of the 1950s, and the antiwar movement of the 1960s, many people who expressed unpopular opinions were discharged from their teaching positions in elementary schools, high schools, colleges, and universities. Bar associations during the 1950s routinely disbarred attorneys daring to defend politically unpopular people and organizations. When the Lockheed Aircraft Corporation discharged eighteen employees in 1949 because it could not be certain of their loyalty, the California Supreme Court justified the action on the grounds that loyalty to the United States took precedence over any free-speech rights guaranteed in the California and United States Constitutions.[34]

Repression Through the Legal System. Given the traditional reverence for the law in American society, the most effective device for quiet repression of dissident individuals and organizations is to define their activities as criminal and to transfer their conflict with the dominant powers from the street and the ballot box into the courtroom. Such a transformation is a powerful tool of official repression, for to define certain activities as criminal, rather than political, accomplishes several things favorable to the status quo.[35] First, "criminalizing" dissent makes it possible to ignore the issues raised by that dissent, to redefine the problem as one that involves the determination of guilt or innocence. In such a setting, the issues are not likely to receive a hearing. Second, "criminalizing" dissent makes it more difficult for dissenters to gain allies for their cause in the larger community. Once persons or groups are officially stigmatized as "criminal," they tend to lose sympathizers. Finally, unless one is armed with a strong character and a powerful supporting ideology, "criminalization" discourages and demoralizes dissident individuals themselves once they find that they are treated as criminals by the police, the courts, and prison personnel. The criminal process isolates people and treats them as individual wrongdoers, cutting them off from the support of their compatriots. As Isaac Balbus puts it:

> Because formal rationality [the law] tends to depoliticize the consciousness of the participants, delegitimate their claims and grievances, and militate against alliances between participants and other nonelites or elite moderates, it is likely effectively to minimize revolutionary potential and maximize long-run legitimacy. . . . As such . . . that form of repression . . . most consistent with the long-run legitimacy of the state is repression by formal rationality.[36]

Examples of repression through formal legal processes abound. As a method for combating the influence of the IWW, many states and communities in the early part of the century passed *criminal syndicalist* laws specifically defining IWW activities as criminal and thus transferring their persecution to the courts. At the federal level, the IWW was brought before the courts and its leaders jailed for "conspiracy" against industrial production and the draft because of their militantly outspoken stance against participation in World War I under terms of the Espionage Act of 1917. Socialist leader Eugene Debs was imprisoned under the same law, as were nearly two thousand other Americans.[37] During the black uprisings of the mid- to late 1960s, "rioters" were treated as common criminals, as persons rioting mainly for "fun and profit,"[38] and a political protest was thereby transformed into a legal question to be dealt with formally and dispassionately. The Cold War era saw a number of statutes passed by Congress, principally the Smith Act, designed to deny political and civil rights to supporters of the Communist Party by making it a crime to *advocate or teach* the overthrow of the government by force. The Supreme Court upheld the conviction of eleven leaders of the Communist Party in *Dennis* v. *United States* (1951) when the petitioners failed to comply with the stringent technical terms of the Smith Act. The Supreme Court has always been a participant, in fact, in the criminalization of radical dissent. In *Pierce* v. *United States* (1920) it upheld the conviction of a man for publishing a Socialist antiwar pamphlet. In *Gitlow* v. *New York* (1925) it upheld the conviction of Gitlow for distributing Communist literature. While the Court has usually reversed these opinions in later cases, what is most significant is their willingness to cooperate with other officials in the repression of dissent during "troublesome" times.

We might also take note of *political trials*, trials which, while ostensibly concerned with the transgression of some statute, are in fact concerned with the control of political dissent. Political trials became especially prominent during the anti-Vietnam War protests and the rise of black militancy. The list is long and familiar—the "Chicago Seven," the "Panther 21," the trial of Dr. Benjamin Spock, the trial of the Berrigans, the Gainesville trial of the leaders of the Vietnam

Veterans Against the War, the various trials of Huey P. Newton and Bobby Seale of the Black Panther Party, and so on. It is largely immaterial that in most of these cases, juries found the defendants innocent of all charges, for the court process, given its length and complexity, dissipated the energies and treasuries of the affected dissident organizations, and transferred the attention of their members and their sympathizers from political organizing to the criminal courts. The speed with which juries have acquitted suggests the flimsiness of the prosecution cases, and raises the possibility that the political trial is designed by officials less for conviction than for harassment and disruption.

Civil Liberties and Capitalism

The picture painted above does not conform to our self-image as a free society, one in which people hold liberties that are inviolate, free from interference either by government or by other persons. How is it that such a state of affairs can exist in a society that professes other ideals, and in a culture dominated by liberalism, with its emphasis on individual freedom?[39]

The answer to the first part of the question causes no insurmountable problem, for it might be argued that no political system, whatever its expressed ideals, will freely allow the organization and political activity of those groups whose stated aim is a change in the regime itself and the underlying system of class relations. The western "democracies" do not differ in this regard from other systems, though repression of dissent is largely hidden behind the rhetoric of freedom and the complexities of the legal code.

As to the second part of the question, you must recall the discussion of liberalism in Chapter 3. It is an inaccurate reading of the liberal tradition to see it as principally committed to absolute individual freedom. From the very beginning, the focus of the liberal tradition has been upon the *rights of property*—the freedom of individuals to buy, sell, and accumulate property without interference. To Locke, the protection of property is the very reason people come together in the first place to form commonwealths, and protecting property becomes the primary function of government. The right to rebel, which is surely the ultimate expression of individual freedom, is limited solely to cases in which property owners are oppressed, in which some government interferes with the inviolable rights of property. In Locke's view, *there is no right of rebellion against property!* Indeed, facing such a threat, governments are justified in suspending all rights and vigorously suppressing it. In Locke's words, faced with such a threat to property, ". . . all former ties are cancelled, and all other rights cease, and every one has a right to defend himself and to resist the Aggressor."

At the very core of the liberal tradition is a basic contradiction: a commitment to freedom and liberty combined with a powerful justification of the forcible suppression of threats to property, of threats to capitalist society itself. Once we are aware of this contradiction, it should no longer surprise us that liberties are available to American citizens only as long as and to the extent that their practice represents no fundamental challenge to the overall system of power and privilege.

The Continuing Importance of Civil Liberties. I must conclude this discussion with an important qualification. While spokespersons for property were the intellectual fountainhead for the ideas of individual freedom, and while they intended to confine liberty mainly to the propertied class, the ideas proved too powerful and appealing to remain there for very long. The freedoms of expression, movement, and assembly so necessary to the practitioners of early market capitalism were eventually seized upon by those groups in society for whom the freedoms were never intended, and the freedoms thereby took on a more democratic cast.[40] Another way to state the same thing is to point out that civil rights and liberties have not so much been freely granted to the American people by the actions of elites as they have been forced by the actions of popular mass movements. One is reminded of the action which forced the original concession for a Bill of Rights, the fight for the abolition of slavery, the long struggle for women's rights, the brave "free speech" actions of the Industrial Workers of the World in the early part of the century, the civil libertarian aspects of the labor movement, and the struggle for the constitutional rights of black and other minority Americans in the 1960s. Because of the existence of this democratic pressure from below and the resultant expansion in the enjoyment of civil rights and liberties, freedom exists in a certain state of tension in the United States. This tension is the result of the contradiction between the private property and class commitments of the liberal tradition, and the general belief among the American people that liberties extend beyond large property holders to all citizens. Such a contradiction heightens the problem of controlling dissent for the government, because it must repel threats or potential threats to the social order without unduly transgressing what the population considers the legitimate exercise of liberties. To do so openly and persistently would very likely undermine the legitimacy of the government itself. Civil liberties thus have the unique and peculiar quality of being at one and the same time a prop of capitalism and a potential tool for expanding the freedom of all citizens. Liberal freedoms are at one and the same time a tool of social control and a potential tool of liberation. How they are used in practice depends heavily on the degree of popular support for the libertarian interpretation of the tradition and on public hostility to government transgressions of agreed-upon limits. Civil liberties thus become ideals well worth fighting for both because of their intrinsic qualities and because they are potential barriers to the full exercise of repression by government.[41]

CONCLUDING REMARKS

We have found that both the letter and the practice of the law in the United States are strongly biased in favor of the interests of powerful economic institutions and individuals. Behind the Fourth of July mystique, the Law Day pronouncements, and the general veneration of the American legal system stands the inescapable reality of unequal power. While none of this implies that the legal order *never* offers protection and sustenance to the weak, or that it may not be better than most other legal orders in the world today, the foregoing discussion may introduce a dose of realism into an area of national life all too often obscured by myopic and wishful thinking.

The discussion also suggests that the basic law and the Constitution are supportive of certain forms of democratic practice and not others—clearly representative and pluralist forms are favored and not the direct, participatory form—and a form of economic system, a capitalist market economy, in which a particular conception of social justice (the classical liberal one) prevails. While the basic law and the Constitution do not forbid the existence of direct participatory democracy in the United States or legislate against the realization of socialist or classical conservative conceptions of social justice, they do stack the deck in important ways against such possibilities.

NOTES

1. From Herbert Jacob, *Justice in America*, 2nd ed. (Boston: Little, Brown, 1972), p. 14, based on the observations of Thurmond W. Arnold, *The Symbols of Government* (New York: Harcourt, Brace, 1935).
2. While the general commitment to property has not wavered, what has changed is the type of property afforded the greatest protection. See Morton Horwitz, *The Transformation of American Law* (Cambridge: Harvard University Press, 1977) for a brilliant exposition of the triumph of large-scale over small-scale property in the law as American capitalism was transformed from laissez faire to concentrated corporate form. Note, furthermore, that property refers to a social relation, e.g., the ability to purchase the labor power of others and to control the process of production (see chapter 5). It does not refer to articles of personal use and consumption.
3. Charles A. Miller, *The Supreme Court and the Uses of History* (Cambridge: Harvard University Press, 1969), p. 181.
4. Since the Bill of Rights (Amendments I through X), was adopted by the first Congress over 200 years ago, only 16 amendments have been made in the Constitution.
5. Samuel Eliot Morison, *The Oxford History of the American People* (New York: Oxford University Press, 1965), p. 274.
6. Unless otherwise noted, all direct quotes in this section on the Constitution are from Jackson Turner Main, *The Anti-Federalists* (Chapel Hill: University of North Carolina Press, 1961).
7. Vernon T. Parrington, *Main Currents in American Thought*, Vol. 1 (New York: Harcourt, Brace, 1927), p. 277.
8. Charles Beard, *An Economic Interpretation of the Constitution* (New York: Macmillan, 1913).
9. Significantly, many prominent proponents of democracy like Thomas Jefferson and Patrick Henry did not attend the proceedings. The latter is reported to have said in explanation, "I smelt a rat."
10. Richard Hofstadter, *The American Political Tradition* (New York: Knopf, 1948), p. 4.
11. Hofstadter, *The American Political Tradition*, p. 11.

12. Ibid., p. 11.

13. See for example Article I, Section 10 (restrictions upon the powers of states).

14. Repealed by the Thirteenth Amendment.

15. Consult the Constitution, a copy of which may be found in the back of this book. For the separation of powers see, in particular, Articles I, II, and III.

16. See Article I for the specification of congressional structure and responsibility.

17. See Article V.

18. See Article II, Section 1.

19. Benjamin Franklin wanted to eliminate all property qualifications for elections to the House of Representatives but was unable to gain the support of his fellow delegates for this radical proposal.

20. Robert Dahl, *Pluralist Democracy in the United States* (Chicago: Rand McNally, 1967), p. 32.

21. See Main, *The Anti-Federalists.*

22. *Class Conflict, Slavery, and the United States Constitution* (Indianapolis: Bobbs-Merrill, 1967) quoted in Michael Parenti, *Democracy for the Few* (New York: St. Martin's Press, 1983), p. 70. For a well argued position opposite to the one taken in this text, see Forrest McDonald, *A Constitutional History of the United States* (New York: Franklin Watt, 1982).

23. Quoted in Ira Katznelson and Mark Kesselman, *The Politics of Power* (New York: Harcourt Brace Jovanovich, 1975), p. 326.

24. Theodore L. Becker, *American Government: Past, Present, Future* (Boston: Allyn & Bacon, 1976), p. 81.

25. It is true that over the course of the past two decades, now that the constitutional framework for modern corporate capitalism is firmly in place, that the Supreme Court has expanded the rights of criminal defendants and increased the constitutional protections for racial and cultural minorities and women. Nevertheless, these important and significant advances have been confined to expanding procedural rights, guaranteeing equality before the law, and opening the opportunities for the practice of formal citizenship, but have not been directed toward establishing substantive and material equality. While dramatic advances have been made in a great many areas of American life through the actions of the Court, the institutions of corporate capitalism and the system of class inequality remain untouched and intact, with the basic framework of the law acting as one of its most fundamental props.

26. On the subject of repression in American history see Robert Justin Goldstein, *Political Repression in Modern America* (Cambridge, Mass.: Schenkman Publishing Co., Inc.); David Kairys, "Freedom of Speech," in David Kairys (ed.), *The Politics of Law* (New York: Pantheon, 1982); and Alan Wolfe, *The Seamy Side of Democracy* (New York: David McKay, 1978). Much of the material in this section is based on Wolfe.

27. Hugh D. Graham and Ted R. Gurr, *Violence in America* (New York: Signet, 1971), p. 750.

28. Wolfe, *The Seamy Side of Democracy*, p. 50.

29. The FBI was intimately involved in Hampton's murder. The Black Panther chief of security, in fact, was an FBI informer and the source of all information supplied to the Chicago police. As *The New York Times* reported (May 7, 1976), "Within days of the raid . . . the Chicago FBI office asked Washington headquarters for a $300 bonus for O'Neal [the informer] . . . and [he] subsequently received the money.''

30. For the most complete compilation of the horrors of the McCarthy period, see David Caute, *The Great Fear: The Anti-Communist Purge Under Truman and Eisenhower* (New York: Simon & Schuster, 1978).
31. *Ibid.*, p. 121.
32. Frances Fox Piven and Richard Cloward, *Regulating the Poor* (New York: Pantheon, 1971).
33. Democratic administrations have also used visa control as a way to keep dangerous ideas from infecting the American people. Note the Carter administration's refusal to issue visas to the eminent scholars Ernst Mandel and P. T. Bottomore.
34. Caute, *The Great Fear*, p. 368.
35. Based on Issac Balbus, *The Dialectics of Legal Repression* (New York: Russell Sage, 1973), p. 12.
36. *Ibid.*, p. 14.
37. The Espionage Act was held to be constitutional in the famous case of *Schenck* v. *United States* in which the supposed great civil libertarian justice Oliver Wendell Holmes enunciated his landmark "clear and present danger" concept. In upholding the conviction of Mr. Schenck, who had been distributing leaflets condemning the war and demanding that the draft law be repealed (he did not advocate any illegal or disruptive actions), Holmes indicated that Schenck's customary free speech rights had no constitutional protection during a war when such speech has the "clear and present danger" of producing "the substantive evils that Congress has a right to prevent." So much for "Congress shall make no law. . ."
38. The quote is a chapter title from the notorious book by Edward Banfield, *The Unheavenly City* (Boston: Little, Brown, 1968).
39. Wolfe, *The Seamy Side of Democracy*, p. 6. Much of the remaining discussion is based on Wolfe.
40. See C. B. MacPherson, *The Real World of Democracy* (Oxford: Clarendon Press, 1965) and Kairys, "Freedom of Speech" for this history.
41. This chapter has focused on issues related to the fundamental law: the Constitution, the interpretation of the Constitution by the Supreme Court, and the status of civil liberties in the United States. The discussion has continually emphasized that the law is not neutral, but is, rather, an instrument of and a creation of the institutions of private economic power. It is important to point out that the more mundane, everyday practice of civil and criminal law is also deeply biased in favor of large scale property and against the poor and the politically powerless. For an introduction to a vast literature on the subject see Jerold S. Auerbach, *Unequal Justice* (New York: Oxford University Press, 1976); Herbert Jacob, *Justice in America* (Boston: Little, Brown, 1978); Leonard Downie, Jr., *Justice Denied* (New York: Praeger, 1971); Kairys, *The Politics of Law*; Richard Quinney, ed., *Criminal Justice in America* (Boston: Little, Brown, 1974); and Edwin H. Sutherland's classic *White Collar Crime* (New York: Dryden Press, 1949).

SUGGESTIONS FOR FURTHER READING

David Caute. THE GREAT FEAR: THE ANTI-COMMUNIST PURGE UNDER TRUMAN AND EISENHOWER. *New York: Simon & Schuster, 1978.* The most complete (and chilling) catalogue of government suppression of civil liberties in the United States during the McCarthy period.

Edward S. Corwin. THE CONSTITUTION AND WHAT IT MEANS TODAY, 13th ed. *Princeton, N.J.: Princeton University Press, 1974*. A classic work that reviews the history of Supreme Court interpretation of the Constitution.

Robert Justin Goldstein. POLITICAL REPRESSION IN MODERN AMERICA. *Cambridge: Schenkman, 1978*. The most complete treatment of the subject of repression in the scholarly literature.

Alexander Hamilton, James Madison, and John Jay. THE FEDERALIST PAPERS, ed. by Clinton Rossiter. *New York: McLean, 1788; New American Library, 1961*. A brilliant and detailed defense of each of the provisions of the Constitution executed by three people actively involved in its writing.

Morton Horwitz. THE TRANSFORMATION OF AMERICAN LAW. *Cambridge: Harvard University Press, 1977*. A brilliant and justly honored book, which examines how changes in the early American economy led to transformations in the case law and in the legal profession.

Herbert Jacob. JUSTICE IN AMERICA, 3rd ed. *Boston: Little, Brown, 1978*. A highly respected review of the court system, which has rightly become a standard work in the field.

David Kairys (ed.). THE POLITICS OF LAW. *New York: Pantheon, 1982*. A collection of essays by radical legal scholars which examines basic legal concepts of the American system, from torts to contracts.

Victor Navasky. NAMING NAMES. *New York: Viking Press, 1980*. A penetrating analysis of the McCarthy era and the creation of a culture of informers.

5

Capitalism:
Theory and Implications

Up to this point, we have examined the American cultural system (liberalism) as well as our basic constitutional/legal framework. I have argued that our culture and legal systems are profoundly and inescapably shaped by their location within a capitalist market economy. It remains for us to ask about the nature of such an economy.

What is capitalism? What are its fundamental characteristics? How does capitalism differ from other economic systems? Does capitalism affect the realization of democracy and social justice? This chapter will examine these complex theoretical questions. If the discussion seems unduly abstract and theoretical, rest assured that without an understanding of capitalism as a system, the remainder of the book and, I must add, American political life, will remain incomprehensible.

CAPITALISM AND ITS RAMIFICATIONS

No simple definition can capture the essential nature of capitalism and spell out its implications. Nevertheless, I shall propose such a simple definition as the *first* step in our analysis of capitalism.

> Capitalism may be defined as an economic system in which one class of individuals ("capitalists") owns the means of production ("capital" goods, such as factories and machinery), hires another class of individuals who own nothing productive but their power to labor ("workers"), and engages in production and sales in order to make private profits.[1]

Some scholars have suggested that modern capitalism is so different from eighteenth century small-scale laissez-faire capitalism that it is an entirely new creature, free from the problems of early capitalism and deserving of new terminology. Hence, the widespread use of terms such as "postcapitalism" or "neocapitalism" to describe it. Certainly capitalism has changed rather dramatically over the past two centuries. Nevertheless, it remains an economic system characterized by a dichotomous class structure based on the division between ownership and nonownership of property, and by a system of market-oriented production for profit.

Such a definition is not merely an academic exercise. It serves to distinguish capitalism from other forms of economic society (both industrial and nonindustrial), and to introduce a consideration of certain social problems associated with all capitalist systems, whether free market capitalism or modern corporate capitalism. I shall argue that the essential, defining characteristics of capitalism—the very way it organizes economic life—inescapably entail severe social and human costs. Market production and the class system, by their very nature, have problems and dislocations that are impossible to evade. One of the most important functions of twentieth-century governments has been to alleviate some of these problems and dislocations.

Capitalism is, then, a social system characterized by a class system based on the ownership of property, and by the production of goods and services for sale in the marketplace. The following discussion elaborates and expands the minimal definition of capitalism already presented, and points out some of its most telling social costs and problems.

THE CLASS SYSTEM

Capitalism is a system in which a relative handful of people own the means by which goods and services are produced and distributed. In this respect, capitalism is not unique. With the exception of some primitive communal societies described by historians and anthropologists, all known historical societies have been characterized by minority ownership of fundamental resources. In classical Roman and Greek society, for instance, only a wealthy and powerful minority of the people owned slaves, the main productive instruments of economic life. In European feudal society, only a tiny minority owned land, the key economic component for agricultural society. In capitalist society, only a small segment of the population owns the main instruments of economic life: factories, machinery, natural resources, land, and investment capital.

Capitalism is a system in which the owning class, by virtue of its ownership of the productive assets of society, determines the overall shape and development of economic life. Whether we refer to the era of small-scale capitalists described by Adam Smith, or to the current era of giant multinational corporations, the shape of economic and social life in capitalist societies is, in the main, determined by thousands upon thousands of private investment decisions. These decisions encompass such diverse activities as plant location, job design, technological innovation, savings, advertising, and lending. Economic life, which is by nature social and interdependent, is determined by the sum total of the decisions of the owning class, and not by the population as a whole through democratic procedures. Decisions that affect the affairs and prospects of society in general are made by economically powerful private individuals who are in no way publicly accountable for their actions.

Capitalism is a system in which the vast majority of the population, not being in possession of the productive assets of society, must sell its labor skills, effort, creativity, and time to the owning class in return for wages and salaries. Capitalism is a system in which a minority of people is able to purchase the labor power of others, and is thereby able to determine the purposes and uses of that labor. It is a system in which a few have the means to buy labor and set it to work. It is a system in which the nonowning majority works for ends and in ways determined by the property-owning minority. Indeed, we may best define *private property* not as a collection of things, but as the ability to buy and live off the labor power of others. Historian R. H. Tawney has made the following observation about early twentieth-century Britain, and it holds just as well for the contemporary United States:

> Regarded as an economic engine, the structure of English society is simpler than that of some more primitive communities. . . . The most salient characteristic of its class structures is the division between the majority who work for wages, but who do not own or direct, and the minority who own the material apparatus of industry and determine industrial organization and policy.[2]

Obviously, the nonowning majority of the population does not sell its labor skills, efforts, creativity, and time for the sheer joy of being directed by others, but is forced to do so by the need to make a living. Particularly in the modern corporate era, with the decline of small business opportunities, few have the opportunity to become owners in their own right, and most must work for others. This transformation of the vast majority of the population into wage laborers is one of the most salient characteristics of capitalist development.

Capitalism is a system built on the continuous appropriation of the production of the many by the few. Capitalism is an economic system whose lifeblood is profit. Without profit, or the prospect of profit, private persons would be either unwilling or unable to invest their surplus savings in business enterprises, a situation that would inevitably lead to stagnation or collapse. Firms within a capitalist economy constantly seek a level of profitability that allows them to maintain themselves or to expand. This outcome is made possible only by keeping the costs of production (the costs of plant and equipment, raw materials, labor, and so on) significantly below the selling price of the goods or services produced. It is necessary for capitalist enterprises, from one point of view, to give back to the workers who directly produce some product or service, *less than the value produced.* For a firm to do otherwise would be suicidal. At the level of society, it is necessary in capitalism that the owning class give back to the working class less in wages and salaries than it realizes from the sale of goods and services. It follows that no matter what the absolute level of wages and salaries may be, either in the firm or in the economy as a whole, the relationship of workers to owners in capitalism is one of continuous and perpetual exploitation; some portion of the value produced by workers is continuously extracted by those who own but do not themselves produce. It is a system described by Tawney as one characterized by that strange "alchemy by which a gentleman who has never seen a coal mine distils the contents of that place of gloom into elegant chambers in London and a house in the country."[3]

Classes and Exploitation

Exploitation, defined as the power of capital to direct production and to live off the labor of others, finds expression in a variety of forms. Consider the issue of inequality. The most obvious benefit to be derived from ownership is that the bulk of the fruits of the economy flow to those who own. All capitalist societies, as a result, are characterized by severe inequalities in income distribution based on the division, primarily, between those who own substantial capital and those who do not. (See Chapter 6 for a more extensive discussion of this issue.) Since access to those goods and services necessary for a decent life are generally available in the United States only to those who can afford to pay for them out of pocket, inequalities of wealth and income are reproduced in most other areas of life. The inegalitarian realities of property are neatly reproduced in such areas as health, education, safety, security, and life style. In a society where most goods and services are available to the highest bidder, it is only natural that those persons with the greatest disposable income enjoy most of the fruits of the economic system.

Whatever its level of affluence and material wealth, capitalism is an inherently exploitive system. Political philosopher C. B. MacPherson has proposed that a truly just and humane society, one without exploitation, would be one in which all persons would have both the opportunity and the means to use and to develop their innate human capacities. He points out that many factors can stand in the way of such development. But above all other obstacles is the lack of access to the facilities for laboring. The development of human capacities requires, as a first order of priority, materials and tools with which to work. The sculptor requires marble and chisels; the architect, T-square and pen; the builder, boards, nails, and hammer. In capitalist society, however, the tools, materials, and other resources requisite to creative and fulfilling work are owned by the few, who retain the economic and legal power to define the purposes for which they can be used. Thus the uneven distribution of property is reflected in the uneven distribution of the opportunity to use and develop capacities. This transfer of human power, as MacPherson points out, is a continuous and inherent one in the relationship between owners of property and sellers of labor. It is exploitive in the sense that one group of people controls access to the means for the development and fulfillment of others.[4]

Modern Times: *human beings as appendages to the productive process*

The relationship is exploitive in another closely related way. Ownership of property wealth confers upon a relative handful of people the means and ability to determine vital elements of other people's lives. For instance, in capitalist societies, owning and controlling a factory gives one the legal right to determine the technical organization of production and the content of work. Nonowners in such a setting (the situation of most Americans) must work for objectives that are not necessarily their own, produce things not necessarily of their choice, and use their skills and creative talents in ways determined by others.

For most people, this has meant working at jobs that are increasingly fragmented, simplified, routinized, and supervised in the name of efficiency and productivity. This has devastating implications for the average American worker.[5] If *homo sapiens* is by nature a free, creative, and independent being, then to work in settings that are controlled, specialized, and routinized is to spend one's life in a manner less than human.[6] Over the past few years, wide-ranging research literature has confirmed that modern forms of work organization tend to run counter to the psychological well-being of most people.[7]

Studs Terkel, in writing about the work experiences of Americans he had interviewed intensively, gives his overall impressions in these words:

This book, being about work, is, by its very nature, about violence—to the spirit as to the body. It is about ulcers as well as accidents, about shouting matches as well as fistfights, about nervous breakdowns as well as kicking the dog around. It is, above all, about daily humiliations. To survive the day is triumph enough for the walking wounded among the great many of us.[8]

It is important to note that the relationship between the owner of capital who buys labor and the worker who sells labor is neither accidentally nor occasionally exploitive, but is so in the very nature of class relationships, and is therefore inherently *antagonistic*. For the owners of capital to significantly increase their profits, they must, among other things, squeeze wage and salary rates—or in the modern parlance, increase productivity (for example, producing more from each worker at a constant labor cost). For the working class to significantly enhance its position in the total economy, it would have to keep for itself a large part of what normally finds its way into profits. For the working class to escape alienating and dehumanizing work settings, it would have to break the monopoly of the capitalist class over the organization of production. In contrast to the usual rhetoric that pervades American thinking (which articulates a vision of unity, commonality, and "one big family"), the interests of owners and the interests of workers are perpetually and fundamentally at odds.

The social class concept—the division of society into two great strata defined by their relationship to the system of production, one *owning* the means of material production and appropriating the surplus created by others, the other *selling* its labor and producing surplus—is the bedrock of my point of view in the analysis of capitalist society. We shall see later how this class division profoundly shapes American politics and public policy.[9]

PRODUCTION FOR THE MARKET

The pervasiveness and importance of the market is unique to capitalism. The objective of economic actors in capitalism is to produce goods and services for sale in the market. It is not to produce goods and services to be used by those who actually make them, or to fulfill some direct human or social need. Rather, the objective is the production of things for sale in the marketplace for the *sole purpose of generating profits*. The drive of capitalist economic life is not toward the useful or beneficial (though since Adam Smith the common assumption has been that such is the normal byproduct of a market system), but toward the marketable and profitable.

Actually, the existence of an all-pervasive market is a rather rare and recent phenomenon in human history. While exchange of goods and services has probably existed in some form in all societies, capitalism is unique to the extent that the market encompasses everything. Under capitalism, for the first time in human history, everything is for sale and has a price, including land and human beings themselves. In traditional cultures, for instance, land is regarded as something holy and sacred, the basis of social life, the link to ancestors, the provider of sustenance, the connector of humans to the natural world. As such, land is not something to be bought and sold in the marketplace. One might just as well sell one's arms, or legs, or children in such societies. Similarly, in traditional cultures, individuals do not exist as separate and isolated beings but as members of a tightly knit community, connected to the life of the community through family, work, ritual, and ceremony. In such societies, it would be inconceivable to consider human labor as something to be priced in the marketplace, to be bought and sold like so many oranges, to be discarded onto the dungheap of unemployment when no one is willing to buy it.

Some Implications of the Market Mechanism

As the reader might suspect, both the contact of modern capitalist societies with traditional ones (for instance, the United States in Vietnam),[10] and the transformation of a traditional society to a capitalist one, are disruptive, disorienting, and even devastating to the members of a traditional society. This was evident in the transformation of European feudalism into market capitalism. The brutality of this transformation is seen most clearly in the *enclosure movement* of seventeenth- and eighteenth-century England. Over these two centuries, the scattered fields that poor but relatively free farmers had worked by traditional feudal right were gathered together into great estates under single owners, enclosed by hedges and fences, and turned over to the raising of sheep. In the process, agriculture was transformed from the production of *use values* (farm products to be consumed by the largely self-sufficient local community), to *exchange values* (wool to be bought and sold in the marketplace). In the process, the rural population was ripped from the land and transformed into a landless mass, "free" to sell its labor in urban centers. The alternative was starvation, the poorhouse, or forced labor. The process was so disruptive and brutal that Sir Thomas More was moved to lament that "sheep are eating men."

Similar stories can be told of all transformations to capitalism. What is so disruptive about the introduction of capitalism is its tendency to destroy all preexisting traditional forms, so that all elements of the social order become marketable commodities. In describing the transition of European societies from feudal to market in form, Karl Polanyi writes that while such an organization of economic and social life was more often than not conducive to miraculous new heights of production, it "was accompanied by a catastrophic dislocation of the lives of the common people."[11] By subjecting every element of society to the market, including individuals in their own labor, it "annihilate[d] all organic forms of existence and . . . replace[d] them by a different type of organization, an atomistic and individualistic one."[12]

Contemporary Social Disruption

Readers might protest that if such descriptions capture the barbarism of the early transformation to capitalism, they no longer make sense of the fully developed, mature capitalism of our own day. To a great extent, the objection is well-founded. This may be so because most remnants of traditional society have all but disappeared from western nations under the steamroller of capitalist development. Nevertheless, the market continues to have fully as many negative effects in our own day, though they may be less obvious. A system of production for profit leads to a set of severe social dysfunctions endemic to capitalism. Let me review just a few.

Business Cycle Instability. Capitalism is inescapably subject to periodic economic crisis. While western governments have, to some degree, enhanced their ability to manage the business cycle, capitalism remains a system wracked by periodic alterations between recession and inflation. Since business investment remains in private hands, directed toward the generation of profit, such investment fluctuates as businesspeople assess the future possibilities of profit. If the profit picture is not encouraging, the rational businessperson saves rather than invests. Businesspeople might put their capital into such unproductive activities as real estate speculation and corporate takeover bids or they may invest in other countries. Should this tendency become generalized throughout the entire economy and should businesspeople as a group reach the same conclusion, economic activity slows, and factories cut back their operations or close. In an economy in which labor is a commodity, workers are then thrown onto the unemployment rolls. As unemployment rises, and as other workers find themselves on reduced hours, the level of consumption in the economy further drops, deepening the recessionary spiral, encouraging more plant shutdowns and layoffs.

As recovery begins, either because of new business investment or, more frequently, because of the economic stimulation of massive government spending as in the Reagan boom of 1983, businesspeople with a large pool of savings from the previous period begin to accelerate their level of investment as the overall profit picture brightens. At this point, two things happen. First, the combination of government spending and new investment soon outstrips the capacity of the system to produce goods, creating serious inflation.[13] At a later stage of the recovery, as production accelerates because of the attractive high prices available for goods, production at some point outdistances the effective demand for goods, leaving excessively large inventories. The next collapse into recession or depression comes as businesspeople throughout the economy cancel orders for new goods, factories slow production or close, workers are laid off, and so on as the cycle repeats itself. The violent up and down swings of the business cycle are characteristic of any and all capitalist societies.[14]

Workplace Tensions. Since labor in capitalism is a commodity to be bought when needed and discarded when no longer required, and since this market relationship leads to highly disproportionate power in the workplace, capitalism is continuously beset by serious tensions at the point of production. Forced to work for ends and in ways not freely chosen by them, workers customarily express their alienation in absenteeism, low motivation, turn-over, slow-downs, and strikes. This not only seriously impairs production, but also forces the creation of an elaborate, top-heavy, and very expensive supervisory structure to keep the production process going.[15]

Externalities. In order to maximize profits, the capitalist firm attempts to keep its production costs to a minimum. Such costs normally include the price of plants and equipment, raw materials, and labor. Unless it wants to lower its level of profit, no rational firm chooses to pay for the social costs or *external diseconomies* of its operations. In order to maximize profits, the firm must ignore the social costs of its activities (whether these costs be pollution, traffic deaths, broken families, or lung cancer) and allow society at large to foot the bill.[16] Unless forced by public or union action, for instance, individual firms rarely—and never at the expense of profit—choose to pay for the damages caused by industrial pollution. To do so would be clearly irrational according to business logic. Unless forced, individual firms rarely make their operations as safe as they might be, given the state of technology; to alter operations in the interests of safety would diminish profits. Such business logic largely explains why the United States, by many measures the world's richest society, suffers by far the highest rates of occupational disease, injury, and death in the industrialized world.

The logic of profit maximization is antisocial because it compels business firms to disregard externalities. Any firm that disregarded its own profit statement out of some sense of social obligation would risk financial disaster or takeover by another firm. Clearly, the issue here is less whether the owners or managers of the firm are good or evil people, but rather the imperatives of any firm in a capitalist market economy.

Waste. Capitalism tends to utilize resources in a highly wasteful and irrational manner. Capitalism remains a system driven by the pursuit of profit. It matters not what is produced and sold, whether it be video games or mass transportation, designer label clothing or medical care, nonreturnable bottles or decent housing, so long as profits are made. In the eloquent and revealing words of one car executive, "at GM we produce profits, not cars."[17]

The irrationality and waste of such a system is surely self-evident. A rational firm, in attempting to make profits in the marketplace, will use whatever methods, produce whatever commodities, and utilize whatever raw materials are required for making profits. The firm cannot allow issues of social waste and irrationality to enter into its calculations, unless they will somehow affect the long-range profit picture of the firm. As a result, the general trend in American industry, agriculture, and transportation in recent years has been to change from the use of relatively efficient, nonpolluting forms of energy to less efficient, polluting ones. Synthetic detergents have largely replaced soap, trucks have largely replaced railroads in shipping, cars have replaced rail travel in public transport,[18] and synthetic fibers have replaced natural ones.[19] Business firms have made such transitions not necessarily out of technological imperatives, but because of essentially correct calculations that more profits were to be made. The effects have been disastrous. While the American population increased 126 percent between 1946 and 1971, for instance, the pollution levels in that same period rose, by some estimates, 2,000 percent.[20] Since 1940, U.S. industry has consumed more primary metals than have been consumed in all of previous history, and the pace of usage is increasing. This consumption of nonrenewable resources is taking place at a time when the limits of these resources are becoming all too evident.[21] In short, what may be rational for the business firm is often wasteful and irrational from a social point of view.

Planned obsolescence is another example of waste. The health of market economies depends on a continual willingness of people to buy goods and services. Therefore, any widespread sense of satisfaction with what one already possesses would be a serious development indeed. Capitalism has evolved a useful method to undermine any such threat to mass consumption: a planned abbreviated life for products. It is a not very well-kept secret that most consumer durable products (such as cars, refrigerators, or washing machines), given present technology, could be made long-lasting and easily repairable. Such a development, of course, would considerably limit the market for new consumer durables as well as for spare parts. Thus, companies not only ignore such improvements, but actually build a maximum life into their products. The first fluorescent light bulbs had a life of 10,000 hours, a period of useful life much too long from the point of view of the Philips Trust (the parent holder). After much investment of time and money, its scientists were able to reduce the life of the fluorescent bulb to 1,000 hours. It was only at that point that Philips felt sufficiently secure about its long-range profit picture to market the bulb.[22]

Capitalism also attempts to accelerate product changeover through advertising and periodic model changes. These are designed to create dissatisfaction in the potential consumer, who is made to feel old-fashioned, a failure as a provider, or deficient in sex appeal without the new model. In addition to the obvious cost of advertising and of retooling industry to produce slightly different models of standard products, valuable resources are wasted as Americans are encouraged to discard older models. Again, what might be rational from the point of view of the firm, or from the point of view of the capitalist economy as a whole, is clearly irrational and wasteful from a human or social point of view.

Finally, capitalism is irrational and wasteful because it conceives of human labor as a commodity to be bought and sold in the marketplace like any other commodity. Because labor is used only if some enterprise is willing to buy it, persistent unemployment is a central characteristic of any and all capitalist societies, especially in the modern corporate economy (as will be seen in a later chapter), where overproduction and underconsumption become ever more serious, and where unemployment as a consequence tends to fluctuate between 6 and 10 percent of the workforce in the best of times.

To understand the relationship between a market system and waste, it is crucial to realize that the seemingly mindless wasting of resources, whether material or human, is intrinsic to and inherent in the market itself. Nothing in the market mechanism plans rational usage or harbors resources for the future. Any concern about depletion of resources, pollution, or unemployment is external to the market, and efforts to act on these concerns, whether by government, unions, or consumers, are external to the market and intrude upon its normal operations.

Social Disintegration. Before abandoning this discussion of the disutilities inherent in capitalism, we might also take note of the problem of social disintegration. Ironically, one of the most powerful and important effects of the operations of a market capitalist economy is its tendency to tear apart all stable communities, traditions, and values. I use the word "ironic" because many of the most vocal advocates of market capitalism are precisely those people who most strongly lament the decline of religion, community, and family in American life, and who tend to place the blame for these trends squarely on the shoulders of modern liberals and other egalitarians with their penchant for schemes to interfere with the free and untrammeled operation of the market mechanism. It is precisely the incredible dynamism of the capitalist economy that represents the main force in the destruction of all stable traditions and institutions. How can local communities remain stable and viable when enterprises are free to come and go, when resources are ruthlessly exploited, when families are uprooted to make way for enterprises, or when people are forced to seek jobs in other regions? It is the pace of technological change and the tremendous mobility of private capital in its unending pursuit of gain that are both the power of the market economy and the essence of its destructiveness. How can traditional values and institutions stand the blows of such a dynamic process? The market creates a society of mobility and change, of competition and self-interest. It creates a society of individual self-seekers without obligations or ties. It destroys the ground upon which people might pause to rest. And most individuals, for better or worse, cannot stand the consequences of such a life. It is reflected in distressingly high rates of alcoholism and drug abuse, in divorce, and interpersonal violence. These are the kinds of costs that represent the dark underside of the glittery, gadget-filled capitalist success story.

CONCLUDING REMARKS

This chapter has described the defining elements of capitalism, how these elements relate to each other, and what some of the ramifications of their operations might be for American society. Such descriptions are important for several reasons:

☐ *To demonstrate the ways in which capitalism is distinguished from other economic systems.* While some of the elements we have described can be found in other economic systems, the combination of market-oriented production and a class system based on property are unique to capitalism. Furthermore, while capitalism has been greatly transformed during its three- or four-hundred-year history, class and market remain its defining characteristics.

The long arm of the consumer economy

☐ *To demonstrate the problematic nature of capitalist economies.* We have examined how the class system and the market produce a set of problems that are inescapable; these include inequality, alienation, instability, unemployment, exploitation, irrationality, and wastefulness. While many of these problems can be found in other types of society, it is only in capitalism that they arise out of the very logic of the system. Furthermore, the problematic nature of capitalist production, being intrinsic to social class and commodity, cannot be changed merely by displacing old piratical entrepreneurs with more humane, Harvard Business School–trained managers. The logic of the economic system forces them to act in very much the same manner.

☐ *To begin to consider the functions of government in the contemporary United States.* One of the most important phenomena that we shall examine is the seemingly inexorable growth in the size and impact of all levels of government in the United States. A substantial part of that growth can be explained by the social havoc wrought by capitalism, and by the problems spun off in its development. Government has been forced to intervene in economic and social life because of mass political pressures, and because of elite fears of mass instability in the face of the problems caused, paradoxically, by the very successes of capitalism.

This chapter has described a *general* theory of capitalist society relevant to any and all market capitalist systems. As such, it remains at a fairly high level of abstraction. The next two chapters will describe more carefully the specific ways in which capitalism operates in the contemporary United States and how these economic processes affect the possibilities for social justice and democracy. Subsequent chapters will analyze how political institutions and government policy are shaped by American capitalism.

NOTES

1. Howard Sherman, *Radical Political Economy: Capitalism and Socialism from a Marxist-Humanist Perspective* (New York: Basic Books, 1972).
2. R. H. Tawney, *Equality* (London: Allen and Unwin, 1952), pp. 58, 66.
3. Quoted in Ross Terrill, *R. H. Tawney and His Times* (Cambridge: Harvard University Press, 1967), p. 167. I do not agree that profit is simply the just reward for productive innovation or for abstinence from the immediate use and enjoyment of wealth. For a devastating refutation of these understandings of profit, see Francis Green and Peter Nore, *Economics: An Anti-Textbook* (London: Macmillan, 1977); and E. K. Hunt and Jesse Schwartz (eds.), *A Critique of Economic Theory* (London: Penguin, 1972).
4. See his discussion of these issues in C. B. MacPherson, *Democratic Theory: Essays in Retrieval* (London: Clarendon Press, 1973). It must be added that in most societies that call themselves socialist, different yet equally serious obstacles to the development of human capacities exist (see chapter 17). For the best comparison of capitalist and socialist societies, see Branko Horvat, *The Political Economy of Socialism* (Armonk, N.Y.: M. E. Sharpe, 1982).
5. See the discussion of the history of work organization and the accelerating pace of the division of labor in Harry Braverman, *Labor and Monopoly Capital* (New York: Monthly Review Press, 1974).
6. Marx referred to this separation between the human essence and the reality of most people's everyday life as *alienation*. For the best introductions to Marx's concept of alienation see Shlomo Avineri, *The Social and Political Thought of Karl Marx* (New York: Cambridge University Press, 1968); Erich Fromm, *Marx's Conception of Man* (New York: Ungar, 1961); and Bertall Ollman, *Alienation: Marx's Conception of Man in Capitalist Society* (New York: Cambridge University Press, 1971). Also see Horvat, *The Political Economy of Socialism*.
7. Paul Blumberg, *Industrial Democracy: The Sociology of Participation* (New York: Schocken Books, 1969); Melvin Kohn, *Class and Conformity* (Homewood, Ill.: Dorsey Press, 1969); Arthur Kornhauser, *The Mental Health of the Industrial Worker* (New York: Wiley, 1965); H. L. Sheppard and N. Q. Herrick, *Where Have All the Robots Gone? Worker Dissatisfaction in the Seventies* (New York: Free Press, 1972); Ronald Mason, *Participatory and Workplace Democracy* (Carbondale, Ill.: University of Southern Illinois Press, 1982); Studs Terkel, *Working* (New York: Pantheon, 1972). For provocative introductions to alternative forms of work organization see Martin Carnoy and Derek Shearer, *Economic Democracy* (New York: M. E. Sharpe, 1980) and Daniel Zwerdling, *Workplace Democracy* (New York: Harper & Row, Colophon Books, 1980).
8. Terkel, *Working*, p. xxxii.
9. Given the general misunderstanding of this fundamental concept, an important qual-

ification is in order. My presentation of capitalist society as composed of two opposed classes is in the form of a model. As with any scientific model, this one does not claim absolute fidelity to all of the details of any particular society. All scientific models are simplifications of reality that advance our understanding by extracting and highlighting the essentials and placing less important matters in the background. I most certainly understand that the actual class structure of the United States is infinitely more complex. I shall explore these issues more closely in the next chapter.

10. For a compelling and poignant description of the impact of the American presence on traditional Vietnamese society, see Frances FitzGerald's *Fire in the Lake* (New York: Vintage, 1973). One should also see the Academy Award–winning documentary film "Hearts and Minds."
11. Karl Polanyi, *The Great Transformation* (Boston: Beacon Press, 1957), p. 33.
12. Ibid., p. 163.
13. To be sure, inflation is also the product of the natural and artificial scarcities and of a phenomenon known to economists as "administered pricing," whereby giant corporate enterprises set their own market prices (see chapter 7).
14. Economic fluctuations occur in socialist countries, but they are distinctly different. Not only are they less severe, but they are characterized by alterations in the rates of real growth, not by absolute declines in output and employment. See Sherman, *Radical Political Economy*, ch. 17.
15. See Horvat, *The Political Economy of Socialism*, pp. 192–198, for elaboration of this point.
16. For the best discussion of these issues see K. William Kapp, *The Social Costs of Private Enterprise* (New York: Schocken Books, 1971).
17. Quoted in William Serrin, *The Company and the Union* (New York: Vintage, 1974).
18. A study by Brad Snell for the Senate Judiciary Committee (1974) reveals that since 1949, General Motors, Standard Oil, and Firestone had been involved in a strategy to buy and to ruin urban rail systems in order to create a market for buses, trucks, and automobiles.
19. Barry Commoner, *The Closing Circle* (New York: Alfred A. Knopf, 1971), pp. 143–45.
20. Ibid., p. 145. During this period, Commoner reports the following increases in production: nonreturnable soda bottles, up 52,000 percent; synthetic fibers, up 5,980 percent; mercury for chlorine detergents, up 3,930 percent; and so on.
21. Stephen E. Harris, *The Death of Capital* (New York: Pantheon, 1977), p. 43.
22. André Gorz, *A Strategy for Labor* (Boston: Beacon Press, 1967), p. 79.

SUGGESTIONS FOR FURTHER READING

Harry Braverman. LABOR AND MONOPOLY CAPITAL. *New York: Monthly Review Press, 1974.* A brilliant analysis of transformations in the world of work.
Milton Friedman. CAPITALISM AND FREEDOM. *Chicago: University of Chicago Press, 1962.* The leading and most influential defense of the competitive free market system by the Nobel Prize–winning economist.
John G. Gurley. CHALLENGERS TO CAPITALISM: MARX, LENIN AND MAO. *San Francisco: The Portable Stanford Series, San Francisco Book Co., 1976.* A useful introduction to the Marxist analysis of capitalist society.
Branko Horvat. THE POLITICAL ECONOMY OF SOCIALISM. *Armonk, N.Y.: M.E. Sharpe, Inc.,*

1982. A monumental comparison and rejection of capitalism and presently existing socialism.

K. William Kapp. THE SOCIAL COSTS OF PRIVATE ENTERPRISE. *New York: Schocken Books, 1971.* A close look at the dark underside of free enterprise.

R. H. Tawney. THE ACQUISITIVE SOCIETY. *New York: Harcourt, Brace & World, 1920.* A classic and still compelling description of the behavioral and attitudinal attributes of capitalism.

Eric Wolf. EUROPE AND THE PEOPLE WITHOUT HISTORY. *Berkeley: University of California Press, 1982.* The best single work charting the rise of the world capitalist system.

6

Economy and Society:
Social Class and
Inequality

> If we made an income pyramid out of a child's blocks, with each layer portraying $1,000 of income, the peak would be far higher than the Eiffel Tower, but almost all of us would be within a yard of the ground.[1]

This chapter is about the great inequalities that characterize life in America. It is about inequalities that doom many to abject poverty and bless more than a few with opulence and leisure. As such, this chapter refutes many of our most cherished, persistent, and deeply held beliefs about our country. It diverges, in particular, from that set of beliefs which holds that we are a middle-class, affluent society, a society in which both poverty and extreme wealth are in steady decline, equality of condition is slowly but steadily becoming a reality, and in which, as a result, most Americans participate in the "American Dream."

As is often the case with widely held myths, some grains of truth can be discerned. Nevertheless, I hope to demonstrate that a surprisingly small percentage of Americans owns a share in the American Dream; that a majority lives in an anxious and desperate economic situation; that the severe maldistribution of American affluence is structured along social class lines; and that this state of affairs is inherent in capitalism.[2]

INCOME DISTRIBUTION

I begin with a consideration of the distribution of income in the United States. I do so primarily because of the obvious relationship between how much money one has to spend and one's quality of life in any market capitalist system. In the

The rich at play

United States, where fewer social services are provided by government than in any other western nation, the relationship between income and quality of life is particularly significant. Americans must pay out of pocket (or through credit borrowing) for most of those benefits that other economically developed societies provide as a matter of right to its citizens (higher education, health care, day care for children, retirement, and so on). It can be said without exaggeration that in the United States one's relative standard of living is more dependent on available income than it is in any other industrial society, whether capitalist or socialist. A consideration of the distribution of income, therefore, provides a necessary opening wedge into the consideration of the distribution of life chances among the population.

Measuring the distribution of income, however, is not an easy task. For one thing, most measures depend upon figures from the Internal Revenue Service, which is itself dependent upon the honest reporting of income, particularly by the very wealthy who have the greatest opportunity to hide their income. Moreover, IRS figures are concerned solely with taxable income. They do not include income derived from such sources as unrealized capital gains, or interest from tax-exempt bonds—income that accrues almost entirely to the very rich. Finally, the IRS does not count as income the rather considerable expense accounts and other income-in-kind that corporations provide to their executives. For all of these reasons, IRS figures considerably *understate* the share of national income that goes to the wealthy. Bureau of the Census figures suffer from similar problems of accuracy. Thus, the reader should keep in mind that the figures presented here are not perfectly accurate, but are often based on estimates and reasoned judgments.

With all of that said, what is striking about all of these data is their general consensus on two points: *the existence of severe inequality in income distribution, and the stability and persistence of that inequality*. Consider the figures published by the Urban Institute based on data from the Bureau of the Census (see Table 6.1).[3] Several observations about these figures are important. First, the inequalities are persistent. Between 1950 and 1984, during a period of unparalleled growth in the American economy, of expansions in educational opportunities, and of government programs designed to assist the poor and the elderly, the poorest 20 percent of American families increased their share of national income (before taxes) by only 0.6 percentage points. The position of the wealthiest 20 percent of families declined only 0.5 percentage points in that same period. In absolute terms and in constant dollars, the gap between rich and poor increased dramatically. The Urban Institute reports that the difference between the median incomes of the top and bottom 20 percent increased from $14,745 in 1960 to $34,489 in 1984.[4]

The reader should also be aware of the rather startling changes that have taken place in the distribution of family incomes during the Reagan years. Using a computer model that is based on data from the Bureau of the Census and which includes government transfer payments and food stamps, the Urban Institute reports that real disposable income increased by 8.7 percent for the top 20 percent of American families between 1980 and 1984 and decreased by 7.6 percent for the bottom 20 percent. The former had almost $3,000 more to spend at the end of the period; the latter had about $600 less.[5]

It is also of more than passing interest that the United States is close to being the most inegalitarian of all of the industrialized nations (France being our only close competitor). The West Germans, for instance, manage to be productive and

TABLE 6.1   Percentage of aggregate income before taxes
received by U.S. families

INCOME RANK	1950	1960	1970	1979	1984[a]
Lowest 20 percent	4.5	4.8	5.4	5.3	5.1
Second 20 percent	11.9	12.2	12.2	11.6	11.2
Third 20 percent	17.4	17.8	17.6	17.5	17.2
Fourth 20 percent	23.6	24.0	23.8	24.1	24.3
Top 20 percent	42.7	41.3	40.9	41.6	42.2

SOURCE: U.S. Department of Commerce, Bureau of the Census, *Current Population Reports*, Series P-60, various years; and John L. Palmer and Isabel V. Sawhill (eds.), *The Reagan Record* (Cambridge, Mass.: Ballinger, 1984).

[a] Estimate, Urban Institute household income model.

prosperous with 36 percent less inequality than us, while the Japanese manage with 50 percent less.[6] Or to take a different measure, the ratio of the income of a family at the ninety-fifth percentile to one at the fifth is 3.0 for Sweden, 5.0 for Great Britain, 5.7 for Denmark, but 12.7 for the United States. It should be further noted that the distribution of income is decidedly more equal in the socialist countries than in capitalist ones (at least when countries at a similar level of economic development are compared).[7] Finally, all of these figures on comparative inequality are from the pre-Reagan years. There is very strong reason to suspect that they would be much worse today.

THE DISTRIBUTION OF WEALTH

As critical as income remains in determining the life chances of Americans, wealth in property is far more important in the long run. I make that claim for several reasons. First, the ownership or nonownership of wealth is the most important determining factor in generating disposable income itself; it is the very basis for income. Having no wealth in property means having to sell one's labor in the marketplace, and for all but a few (doctors, lawyers, athletes, corporation executives, or fashion models, who happen to have highly prized skills or personal assets), high incomes are an impossibility. To have made but $32,000 in 1980 put one among the top 20 percent of families in the United States. While a few very high incomes are based purely on salary (professional athletes, for instance), most are based on wealth in property. For those families who make over $200,000 a year, almost three-fourths of all income is generated from property ownership. For families lucky enough to take home in excess of $1,000,000 annually, over 90 percent is generated from the sale or use of property (real estate, corporate stock, savings accounts, bonds, and so on). It should not be surprising to learn that an almost perfect correspondence exists between annual earnings and the ownership of property in the United States. Those without property tend to have very low incomes; those with extensive property tend to enjoy high annual incomes.

In an economy where labor is a commodity to be bought and sold, wealth in property acts as a shield against insecurity. To sell one's labor is to be vulnerable. Except for those few salaried persons who have stabilized their employment situation through some kind of tenure arrangement, wage and salary workers tend to be tied to the fluctuations of the business cycle. Even people with substantial salaries can and do lose their jobs. The issue is put in characteristic fashion by iconoclastic economist Ferdinand Lundberg, who has bluntly observed:

> For my part, I would say that anyone who does not own a fairly substantial amount of income-producing property or does not receive an earned income sufficiently large to make substantial regular savings or does not hold a well-paid securely tenured job is poor. He may be healthy, handsome and a delight to his friends—but he is poor. By this standard at least 70 percent of Americans are certainly poor, although not all of these by any means are destitute or poverty-stricken. But, as was shown in the 1930s, Americans can become destitute overnight if

deprived of their jobs, a strong support to mindless conformity. As a matter of fact, many persons in rather well-paid jobs, even executives, from time to time find themselves jobless owing to job discontinuance by reason of mergers, technical innovation, or plant removal. Unable to get new jobs, they suddenly discover, to their amazement, that they are really poor, and they also discover by harsh experience to what specific conditions the word "poverty" refers. And even many of those who never lose their jobs often discover in medical and similar emergencies that they are as helpless as wandering beggars. They are, in fact, poor. In such eventualities the man of property is evidently in a different position. He is definitely not poor.[8]

Finally, and perhaps most important, to own substantial property in the United States is to be in a position to control major social institutions. Only those who are wealthy in property have the income, assets, technical assistance (lawyers, accountants, financial consultants, and so on), investment capability, and time necessary to control corporations, banks, foundations, universities, the political process and news media. To own wealth in property is to be among the potential directors of the social order. To be only a wage and salary earner is to be one who is largely directed and controlled by others. In a purported democracy, this great maldistribution of wealth ought to be (but is not) a matter of great public concern.

The Nature of the Distribution

The distribution of *wealth* thus tells us much more about who wins and who loses in American life and about who controls and who is controlled than does the distribution of *income*. Unfortunately, accurate information about the distribution of wealth is even more difficult to come by than information about income, since wealth is more easily hidden. Information about the property holdings of Americans is nowhere consistently and periodically collected. No bureau or branch of the federal government requires Americans to declare what they own. Those few who have plunged into the investigation of wealth have been hampered by the many ingenious devices for hiding wealth. Nevertheless, as precarious as the data are, and knowing that the figures probably *understate* the holdings of the very wealthy, every government and scholarly study of the distribution of wealth shows an astounding maldistribution, so extreme that it makes income inequality look quite tame by comparison (see Table 6.2).[9]

The meaning of the figures is clear. In 1962, a tiny minority of wealth holders, no more than 5 percent, owned *half* of the total personal wealth in the United States. Perhaps more important, given the decisive nature of the corporation in the American economy (see Chapter 7), this tiny group owned virtually all privately held corporate stock. Despite the constant refrain of "stockholder democracy" found in business publications, the bottom 95 percent of the population was left with only 17 percent of corporate stock, the bottom 80 percent with an almost laughable 4 percent. Figures based on an evaluation of estate tax returns estimate that the top .05 percent (one-twentieth of one percent) of the population

TABLE 6.2   Distribution of various types of personal
wealth, 1962 (percentages)

	WEALTHIEST 20%	WEALTHIEST 5%	WEALTHIEST 1%
Total U.S. wealth	76	50	31
Total corporate stock	96	83	61
Total assets of businesses and professions	89	62	39

SOURCE: Frank Ackerman et al., "Income Distribution in the United States," *Review of Radical Political Economics*, 3, 3 (Summer 1971); based on data from Dorothy S. Projector and Gertrude Weiss, *Survey of Financial Characteristics of Consumer*, Federal Reserve System, 1966; and Irwin Friend et al., *Mutual Funds and Other Institutional Investors: A New Perspective*.

today holds about one-fifth of all corporate stock, two-thirds of all state and local tax-free bonds, and two-fifths of all bonds and notes.[10] It should also be obvious that only a very few receive the great bulk of the income generated by property. Thus, the top 5 percent receives 64 percent of all income from stock dividends, 30 percent of all interest, 64 percent of trust income. In 1984, according to *Forbes* magazine, the wealthiest 482 individuals and families in America controlled $2,200 billion in business assets, or about 40 percent of all nonresidential private capital in the nation.[11] The trend over the past decade, moreover, seems to be toward an ever greater concentration of wealth, a trend that has accelerated under Ronald Reagan because of changes in the tax laws (estate tax, accelerated depreciation, and so on).

The average American, on the other hand, has little or no wealth of which to speak, no cushion upon which to rest should he or she lose a job or suddenly face a major medical bill. Over half of the population in 1977 had a total net worth of under $3,000! The United States government also reports that 30 percent of Americans had less than $500 in liquid assets in that same year, while another 22 percent had less than $2,000. At the top of the pyramid, the top 10 percent of the population had about 75 percent of all savings.

THE INCIDENCE OF POVERTY

No discussion of wealth and income distribution would be complete without some consideration of the continuing and recently escalating problem of poverty in the United States. Although absolute income levels may be on the rise for the entire population, we must not succumb to the illusion that inequality is thereby shorn of its adverse consequences. What is most evident when looking at the poverty figures is the tenacity of poverty amid affluence in the United States, and the very large number of Americans who hover precariously near its edges.

One of the problems we face in the analysis of poverty is that no general consensus exists about either its definition or how to best measure its scope. The least adequate measure is the one used by the Social Security Administration (SSA). Not surprisingly, since it is the most optimistic measure, it is the one most widely used by the government (see Table 6.3 and Figure 6.1).

From the SSA measure several things become immediately apparent. First, during the 1960s there seems to have been a significant and steady decrease in the number of Americans who fell below the poverty line. Second, during the 1970s there was a perceptible leveling off of these trends and the appearance of a plateau upon which the poverty figures rested. (What this means, given an

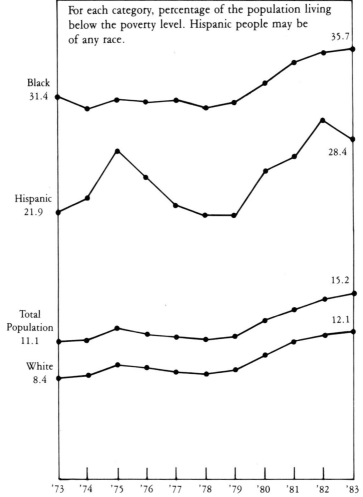

SOURCE: *The New York Times,* August 3, 1984, based on data from the U.S. Bureau of the Census. Reprinted by Permission.

FIGURE 6.1   Poverty Rates in the U.S., 1973–1983

TABLE 6.3   U.S. population below SSA poverty line

YEAR	PERCENTAGE OF POPULATION BELOW SSA POVERTY LINE
1960	22.2
1965	17.3
1968	12.8
1972	12.0
1973	11.6
1974	11.6
1977	11.6
1980	13.0
1982	15.1
1983	15.3

SOURCE: U.S. Bureau of the Census, *Current Population Reports,* Series P-60, various years through 1984.

expanding population, is an increase in the absolute number of people defined as poor. Between 1972 and 1977, there was an increase of 1.7 million such people.[12]) Third, in very recent years, the percentage of those falling below the poverty line has increased dramatically. Between 1982 and 1983 alone, the poverty rolls increased by almost one million people. Between 1980 and 1984, it increased by almost six million. By 1984, almost one-fourth of all American children were found to be living in poverty.

These official poverty figures substantially understate the number of people living in poverty conditions. The Social Security Administration poverty measure is constructed for families of different sizes by multiplying the Department of Agriculture's "emergency food budget" by three. The number three is used because a 1955 study showed that the average American family spent about one-third of its budget on food; thus, a total budget would be the food budget multiplied by three. Several things are critically amiss with this measure. First, the food budget used is an "emergency" budget, and by that the Department of Agriculture means a diet for temporary emergencies. It has never been suggested that human beings can maintain life on such a diet over the long run. Furthermore, a more recent study demonstrates that Americans spend only about one-fourth of their budget on food, so the multiplier used should properly be four. In other words, given a more reasonable food budget and a multiplier of four, the poverty line, even using the government's own assumptions, should be considerably *higher*. It is obvious that given a higher poverty line, a much greater percentage of the population—well over 20 percent—would fall beneath it.

During the Reagan years, the poor got poorer and more people became poor. Immediate prospects for this group, moreover, do not look promising. First, because the poor are outside the mainstream of the economy (they are often displaced "smokestack" industry workers, low-paid service workers, minority

teenagers, female heads of households, street people, and residents of permanently depressed regions like Appalachia) they have been largely unaffected by
the vigorous economic growth of recent years. Various recoveries, that is to say,
have left them untouched. Second, programs to assist the poor and the near-poor,
from food stamps to Medicaid, have borne the brunt of the Reagan ideological
and budgetary axe. Programs for these groups have been seen by policy-makers
in the Reagan administration as unsuitable and counterproductive in a free-
enterprise economy (to the extent that they sap initiative, self-reliance, etc.) and
far too expensive in an era of record-setting budget deficits. The Congressional
Research Service has reported, for instance, that during the 1981–82 recession,
almost 600,000 people fell into the poverty category because of federal budget
cutbacks.[13] Squeezed between a rapidly changing American economy and an un-
sympathetic and unsupportive federal government, the plight of the poor in
America is likely to worsen in the future.

Poverty Among Black Americans

The situation is even more desperate for specific groups within the population,
including the elderly, female heads of households,[14] and blacks. The situation of
black Americans is particularly instructive (and says much about the tenacity of
the class system). After at least a decade and a half of protest, political advance,
and massive federal government intervention and assistance, the depressed economic picture for blacks remained relatively unchanged throughout the 1970s and
deteriorated in the 1980s. For a very long time now, the median family income
for blacks has hovered between 55 and 60 percent that of whites, and, in
recent years, has moved toward the lower end of the range. Well over one-
third of all black families fall below the government's official poverty line, while
only a handful exceed the "intermediate" income budget of the Bureau of Labor
Statistics. Only 30 percent of black American families find themselves above the
median income. Figures on the ownership of property are even more distressing.
Only about 3.7 percent of the black population are self-employed proprietors
(mostly of small and marginal businesses). That 3.7 percent, it is estimated by
economist Henry Terrell, owns no more than 1 percent of the equity of American
businesses and farms. As for wealth in general, blacks own no more than 0.1
percent of stock holdings.[15]

The situation of the black population is a particularly graphic demonstration
of the impact of the social class system. The depressed economic condition of
blacks is the result of two related factors. First, blacks do not own property to any
appreciable degree. They are therefore denied all of the financial advantages that
naturally accrue to property in a capitalist system—the ability to live off the labor
of others, the power to direct production, and the ability to ride out fluctuations
in the business cycle. Second, the black population is almost totally dependent
on wages and salaries. If one puts aside for a moment those blacks who are unemployed, on welfare, or on social security, over 96 percent of black families de-

Black poverty remains a fact of life in the United States

pend entirely on wages and salaries.[16] They are largely dependent, that is to say, on their ability to sell their labor in the marketplace. Since they are a population with educational and skill levels below the national average, a population with low seniority, faced with severe competition for unskilled and semiskilled jobs by a large pool of unemployed and underemployed labor, and faced, too, with persistent job discrimination, they have not been able to sell their labor for a satisfactory price. The black labor force remains a commodity for which the owners of property have not had to pay a high price. Black families have the great misfortune of being a cheap commodity in a capitalist economy.

THE DISTRIBUTION OF GENERAL SOCIAL BENEFITS: THE CASE OF HEALTH

The above data demonstrate the existence of a highly unequal distribution of wealth and income in the United States. Furthermore, there are no discernible trends toward a narrowing of the gap between rich and poor. Indeed, the income and wealth gap appears to have been widening significantly in recent years. As I have attempted to point out, income and wealth distribution are not only of interest in and of themselves, but also for their implications for the quality of life of different groups within society. Whether one measures it in terms of access to security, legal justice, nutrition, housing, or political power, quality of life remains tied to income and hence to property.

Up to this point, the analysis has merely claimed that a relationship exists between quality of life and class position. While this relationship seems self-evident, I have yet to offer any concrete evidence. Unfortunately, there is no easy way to measure quality of life. Nor can I go through every possible component of the quality of life, measure their distributions, and add them all together. Rather, what is needed is some single indicator of the quality of life, some component considered so central and important by reasonable people that it can represent the overall concept.

Health is a nearly perfect measure of the quality of life. First, without reasonable health, a person is largely barred from enjoying whatever other things are considered part of the good life. Second, the state of health of a given social group is greatly influenced by all of the other component parts of the quality of life, such as nutrition, security, good housing, and clean air. Finally, health is an important indicator of the quality of life simply because most people believe that it is. In one opinion study after another, Americans (as well as other peoples) place good health at or near the top of their list of hopes and aspirations. For these three closely interconnected reasons, I believe that it is reasonable to use health as an indicator of the quality of life, and as a useful measure by which to compare social groups.

The State of American Health

Americans spend an enormous amount of money on medical care. Health care expenditures by government and by private individuals have increased by an average of 10 percent per annum since the mid-1960s, exceeding $330 billion by 1982, and accounting for almost 11 percent of the Gross National Product.[17] And yet, strange as it may seem, in comparison to other advanced industrial countries, America has a dismal health record. The United States ranks only fifteenth in the world in infant mortality, and only sixteenth in average life expectancy. Twenty countries have fewer cases of heart disease, and twelve have fewer cases of ulcers, diabetes, cirrhosis of the liver, and hypertension. Deaths among women in childbirth exceed that of one hundred other countries. As one scholar has bluntly pointed out, "While the medical profession of the United States is extraordinarily rich and its medical scientists are dominant in international research . . . citizens of the United States . . . are among the least healthy people in the industrialized world."[18] If health is an indicator of quality of life, then one would be forced to conclude that behind the glitter of the American dream stands a more sobering reality.

The Maldistribution of Health

As bad as the general situation might appear, the maldistribution of health among the population is even more striking. Hidden behind the overall American averages are the severe inequalities prevalent among population groups. The officially designated poor in the United States suffer *twice* the infant mortality rate of the remainder of the population, *twice* the postneonatal mortality rate, and half again as many mortalities at all age levels.[19] There is evidence to suggest, moreover, that this historic ratio of the health of the poor to that of the national average has changed for the worse over the past decade and a half despite increases in medical expenditures at all levels.[20] If we compare the situation of the poor not to the national average but to advantaged groups, the data are even more jolting. One medical demographer has pointed out "that there are a number of northern ghetto census tracts in which the infant death rate now exceeds one hundred deaths for every thousand live births."[21] This rate is *ten* times the rate in the wealthy suburb of Scarsdale, New York.

There is no incontrovertible explanation for the wide disparities in health among population groups in the United States. However, two explanations stand out from the many possibilities: the commodity nature of health care, and the human pathology of social class. One of the principal problems of health care distribution in the United States is that such care is considered not a right of all citizens, but something that is bought and sold in the marketplace. Doctors are, by and large, professionals who sell their services to those who can afford to pay the bill. "Most medical practitioners are private entrepreneurs, and good health is considered a commodity."[22] It goes almost without saying that those with the greatest disposable income will be those for whom the medical profession is most solicitous. Just as the poor and the near-poor have limited access to the goods and services of American life, so too are they denied access to the best in medical care. The result is that "how long a person will live, the disease he will have, the type of treatment he will receive, and the cause of his death are strongly influenced by the amount of money these is to spend on health."[23] Without the necessary fees to buy medical services, the poor and the near-poor must depend on charity, on the fragmented care of the outpatient clinic, or on the wards of the large, urban, public hospitals in which care is episodic, not coordinated over the long term as it is for the more affluent. Where health is a commodity, those who are weak in the marketplace invariably suffer. The rapid rise of "for profit" hospital chains is likely to make matters even worse in the years ahead.

Some observers argue that disparities in health have little to do with access to medical care, but are more strongly related to the different ways of life of groups in the United States. They point out that poor nutrition, inadequate housing, and interpersonal violence have more to do with health or its absence than does the accessibility to medical care. While acknowledging that medical care is severely maldistributed in the United States, these scholars point out that class differences in health are so pronounced even before people come into contact with the medical system that the system can do little to overcome the inequalities. Infant mortality, for instance, is directly related to birth weight. Doctors can do little about low birth weight, for such a deficiency is tied to the quality of nutrition, housing, air quality, and sanitation. Many deaths among black children are tied to lead poisoning, caused by high levels of pollution in central cities and by eating peeling wall paint; doctors can do little once lead poisoning is well advanced.

No matter which explanation of health inequality is most convincing, it remains indisputable that wealth and income differences relate strongly to differences in the overall quality of life in the United States. It also remains the case, given the commodity nature of medical care and class differences in access to the means of good health, that any explanation of the severe inequalities existing in the overall quality of life in the United States must center on its organization as a capitalist market society.

CONCLUDING REMARKS

In this chapter I have examined the widespread inequalities in the distribution of advantages in the United States. Focusing on the health sector, I have attempted to show how wealth and income disparities translate into disparities in the overall quality of life among the American population. I have also suggested that these disparities are tied to the existence of social classes as defined in Chapter 5. How so? How is inequality derived from social classes in capitalism?

First, it is clear that the decisive distinction between those who receive substantial incomes and those who receive merely adequate incomes (to say nothing of those with inadequate incomes) is their relative access to private property. To have access to substantial property is to enjoy the possibility of high income. To be without property is to be largely cut off from such a possibility unless and to the extent that one's labor is highly valued by property owners. Stratification of incomes within the nonpropertied group is tied to the wage labor system, in which labor's relative attractiveness to property, and its relative scarcity as a commodity, determines its market value. Thus skills that directly advance the interests of the holders of private property (tax lawyers, accountants, and the like) receive substantial remuneration, while easily replaceable unskilled and semiskilled labor inhabit the lower strata of the income pyramid.

Second, the social class system structures inequality because of its intergenerational character. That is to say, while inequality does and has always existed in every known society, our own system of inequality may best be understood in social class terms because of its persistence across successive generations. The sons and daughters of the rich and privileged retain a very high probability of continuing their way of life in our system, as do the sons and daughters of the poor because the parents of the former may transfer their property to their offspring whereas the latter have nothing to transfer. *Forbes* magazine's annual survey of the American wealthy reports that each and every one of its richest 82 families in 1984 attained its lofty position by virtue of inheritance.[24]

The existence of great inequalities, whether or not the reader chooses to believe that inequality is derived from social classes, raises important issues in terms of the overall analysis in this book. First, the existence of great inequalities raises the issue of social justice in America. To the socialist, the very existence of such inequalities signals the absence of justice. On the other hand, the classical liberal would want to know whether such inequalities arise from the natural operations of a free market, while the classical conservative would focus on whether they reflect natural merit and provide the resources whereby the fit might govern. Second, the existence of great inequality raises the issue of the vitality of democracy, for it has the potential for being translated into highly disproportionate political power, a fact which makes the attainment of either participatory, representative, or pluralist democracy highly problematic. Third, and finally, the existence of great inequality and the social tensions that exist between groups and classes provides much of the public-policy agenda for government in the United States. I shall have much more to say about each of these issues in subsequent chapters.

NOTES

1. Paul Samuelson, *Economics*, 6th ed. (New York: McGraw-Hill, 1964), p. 113.
2. Philip Green has aptly termed capitalism "systematized inequality." See *The Pursuit of Inequality* (New York: Pantheon, 1981), p. 1.
3. The Urban Institute calculations include government transfer payments such as social welfare and Social Security as well as the market value of food stamps.
4. Marily Moon and Isabel V. Sawhill, "Family Incomes," in John L. Palmer and Isabel V. Sawhill, *The Reagan Record* (Cambridge, Mass.: Ballinger, 1984), pp. 322, 352.
5. *Ibid.*, pp. 320, 321.
6. Malcolm Sawyer and Frank Wasserman, "Income Distribution in the OECD Countries," *OECD Economic Outlook* (July 1976), p. 14.
7. See the summary of this literature in Charles Lindblom, *Politics and Markets* (New York: Basic Books, 1977), ch. 20.
8. Ferdinand Lundberg, *The Rich and the Super-Rich* (New York: Bantam, 1968), p. 23.
9. Because of the great difficulties involved in unearthing information about wealth, the rather ancient data reported in this table remains the best that are available to us.

10. Maurice Zeitlin, "Who Owns America?" *The Progressive* (June 1978), pp. 14–19. The remaining figures in this section are also from Zeitlin.

11. Lester C. Thurow, "The Leverage of Our Wealthiest 400," *The New York Times* (October 11, 1984).

12. U.S. Bureau of the Census, "Money Income and Poverty Status of Families and Persons in the U.S.," *Current Population Reports*, Series P-60, No. 116, July 1978.

13. "Study Says the Budget Made 557,000 Poor," *The New York Times* (July 25, 1984), p. 1. There are many conservative economists who claim that if the value of noncash benefits like food stamps, Medicaid, and rent supplements were included, the percentage of the officially designated poor would be as low as 10 percent. It is not clear, however, why such economists would not do the same for more advantaged groups in their calculations of income distribution and include deductions for mortgage interest payments, unrealized capital gains, company medical and insurance plans, and the like.

14. The median income of female-headed households in 1982 was less than half of the national median income for all families. Over 35 percent of female-headed households fell below the official poverty line. See U.S. Bureau of the Census, *Current Population Reports*, Series P-60. As with other especially disadvantaged groups, the situation of female-headed families significantly deteriorated during the Reagan years. The income of the average family in this category fell nearly 5 percent between 1980 and 1984. See Moon and Sawhill.

15. See Lloyd L. Hogan, "Blacks and the American Economy," *Current History* (November 1974), pp. 222–34.

16. *Ibid.* The black unemployment rate held for years at a relatively constant factor of *twice* the overall unemployment rate. See Lester Thurow, "The Economic Progress of Minority Groups," *Social Policy*, March/April 1976, p. 5. In 1981, however, it increased to about two and a half times the national rate and has remained there ever since. See the *National Journal*, February 7, 1981, p. 238; and Tom Wicker, "Still Two Nations," *The New York Times* (January 23, 1983).

17. *Statistical Abstracts of the United States 1984* (Washington, D.C.: U.S. Bureau of the Census, 1983), p. 303.

18. Michael Michaelson, "The Coming Medical War," *New York Review of Books*, July 1, 1971, p. 32.

19. *Statistical Abstracts . . .* , p. 73.

20. *Science News* 119 (January 24, 1981), p. 59.

21. Reported in Howard Zinn, ed., *Justice in Everyday Life* (New York: Morrow, 1974).

22. Robert Bazell, "I'm Sorry, The Doctor Is Out Making Money," *New York Review of Books*, July 1, 1971, p. 32.

23. Robert Eichhorn and Edward G. Ludwig, "Poverty and Health," in Hanna Heissner, ed., *Poverty in the Affluent Society* (New York: Harper & Row, 1966), p. 172.

24. Thurow, "The Leverage of Our Wealthiest 400."

SUGGESTIONS FOR FURTHER READING

Anthony Giddens and David Held (eds.) CLASSES, POWER AND CONFLICT. *Berkeley: University of California Press, 1982.* A comprehensive collection of classical and contemporary works on the meaning and implications of social class and stratification.

Philip Green. THE PURSUIT OF INEQUALITY. *New York: Pantheon, 1981.* A powerful critique of the various defenses of inequality.

Ferdinand Lundberg. THE RICH AND THE SUPER-RICH. *New York: Bantam, 1968.* An entertaining look at America's first families and the institutions they run.

Francis Parkin. CLASS INEQUALITY AND POLITICAL ORDER. *London: Paladin, 1972.* Most notable for its comparative analysis of social class in the U.S., Western Europe and Eastern Europe.

Eric R. Wolf. EUROPE AND THE PEOPLE WITHOUT HISTORY. *Berkeley: University of California Press, 1982.* How the expansion of the capitalist mode of production has transformed social structure on a world scale.

Erik Olin Wright. CLASS, CRISIS AND STATE. *London: New Left Books, 1978.* A book notable for its innovative and imaginative approaches to social class and its use as a tool of analysis of social change.

Maurice Zeitlin, ed. AMERICAN SOCIETY, INC.: STUDIES OF THE SOCIAL STRUCTURE AND POLITICAL ECONOMY OF THE UNITED STATES, 2nd ed. *Chicago: Rand-McNally, 1977.* An important collection of theoretical and empirical materials relating to income, wealth, and the social class structure.

7

Economy and Society:
The Giant
Corporations

The Nation-State will not wither away. A positive role will have to be found for it.[1]

The history of capitalism is the history of the ever greater concentration of economic power into fewer and fewer enterprises. The history of capitalism in the United States is no different and can best be seen in the evolution of the modern corporation and the corporate sector of the American economy. To understand the modern corporation, its operations, the scale of its economic reach, and the impact of its activities upon everyday life, is to understand much (though not all) of what there is to know about American life. I made the claim in Chapter 1 that an appreciation of capitalism is a prerequisite for coming to terms with American social, economic, and political life. This chapter adds the additional claim that to understand the corporation is to begin to understand the nature of capitalism in the United States.

The corporation is also central to an analysis of the American social class system, briefly sketched in Chapters 5 and 6. I say this because of the virtual identity of the giant corporations and the capitalist class. First, the wealth and power of that class is based primarily on its ownership and control of corporations. Second, the corporations have come to act in ways that traditional economic theory has always attributed to the owning class: corporations save, invest, organize production, assume risks, and accumulate capital, and not the individual owner or entrepreneur. As such, the modern corporation has become nothing less than the institutional expression of the capitalist class and its functions.

111

An extensive examination of the giant corporations thus seems in order from several perspectives. Understanding the giant corporations will advance our understanding of the American economy and class system, which together form much of the basic environment within which citizen politics and the struggles over government policy take place. In many and complex ways, giant corporations provide the material and cultural environment within which Americans play out their private and group lives.

WHAT IS A CORPORATION?

There are a number of ways to examine incorporated business enterprises. The first—and the least revealing—is to define it in formal, legal terms. As a legal entity, a corporation is distinguished from other enterprises by the following features:

1. *Joint stock ownership.* The corporation is the product of the pooled resources of many owners, with ownership rights freely transferable between persons. This enables a corporation to attract additional investors, easily and without legal complication, and to pool their combined capital.
2. *Identification as a person under the law.* In the Anglo-Saxon legal tradition, corporations are considered "persons" and enjoy rights similar to citizens. This traditional view, frequently reaffirmed by American courts, affords the

The architecture of corporate power

corporation certain protections against other businesses, persons, and the government itself.

3. *Continuous legal personality.* This feature gives the corporation a great deal of continuity and permanence. Unlike the partnership or single enterpreneurship, an incorporated entity does not dissolve with the death of any owner. Owners may come and go, but the corporation continues.

4. *Limited liability.* No owner is liable in a financial sense for any losses other than his or her own investment. Thus, investment risk decreases considerably and the corporate business enterprise can attract capital more easily than other forms of business.

In the Anglo-Saxon legal tradition, a corporation was a joint stock enterprise drawn up by private individuals. It was chartered by government to serve some public purpose, whether canal building, charity, support of the arts, or adding to the economic health of the community. Incorporation charters were quite specific about the purposes to be served and were granted for specified periods of time, with renewal dependent upon suitable performance of the promised public purpose.

Modern corporations bear little resemblance to this archaic institution. From at least the late nineteenth century, when, in order to attract business to their states, New Jersey and Delaware wrote extremely lenient and permissive incorporation laws, corporations in the United States have not been required to serve any public purpose. In contrast to early incorporation statutes, modern incorporation statutes tend to be perpetual, global, and without any stated public purpose. As a rule, in order to be granted a charter, the potential corporation need only specify structure, procedures for the issuance of stock, the location of the principal officer of the corporation, and the names of the directors. Modern incorporation laws thus preserve the considerable business advantages provided by legal identity—mainly joint stock ownership and limited liability—while eliminating any promised public purpose as a condition for existence.[2]

The Size of Corporations

While important, legal definitions of the corporation are not nearly as compelling as those which focus on their size, reach, and impact as economic institutions. Most difficult to grasp is the sheer magnitude and concentration of the corporate economy, but the following comparisons can give us some indications.

The United States has been called a "business civilization." That description is undeniably apt when we note the impressive number of businesses that dot the American landscape. In 1980, fully 16.8 million businesses were in operation, with total receipts of $7.2 billion. *Incorporated* businesses—businesses that account for no more than 16 percent of the total—accounted for 89 percent of all sales and 79 percent of all business profit.[3] Though comprising but a small portion of all enterprises, corporations account for most of the assets, sales, and profits of the system as a whole. At one level of analysis, we have what amounts to a two-tiered economy in the United States composed of a numerically superior sector (single proprietorships and partnerships) and a numerically inferior but economically dominant sector (incorporated business).

Most corporations are relatively small operations. What one finds *within* the corporate sector is another two-tiered division. Within the corporate sector, a tiny handful of enterprises is responsible for the bulk of economic activity. Table 7.1 compares the positions of the first 100 largest firms to the top 500 largest manufacturing corporations.

Several things are noteworthy about this table. First, economic concentration accelerates tremendously toward the top of the rankings. Whether in sales, profits, or assets, the first 100 firms in manufacturing account for about two thirds of all the economic activity of the top 500. Moreover, the historical trend toward concentration has continued apace in recent years with the relative advantage of the first 100 increasing in the early 1980s. We can see these trends toward ever greater concentration illustrated in the graph on page 115, prepared for the House Committee on Small Business (Figure 7.1). It demonstrates that, whatever the measure used, concentration is an ever more salient fact about the corporate economy.

The concentration characteristic of the industrial sector of the economy is neatly replicated in every other sector of the economy, including utilities, retailing, insurance, transportation, and commercial banking. Indeed, Table 7.2, which compares the asset size of the ten largest and second ten largest enterprises in each of these areas suggests that concentration is *least* advanced in manufacturing. Banking and insurance take that honor, a fact that is especially important in light of their control of the nation's pension funds and trust accounts.[4]

Mergers

There is no reason to suspect that the movement toward concentration is a transitory phenomenon. Corporate mergers have always been a part of the business system and they continue unabated. The precise form, purpose, and mechanics of the merger process have changed, however, over the years. In the late nineteenth century, horizontal mergers (between competing firms in the same line of production) were most common. In the 1920s vertical mergers (between firms related to each other as suppliers, producers, and/or marketers) were the norm. In the 1960s and 1970s, conglomerate mergers (between firms that are totally

TABLE 7.1   The top 100 as a percentage of the
top 500 manufacturing corporations

	1980	1982
Sales	67.6	68.6
Profits	66.0	70.4
Assets	65.0	67.1

SOURCE: *Statistical Abstracts of the United States, 1984*, p. 546.

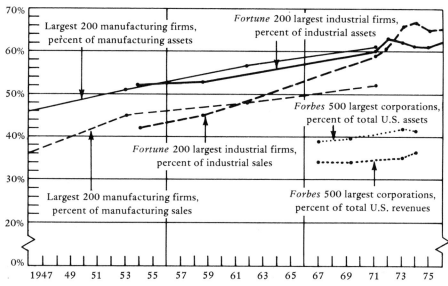

Source: "Conglomerate Mergers," *Report of the Committee on Small Business,* U.S. House of Representatives, October 2, 1980, p. 52.

FIGURE 7.1   Trends in aggregate concentration, by various measures

unrelated in any technical sense, primarily motivated by tax savings and the need to gain adequate cash flow) have become most common. Economic concentration, which is the outcome of such mergers, remains unaltered. In fact, mergers are now so easily achieved and provide such advantages that the rate of mergers has

TABLE 7.2   Size by Total Assets of First Ten and Second Ten Largest American Corporations in 1983, by Sector

	INDUSTRIAL	INSURANCE	RETAILING	UTILITIES	TRANSPORTA-TION (BY OPERATING REVENUES)	COMMERCIAL BANKING
Top Ten (in billions)	329	322	143	269	49	729
Second Ten (in billions)	163	73	55	74	14	238
Ratio of Top to Second Ten	2.02:1	4.41:1	2.6:1	3.64:1	3.50:1	3.1:1

SOURCE: Figures calculated from the special issue on "The Top 500," *Fortune,* April 30, 1984.

actually been accelerating in recent years. Many analysts have now begun to use the term "merger mania" to designate the most feverish corporate merger wave in American history.[5] The mania is at such a peak in the oil industry that many political and business leaders have advocated a moratorium on mergers. Between 1978 and 1981 alone, over $100 billion in corporate resources were used for acquiring *existing* corporate assets rather than for the creation of new plants and equipment.[6] The rate of mergers has significantly increased during the 1980s because of the unprecedented support for mergers by the Reagan administration. The rate of mergers was higher in 1983 than in any year since 1973.

DuPont's takeover of Conoco Oil Company in 1981 for $7.3 billion and U.S. Steel's acquisition of Marathon Oil were but the tip of a vast iceberg. The year 1981 saw over one hundred mergers with purchase prices in excess of $100 million. Figure 7.2 graphically illustrates the accelerated pace of the merger mania, the end results of which are predictable. Recent evidence bears out the supposition that giant enterprises account for an ever greater share of total economic activity in the United States (Figure 7.3).

The curious reader might ask how this can be so, given the most stringent antitrust statutes of any western nation. The answer, quite simply, is that antitrust laws are rarely enforced and, with a few notable exceptions, were probably never

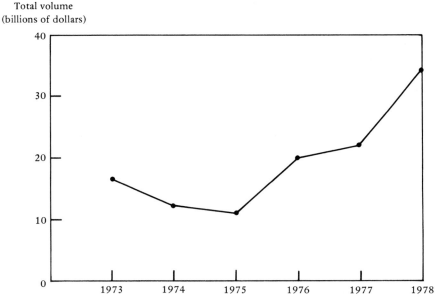

Total volume
(billions of dollars)

Source: "Conglomerate Mergers," *Report of the Committee on Small Business,* U.S. House of Representatives, October 2, 1980, p. 50.

FIGURE 7.2   Total value of announced corporate mergers and acquisitions

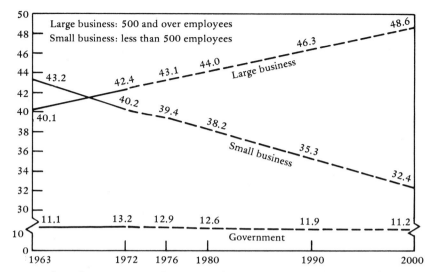

Source: "Conglomerate Mergers," *Report of the Committee on Small Business*, U.S. House of Representatives, October 2, 1980, p. 3.

FIGURE 7.3   Percentage share of GNP by small business and large business, and preliminary estimates for 1976–2000

meant to be. From 1950 to 1967, one of the most active merger periods in history, only 199 cases were filed by the antitrust division of the Department of Justice, and only half of the suits involved companies with more than $100 million in sales. Given the fact that the Department of Justice does not always win in the courts,[7] and that the courts tend to be lenient even when it does, it is not surprising to learn that companies were forced to divest themselves of something in only forty-eight cases.[8] Even these divestitures can be illusionary. Many times a company will undertake mergers with several companies at once in the hope that, if challenged, it will be forced to divest itself only of those acquisitions that it never wanted in the first place. In a notable case just a few years ago involving ITT, the most aggressive and successful conglomerate in recent business history, the government and ITT agreed to a "consent decree." The decree allowed ITT to acquire the giant Hartford Insurance Company, but disallowed the acquisition of the Automatic Canteen Corporation and Grinnell Corporation. In business circles it is well understood that Hartford, with its enormous cash flows so useful in making further take-over bids, was the main target from the very beginning.

The most famous example of the ineffectuality of the antitrust statutes—even when vigorously enforced—was the forcible dismemberment of John D. Rockefeller's Standard Oil Trust in 1911. While the dissolution was dramatic, the newly formed companies essentially remained in the hands of the same people. They have acted toward each other in a most cooperative manner to the present day.

The three major spinoffs of the dissolution—Exxon, Mobil, and Socal—have been intimately tied to each other through their boards, through Rockefeller banks, and through joint exploration, transportation, and refining ventures. With cases such as this one and ITT, which are by no means uncommon, it is no wonder that antitrust laws have never been a serious barrier to concentration of firms.[9]

It is insufficient to say that antitrust laws are indifferently enforced, for the question remains: "Why are such laws unenforced?" My provisional answer is that the corporations are so economically, socially, and politically powerful that no administration would have the capacity, to say nothing of the will, to pursue vigorously a policy of decentralizing the American economy.[10]

Interlock and Concentration

I have portrayed the concentrated American economy by pointing out the proportion of assets, sales, or profits accounted for by relatively few firms. Such a picture certainly clashes with the traditional concept of the American economy, one of intense competition between small to medium-sized firms. Many economists argue, however, that even with the transformation of the firm, competition remains a reality, though it is competition between giants rather than pygmies. This view is misguided because it fails to recognize the many ways in which the dominant firms in the economy act cooperatively and collusively, rather than competitively. The intimate ties and subtle cooperation between firms take a variety of forms: trade associations; representation by common law firms, banks, or investment houses; price leadership; prior consultations. By far the most pervasive and important method to transcend competition is the interlocking directorate.

In the interlocking directorate, officers or directors of one firm sit as members of the board of directors of another firm. Interlocked directorates involve firms related to each other in a variety of ways: as supplier-manufacturer, as manufacturer-customer, as lender-borrower, or even as competitors. Although the Clayton Antitrust Act makes it illegal for firms that are direct competitors to be interlocked, the law is circumvented most often by the formation of interlocks through third institutions, usually a bank, investment house, or law firm.

How extensive is the phenomenon of interlock? Surely, if only a few firms are involved, particularly firms with few assets, we need not be unduly concerned. As one might have guessed given the advantages to be had from collusion, the phenomenon is quite widespread among the largest corporations. In the most important study of the subject, economist Peter Dooley reports that of the 250 largest industrial, merchandising, transportation, financial, and utility corporations in 1965, only 17 were not significantly interlocked with others. This represents a level of interlock greater than that found in studies in the mid-1930s.[11] Dooley finds, moreover, that interlocks characteristically occur among the largest manufacturing firms and financial institutions (banks and insurance companies). None of this is surprising given the mutual advantages involved. For financial institutions, interlock with nonfinancial corporations offers inside information in managing their investment portfolios, as well as significant sources of deposits.

For nonfinancial corporations, interlock with banks provides ready access to loans and to financial expertise and counseling. The Patman Subcommittee of the House of Representatives reported widespread consultation between management, directors, and large institutional investors on "any major corporate decision, such as a proposed merger, a new stock issue proposal or any pending decision which may seriously affect the company's operations."[12]

By any measure, then, the corporate economy of the United States is characterized by very heavy concentration at the top, a concentration enhanced by intercorporate "incest" and cooperation through many means, including price leadership, trade associations, and joint ventures. Such a state of affairs has prompted some economists to label this most decisive sector of the American economy *monopoly capitalism*.[13]

SOME IMPLICATIONS OF CORPORATE ECONOMIC POWER

The previous discussion of concentrated corporate power is of more than academic interest. Such concentrated power has wrought a profound transformation in the American economy, a transformation that deeply affects the quality of life of the American people and the degree of control they are able to exercise over their destinies. Since the formation of the great trusts of the late nineteenth century, the division of the American economy has gradually evolved into two distinct segments—one competitive and of declining importance, the other monopolistic and dominant in the economy. The competitive sector, the sector that encompasses most of the business firms in the United States, is characterized by small-scale production, local markets, low productivity, unstable and irregular markets, and high rates of business failure. The businesses in this sector are also largely nonunion and thus characterized by poor wages and working conditions. Women and minority group members comprise the majority of employees. Such small-scale enterprises include restaurants, drugstores, repair shops, small manufacturers, and clothing stores. The concentrated corporate sector of the economy comprises a relative handful of enterprises, yet accounts for most business activity in the United States. Firms of this sector are capital- and technology-intensive, characterized by large-scale production and exchange, high productivity, national and international markets, and relatively stable market relations.[14] This sector is almost completely unionized. The competitive sector includes firms forever buffeted by market forces. By virtue of their economic power and their intimate relationships with other corporations, firms in the corporate sector exercise significant (though not total) control over their own market situations, rather than remaining victims of its impersonal and disciplining processes.

The appearance of this concentrated and by now dominant sector in the economy represents a remarkable change, not only in the organization of capitalism but in the degree to which private business decisions affect the public well-being. The direction of economic life today is no longer the product of millions of transactions among thousands of firms operating through an impersonal marketplace. Rather, the main directions of economic life, and thus of social life in general, are a product of the planning processes of the great corporate firms, and rest in the hands of relatively few people who sit in executive offices and boardrooms. Decisions made by the executives and owners of the great corporations have more direct and lasting effects upon the quality of life of Americans than decisions reached by any other set of decision makers (including government officials), and in rendering these decisions, many of which have socially irrational and harmful effects, they are responsible to no one but themselves.

I do not mean to imply that corporations act immorally or illegally in these or other matters. I am only suggesting that in the course of their everyday business activities, given their size and concentration, corporations shape and alter the world around them with profound effects on the population. Government responds *ex post facto* to the problems generated by corporate action: the corporations act, and government deals with the consequences of those actions as best it can. A few examples might help to illuminate this point.

It is normal, legal, and rational business behavior for corporate managers to attempt to maximize their return on investment, even if local employment suffers as a result. The shoe and textile industries have largely abandoned the New England states for the South, where antiunion sentiment has kept wages low, while steel firms have been closing their gates all over the upper Midwest. Other corporations are accelerating the trend to transfer manufacturing processes to places like South Korea, Taiwan, and Indonesia, where wages are even lower, thus exporting significant numbers of jobs.

It is not unusual for a corporation to deplete and close one of its divisions or new acquisitions (thereby increasing unemployment) in order to use its liquid assets to finance further acquisitions. In 1977, the profitable Youngstown Sheet and Tube Company announced its closing, resulting in the immediate loss of 5,000 jobs in that already depressed section of Ohio. The company closed after its parent company, Lykes Brothers, Inc., used its treasury to finance further acquisitions. As *Business Week* put it, "The conglomerateur's steel acquisitions were seen as cash boxes for corporate growth in other areas."[15]

These examples are symptomatic of general trends in the behavior of American corporations which have been systematically exporting capital, manufacturing facilities, and manufacturing jobs since the early 1970s. They have done so in an effort, rational for the corporation but not necessarily for the American economy, to maximize short-term profit margins, a form of managerial behavior that is much admired and highly rewarded in the business world. When not exporting investments, American corporations have increasingly engaged in what some have called "asset rearrangement" and in real estate speculation. They have not been willing, on the other hand, to channel very much of their capital into the formation of new plant and equipment. The result has been a virtual collapse in the growth of American productivity and a significant and escalating loss of world markets to other nations, particularly Japan.[16] One student of the American auto

Setting corporate policies: private decisions with public consequences

industry tells a story that vividly demonstrates how American corporations, interested in short-term profit maximization, reward irrational managerial behavior:

> . . . At one time, the assembly plant in Tarrytown, New York, year in and year out, produced the poorest quality cars of all 22 GM U.S. car assembly plants. In some instances, Tarrytown cars were so poorly built, the dealers refused to accept them. At the same time, it had the lowest manufacturing costs in General Motors. So the Tarrytown plant manager was getting one of the biggest bonuses of all the assembly-plant managers while building the worst cars in the company.[17]

It is hardly surprising that, while the American auto industry remains profitable, it steadily loses domestic and international markets to the Europeans and the Japanese.

The modern corporation has assumed a form so large, concentrated, and interlocked with other giant enterprises that its every act has consequences for human populations far beyond its own walls. Government finds that it can at best act *ex post facto,* or, more commonly, that attempts to regulate the consequences of corporate decision making are beyond its capacity. Private corporations define the contours of American life. Though the ways in which they do so are too abundant to discuss at any length, I list some of the most important ones.

1. Corporations determine research and development priorities and regulate the pace and form of technological development and its introduction into the production process. If it is not convenient for a certain new technology to be introduced, it can be suppressed.
2. Corporations, as a necessary part of selling their products to a near-satiated public, bombard the population with continuous advertising messages designed to induce consumption. It is reasonable to suggest that such corporate behavior is an important contributor to the pronounced materialism of American life.
3. Corporations, through location, investment, and lending policies, largely determine the shape of urban and regional development in the United States, as well as the economic health of local communities.
4. Corporations largely determine the form and priorities of transportation in the United States. Given the power of the "auto-industrial complex" (autos, oil, auto parts, and highway construction corporations), this has meant an emphasis upon the private car and the de-emphasis of cheap, efficient mass transportation.
5. Corporations substantially determine the quality of the environment for the American population. We are becoming increasingly aware that levels of health and the incidence of illness have less to do with the availability of medical care than with stress, pollutants, and carcinogens in the environment. The incidence and distribution of such health detriments may be almost entirely attributable to decisions made by corporations on production and distribution of goods and services.
6. Corporations determine the substance of the working lives of most Americans, since the power to design and establish the technology, methods, and processes of work related to production, distribution, and marketing rests in the hands of those who own and control the corporation.

CORPORATE POWER AND DEMOCRATIC CONTROL

☐ "Moral principles are at the base of all permanent business success—they go together. In the long run, every business question, every public question must be settled by what is right and what is wrong." Quotation from Judge Elbert H. Gary, United States Steel Corporation.[18]

☐ The Firestone Tire Company is reported to have known of design defects in its Radial 500 tire six years before taking it off the market.[19]

☐ "In the 1960s, General Motors spent some 250 million dollars to change its corporate identity signs, the new motto being emblazoned across the country in blue and white. 'GM—Mark of Excellence.' the cost was many times the amount—15 million to 25 million dollars—then being spent each year to produce a pollution-free automobile."[20]

☐ "Lomotil, an effective anti-diarrhea medicine sold only by prescription in the

U.S. because it is fatal in amounts just slightly over the recommended doses, was sold over the counter in Sudan, in packages proclaiming it was 'used by astronauts during Gemini and Apollo space flights' and recommended for use by children as young as 12 months.''[21]

☐ In late 1984, a release of a cloud of cyanide gas from a Union Carbide plant in Bhopal, India, killed over 2,000 men, women, and children. Preliminary reports suggest serious shortcomings in plant design and safety procedures.

Each and every corporate action may not necessarily have adverse consequences for human populations. But whether consequences are negative or positive on balance, there are consequences of corporate behavior that matter to others. Giant corporations are so economically powerful, and the scope and reach of their operations are so vast, that their everyday, routine decisions, which are always made pragmatically, in accordance with normal business logic, have impact throughout the entire community. Corporate executives make decisions about investments, plant location, production levels, advertising appeals, pricing, work assignments, and the like, and Americans (as well as many others around the world) alter their lifestyles and aspirations accordingly, as a matter of course.

What are we to do with this concentrated power? How do we keep it under control, to ensure that these institutions serve decent public purposes? The answer is of obvious and compelling interest in a society that prides itself on being democratic in form and operation, for concentrated and uncontrolled power is the very antithesis of democracy.

The traditional answer to the problem of the control of corporate power and influence has been the market mechanism. Through its unswerving laws and neutral operations, the market theoretically ensures that the direction of production is consistent with popular wants and demands. Yet the corporations are so powerful that they can often transcend the market and its disciplinary power.[22]

Another response to the problem of control of corporate power is the countervailing and democratic power of government to compel the giant corporations to act in ways beneficial to the public. Yet government often acts more as a helpmate to wealth and power than as a countervailing institution. Government, taken as a whole, must be seen more as the instrument of the corporations and not as their antithesis. Later chapters will expand upon this view.

Neither the market nor government seem to be effective instruments of democratic control. What are we to do with these rather frightening facts? According to many social theorists, we have nothing to fear. While generally acknowledging the scale of corporate concentration and influence, they claim that the corporation is tied to decent public purposes *through internal changes in the corporation itself.* This alteration in corporate motivation and behavior is derived, it is claimed, from the declining importance of ownership in the corporation and the emergence of technically trained, nonowning and hence, more responsible managers at their helm. Let us turn to a more detailed description of this theory of the *managerial revolution,* and consider the validity of its claims.

The Managerial Revolution

The theory of the managerial revolution is constructed upon three hypothetical changes said to affect the giant corporations:

1. *The dispersal of stock ownership.* Unlike the situation during the late nineteenth century when corporations first began to consolidate their power, stock ownership is now widely dispersed throughout the population and is growing more dispersed every year. Such a development heralds widespread popular control of the corporation, and even what some have called *stockholder democracy.*[23] In an intriguing variation on this theme, Peter Drucker argues that corporations are indirectly owned by the American people through the pension fund system.[24]

2. *The separation of ownership and control.* The broad dispersal of stock ownership, it is claimed, is so advanced that it has broken the hold of any single owner, or set of owners, on the corporation. Owners are now either content to withdraw from the operations of the corporation to enjoy their dividends and capital gains, or are forced to do so. In their stead, at the control levers of the modern corporation, is a group of professional, nonowning managers.

3. *The decline of the profit motive.* The disappearance of owners from active control of the corporation, it is claimed, fundamentally alters the central motivations of corporate behavior. Managed in the past by the direct owners who held a strong vested interest in that ownership, corporations formerly pursued the goal of maximum profits at the expense of all other goals. Modern corporations, managed by people with no stake in ownership, it is claimed, are motivated primarily by the desire to attain the greatest possible rate of corporate growth as measured in sales, a goal that requires only reasonable and stable profit rates, not maximum profits.

With the decline of the profit motive, to which most of the evils of corporate behavior have been attributed in the past, the corporation becomes more socially responsible. The corporation becomes an institution concerned primarily with meeting the professional standards of its managers, experts, and technicians, and with balancing the claims of its technostructure, stockholders, workers, and consumers. It becomes, in this view, an institution that is balanced, shorn of damaging motives, open to a variety of influences, and thus unable to run roughshod over the public. A measure of democratic control has been introduced, that is to say, though in a subtle and indirect manner.

Factual Problems in the Managerial Theory

No evidence exists to substantiate the managerial theory. Though an increasing number of Americans own stock in corporations, the vast majority own but a few scattered shares. Stock ownership is concentrated in very few hands. Almost 200 million people own no stock, and most of the remainder owns little to speak of. "Stockholder democracy" seems a strange and inappropriate term for such a pattern of distribution. Ironically, the slight dispersal that has occurred has probably enhanced the position of major stockholders, who now require a lower percentage of voting stock to exercise control in a corporation than they did in the past. When one also considers the many existing coalitions of large stockholders, the vaunted dispersal of stock ownership begins to appear less than claimed.

The separation between ownership and control, so central to the managerial and responsible corporation thesis, cannot be proved since reliable data are extremely difficult to come by. Family ownership groups do not freely advertise their control of corporations, nor are sociologists invited to unearth the information. In perusing proxy statements and SEC reports, it is not easy to know which major stockholders are related by marriage. Nor is it evident, without careful research, which executives or directors are nominees or representatives of ownership groups, for they need not publicly state that fact. It is difficult to determine which ownership groups have bank representatives among the directors of a corporation (because of bank management of trust funds). Nor is it easy to assess the impact of the control of corporations by owning families through such devices as foundations, family holding companies, or trust funds.

The complexities of unearthing data are illustrated by findings about the American Telephone and Telegraph Company, published a few years before its divestiture. AT&T listed its largest stockholder as Kabo and Company, and its fourth largest as Cudd and Company. Investigation revealed the former to be the nominee of Bankers Trust Company of New York, and the latter the nominee of the Chase Manhattan Bank. Cede and Company, which was listed as one-third owner of Eastern Airlines, is a technical partnership organized by the Depository Trust Company of New York for unnamed investors.[25]

There is no clear distinction, moreover, between owners and managers. Simply put, the managerial group in the United States "is the largest single group in the stockholding population, and a greater proportion of this class owns stock than any other."[26] Managers are, in fact, members of the owning class. This holds true whether entry into ownership was through birth or through reward after reaching high executive positions. To suggest that the chief executives of the top fifty corporations, who, on the average, own over three million dollars in their company's stock, are neither tied to the ownership of the corporation nor interested in profits is to invite disbelief. Owners and managers are not two distinctly separate groups with divergent interests and goals, but a single one. In the perceptive words of economists Paul Baran and Paul Sweezy, "The managerial stratum is the most active and influential part of the propertied class . . . and function[s] as the protectors and spokesmen for all large-scale property."[27]

Corporate Motivation and Behavior

What about the presumed revolution in corporate motivation and behavior, a revolution based on the rather flimsy argument for the separation of ownership and control in the major corporations? Let us for a moment assume that such a separation does indeed exist, that corporations are run not by owners but by non-owning professional managers. Does it follow that the managerial group is free from the tie to the profit motive? The answer must be *no*.

The claim that the modern corporation has de-emphasized the profit motive is absurd from several points of view. Without high profits, corporations would not have those funds necessary for technological innovation and expansion that are, according to many, their main goals. Moreover, any long-term deviation from profit-maximizing behavior would lead to difficulties in securing loans in capital markets, as well as to declines in stock prices, a situation that would not only be of some concern to major stockholders and lien holders, but would make the corporation an immediate target for takeover by another firm. Finally, extensive research as well as ordinary observation of everyday behavior establishes that the single most important determinant of executive compensation and status is company profitability.[28] Even if managers are in no way members of the owning group, they are forced by the business environment to act very much like owners. The profit motive remains central to their business behavior. Recent attention to the problem of short-term profit perspectives and nonproductive asset rearrangement by corporate executives suggests that even writers in the business press no longer subscribe to the theory of the managerial revolution and the socially responsible and responsive corporation.

Changes in corporate motivation have been merely *inferred* from the pseudofact of separation of ownership and control. It has never been carefully and systematically demonstrated that the modern corporation is more socially responsible and responsive than were earlier business enterprises. The evidence of our senses relative to corporate social responsibility is far more compelling. Note, for example, the widespread price fixing in many industries; the generation of superprofits in the oil and drug industries; the suppression of safety and pollution controls in the auto industry; the widespread disregard of occupational safety laws in the United States; the indiscriminate use of untested additives in the food industry; the irresponsible behavior of the nuclear and chemical industry; the widespread practice of "under-the-table" contributions to domestic and foreign politicians. Until persuasive evidence proves the existence of a reformed and responsible corporation, the informed citizen must conclude that we are faced with the traditional creature, though deodorized by high-priced public relations firms.

CONCLUDING REMARKS

Americans often pride themselves on being members of the largest, most enduring, and most successful democracy in the world. Yet their lives, to a great degree, are channeled, shaped, and determined by the decisions of a very few people sitting in the board rooms and executive suites of the giant corporations, over whom they exercise little control. Neither the market nor internal corporation changes in motivation allow Americans to impose decent public purposes or responsibility upon the monopoly sector; nor does government look promising as an alternative control mechanism. Indeed, I shall attempt to demonstrate in later chapters that government tends to act not as the instrument of the public counterposed to business power but as the protector, helpmate, and instrument of the corporations. It appears as if the corporation fits very uncomfortably into any known conception of democracy.

NOTES

1. Quotation from the chairman of the Unilever Corporation. Cited in Richard J. Barnet and Ronald E. Müller, *Global Reach: The Power of the Multinational Corporations* (New York: Simon & Schuster, 1974), p. 21.
2. For an interesting discussion of these changes in corporate law, see Ralph Nader and Mark Green, "Federal Chartering and Corporate Accountability," in Philip Brenner et al., *Exploring Contradictions: Political Economy in the Corporate State* (New York: David McKay, 1974).
3. *Statistical Abstracts of the United States,* 1984 (Washington, D.C.: Bureau of the Census, 1983), p. 532.
4. For further information on the nation's banks, see the Patman Committee Staff Report for the Domestic Finance Subcommittee of the House Committee on Banking and Currency, 90th Congress, 2nd Session, *Commercial Banks and Their Trust Activities* (Washington, D.C.: U.S. Government Printing Office, July 1968); Barnet and Müller, *Global Reach,* pp. 233–35; and Dye, *Who's Running America?*
5. See Sidney Blumental, "Mergers," *The New York Times,* August 15, 1981, Op-Ed page.
6. Ira C. Magaziner and Robert B. Reich, *Minding America's Business* (New York: Harcourt Brace Jovanovich, 1982), p. 117.
7. Under present law, the antitrust division must prove conscious and deliberate efforts to monopolize some market.
8. Barnet and Müller, *Global Reach,* p. 231.
9. The Reagan administration has proved to be even more tolerant of or indifferent to mergers between the giants. This is demonstrated by the dramatic *decrease* in the rate of government challenges of mergers under the antitrust statutes in the very first year of his presidency (see the *National Journal,* April 4, 1981, pp. 573–77) and the termination of the case against IBM. Even the dissolution of AT&T was illusionary, for it allowed the firm to spin off its least profitable divisions (local phone companies) and to keep its most profitable ones.
10. Much of the remainder of this book is an elaboration of this point.
11. "The Interlocking Directorate," *American Economic Review* 59:3 (June 1969), pp. 314–323.
12. *Commercial Banks and Their Trust Activities,* p. 3. Banks are also represented on the boards as major stockholders.
13. It should go without saying that these giant corporations are global enterprises, their operations not confined to the United States. Indeed, several American corporations, including the Chase-Manhattan Bank, do more business and earn more profits abroad than at home.

14. Though to be sure, American firms have been having their troubles in international markets since the early 1970s.
15. This story is told in "Fear Alley, U.S.A.," *Commonweal,* November 11, 1977, pp. 720–22.
16. This world in which the productive competence of the American economy erodes while the major corporations continue to make record profits is brilliantly described by economist/industrial engineer Seymour Melman in his book *Profits Without Production* (New York: Knopf, 1983). Very much the same story is told in Barry Bluestone and Bennett Harrison, *The Deindustrialization of America* (New York: Basic Books, 1982) and Ira C. Magaziner and Robert B. Reich, *Minding America's Business* (New York: Harcourt Brace Jovanovich, 1982). Between 1965 and 1979, productivity in manufacturing grew 13.7 percent in Japan, 7.3 percent in West Germany, but only 2.3 percent in the United States. The U.S. also has, compared to Japan and West Germany, the oldest stock in manufacturing equipment and the lowest level of civilian research and development expenditures. See Melman, pp. 163–171.
17. Patrick Wright, *On A Clear Day You Can See General Motors* (New York: Wright Enterprises, 1979), p. 211.
18. Ida Tarbell, *The Life of E. H. Gary* (New York: Appleton, 1925), p. 250.
19. Reported in the *Akron Beacon Journal,* December 23, 1978, p. 1.
20. William Serrin, *The Company and the Union* (New York: Vintage, 1974), p. 112.
21. *Mother Jones Magazine,* November 1979, p. 24.
22. For a recent assessment of the shortcomings of the market mechanism as a control on corporate behavior see Charles Lindblom, *Politics and Markets* (New York: Basic Books, 1977).
23. Neil H. Jacoby, *Corporate Power and Social Responsibility* (New York: Macmillan, 1973).
24. See Peter Drucker, *The Unseen Revolution* (New York: Harper & Row, 1976).
25. *The New York Times,* January 9, 1977.
26. Gabriel Kolko, *Wealth and Power in America* (New York: Praeger, 1962), p. 67.
27. Paul Baran and Paul Sweezy, *Monopoly Capital* (New York: Monthly Review Press, 1966), pp. 34–35.
28. See discussion of this point in Edward S. Herman, *Corporate Control, Corporate Power* (New York: Cambridge University Press, 1981). Also see the works cited in note 16.

SUGGESTIONS FOR FURTHER READING

Paul Baran and Paul Sweezy. MONOPOLY CAPITAL. *New York: Monthly Review Press, 1966.* The leading Marxist analysis of the modern corporate-dominated economy.

Adolf Berle, Jr., and Gardiner C. Means. THE MODERN CORPORATION AND PRIVATE PROPERTY. *New York: Macmillan, 1932.* The classic statement of the managerial revolution in the modern corporation.

Peter Collier and David Horowitz. THE ROCKEFELLERS: AN AMERICAN DYNASTY. *New York: Holt, Rinehart & Winston, 1976.* A lively and highly informative portrait of one of America's leading owning families and the creation of a corporate empire.

Peter Drucker. THE UNSEEN REVOLUTION. *New York: Harper & Row, 1976.* A book by a longtime celebrator of corporate business enterprise, in which the argument is made for the democratic control of the corporations through pension funds.

John Kenneth Galbraith. THE NEW INDUSTRIAL STATE. *New York: Signet, 1967.* A rosy portrait of the function of the giant corporation in American life.

Edward S. Herman. CORPORATE CONTROL, CORPORATE POWER. *New York: Cambridge Univesity Press, 1981.* An analysis of the theory of the separation of management and control and its presumed effects, by a professor at the Wharton School of Finance.

Ira C. Magaziner and Robert B. Reich. MINDING AMERICA'S BUSINESS. *New York: Harcourt Brace Jovanovich, 1982.* A provocative examination of how irrational managerial behavior in America's corporations has contributed to the erosion of our position in world trade.

Seymour Melman. PROFITS WITHOUT PRODUCTION. *New York: Alfred Knopf, 1983.* Melman shows how the obsession with short-term profitability in American corporations has eroded the industrial base of the United States.

Part

III

The Political

Process

This section focuses on the various instruments of democratic politics available to the American people and asks how useful they are for transmitting popular aspirations, interests, and wants to government decision makers. We shall see that they are less than optimal because of the distorting effects of unequal economic power.

8

The Group Process
and the Politics
of Unequal Power

We have learned that American politics is practiced in a society where prevailing economic and social structures guarantee significant inequalities in the material conditions of the people and great disproportionalities in power among them. More specifically, I have attempted to establish the following general points:

1. Capitalism is the basic factor shaping the possibilities and problems of life in the United States.
2. Being capitalist, the United States is organized around the basic division between those who own property and those who do not—an unequal division that pervades all aspects of life, including the legal and constitutional systems.
3. The culture of liberalism supplies the basic political, social, and economic ideas and values of the American system and helps sustain and legitimate capitalism and its system of class inequality.
4. The principal features of modern capitalism in the United States are the concentration of economic power into an ever smaller number of giant corporations and the domination of most aspects of American life by them.

This picture of life in the United States, needless to say, neither conforms to conventional notions about our society nor gives much comfort to those citizens who might be concerned about problems of social justice and democracy.

In this part of the book we turn our attention to the problem of democracy. How is it, in a society of highly unequal economic and decision-making power, that we can continue to call ourselves a democracy? What is it in our political system that allows the American people to keep government decision makers responsible for their actions and responsive to popular interests and aspirations? How effective are the conventional instruments of the American political system in ensuring democratic accountability? Does our political system provide mechanisms by which the inequalities in society are counteracted, ensuring civic equality, or do some persons, groups, and classes exercise disproportionate influence over the civic affairs of the nation? Whose voice, in the end, is heard in government?

Democracy, we have seen, has several competing definitions. Recall that direct-participatory democracy is about face-to-face deliberation; that representative democracy is about elections, petition, and the relationship between representatives and the electorate; and that pluralist democracy is about the vitality and openness of the process of group competition and bargaining. What all three have in common is an understanding that democracy is about popular control of political leaders and their actions, or conversely, leadership accountability to the public. If the United States is a democracy, how is this control and accountability achieved? Political scientists generally argue that this is achieved in the United States by means of two principal mechanisms: popular elections and the activities of interest groups. I would add a third, namely mass movements. In this part of the book, we examine each of the three. We shall look at the election process and its trappings (voting, political parties, and public opinion) in Chapter 9. In Chapter 10 we shall look at the dynamics and impact of mass movements. In this chapter, we shall look in detail at the group process—how it reflects the economic organization of society and how it profoundly affects the operations and outcomes of government.

THE GROUP PROCESS

For many years, the vogue in the political science discipline has been to understand the interest group as the principal instrument of democracy in the United States, surpassing the election in many respects as the key to democratic accountability.[1] Not satisfied that elections play the role assigned to them in democratic theory, mainstream political scientists have overwhelmingly subscribed to the theory of democracy known as pluralism, in which the clash, the bargaining, and the compromises struck among the thousands of interest groups active in America become the essence of democratic politics. From this point of view, interest groups (also known as *pressure groups* or *lobbies*) are the principal mechanism by which Americans make their preferences known to government policy makers on a day-to-day basis, communicate their needs and interests, and monitor the activities of politicians. Interest groups, from the point of view of pluralists, are considered more viable tools of democratic politics than elections because they allow people to be continuously and directly involved in the political process as compared to the intermittent involvement offered by elections.

I believe this theory of the political process to be deeply flawed, primarily because of its failure to take into account the highly unequal influence of social classes or to recognize the disproportionate political power exercised by the giant corporations and their ancillary organizations. Rather than being broadly representative of the American people, the group system involves but a tiny and privileged segment of the community. In the classic words of E. E. Schattschneider, "The flaw in the pluralist heaven is that the heavenly chorus sings with a strong upper class accent."[2] All of the available evidence indicates that the organized groups which influence government and political parties are primarily composed of Americans from the most privileged sectors of the social stucture. It is also undeniably the case that the vast majority of the organizations active in the interest group system represent various factions of the business community. While there are, to be sure, many labor unions, charitable institutions, churches, and consumer groups at work in this arena,[3] the groups most active on a continuous basis and having the best-established relations with government agencies are business groups, usually the most powerful ones in each sector. These range from organizations of specific producers (wheat producers, toy manufacturers), to organizations representing a specific industry (the Petroleum Council, the Farm Bureau), to organizations representing the business class as a whole (the Advertising Council, the Business Roundtable, the Business Advisory Council).

Most political science textbooks focus on describing the broad range of interest groups that are active in American politics and leave the impression of a vast, diverse, open, and relatively egalitarian process in which all or at least most can take part. The approach I take here is quite different and more consistent with the available evidence about the interest group system. I have tried to point out that American society is structured by a social class system defined by the ownership and nonownership of property. In this chapter, I shall analyze the interest group system through the analytical lens of social class. I shall, that is to say, explore the issue of how class power shapes American politics through the group process. I shall explore the issue of relative class power and influence in the political process. I shall do this by examining the interest group activities of the main institutional expressions of each of the two great classes in any capitalist society: the giant corporations as representative of the owning class and the labor unions as representative of the working class. I shall examine the bases of power of each set of institutions, their manner of participation in the political process, and the extent of influence each one exercises in the councils of government. I shall conclude that the predominant power exercised by the corporations in the economy is almost perfectly mirrored in the interest group system, a finding that raises some serious and disturbing questions about the health of democratic politics in the United States.

THE BACKGROUND
OF POLITICAL DECISION MAKERS

An interesting way to begin is to ask questions about the relative receptivity of public officials to the competing appeals, demands, and requests of interest groups. Clearly, government policy is constructed out of the many policy decisions made by the few people occupying the seats of power in the legislative, judicial, and executive branches of the federal government. Since it is reasonable to assume that the behavior of such persons is affected by the values, goals, and interests— the notions, prejudices, inclinations, and biases—that they bring with them to government service, it would be instructive to first ask who they are and where they come from.

The evidence indicates that the persons who staff the major political decision-making posts in the federal government are overwhelmingly from the upper business and professional classes. Indeed, in a system that calls itself democratic, government officialdom is strikingly unrepresentative when compared with the American population as a whole. It is apparent, for instance, that women and racial minorities are conspicuously absent among the most important government officials. In the Ninety-ninth Congress (1985–86), women, blacks, and Hispanics, who together form an overwhelming majority in the nation, accounted for only 10 percent of all House and Senate members. Less widely known is the relatively narrow class and occupational strata from which most government decision makers are recruited. There is a mythology, much believed among business leaders and scholars alike, that businesspeople either have skills and characteristics unsuited to politics ("A genius in the business office may be, and often is, utterly unable outside of it to say boo to a goose. . . . Knowing this, he wants to be left alone and to leave politics alone")[4] or hold politicians and politics in contempt ("interfering meddlers who have never met a payroll"), and thus choose to renounce the world of government and politics. The evidence, however, suggests otherwise. It reveals that a strong preponderance of businesspeople, especially businesspeople from the most powerful corporations, staff virtually all top decision-making posts in the federal government.

Congress is a case in point. Our most representative institution is by no stretch of the imagination "representative" in anything but a nominal sense. This may be demonstrated by looking at the backgrounds of U.S. senators and members of the House of Representatives. One way to do this is to compare the occupations of the fathers of recent members of Congress to the general distribution of occupations in the population in the year 1910. Note the figures in Table 8.1, which demonstrate the very heavy overrepresentation of the professions and businesses among the fathers of contemporary members of Congress and the severe underrepresentation of the working class. We may also examine the background of members of Congress by taking note of their own occupations prior to their elec-

A meeting of the Reagan cabinet: blurring the distinction between public and private elites

TABLE 8.1   The social background of representatives
and senators: occupation of fathers

OCCUPATION	POPULATION, % (1910)	SENATE, % (1964–1970)	HOUSE, % (1964–1970)
Professional and technical	10	37	30
Proprietor, manager	2	29	44
Farmer, farm worker	16	15	14
Manual, service, and white collar workers	72	19	12

SOURCE: From Thomas Dye and Harmon Zeigler, *The Irony of Democracy,* © 1970; and Richard Zweigenhaft, "Who Represents America?" *The Insurgent Sociologist* 5:3 (Spring 1975). Reprinted by permission of Wadsworth Publishing Co., Belmont, California, and *The Insurgent Sociologist.*

TABLE 8.2   Members' occupations, Ninety-ninth Congress

| | HOUSE | | | SENATE | | | CONGRESS |
	D	R	TOTAL	D	R	TOTAL	TOTAL*
Aeronautics	0	3	3	1	1	2	5
Agriculture	11	13	24	2	5	7	31
Business or Banking	68	76	144	12	18	30	174
Clergy	2	0	2	0	1	1	3
Education	24	13	37	3	7	10	47
Engineering	1	3	4	0	1	1	5
Journalism	11	10	21	6	2	8	29
Labor Officials	2	0	2	0	0	0	2
Law	121	69	190	32	29	61	251
Law Enforcement	6	2	8	0	0	0	8
Medicine	1	2	3	1	0	1	4
Military	0	1	1	0	1	1	2
Professional Sports	2	1	3	1	0	1	4
Public Service/Politics	42	23	65	4	7	11	76

*Because some members have more than one occupation, totals are higher than total membership.

SOURCE: *Congressional Quarterly Weekly Report* (November 10, 1984), p. 2922.

tion. It is readily apparent in Table 8.2 that the population from which representatives and senators are recruited is but a very narrow slice of the population taken as a whole. Exactly two-thirds of all members of the Ninety-ninth Congress come from backgrounds in law, business, and banking.

The class bias in the makeup of courts is, if anything, even more pronounced, particularly in the upper levels of the federal judiciary. As one political scientist has pointed out:

> Throughout American history there has been an overwhelming tendency for presidents to choose nominees for the Supreme Court from among the socially advantaged families. . . . In the earlier history of the Court [the nominee] very likely was born in the aristocratic gentry class, although later he tended to come from the professional upper-middle class.[5]

It has often been said that social background has little to do with judicial behavior since one can find many cases in which the courts have taken positions favorable to the interests of the poor, racial minorities, and the working class. While such cases certainly exist (the Warren Court decisions in the areas of civil rights and civil liberties being the most dramatic), the history of the courts has been, on balance, deeply conservative. The Warren Court era, in fact, is best understood as an exception to the general rule—a temporary aberration. From the Dred Scott decision of 1857, which defined runaway slaves as property and not persons; to the protection of business from state government regulations in the late nineteenth century; to the suppression of labor union organizing in the same period through the use of the injunction and the antiunion interpretation of the Sherman Antitrust Act; to the support of government prosecution of domestic dissidents at the end of both world wars; to the approval of the internment of Americans of Japanese descent during World War II; to recent court approval of most of the instruments of the Reagan administration's antilabor offensive— the courts have demonstrated their pro-property class orientation. They have done so, in my view, because of the social class backgrounds of judges, and because of the inherent property biases of the law itself, a subject already considered in Chapter 4.

Social class disproportionality among policy makers in the executive branch is even more striking, especially with regard to the open linkages with the corporate sector. The representatives of the corporate capitalist class occupy virtually all key positions in the executive, the branch that has become the most important policy maker in the federal government. If one examines the heads of the major executive departments, the unrepresentativeness of executive leadership is simply overwhelming. One exhaustive examination covering the years 1897 to 1973 found that *90 percent* of all cabinet officials were either members of the social elite (listed in various social registers, members of exclusive private clubs, or graduates of exclusive prep schools and/or colleges), or of the business elite (defined either by membership on a corporate board of directors, or by partnership in corporate law firms), or both. Such officials were almost exclusively members of high-status Protestant denominations, belonged to managerial, professional, or business families, and were descended from northern European or English ancestors.[6]

Historian Gabriel Kolko has examined the composition of the foreign policy-making elite, which he defined as the top officials in the departments of State, Defense, War, Treasury, and Commerce, the Central Intelligence Agency, the Export-Import Bank, and a series of ancillary agencies. Kolko concluded from his research that "foreign policy decision-makers are in reality a highly mobile sector of the American corporate structure."[7] He found that between 1944 and 1960, almost 60 percent of all foreign policy decision-making posts were held by people on loan to the government from either corporate law firms, investment and banking houses, or industrial corporations. The continuity of American foreign policy, despite periodic changes in administration from Democratic to Republican, is perhaps traceable to the fact that representatives from the upper reaches of the law, finance, and industry staff the foreign policy machinery no matter which party is in office. Note, for instance, the backgrounds of key foreign policy cabinet members (Table 8.3) in recent administrations.

Having proclaimed his admiration and support for the giants of American business,[8] Ronald Reagan has, as expected, also filled his administrative leadership positions from the vast pool of talent in the corporate sector, though he has tended to make his selections from a part of that sector that has never before been prominent in government—from sun-belt industry, real estate, and finance, from

TABLE 8.3   Institutional Affiliations of Key Foreign Policy Secretaries
(through January 1983)

SECRETARY OF DEFENSE

Robert S. McNamara (1961–1967)
President and member of the board of directors of the Ford Motor Co.; member of the board
of directors of Scott Paper Co.; president of the World Bank; president of the International
Finance Corp.

Clark Clifford (1967–1969)
Senior partner of Washington law firm Clifford and Miller; member of the board of directors
of the National Bank of Washington, the Sheraton Hotel Corp., Knight Newspapers, Riddle
Publications, and Phillips Petroleum Corp.

Melvin Laird (1969–1973)
Member of Congress; member of the board of directors of Northwest Airlines, Metropolitan
Life Insurance, Investors Mutual, Investors Stock Fund, and Communications Satellite Corp.

Elliot Richardson (1973)
Partner of the law firm of Ropes, Gray, Best, Coolidge & Rugg; trustee of Radcliffe College
and Massachusetts General Hospital; member of the board of overseers of Harvard College;
director of the Harvard Alumni Association.

James R. Schlesinger (1973–1975)
Former director of the Central Intelligence Agency; former chairman of the Atomic Energy
Commission; senior staff of the Rand Corporation.

Harold Brown (1977–1980)
Former president of the California Institute of Technology; member of the board of directors
of IBM and the Times-Mirror Corp.; former secretary of the Air Force; United States
representative to the SALT I talks under President Richard Nixon.

Caspar Weinberger (1981–   )
Former counselor to the President; Secretary of HEW; vice-president of Bechtel Corp.; director of Pepsi Co. and Quaker Oats Co.; former member of Trilateral Commission.

SECRETARY OF THE TREASURY

C. Douglas Dillon (1961–1965)
Member of the New York Stock Exchange; president of the U.S. and Foreign Securities
Corp.; director, vice-president, and chairman of the board of Dillon, Reed & Co.; trustee of
the Groton School; member of the board of governors of the New York Hospital; trustee of
the Metropolitan Museum of Art.

Henry H. Fowler (1965–1969)
Member of the law firm of Covington, Burling, Rublee; senior member of the law firm of
Fowler, Leva, Hawes & Symington; director of the Norfolk & Western Railway; general part-
ner of Goldman, Sachs & Co.; member of the board of directors of Corning Glass Works,
U.S. Industries, Foreign Securities, and Dereco Corp.; trustee of the Alfred P. Sloan Founda-
tion and the Carnegie Endowment for Peace.

(Continued)

TABLE 8.3   *(continued)*

SECRETARY OF THE TREASURY

David M. Kennedy (1969-1970)
Member of the board of directors of the Husky Oil Corp., Abbot Laboratories, Adela Investment, Commonwealth Edison, and Communications Satellite Corp.; chairman of the board of Continental Illinois National Bank & Trust; trustee of International Harvester, Pullman Co., U.S. Gypsum Co., and Equitable of Iowa; chairman of the Council of the Graduate School of Business of the University of Chicago and George Washington University; chairman of the Government Borrowing Committee of the American Bankers Association.

John B. Connally (1970-1972)
Member of the law firm of Bowell, Wirtz & Rauhut; senior partner of the law firm of Unison, Elkins, Searls & Connally; member of the board of directors of New York Central Railroad, First City National Bank of Houston, Texas Instruments Corp., Halliburton Co., General Portland Cement Co., Gibraltar Savings Assoc., Mid-Texas Communications Systems, Inc., Houston Medical Foundation, Texas Research League, and Texas Heart Institute; trustee of the U.S. Trust Co.

George P. Schultz (1972-1974)
Co-chairman of Automation Fund Committee for Armour & Co.; president of the Industrial Relations Research Assoc.; member of the board of directors of Borg-Warner Corp., J. I. Case, Stein Roe & Farnham Stock and Balanced Funds, General American Transportation, Chicago Assoc. of Commerce and Industry; dean of the University of Chicago Graduate School of Business.

William E. Simon (1974-1978)
Senior partner in charge of the Government Bond Department and the Municipal Bond Department of the New York City investment firm of Salomon Bros.; board of governors of the Executive Committee, Securities Industry Assoc.; assistant vice-president and manager of the Municipal Trading Department, Union Securities; vice-president of the investment banking firm Weeden & Co.; founder of the Association of Primary Dealers in the U.S.; member of the advisory board of lower Manhattan, Chemical Bank; member of the Bond Club of New York; member of the board of governors of the Municipal Bond Club of New York (president, 1971–1972); trustee of Lafayette College.

Warner Michael Blumenthal (1978-1979)
Former president of the Bendix Corporation; former vice-president of Crown Cork Co.; trustee of Princeton University and the Council on Foreign Relations.

Donald Regan (1980-1984)
Chief executive officer of Merrill Lynch and Co.; vice chairman of the New York Stock Exchange; trustee of the Charter & Merrill Trust; chairman of the board of trustees of the University of Pennsylvania; member of the Business Roundtable and the Council on Foreign Relations.

James Baker (1985-   )
Princeton; U.S. Marine Corps; member law firm of Andrews, Kurth, Campbell, and Jones of Houston; trustee Woodrow Wilson Center.

TABLE 8.3   *(continued)*

SECRETARY OF STATE

Dean Rusk (1961–1969)
President of the Rockefeller Foundation.

William P. Rogers (1969–1974)
Partner of the law firm of Dwight, Royall, Harris, Koegal & Caskey; member of the board of directors of Standard Oil of Ohio; trustee of the New York Racing Association; director of the Gannet Corp.

Henry Kissinger (1974–1978)
Professor, Harvard University; director of the Special Studies Project, the Rockefeller Brothers Fund.

Cyrus Vance (1978–1980)
Senior partner in the New York law firm of Simpson, Thacher and Bartlett; member of the board of directors of IBM and Pan American World Airways; trustee of Yale University, the Rockefeller Foundation, and the Council on Foreign Relations; former secretary of the Army under President Lyndon Johnson.

Alexander Haig (1981–1982)
Former chief of the White House staff; former Supreme Allied Commander Europe (SHAPE); president, chief operating officer, and director of United Technologies Corp.

George Schultz (1983–   )
Princeton, MIT; director and president, Bechtel Corp.; director of General Motors and Dillon, Reed and Co.

SOURCE: *Who's Who in America,* 42nd ed. (Chicago: Marquis, 1984).

aerospace and energy corporations, and from conservative, corporate-financed foundations and think-tanks.

The general relationship between social class and public office is best summed up by the following observation from one prominent student of western governments:

> What the evidence conclusively suggests is that in terms of social origin, education and class situation, the men who have manned all command positions in the state system have largely, and in many cases overwhelmingly, been drawn from the world of business and property, or from the professions.

> . . . In an epoch when so much is made of democracy, equality, social mobility, classlessness and the rest, it has remained a basic fact of life in advanced capitalist countries that the vast majority of men and women in these countries has been governed, represented, administered, judged, and commanded in war by people drawn from other, economically and socially superior and relatively distant classes.[9]

If there were no class divisions in American society, or if people were not assorted into a complex variety of religions, ethnic groups, occupations, and races— if, in short, Americans were a homogeneous people with no differences in situation, needs, interests, and demands—then the background of decision makers would make no practical difference. Since such is obviously not the case, it is of more than passing interest that the vast majority of political decision makers in the United States come from an exceedingly narrow, powerful, and privileged slice of American society. This fact alone at least partially explains the social class biases so often encountered in the politics of the federal government.

THE POLITICS OF CORPORATE POWER

To a very great extent (as pointed out in Chapter 7), the decisions made by the owners and managers of the giant corporations about a wide range of business matters, simply because of the vast size of corporations, cannot help but shape the character of all of American society. Their decisions about investment, job design, technological innovation, plant location, and financing provide the context within which Americans work and play, create the set of problems that largely define the sphere of activities of the government, and set the boundaries for what is politically possible. Labor unions in the United States, on the other hand, have virtually nothing to say about any of these issues, while government has but a minor voice, usually after the fact.

American corporations also exercise power in politics and public affairs in ways that are even more direct. In this section, I examine some of the more important forms and sources of corporate political power and illustrate why the eminent economist, Charles Lindblom, was forced to conclude his recent book, *Politics and Markets,* with the following observation: "The large private corporation fits oddly into democratic theory and vision. Indeed, it does not fit."[10]

Organizational Resources

The most obvious source of political and social power for the giant corporation is the enormous wealth to which it has access because of its dominant position in the American economy. There is no need to belabor the point, but it is useful to recall that if one were to lump together a handful of the largest banks, utilities, insurance companies, food marketers, and transportation companies along with the top two hundred industrial firms, one would have a group that accounts for the predominant portion of all economic activity in America, whether measured by output, receipts, or profits. These giants of business enterprise derive enormous sums of money from their market domination, which their owners and managers are free to use in whatever manner they choose. While they undoubtedly channel much of it toward further efforts at market domination, most of the expenditures in one way or another add to the sum of their political and social power. Some obvious examples include the vast expenditures on advertising, which are aimed not only at product differentiation but also at company image and the legitimacy of the corporate system in general; the ownership of many of the key sources of information dissemination—newspapers, book publishing companies, and radio and television stations; the shaping of educational curriculum through philanthropic activities; the influencing of political candidates at local, state, and national levels through campaign contributions; and the establishment of trade associations, lobbying groups, and political action committees to influence government officials. No other group or set of groups can match the scale of these expenditures. Several scholars estimate that corporations spend more than fifty times as much money as labor unions in efforts to influence legislation and administrative action.[11] Given the recent corporate offensive which has placed business in its best position since the 1920s[12] (to be reviewed in this section), it is reasonable to suppose that the disproportionality in resources and expenditures is even more serious today.

These giant enterprises may also be understood as complex organizations of skilled manpower, as aggregations of professional, scientific, and technical talent. In a society that increasingly rewards the groups and institutions that have access to knowledge (e.g., to plan, cope, and innovate), the giant corporation enjoys distinct advantages. To be sure, other complex organizations exist in our society, but with the possible exception of the federal government, no other set of organizations has assembled within it such a wide range of skills and talents. The giant corporation is able at literally a moment's notice to call together scientists, engineers, lawyers, accountants, social scientists, management experts, and systems analysts and to direct them toward any problem deemed appropriate by corporate management, whether it be new product development, basic research, public relations, oveseas expansion, or negotiation with government bureaus and regulatory agencies. The great corporation holds distinct advantages over other organizations and institutions since it has at its disposal almost unlimited funds and an unmatched collection of skills and talents, all of which can be used at the discretion of its owners and managers, who are relatively free from public scrutiny and control. For its antitrust battle with the federal government in the 1970s, IBM was able to mobilize more in-house lawyers than were available to the *entire* antitrust division of the Department of Justice.

The reach and influence of the giant corporations is so great that it is able to mobilize a vast number of people for political action at literally a moment's notice. Corporations like IBM, American Express, General Electric, Coca-Cola, General Motors, and the like, with networks of plants, suppliers, retailers, employees, subcontractors, salespeople, distributors, and stockholders in every congressional district in the nation, have learned how to orchestrate coordinated "grass-roots" lobbying efforts through telephone banks and direct-mail campaigns. At its most sophisticated, these "grass-roots" efforts are able to mobilize corporate networks in specific districts whose legislators sit on decisive congressional committees. This was used very effectively, for instance, by the Natural Gas Supply Association in its successful effort to decontrol the natural gas industry.[13] Corporations have also systematized methods to raise money from their employees and stockholders in order to fund a wide range of political action committees.

While corporations have always held such advantages over other groups and institutions, the resources devoted to government and politics by corporations have dramatically escalated in recent years.[14] Corporations increased the number of their public affairs offices in Washington fivefold between 1968 and 1978, from one hundred to five hundred. They also increased the size of their Washington corporate offices by a factor of 3 during the same period. Over 2,500 corporate trade associations are now headquartered in the nation's capital. The Washington, D.C., bar nearly doubled in the same period with its main business related in one way or another to the growing corporate interest group presence in Washington. No other sector of the population can match big business in forming and financing a multitude of organizations whose activities directly or indirectly influence government and politics in the United States. The *Encyclopedia of Associations in the United States* devotes 17 pages to labor unions, 60 to public affairs organizations, 71 to scientific and technical organizations, but 256 pages to national business associations.[15]

The corporate presence in Washington has also taken the form of organizations designed to speak to various government officials and bodies as the voice of the corporate class as a whole. Such groups would include the National Civic Federation, founded by J. P. Morgan and August Belmont near the turn of the century, which was influential in many of the ''reforms'' of the Progressive era; the American Association of Labor Legislation, which helped create the modern legal structure of labor-management relations; the Committee on Economic Development, which influenced the economic policies of the postwar years in the forties; the Council on Foreign Relations, which helped shape the main contours of American foreign policy for two-and-a-half decades after the second World War; and the Business Advisory Council, which was regularly consulted by presidents from Truman to Nixon. Today the most prominent of these groups is the Business Roundtable, founded in 1972, and based on the principle that the chief executive official (CEO) of each of the major corporations be personally and actively involved. Wayne Valis, in Mr. Reagan's Office of Public Liaison, has suggested that ''The resources of the coalition [The Roundtable] are almost scary they are so big.''[16] Its purpose is not only to lobby for the corporate point of view in Washington but also to shape public opinion on the issues relevant to corporate interests and to further the political education and class unity of the CEO. As Vogel suggests, ''The Roundtable deliberately seeks to avoid advancing the narrow economic concerns of particular companies and industries in order to address issues of a more class character.''[17] Key principals in the creation of the Roundtable were Bryce Harlow of Proctor and Gamble, W. B. Murphy of Campbell Soup Co., Roger Blough of U.S. Steel, Fred Borch of General Electric, and John Harper of Alcoa.[18]

Deference to the Business Point of View

Another source of corporate power and influence is the general legitimacy enjoyed by the business system in the United States and the traditional preference for private over public undertakings. The traditional preferences are no doubt reinforced by the fact that, for many people, the economic system has delivered the goods and that for many Americans "free enterprise" has been the primary engine in generating prosperity. While bearing only the most fleeting resemblance to the small enterprises appropriate to Adam Smith's free laissez-faire economy, the giant corporation retains much of the generalized good will directed toward the business system: Americans seem to favor the large corporation as a variant of free enterprise.

The legitimacy of the corporate sector is further reinforced by the fact that the financial well-being of a significant number of Americans is tied to the financial well-being of giant corporations. Corporations are vast organizations that in their wide-ranging activities affect the lives of many people. American Telephone and Telegraph employs over 1,000,000 people; General Motors over 800,000; Ford and General Electric over 400,000; IBM over 300,000. Besides the direct dependence of these people on the health and profit position of the companies for which they work, a much wider circle of people is affected. Each of the major corporations has scores of companies employing thousands of people to which it subcontracts its work, and they also are dependent on the giant corporation. To this list of affected persons and communities one can add the numerous stockholders of corporate stock and the citizens of the many local communities where plants are located. To a large extent, the economic position of merchants, lawyers, doctors, bankers, realtors, and homebuilders in localities dominated by large plants is a direct function of the well-being of the company. All these factors lead to a deep reservoir of support among the American public for public policies beneficial to the profitability of big business.

Another critical source of corporate power is the commitment of all public officials to the existing economic and social system. While there are differences, to be sure, between liberals and conservatives, and Democrats and Republicans in American politics, these differences never extend to fundamentally divergent and opposed views of the ongoing economic and social order. Differences of opinion, often strongly held, concern issues like taxation, the scope of the welfare state, the degree to which government ought to regulate the economy, enforcement of drug laws, and the rights of black Americans. With rare exception, however, political office-holders do not pose basic challenges to the corporate system regardless of their particular party or philosophic label. Radical proposals for massive income redistribution or for the curbing of corporate autonomy and the substitution of public control over the basic questions of production (what to produce, how much to produce, and how to produce) are absent from the American scene. While debate among politicians has been intense on many issues, it has been about different conceptions of how to run the same economic and social system and not about radically different social systems. As Robert Heilbroner has pointed out, "The striking characteristic of our contemporary ideological climate is that the dissident groups, labour, government, or academics, all seek to accommodate their proposals for social change to the limit of adaptability of the prevailing business order."[19]

The necessity faced by political leaders to maintain the health of the economic system gives tremendous influence to big business because in order to maintain economic health, leaders must maintain *business confidence*. For political leadership there is no way to escape this constraint. Given the importance of big business to the American economy and the relative autonomy of business decision making, the cooperation of business leaders is required to maintain economic vigor and expansion. Reformist presidents have learned that business investment is the key ingredient in the health of the American economy and that precipitous actions on their part to restrain business usually result in serious declines in the most important economic indicators. President Kennedy in his first eighteen months in office hurt business confidence by his efforts to diminish the influence of the Business Advisory Council, a powerful collection of business leaders, and by his emotional public debate with United States Steel Chairman, Roger Blough, over steel price increases. The painful economic consequences of his lukewarm support of business influenced him to court big business actively for the remainder of his presidency, to restore the Business Advisory Council, and to allow price increases in steel only a year after the confrontation. Similar stories could be told about Lyndon Johnson and Jimmy Carter with only the small details being different.

Charles Lindblom has brilliantly illuminated what is at issue here. Since the health of the economy and the well-being of most of the population depends on big business, but since it cannot be forced to invest and produce in ways that serve these goals, government must constantly offer inducements to business. The particular forms of inducements are as varied as stories on the front page of any newspaper: tax breaks, investment credits, subsidies, pollution control waivers, extensive consultation, protection of overseas investments, and the like. What is striking is that no other important set of actors in society requires similar inducements. Workers, for instance, must work; they have no other choice if they want to feed and house themselves and their families. Corporations, on the other hand, may choose to invest overseas or in speculative real estate rather than in job-creating plant and equipment, transfer their liquid assets into Japanese yen, or slow the pace of technological innovation. The business point of view must be attended to before any other because its interests in a capitalist economy come to be perceived as equivalent to the interests of American society and its people. As Lindblom points out:

> In the eyes of government officials . . . businessmen do not appear simply as the representatives of a special interest, as representatives of interest groups do. They appear as functionaries performing functions that government officials regard as indispensable. When a government official asks himself whether business needs a tax reduction, he knows he is asking a question about the welfare of the whole society and not simply about a favor to a segment of the population, which is what is typically at stake when he asks himself whether he should respond to an interest group . . . collaboration and deference between the two are at the heart of politics in such systems. Businessmen cannot be left knocking at the doors of the political systems, they must be invited in.[20]

Molding Citizen Attitudes

The general legitimacy of the business point of view is not only a product of the centrality of the major corporations to the economic well-being of many Americans but also a product of a careful and massive effort at influencing public opinion. These expensive and extensive efforts are on a scale that cannot be even remotely matched by any other set of institutions in America. The efforts at opinion formation by labor unions, for instance, are comparatively so small as to pale into insignificance.

Advertising. Americans do not need to be reminded that the pervasive quality of corporate advertising is perhaps the single most salient feature of American culture. There is no escaping advertising. It assaults us at every turn: television, radio, magazines, direct mailings, telephone solicitations, neon signs, and billboards. It is not unreasonable to propose that advertising is not a mere adjunct to mass media in the United States—it is its most evident quality.

Advertising, of course, is largely concerned with the attempt to sustain and expand the sales of particular products. A significant portion of the total advertising budget of the major corporations, however, is directed toward convincing the public of their benevolent intentions and good works (e.g., support of the arts, protection of the environment, encouragement of racial equality, and the like) and to persuade it of the correctness of the corporate viewpoint on the major issues of the day. One estimate holds that corporate advocacy advertising (as opposed to product-oriented "institutional advertising") exceeds $1 billion.[21] Mobil Oil Company spends almost $4 million annually on ads in the newsmagazines, on the Op-Ed page of *The New York Times,* and on television extolling free enterprise, private initiative, and limited government. Other chemical and oil companies feature advertising announcing their concern for the environment (on the front page of the same newspaper where such ads appear one finds stories about oil spills and the dumping of toxic wastes).

Ownership of the Mass Media. While no one can deny that various points of view may be heard in the United States (if one searches strenuously enough), the pervasiveness of the corporate point of view is virtually assured by ownership patterns in the mass media. The major mass media do not show any proclivity to be critical of the corporate system; or to be supportive of the labor movement; or to be favorably disposed to print, broadcast, or televise radical points of view because the media tend themselves to be organized as powerful business conglomerates, owned and controlled by a handful of people and institutions. It is now common for empires such as Hearst or Gannett to own daily newspapers, local radio and television stations, book publishers, film production facilities, and so on, and for major corporations like Gulf and Western to own media outlets such as Paramount Pictures, Simon & Schuster, and Pocket Books. Also, since newspapers, magazines, and television stations depend almost entirely on their advertisers in the business world, they are unlikely to become the voice of dissenting points of view on a regular basis.

Access to Educational Institutions. Compared with potentially competing interests like environmental and consumer protection groups or labor unions, large business enterprises have ready access to educational institutions at all levels. In almost every school system in the country, slick educational materials for the classroom, designed, produced, and distributed by the corporations, are in widespread use. In Dallas, Salt Lake City, Boston, and Denver, extensive "adopt-a-school" programs are in place in which representatives of local and national corporations "inform" school children about the virtues of free enterprise and the problems of government interference (labor unions, needless to say, have not generally been invited to present their views). Prestigious universities are increasingly prone, as public sources of financing begin to diminish, to accept corporate grants of money to establish research programs, business-oriented curriculum, and even endowed chairs of free-enterprise studies, the purpose of which, according to *Management Today,* is "to counter-attack the lamentable public standing of business."[22] Corporations and foundations closely connected to them also finance "executive-on-campus" programs, faculty-business seminars, contests for students, pro-business campus newspapers, and other programs too numerous to mention. Needless to say, nothing comparable is possible on the part of organizations representing other sectors of society.

Think-tanks. While they have always been around in one form or another, a number of corporation-funded, pro-business think-tanks have been playing an almost incalculable role in the shaping of elite opinion in recent years. The most prominent among them are the conservative, anticommunist Hoover Institution located at Stanford University; the American Enterprise Institute, which supplied much of the staff and many ideas for the Reagan administration and which has seen its budget of $879,000 and staff of 19 in 1970 expand to $10.4 million and 135 in 1980;[23] and such militantly antigovernment regulation, pro–big business organizations as the Institute for Contemporary Studies, the International Institute for Economic Research, and the Institute for Educational Affairs, among many others.[24] Especially prominent during the Reagan years was the Heritage Foundation which, supported by Coors, the Scaife Foundation, Mobil Oil, Gulf, and Dart Industries, enjoyed annual 40 percent increases in its budget throughout the late 1970s and early 1980s.[25]

Political Action Committees. There has recently been an unprecedented growth in the number, size of budgets, and expenditures of corporate, conservative, and pro-business political action committees (PACs).[26] In 1974, for instance, there were but eighty-nine corporate PACs. By 1984 there were over 2,000 of them. Closely allied trade-membership-health PACs increased from 318 to almost 1,000 during the same period. Expenditures of these combined groups grew from about $8 million to over $90 million. The objective of these PACs has been to propagate and widely disseminate a pro-business, antiwelfare state point of view on a wide range of public issues and to support political candidates supportive of such views. In just two years, between 1980 and 1982, overall PAC spending on congressional races increased by 46 percent with most of the increase accounted for by business-oriented PACs.[27]

To be sure, many different kinds of groups and associations are free to create their own PACs and a great many do. The landscape is dotted with PACS created by labor unions, environmental groups, antinuclear organizations, and more. Nevertheless, and with that said, what is most apparent in the system is the overwhelming preponderance of corporate, pro-business, antiwelfare state, and conservative PACs. Note Tables 8.4 and 8.5. The former table indicates that corporate and association PACs raised well over twice the money during the 1984 elections as did labor, while ideological PACs, most of which are conservative and pro-

TABLE 8.4   Money raised by political action committees
for 1984 elections, by category

Ideological	$63.2 million
Corporate	47.7 million
Association	42.7 million
Labor	35.7 million

SOURCE: Federal Election Commission, reported in *The National Journal* (November 10, 1984), p. 2171. Reprinted by Permission.

TABLE 8.5   The twenty-five largest PACs (1984 elections)

National Conservative Political Action Committee	$16,258,217
National Congressional Club	5,172,546
Fund for a Conservative Majority	4,873,853
Republican Majority Fund	4,200,983
Realtors Political Action Committee	3,905,734
American Medical Association	3,713,984
NRA Political Victory Fund	3,172,401
Ruff Political Action Committee	2,981,095
Fund for a Democratic Majority	2,697,970
National Education Association	2,299,751
National Committee for an Effective Congress	2,242,272
Citizens for the Republic	2,170,020
National PAC	1,841,782
Campaign for Prosperity	1,773,399
National Association of Home Builders	1,653,585
International Longshoreman's Association	1,692,284
United Auto Workers	1,641,381
Machinists Non-Partisan Political League	1,639,210
United Food and Commercial Workers	1,614,361
National Association of Retired Federal Employees	1,537,373
Associated Milk Producers Inc.	1,551,618
Seafarers Political Activity Donation	1,480,384
Transportation Political Education League	1,463,363
Democratic-Republican Independent Voter Education Committee	1,425,925
Communications Workers of America	1,396,293

SOURCE: *The National Journal* (November 11, 1984), p. 2171. Reprinted by Permission.

business in orientation, also far outstripped labor. The latter table, which lists the top twenty-five PACs, dramatically demonstrates the favored position of business and conservative PACs. That is to say, while a handful among them represent labor unions and espouse liberal ideas and programs, most of them, especially the very largest, represent business and professional groups and/or espouse conservative and Republican points of view.

In this section, we have seen a few of the many ways in which the corporations attempt to shape citizens' and politicians' perspectives on the issues of the day. The instruments of persuasion are many. We have touched on only a few. The messages conveyed, however, are fairly consistent. First, the major corporations attempt to identify themselves with those values most cherished by the American people: freedom, abundance, efficiency, democracy, environmental protection, and philanthropy. Second, the public is admonished to let business do what it knows how to do in perpetuating these values, a task it can accomplish only to the extent that government interference is kept to a minimum. Third, certain issues potentially threatening to big business like wealth and income distribution, corporate-government linkages, planning in the public interest, and so on are virtually ignored. Now it is certainly the right of corporations to so act. Indeed, no rational person could reasonably expect otherwise. Nevertheless, the molding of public opinion in the United States takes on a decidedly uneven cast given the relative distribution of resources among social classes and groups. As Charles Lindblom points out, " . . . core beliefs [in the United States] are the product of a rigged, lopsided competition of ideas."[28]

Corporate Power Reconsidered

The power base of the corporations is indeed awesome. They control more financial resources than rival organizations and institutions; they exercise control over an unmatched collection of skills and talents; they enjoy wide-ranging support from both the general public and political leadership; and it is widely believed that their well-being is essential to the well-being of all Americans. Given this set of advantages, it should come as no surprise to learn that corporate managers and owners enjoy relatively free access to the important councils of government, where their views, interests, and demands are incorporated into the complicated calculus by which decisions are made.

This story of access, sympathy, and collusion represents the general, long-term tendency in the relationship between big business and government. It does not preclude the possibility of short-term reversals—periods when government takes on a mildly antibusiness posture. One might point to some of the policies of Roosevelt's New Deal after 1935 when he loosed the antitrust division of the Department of Justice on several corporations and sprinkled his speeches with references to "economic royalists," though not much came of either. One might point also to the decade of the seventies when public opinion turned sharply against big business and created an atmosphere conducive to the passage of various federal and state laws controlling business activities that directly affected the environment, occupational safety, political campaigns, the consumer, racial equality, and so on. Again, however, this decline in business power proved to be short term. Note how the Reagan administration dramatically reversed the effects of these various laws by slowing investigation and enforcement, by slashing budgets of all the regulatory agencies, and by appointing to leadership positions in the various agencies persons friendly to the corporate point of view and hostile to the laws they were charged with administering (Watt at the Department of the Interior, Gorsuch at the Environmental Protection Agency, Auchter at the Occupational Safety and Health Administration, Baxter in the Anti-Trust Division of the Justice Department, Miller at the Federal Trade Commission,[29] and others). This turn of events was entirely predictable since no government in a market capitalist society can, in the long run, be hostile to the interests and wishes of its largest business enterprises.

THE MYTH OF LABOR UNION POWER

American workers and labor unions find themselves face-to-face with concentrated national and multinational corporations in the economy and in the workplace; with a set of government policy makers whose upbringing, training, and career are in sharp contrast to its own; and with a powerful, wealthy, and mobilized pro-business, antilabor political apparatus. What countervailing power, other than the votes of its members, is the American working class able to mobilize in the service of its concerns and interests? In particular, what influence do labor unions and the labor movement exercise in the political process? This section attempts to evaluate the political capacity of the American working class.

Most Americans, including more than a few labor union members, consider unions to be too powerful and socially irresponsible. Most of this opinion seems to be based on recurring stories of union featherbedding, widespread corruption, financial contributions to political campaigns, economic pressure on small businesses, extensive lobbying efforts in Congress, strikes of national consequence, and more. Although popular conceptions have some basis in fact—labor unions do often exercise considerable economic, social, and political power—the extent of that power is greatly exaggerated in the common perception, and is of little consequence when compared with that of the giant corporations.

Political Impotence

We can best see this relative lack of sustained power on the part of organized labor in the story of its failed efforts to reform federal labor laws over the last three decades. Its most important target in these efforts has been the Taft-Hartley Act of 1947, the purpose of which was and is to deradicalize the labor movement and to undermine working class solidarity. Passed by a conservative, Republican-dominated Congress, in response to labor advances during the New Deal and to labor militancy and strikes during and immediately after the second World War, the act contained the following provisions: it required all labor union leaders to file an anticommunist disclaimer; it outlawed sympathy strikes, supportive boycotts, and mass picketing; it placed restrictions on political contributions; it banned the "closed shop" and allowed states to pass "right to work" laws banning "union shops"; it made union leadership legally responsible for "wildcat" strikes; and it allowed the president to impose an eighty-day "cooling off" period on strikes with national consequences. Whatever one thinks of the legislation, organized labor has consistently interpreted it as harmful to its long-term interests and has considered it to be its primary target for legislative reform. Nevertheless, despite the putative power of the labor movement, the unions were unable to prevent its passage in 1947 and have failed miserably ever since in their efforts to overturn it. They failed even in those years when a Democratic president was in office and a strong liberal Democratic majority controlled Congress (in 1965 during the presidency of Lyndon Johnson and during Jimmy Carter's term from 1976 to 1980).

This is no small matter. If organized labor is as powerful as it is often per-

Air traffic controllers strike

ceived to be, then one would expect to see some results in precisely that area of public policy it has consistently regarded as vital to its interests, and for which it has mobilized its resources. There are other indicators, furthermore, suggesting that the labor movement is relatively weak in political terms in the United States. Compared with the western European democracies, the United States is strikingly unique in the degree to which labor is unrepresented in government policy-making positions. Virtually no working class people at all fill such positions, let alone active union members. In Sweden, to take a contrasting case, over one-half of the deputies of the Social Democratic party (the majority governing party in Sweden for much of the last four decades) have traditionally been from the unions. Most other western European nations are also characterized by significant numbers of labor union members in parliamentary office. The United States is virtually unique in the western world in not having a major political party that sees itself and that is universally perceived to be the political voice of the labor movement. While some would interpret the Democratic party as such an organization,[30] its diverse constituency and vague programmatic commitments make it a pale imitation of such parties as British Labour, the socialist parties of Sweden, Denmark, and Greece, or the communist parties of Italy and France. Not surprisingly, the absence of such a party in the United States results in the lowest level of "class" voting among all of the western democracies. That is to say, workers in the United

States are less likely to vote consistently for parties of the Left than in comparable industrialized countries.[31]

All the above indicators suggest a labor movement in the United States that exercises something less than awesome political power. The reasons for this are not difficult to discern: the pervasive character of business civilization and the power of the corporations; the feeble and declining character of union organization; and the apolitical, "bread-and-butter" character of the labor movement in the Unites States.

Declining Membership

Compared to other western democracies, labor union membership in the United States relative to the total workforce is extremely small and declining. Even at its height in the mid-fifties, no more than one-third of nonagricultural employees in the U.S. were union members and that figure may have fallen to less than 20 percent today. (As a point of comparison, almost 80 percent of nonagricultural employees are union members in Sweden.)[32] This decline has been caused by a combination of changes in the nature of employment, in effectual and halfhearted efforts to organize the unorganized, and growing worker cynicism about the benefits of unionization.

Most important, it is precisely in those industries where unions have traditionally been the strongest where automation, capital flight, and plant closings have sharply reduced the need for blue-collar workers. From 1947 to 1980, white-collar employment—that is, professional, technical, clerical, and sales workers—rose by over 12 million, while blue-collar employment fell by four and a half million.[33] Today, well over 50 percent of all workers fall into the white-collar category, where American labor unions have been only fitfully successful. Although there are growing trends toward unionization of some white-collar groups such as teachers and other government workers, the pace of unionization lags far behind the rate of creation of white-collar jobs.[34] Organized labor is also hurt by the movement of industry to the south where unionism is weak and antiunion sentiment is substantial and to the Third World where wages are but a fraction of wages in the United States.

The results for the labor movement have been predictable and disastrous. Strong membership declines have been reported among those unions that have historically been the largest and strongest in the nation: the United Steelworkers, the International Ladies Garment Workers Union, the International Electric Workers, the Brotherhood of Railroad Trainmen, and the United Auto Workers. The International Association of Machinists and Aerospace Workers lost 150,000 workers between 1969 and 1979, representing one-quarter of its membership. The Teamsters have seen their membership drop from 2.4 to 2.0 million in less than a decade.[35] Between 1980 and 1982 alone, the AFL-CIO as a whole lost almost a million members.[36]

Bread and Butter Unionism

The political power of labor unions is thus crippled by its lack of representation in government, the absence of a closely aligned political party, its ability to mobilize votes, and its rapidly declining membership base. The labor movement is further constrained in the exercise of power in the political arena by the historic bread-and-butter character of the organized unions. That is to say, the self-defined mission of the leadership of the American labor movement has been to maximize the wages and benefits of its members; to cooperate when possible with big business to create conditions of profitability, in order to make wage and benefit gains possible; and to remain relatively (as compared with unions in the other western democracies) apolitical, especially eschewing the creation of a class-based political party. While a handful of class-oriented and even radical labor unions have existed in the American past (e.g., the Knights of Labor in the late nineteenth century, the Industrial Workers of the World in the early twentieth century, and several CIO unions during the Great Depression of the 1930s), a combination of outright repression by government and business (see Chapter 4), as well as the hostility of established unions in the American Federation of Labor, destroyed them. What is left in the wake is a timid and conservative labor movement.

The failure of an alternative political vision and therefore of a countervailing power to that of the corporations is partially attributable to the acceptance of business values by union members and leaders. Historically, the mainstream of American unionism (personified by Samuel Gompers) has basically accepted the American business system and has struggled to secure a place within it. The commitment to business values is dramatically demonstrated by the fact that unions have themselves begun to invest in big business. As the pension and welfare funds of unions began to accumulate, and lacking any antibusiness class consciousness, labor leaders naturally turned to big business as the "soundest" investment. The potential for big labor to become a significant countervailing political force in society is called into question when its own financial position as a set of organizations is based on the health of the corporate sector of the economy.

It is hardly surprising, then, that the president of the AFL-CIO, Lane Kirkland, is a man with a long history of close working relations with the major corporations and their political organizations.[37] Kirkland has been a member of such corporate political, research, and philanthropic organizations as the Council on Foreign Relations, the Tri-Lateral Commission, the Rockefeller Foundation, the Commission on Foundations and Private Philanthropy, and the militant Cold War organization, the Committee on the Present Danger. In light of such facts, the standing of the AFL-CIO as an independent and countervailing (to corporate power) political force seems unlikely and even mildly fantastic.

The Revival of Antiunionism

In the 1970s and continuing into the 1980s, corporate America launched its most ferocious antiunion drive since the 1920s. The drive took the form of an ideological attack on unionism in a wide range of media outlets; the dissemination of PAC campaign money to openly antiunion candidates; the use of Chapter 11 bankruptcy to abrogate union contracts; the use of "union-busting" consultants on a widespread basis in collective bargaining elections; reinvigorated efforts to force decertification elections; and an explicit willingness to engage in unfair labor practices as defined under terms of the National Labor Relations Act. The last is particularly interesting. When the National Labor Relations Board (NLRB) finds evidence of unfair labor practices (firing employees for union activities, for instance), it can order the reinstatement of workers and award back pay. The incredible increase in the number of reinstatements and the size of awards (the number of reinstatements increased from 2,723 in 1970 to 8,592 in 1980)[38] is one indicator of change in corporate behavior and a vivid demonstration that the cost of sanctions to business is less than the gains to be made by weakening and destroying unions. The antiunion drive was given a significant boost by the election of Ronald Reagan in 1980. President Reagan's contribution was twofold: the destruction of the air traffic controllers union (PATCO) in 1981 and a pattern of appointments to the NLRB which gave it a pro-business caste for the first time in memory.[39] Reagan appointments to the NLRB included Donald Dotson, labor counsel to Westinghouse and Western Electric; Robert Hunter, aide to Senator Orrin Hatch, a leader in blocking the 1978 Labor Reform Act; and Patricia Diaz Dennis of ABC. Reagan also appointed Hugh Reilly as head of the NLRB enforcement division. Reilly came to the NLRB from the rabidly antiunion National Right to Work Legal Defense Foundation. The contemporary situation of American labor unions is seen in its virtually helplessness before this combined business-government onslaught.

CONCLUDING REMARKS

We have learned in this chapter that the general distribution of political power between the two great and competing social classes that comprise the heart of American society is highly unequal. We have learned that the power of the working class, operating through its main organizational expression, the labor unions, is but a pale reflection of that exercised by giant corporations. Thus the scale of disproportionate power that corporations enjoy as a matter of course in the operations of the marketplace economy is neatly replicated in the world of government and politics. What about the vote, however? In a democratic country, is it not the case that economic power can be tamed by political officials whose tenure in office is entirely dependent on the good opinion of voters? Are not elections an effective and efficient instrument whereby concentrated and disproportionate economic and social power are brought under control and made responsible? It is to a more detailed consideration of these and related issues that we turn in the next chapter.

NOTES

1. The seminal works in this field are Robert Dahl, *Who Governs?* (New Haven: Yale University Press, 1961), and David Truman, *The Governmental Process,* 2nd ed. (New York: Knopf, 1971), though the basic assumptions and views pervade the work of most political scientists of the post–World War II era.
2. E. E. Schattschneider, *The Semisovereign People* (New York: Holt, 1960), p. 35. I would add that the chorus sings with a strong business and corporate accent.
3. Needless to say, those members of society who are not organized at all are virtually without influence.
4. This pointed observation was made by economist Joseph Schumpeter and is quoted in Ralph Miliband, *The State in Capitalist Society* (New York: Basic Books, 1969), p. 56.
5. R. Schmidhauser, "The Justices of the Supreme Court," *Midwest Journal of Political Science* 3 (1951), p. 45.
6. Beth Mintz, "The President's Cabinet, 1897–1973," *The Insurgent Sociologist* 5:3 (Spring, 1975).
7. Gabriel Kolko, *The Roots of American Foreign Policy* (Boston: Beacon Press, 1969), p. 17.
8. Reagan symbolically placed a portrait of Calvin Coolidge in a prominent place in the Cabinet Room of the White House. Coolidge is most famous for his pithy phrase, "The business of America is business."
9. Miliband, *State in Capitalist Society,* p. 67.
10. Charles F. Lindblom, *Politics and Markets: The World's Political-Economic Systems* (New York: Basic Books, 1977).
11. Francis X. Sutton et al., *The American Business Creed* (Cambridge: Harvard University Press, 1956), p. 292.
12. Thomas Byrne Edsall, *The New Politics of Inequality* (New York: W. W. Norton, 1984), p. 107.
13. *Ibid,* p. 111.
14. Most of what follows in this paragraph is based on David Vogel, "How Business Responds to Opposition," paper delivered at the 1979 annual meeting of the American Political Science Asociation; and Edsall, *The New Politics of Inequality.*
15. Lindblom, *Politics and Markets,* p. 197.
16. Sidney Blumenthal, "Whose Side Is Business On Anyway?" *The New York Times Magazine,* October 25, 1981, p. 92.
17. Vogel, "How Business Responds to Opposition," p. 21. Two political scientists have reported research indicating that the Roundtable was instrumental in "destroying the Labor Law Reform Bill, undermining the consumer protection agency proposal, turning back common situs picketing initiatives, rewording one of the clean air acts, designing the first Carter tax program, promoting natural gas price deregulation, blocking attempts to audit the Federal Reserve, bottling up antitrust bills in the House and Senate, even excising all references to antitrust from Carter's 1979 State of the Union Message." See Thomas Ferguson and Joel Rogers, "The Knights of the Roundtable," *The Nation,* December 15, 1979, p. 621.
18. Edsall, *The New Politics of Inequality,* p. 121.
19. R. L. Heilbroner, "The View from the Top: Reflections on a Changing Business Ideology," quoted in Miliband, *The State in Capitalist Society,* p. 72.

20. Lindblom, *Politics and Markets,* p. 175.
21. Subcommittee on Commerce, Consumer, and Monetary Affairs, of the House Government Operations Committee, 1978.
22. David Vogel, "Business's New Class Struggle," *The Nation,* December 15, 1979, p. 628.
23. Edsall, *The New Politics of Inequality,* p. 120.
24. The patrons of IEA include American Brands, Bendix, Coca-Cola, Dow, Ford, General Motors, Nestlé, Pfizer, and United Telecommunications. Its mission seems to be the distribution of small grants to neoconservative scholars, probusiness campus newspapers, small magazines and journals with a business point of view, and the like. See Peter Stone, "The IEA: Teaching the Right Stuff," *The Nation,* September 19, 1981, pp. 231–234.
25. Edsall, *The New Politics of Inequality,* p. 117.
26. "A PAC is simply the political arm of a business, labor, professional or other interest group, legally entitled to raise funds on a voluntary basis from members, stockholders, or employees in order to contribute funds to favored candidates, or political parties." James MacGregor Burns, Jock W. Peltason, and Thomas E. Cronin, *Government by the People* (Englewood Cliffs, N.J.: Prentice Hall, 1984), p. 167.
27. *The National Journal* (October 27, 1984), p. 2171.
28. Lindblom, *Politics and Markets,* p. 212.
29. Immediately upon assuming office as chairman of the FTC, James C. Miller III said that "the commission should no longer protect consumers from defective products and unsubstantiated advertising claims," *The New York Times,* October 25, 1980, p. 8.
30. See J. David Greenstone, *Labor in American Politics* (New York: Knopf, 1969).
31. See Robert Alford, *Party and Society* (Westport, Conn.: Greenwood Press, 1973), for an analysis of class voting in several western countries. It may well be that an important factor in the electoral behavior of the American working class is that the Democratic party is not really a party of the Left.
32. Walter Korpi, *The Working Class in Welfare Capitalism* (London: Routledge and Kegan Paul, 1978), p. 62.
33. *Statistical Abstracts of the United States, 1980,* p. 411, U.S. Bureau of the Census.
34. Even this area of slow growth has been significantly decelerated by the action of the Reagan administration in firing striking air traffic controllers and decertifying their union [The Professional Air Traffic Controller's Organization (PATCO)].
35. William Serrin, "Where Are the Pickets of Yesteryear?" *The New York Times,* May 31, 1981, p. 22F.
36. Edsall, *The New Politics of Inequality,* p. 170.
37. See "Lane's Friends," *The Nation,* January 19, 1980, pp. 37–38.
38. Edsall, *The New Politics of Inequality,* p. 152.
39. The NLRB ruled in 1984, for instance, that it was permissible for companies to move their operations from a union to a nonunion plant. This decision is expected to accelerate the trend by which companies move to nonunion areas to avoid having to bargain with unions. *(The New York Times,* Jan. 15, 1984, p. 1.) The NLRB has also significantly lengthened the time it takes to rule on unfair labor practice cases, which puts individual workers in great difficulty.

SUGGESTIONS FOR FURTHER READING

Stanley Aronowitz. FALSE PROMISES. *New York: McGraw-Hill, 1973.* A provocative interpretation of the American working class and the weaknesses of organized labor.

Stanley Aronowitz. WORKING CLASS HERO. *New York: Pilgrim Press, 1983.* An analysis of the political decline of labor and a pragmatic program for revival.

Thomas Byrne Edsall. THE NEW POLITICS OF INEQUALITY. *New York: W. W. Norton, 1984.* The best contemporary consideration of the political roles of American corporations and labor unions.

J. David Greenstone. LABOR IN AMERICAN POLITICS. *New York: Knopf, 1969.* Slightly dated although still the single best analysis of the relationship between organized labor and the Democratic party.

Charles Lindblom. POLITICS AND MARKETS. *New York: Basic Books, 1977.* A controversial but convincing analysis of the incompatability of the giant corporations and democracy.

Ralph Miliband. THE STATE IN CAPITALIST SOCIETY. *New York: Basic Books, 1969.* A modern classic that focuses on the political power of the capitalist class and its role in the formation of public policy.

Peter Steinfels. THE NEOCONSERVATIVES. *New York: Simon and Schuster, 1979.* A devastating critique of the new corporate intellectuals.

Erik Olin Wright. CLASS, CRISIS AND THE STATE. *London: New Left Books, 1977.* A collection of thought-provoking theoretical essays about class structure, political struggles, and capacities.

9

Elections Amidst
Inequality

We have learned so far in this book that the American economic, social, cultural, and legal systems are heavily biased toward the needs, interests, and wants of the most privileged individuals, groups, and classes in the nation. We have learned, furthermore, that the interest group system, one of the purported pillars of democratic politics in the United States, is itself biased to the extent that the "heavenly chorus" sings with a distinctly upper class and corporate accent. We have learned, that is to say, that corporations are organized for the exercise of political power in ways which no other group can begin to match, and that the exercise of political power by the working class through its unions, on the other hand, is relatively anemic. The prospects for social justice and democracy in such a setting, no matter how these terms are defined, do not look terribly promising. How, then, are we justified in calling ourselves citizens of a democracy?

It is generally assumed by lay people and professional political scientists alike that *free elections* are the main guarantee and touchstone of democracy. It is the election, open to all on a one-person, one-vote basis, that compensates for the many other inequalities in American life and that allows every citizen to exercise a voice in the affairs of governance. As one scholar has put it, "elections are the unique institution of democracy and a viable democracy requires meaningful elections."[1]

> The right of citizens to choose their leaders is the cornerstone of democratic government. . . . Elections offer the individual an effective opportunity to register his support for an incumbent leader or indicate his preference for change. In the

160

hands of the democratic citizen, the ballot is the most potent weapon for ensuring democratic government.[2]

In this view, elections serve to keep political decision makers responsive and responsible to ordinary citizens; elections link elites and nonelites and thereby make democracy a living reality. At work is a "law of anticipated reactions" in which political leaders conduct government business with an eye constantly fixed on the next election. Politicians heed popular interests and aspirations not necessarily because they are moral, patriotic, or socially concerned persons, but because they must eventually face the public at the ballot box. Elections force politicians to be attentive and responsible because they want to stay in office.

Most of this common-sense wisdom about elections has rarely been put to the test, however. It is merely assumed as part of the American folklore that elections are influential and controlling, that they hold political decision makers responsible, and that they help ensure that public policy conforms to public expectations. Is this true in practice in the United States? Do elections play the important role assigned to them in democratic theory? Is representative democracy alive and well in the United States? In this chapter, we turn our attention to considering these questions. We shall learn that elections are limited as instruments capable of linking elites and nonelites in the United States because of the "spillover" effects of social and economic inequality; the weak accountability of politicians; and the insulation of most decision makers from the potential sting of the voter. We shall learn that elections in the United States, while not devoid of certain democratic qualities, are, to a great extent, a form of mass entertainment serving to placate and mystify. Lamentably, they have not been a means by which ordinary citizens have been politically *empowered*, though the possibility remains that elections might serve such a purpose, given the proper environment.

MONEY IN AMERICAN ELECTORAL POLITICS

It would surely be a cause for wonder if the formal equality of a one-person-one-vote election system were not somehow tainted by the great inequalities that characterize every other area of American life. In this section, I examine the many ways in which disproportionate economic power is translated into disproportionate electoral power.

The Need for Money

It has been said that money is the mother's milk of American politics. With wealth and income distributed as they are in America, it should have also been said that this mother's milk is enjoyed by some and not others. Nevertheless, there is plenty of it. Richard Nixon's presidential campaign in 1972 cost $60 million. The presidential primary campaigns of both parties in 1976 cost over $66 million. The primary and national races in 1980 (including congressional races) topped the $500 million mark. The average campaign cost of a first-term member of the House increased from $100,000 in 1972 to $300,000 in 1982. In the same year, the average Senate candidate spent $1.7 million. In 1984, one senator, Jesse Helms, spent over $13 million in his race against Governor Hunt while John D. Rockefeller IV spent nearly $8 million to win his senatorial seat in the relatively small state of West Virginia.

Modern political campaigns, it is fair to say, cost a great deal of money and, because of the growing trend toward electronic campaigning, become more expensive with each electoral cycle. Political candidates now have the capacity to blanket their constituencies with their images and messages on a daily basis, to continuously monitor the effects of these images and messages, and to change them when needed. Campaign advertising and fund-raising appeals can now be electronically targeted to specific groups. Long gone are the "back-porch" campaigns and the lengthy "whistle-stop" tour. This is the age of the 60-second television spot, radio jingles, billboards, bumper stickers, issue and candidate polling, direct-mail computerized fund raising, professional campaign consultants, the campaign advertising agency, video cassettes, electronic mail, multicity video conferencing, and the like. Senator Richard Lugar of Indiana spent over $3 million in his 1982 race with less than $100,000 of the total cost going for traditional items like political meetings and campaign paraphernalia. Pete Wilson spent over half of his $7 million budget on television in his successful bid for California's senatorial seat.[3] The new technology, it need hardly be said, is extremely costly and becoming more so each year. By 1980, for example, a 60-second spot in a single prime television market such as Boston cost almost $8,000 (not counting production costs), while a single interview by a pollster cost $16 (a national poll might include about 4,000 people; a state poll might include up to 2,500 people).[4] To campaign for political office in the United States today requires either a great personal fortune or access to a great deal of money from other persons and groups.

Where Does the Money Come From?

Money in elections tends to be interested money. It is contributed, that is to say, by people who have an interest in who is elected and how politicians behave once in office. It matters a great deal, therefore, where this money comes from. Not surprisingly, given the nature of the distribution of wealth and income in the United States, the mother's milk of modern election campaigns comes mainly from the most privileged and powerful individuals, groups, and institutions in the nation, a fact that profoundly shapes the public agenda and the content of public policy.

There is one partial exception to this rule, however. The national presidential campaign is partially funded by matching funds from the federal treasury. Under provisions of the 1974 Campaign Finance Act passed in the wake of the Watergate affair,[5] the public subsidized over 50 percent of campaign costs during the 1976 presidential race between Gerald Ford and Jimmy Carter. The presidential election had seemingly been wrested away from private, interested money and put on a firm public footing, open to all legitimate contenders. The first publicly funded presidential election in 1976 proved to be the high-water mark of tax-supported campaigns, however, for the percentage of public support in presidential campaigns has been steadily dropping. This may be attributed to successful efforts by candidates to by-pass the spending limits in the legislation. They have done so primarily through the device of "independent" campaign organizations, which are committed to the election of a particular candidate but not formally associated with the candidate, free to raise and spend money virtually at will. These parallel campaign organizations are often more important and influential than the official party and candidate organizations. In the 1980 presidential election campaign, for example, Americans for Change spent over $100,000 in Houston in support of Ronald Reagan. This organization funneled the remainder of its nearly $1 million campaign chest to districts in ten states where it perceived the outcome to be close. In that same election, the National Conservative Political Action Committee spent over $2 million in pro-Reagan, and anti-Carter spots in what it considered crucial swing states. The Fund for a Conservative Majority (pro-Reagan) conducted its own $2 million campaign while Americans for an Effective Presidency (also pro-Reagan) ran its own for $1.27 million.[6]

Putting aside the decreasingly important public tax support for presidential campaigns, most election money in the United States comes from groups and individuals that have money to give in the first place. That includes, in a proportional sense, a very small number of individuals and groups who are *not* a random selection of the nation's individuals and groups. Not surprisingly, individuals who contribute to political campaigns tend to be far richer than the average American citizen. In the 1980 election, less than 7 percent of adult Americans contributed money to political campaigns; almost all of them were to be found in the upper third of income earners.[7] The Republicans have been especially closely tied to this segment of the population. When Republican National Committee fund-raising lists were put together in the 1960s, they were based on lists of Carte Blanche credit card holders, subscribers to *The Wall Street Journal*, and clients of investment and brokerage firms.[8]

Increasingly important as sources of support for candidates, political parties, and "independent" campaign organizations are the ubiquitous political action committees. PACs currently provide over a third of all campaign money in American elections and their role becomes more important with every election. Their relative share of campaign funding has increased *tenfold*, in fact, over the last decade. We know already, moreover, from the discussion in Chapter 8, that PACs are hardly representative of the broad range of interests and opinions that exist in the United States.

The PAC system, so central and increasingly important in our elections, is biased in a number of obvious ways. First, the system tends to better represent the rich than the poor. Few PACs exist to defend the interests of those below the poverty line, or welfare recipients, or female-headed, single parent households, or the unemployed. Second, the system tends to better represent producer groups (steel makers, wheat growers, chemical companies, and so on) than consumer groups, although a handful of PACs exist to protect and advance the interests of the latter. Third, as we have already seen, the PAC system tends to better represent business corporations than labor unions, even though, ironically, the very first political action committees were created a generation ago by the unions. Fourth and finally, the PAC system is disproportionately tilted toward conservative as opposed to liberal ideological organizations with the National Conservative Political Action Committee being the most prominent.[9]

If money contributed to election campaigns in the United States tends to be interested money, as I strongly believe, then the pattern of contributions helps to give a particular tone and shape to our governing institutions. If politicians are significantly and increasingly beholden to wealthy and near-wealthy individuals, and to corporate, producer, and conservative groups, then we can expect that public policy in the United States will significantly and increasingly favor the already privileged and powerful and ignore or actively disfavor the underprivileged and weak. I will show in Chapters 13 and 14 that this is indeed the case.

Who Gets the Money?

The privileged and the powerful are not only favored by prevailing patterns of fund raising, but also gain an additional advantage from prevailing patterns of campaign expenditure. This is hardly surprising since the very same individuals and groups that dominate fund raising also dominate decisions about the use of such funds. This is almost uniquely possible in American elections because the major political parties in the United States are virtually powerless as organizations. It would not be an exaggeration to suggest, in fact, that political parties, as such, do not exist in the United States. Each of the major parties is little more than a very loose coalition of independent state and local party organizations, along with scores of sympathetic and traditionally allied interest groups. These various fragments come together every four years to nominate a presidential candidate and to construct a relatively meaningless party platform. Neither party is controlled at a national level by a central party organization, though the presidential candidate can often gain some cooperation from his decentralized fragments during the short months of the campaign. The Democratic and Republican national committees wield little influence or power over the far-flung party coalitions. While the 1974 campaign finance reforms gave the national committees a slightly more significant role in the collection and distribution of campaign funds, the respective party committees are responsible for only a very minor portion of total campaign spending. Money for candidates and campaigns is generally raised locally and regionally from private sources, further contributing to the organizational fragmentation of the parties and the inability of central party organizations to nominate candidates and conduct campaigns. No mechanisms exist, either in law or in practice, which compel those who finance campaigns to channel funds through the national committees of the Republican and Democratic parties. Indeed, matters are so extremely fragmented that not even local party organizations are able to completely control the nomination and campaign process, given that contributions, whether from rich individuals or powerful corporate political action committees, are directed toward individual candidates.

In the main, then, wealthy and near-wealthy individuals and PACs control the distribution of campaign funds. In effect, by controlling the most important resource of political campaigning, they very largely decide who shall run and who shall not run for political office in the United States. They largely determine who has access to political decision makers and who does not; whose point of view and interests are attended to and whose are pushed aside. Political scientists and journalists have largely missed this obvious point because of the prevailing evidence that PAC money, in particular, is as likely to go to Democrats (supposedly, the party of the underdog) as to Republicans. The distribution of campaign money, that is to say, is relatively even-handed between the parties and therefore, in the opinion of political scientists and journalists, not important in shaping the national political agenda and public policy. It is the pattern of distribution within and between the parties, however, that gives the game away. Let's look more closely at who gets campaign money.

Most PAC money goes to incumbents, regardless of party. The reason is obvious. When they choose to run, incumbents in Congress, in particular, almost always win. Congressional incumbents, furthermore, already hold power and are people to be reckoned with. Those with a strong interest in the legislative agenda find it prudent to keep on the good side of powerful members of the House and the Senate, whether Democrat or Republican, liberal or conservative, so as to maintain their ear and good will. This is especially the case when it comes to party leaders, committee chairpersons, and members of important congressional committees. House Appropriations Committee Chairperson Jamie Whitten received over 75 percent of his campaign funds from PACs in 1982, while House minority leader Robert Michel received 68 percent of his from similar sources. Democratic and Republican members of the House Ways and Means Committee, during the course of their consideration of the Reagan tax cut bill of 1981, found their own war chests enhanced to the tune of $2.5 million for the 1982 campaign.

This system is entirely nonpartisan; Republicans have no great advantage over Democrats. To be nonpartisan, however, is not to be unbiased. It is a system that is, in the final analysis, open to all with the resources to play the game. Political scientist Frank Sorauf, concluding a study of PACs for the Twentieth Century Fund, says that "most PACs have parent organizations, and most of those organizations have legislative interests and Washington representations. . . . Supporting incumbents is thus a strategy of risk avoidance, of consolidating and protecting influence already won; it is the strategy of the already influential."[10] While a handful of consumer, liberal, and union groups are able to pay the tariff, it is a game played primarily by the privileged and the powerful: namely, business corporations and corporate funded, pro-business, ideological groups.

While most campaign money quite understandably goes to incumbents, some of it does not. In these cases, the evidence seems to suggest the existence of a pattern of giving that very strongly favors Republicans over Democrats and conservatives over liberals, reinforcing a general pattern that gives pro-business, antiwelfare state perspectives strong advantages in the political process. Journalist Thomas Byrne Edsall reports that about 90 percent of all of the PAC dollars not going to incumbents went to Republican and conservative candidates in close contests in the 1980 and 1982 elections.[11]

Money and the Molding of Public Opinion

Economically powerful individuals and groups protect and advance their interests not only by funding American elections and guaranteeing access and a sympathetic ear but also by using their economic power to shape public and elite opinion concerning the issues of the day. When they are successful in these efforts,[12] they very much control the political agenda—those problems and concerns which come to public and elite attention and become issues for public debate. There is no great mystery to all of this. As suggested in Chapter 8, the corporations, in particular, have resources available to them that cannot be matched by any other private institution or set of institutions. Corporations can take their message to the public through advocacy advertising and through the funding and wide dissemination of the products of pro-business "think tanks"; they can support favorable research, contribute to and shape the content of higher education, and launch a multitude of political action committees. Most importantly, the mass media are themselves parts of gigantic corporate empires and, while a few among them may experience an occasional episode of "muckraking," these media are firmly, in the long run, entrenched in the camp of the powerful.[13] While making occasional appearances here and there, the media rarely convey union or minority points of view, feature articulate spokespersons for dissident points of view, report European and Third World perspectives critical of American policy, root out fundamental causes of problems like pollution (though they often show surface details), examine workplace issues such as job safety and alienation, or challenge the basic antisocialist, anticommunist assumption of American foreign policy. The media environment within which the American people conduct their political life is defined, then, by either a singular and safe point of view or by escapist and trivialized entertainment.

None of this is to say that the wealthy and the powerful win every time or that they are able to manipulate and control every idea held by the American people. It is to say, however, that in the long run and on the important issues, the opinion and idea environment in which the average citizen learns and deliberates is heavily biased. There is, as suggested in Chapter 3, a strong ideological consensus in this country built upon the ideas promulgated by classical liberal thinkers like Adam Smith and John Locke and carried forward into the present by those with an interest in sustaining the privileged position of large holdings of private property. There exists in the United States what political scientist Walter

Dean Burnham calls an "uncontested ideological hegemony,"[14] an ideational environment characterized by the tradition of individualist liberal capitalism and its belief in the market, private property, competition, individual initiative, and limited government. This "uncontested hegemony" links political democracy to free enterprise, teaches that "what is good for General Motors (or other corporations) is good for America," and either removes such issues as public control of corporations or income redistribution from public debate or links them to communism. These "constrained volitions," as political scientist Charles Lindblom calls them,[15] mean that political debate and electoral contests are carried out in the United States within a context in which certain issues, viewpoints, and candidates are considered to be "out of bounds," not part of the legitimate game.

Many political scientists, journalists, and commentators understand democracy to be at work in American politics and election campaigns when it can be shown that a close match exists between public opinion and the positions of political parties, the behavior of candidates, and the content of public policy.[16] Such an interpretation is, I believe, untenable when it can be shown that public opinion is itself the product of a process in which wealthy and powerful individuals, groups, and institutions wield disproportionate power.

Money in Electoral Politics Reconsidered

As we have seen, American elections are fueled by large amounts of money. The sources of this vast ocean of money as well as its distribution to candidates are largely controlled by a small subset of the American population. The cultural and ideological environment in which elections are conducted, furthermore, is largely shaped by these same individuals, groups, and institutions. The result of this rigged game is entirely unsurprising: both major political parties, as well as their leading candidates for political office, are particularly attentive to the requirements of the business and financial community. They may disagree about what policies are most likely to work (as in debates over Keynesian, monetarist, and supply-side policies, for instance), whether domestic or international firms should be favored (as in debates over tariff policy), or the degree to which government should help firms maintain their market positions (as in the deregulation debate), but there is no doubt about whose interests or values are to be served. The fundamental similarities between the parties and the nature of their basic commitments are captured in the following observations, one by a leading student of corporate opinion, the other, by an outspoken labor leader.[17]

> Top executives may still be Republican, but they are no longer *partisan*. Professional managers who deal with the big world, most of them have come to think it does not usually make all that much difference which party wins, and indeed that business and the country often fare better under the Democrats. Observes Rawleigh Warner, Jr., the chairman of Mobil: "I would have to say that in the last ten to fifteen years, business has fared equally well, if not better, under Democratic administrations as under Republican administrations." Other top executives echo Warner's sentiments.[18]

What separates the Democrats from the Republicans is the windowdressing—the Democrats want it and the Republicans don't. . . . We don't have a 2-party system in this country. We have the Demopublicans. It's one party of the corporate class, with two wings—the Democrats and Republicans. They both say the other can't do the job for working people, and they're both right.[19]

These views are not meant to suggest that parties and candidates never disagree on policy or never change their stands. As to the former, the biennial and quadrennial fireworks of American elections is proof enough that disagreement often exists, though campaign heat is almost always generated by disagreement over means and not fundamentals.[20] As to the latter, to be fixed in commitment to the interests of the business community does not mean that parties and candidates are fixed forever on particular policies. Candidates and parties may simply disagree about what is necessary. More typically, however, parties and candidates propose new and different policies when the economic environment changes to such an extent that old policies become irrelevant or counterproductive. Typically one party will take the lead to reshape public policy, with the other party following in its wake. In 1896, for example, the GOP was able to formulate an approach to rising populism and the emerging corporate economy that enabled it to define the terms of public debate for a generation. The crisis of the Great Depression moved first Democrats and then Republicans toward policies favoring government economic management, social insurance for old age and unemployment, and collective bargaining (while they continued to fight vigorously over the details of implementation). GOP candidate Wendell Wilkie's positions in the 1940 election were barely distinguishable from those of Franklin Roosevelt. He claimed to love the New Deal as much as FDR but promised to run it better. By the 1984 election, the center of gravity of American politics had shifted so far to the right that the Democratic party was barely distinguishable from the Republican party as its candidates all affirmed their allegiance to balanced budgets, cut-backs in social programs, family values, patriotism, a strong military, toughness in Central America, and the efficiencies of the marketplace. By 1984, the Democrats were promising the American people Reaganism without Reagan.[21]

PROBLEMS OF POLITICAL ACCOUNTABILITY

In this chapter, we are examining the degree to which elections in the United States force political leaders to be attentive to the wishes of the American people. We have seen, so far, that the distribution, use, and control of money in the electoral process are such that a reasonable person would be forced to conclude that the electoral process tilts strongly toward the interests of the already privileged and powerful in American life. Disproportionalities of power in economy and society, that is to say, seem to "spill over" and contaminate the democratic qualities of our elections. Are they fatally contaminated? Let us examine elections and the political parties more closely. Perhaps they are able to transcend the democratic limitations created by economic inequality.

I will start by asking what parties and elections would have to look like if they were to truly be vehicles by which political decision makers were kept responsible and responsive to the American people. At a minimum, it seems to me, democracy would require that the following standards be met:

1. Candidates and parties should present clear policy choices to the American people and these policy choices should concern important issues. Elections, that is to say, should be *competitive* and *nontrivial*.
2. Once elected, officials should try to carry out what they promised during their campaign.
3. Once elected, officials should be capable of transforming campaign promises into binding public policy.
4. Elections should generally influence the behavior of those elites who are responsible for making public policy.

Clearly, if any of these four standards are not met, then the link between mass public and political decision makers is more tenuous than is normally assumed. The controlling function of elections, their use as instruments of accountability, becomes problematic in the absence of any one of the four standards.

Competitive, Nontrivial Elections

Any consideration of elections and their meaning must necessarily begin by examining the political parties that are the institutional core of American elections. After all, it is the parties that organize and conduct elections, recruit candidates, and staff political offices. A clue to the close affinity between political parties and elections may be found in the fact that parties are organized almost exclusively by election districts all across the United States, ranging from party committees for the smallest districts, all the way to the national committee concerned primarily with presidential and major senatorial races. Given our basic concern with elections as instruments of popular democratic control, and the close identification in an institutional sense of elections and political parties, what can be said about political parties that might shed light on the issues under consideration in this chapter? What sort of institutions are they?

A Two-Party System. In many ways, the most important fact about the American party system is that it is a two-party system. More so than in any other western nation, the contest for political office in the United States has been the province of only two major parties. Since the election of Abraham Lincoln in 1860, no party other than the Democrats or the Republicans has held, or even seriously bid for, the office of president. Since that same election, no other party besides the two major ones has controlled either house of Congress, or come close to doing so. While several attempts at third-party insurgency have taken place in American history (such as the Populists, the Progressives, the Dixiecrats, and George Wallace's American Independent Party), it can be safely said that nowhere in the western world have third parties been so inconsequential.

Broad Coalitions. Each of the two major American political parties is broadly coalitional in character. Lacking central direction or strict membership requirements, and competing for office in single-member, winner-take-all election districts, each party attempts to build as broad a coalition as it can, and to appeal to a diversity of groups. If they want to win elections, the parties have no choice but to attempt to pull within their orbit as many elements in the population as they are able; they attempt to prevent action or words by their candidates and lenders that would drive away important blocs of voters. The Democratic party, while sometimes brandishing its banner as the party of the underdog, tries also to appeal to the great middle- and upper-middle classes as well as to the business community. Republicans expend tremendous energy in trying to attract (quite successfully of late) the support of ethnic labor unionists and other blue-collar workers. Both parties solicit and welcome Italians, blacks, housewives, Jews, Hispanics, Irish-Catholics, ''yuppies,'' and more. Each is a vast umbrella for a broad range of groups, individuals, and voting blocs.

Ideological Consensus. It is often said that American political parties, being broadly coalitional in character, must of necessity be nonideological. In a country as pluralistic as our own, it is argued, for a party or candidate to stand on principle or ideology is to risk shattering these diverse groupings of electoral support. I would pose the issue of ideology in a slightly different way. I would suggest that the two major American political parties are strongly ideological—anyone who believes that they are devoid of ideology is invited to read the 1984 platform of the GOP. However, they are not in ideological competition with each other. The American parties do not confront each other in the manner of European and Latin American parties—Catholic parties against communist or socialist parties, labor parties ranged against free-enterprise parties—yet they remain ideological. Only in the American case, the parties share very much the same fundamental values and commitments. While the difference between the parties is not entirely trivial, the areas of overlap are much more notable.

The results of ideological consensus may be seen quite vividly in American presidential elections. While substantial conflict between the parties may often be visible during election campaigns, the conflict is never over the fundamentals of the American system. Elections, by and large, do not focus debate on such issues as the distribution of wealth, income, and power in American society, the control of monopoly capitalism, the nature of work, the control of technological change, or alternatives to present global strategy. Nor do the parties differ, except in details and rhetoric, over such givens as the primacy of private property, the beneficial nature of the free-enterprise system, and the maintenance of law and order in the face of dissent. As Gerald Pomper has pointed out, ''Politics can

Jim Crow: the price of compromise

affect changes but, viewed in the context of the total environment, these changes must be marginal and incremental."[22] Or, as another political scientist has described it, the only thing that an election can do is change the government, or part of the government. It cannot change the regime.[23]

To be sure, campaigns are often intense and even bitter. To be sure, an *occasional* national election has decisively determined the direction of national policy (the elections of 1860, 1896, and 1936 come to mind while 1980 may yet qualify), though even that remains arguable. Nevertheless, national election campaigns remain for the most part separate from, rather than engaged in, the decisive and fundamental issues of the day.[24] As one scholar has pointed out, no one would have imagined that slavery and abolition were the central national issues between 1830 and 1860 if one examined only the content of election campaigns. Little about the problems of monopoly and of the new corporations could be discerned in the materials and rhetoric of national elections in the late nineteenth century.[25]

By and large, then, the American party system does not allow political campaigns that sharply define, articulate, and contest issues of policy and principle. Rather, it actually suppresses and mutes the issues. As Walter Dean Burnham points out, "Rather than promoting competition over national goals and programs, the parties reinforce societal consensus and limit the area of legitimate political conflict."[26] That is not to say that campaigns are not often hard-fought and bitter, but for the most part even these infrequent campaigns tend to focus on trivial issues of personality or symbols. To the extent that American political

Questioner —
"I'm disappointed you failed to speak out while the government was spending $140 billion and 50,000 lives in Vietnam."

Rockefeller —
"I can see you never ran for political office, young man."

Reprinted by permission of Newspaper Enterprise Association

parties avoid ideological and programmatic issues (since they are in agreement on the fundamentals) or, in another sense, prevent many problems and concerns from becoming political issues at all, there is much truth to the traditional characterization of the parties as "Tweedledum and Tweedledee." It makes comprehensible (though no more acceptable) Ted Lowi's profound question about American life and politics: "Why do we have so many problems and so few issues?"[27]

Perhaps we can grasp the essence of these observations by examining the presidential campaigns of the past generation, where there was either general agreement between the candidates or the conflict was over relatively trivial issues.[28]

1952: Eisenhower and Stevenson. While some issues were evident in this campaign, the election centered on the powerful and compelling personality of Dwight

Eisenhower. At the issue level, Eisenhower promised to end the Korean War by going to Korea (Stevenson also promised to end the war), and by turning his attention to "communism in government," a "problem" that had already been tackled with enthusiasm by the previous Democratic administration, one that was not repudiated by Stevenson, and one that did not interest many Americans.[29] While there was some conflict in the election, there was little reason to choose between the two candidates at the level of the issues, other than the traditional one of substituting a new group of "outs" for the current incumbents. The Republican campaign slogan, "It's time for a change," and the Democratic slogan, "You never had it so good," suggest the paltry level of political debate in the campaign.

1956: Eisenhower and Stevenson. For all practical purposes, this was a noncampaign in terms of issues. Even in the wake of the momentous events and political turmoil surrounding the 1954 Supreme Court decision *Brown* v. *Board of Education*, that outlawed legally mandated racial segregation, neither candidate offered an unambiguous position on the race issue. Clearly articulated and differentiated positions on less important issues were also absent. Party energies and the attention of the public concentrated on the personality of President Eisenhower, Republicans pointing out the leadership qualities of the president ("I like Ike") and Democrats raising questions about his health and competency.

1960: Kennedy and Nixon. The Republican and Democratic party platforms for 1960 were, for all intents and purposes, identical. During the campaign, the two candidates were indistinguishable on most issues. Where they differed, strangely enough, was over Kennedy's attempt to out-Republican the Republicans on issues of anticommunism and national defense, with Kennedy taking traditional Nixon positions on Cuba, Formosa (Taiwan), and the Soviet Union. The main issue in the campaign was Kennedy's religion. All that the campaign settled was that a Catholic could be president, which, while symbolically important, was substantively insignificant.

1964: Johnson and Goldwater. Here was one of the few elections in which the parties stood in sharp contrast to each other on the issues. It is one of those proverbial exceptions that proves the rule. The campaign was fought at the level of the issues in the early stages only because the Republican party was captured by one of its coalition partners, which resolutely refused to accommodate or compromise with other elements of the party or to stay in the ideological mainstream of the two-party system.[30] The price of ideological divergence was high: the splintering of the Republican party, the defection of many groups and voting blocs to the Democrats, and one of the most ignominious electoral defeats in American history.

1968: Nixon and Humphrey. At a time when the American people were engaged in a divisive, intense, and emotional debate about Vietnam and American foreign policy, the candidates were almost indistinguishable from each other on these issues. The only perceptible difference was Nixon's claim to have a "secret plan" to end the war.

Nixon's fuzziness on foriegn policy issues was only part of a larger approach to the campaign. It is reported that Nixon pursued a conscious strategy of avoiding the issues, feeling strongly that he had lost the 1960 election to Kennedy because of his attention to them, when Kennedy focused on appearance, public relations, and good marketing strategies. Nixon is reported to have said prior to the 1968 campaign that he would never again make that mistake. He was true to his word, launching the most sophisticated television candidate packaging campaign ever conducted up to that point.[31]

Hubert Humphrey, the losing Democratic candidate, perhaps best articulated the meaning of the election and of the debate on the issues when he declared to his supporters that Nixon's election was no cause for consternation or alarm. He was able to make such a statement, he said, because it didn't matter in the long run which candidate was victorious. "We're . . . aware of the necessity for leaders of the parties to pull together on matters of great national concern. . . . We've got a President. He's going to have my help."[32] While perhaps a laudable sentiment at one level, it suggests the essential triviality of elections at another level.

1972: Nixon and McGovern. This election appeared at first glance to reenact the 1964 ideological election, only this time with the roles of the parties reversed. Appearances, however, were deceptive. In his successful campaign for nomination, Senator George McGovern seemed to take significantly more liberal positions than other major Democratic politicians with respect to counterinsurgency, war, foreign policy, business regulation, and taxation. The people who worked for him, and who in a very real sense made his nomination possible, had every reason to believe that the campaign would be fought on the issues and that it would stress a clearly liberal program against the clearly conservative program of the Republicans. As the imperatives of *winning* took over his campaign, however, McGovern began to back away from his previous positions. His various tax proposals were scrapped. He insisted, despite his opposition to government policy in Vietnam, that he fully accepted the traditional goals and commitments of American policy—but, he argued, they could be accomplished more efficiently and at lower cost. His antibusiness rhetoric was reversed in the midst of the campaign, with a full-page ad in *The Wall Street Journal* and a series of speeches before business groups proclaiming his faith in American corporate enterprise. His most powerful issue, the war in Vietnam, was effectively eliminated when presidential advisor Henry Kissinger announced at the Paris negotiations two days before the election that "peace was at hand."

For his own part, President Nixon resolutely refused to debate the issues. He relied, instead, on his by now very effective media managers and on acting "presidential" and statesmanlike, above the political fray. By minimizing news access to Nixon's administration, by allowing him to appear before the public only in carefully orchestrated media events, Nixon strategists literally forced journalists to focus their attention on the McGovern campaign for want of anything else to do. The campaign news coverage became dominated by McGovern news, none of it good—party defections, McGovern indecisiveness, the Eagleton affair, and so on.

The attitude of the president and his advisors toward elections is perhaps best summed up by an incident that occurred about four months after the campaign. When questioned by news reporters about why the president had not mentioned his plan to dismantle the Office of Economic Opportunity and to drastically cut funding for other domestic programs, presidential communications director Herbert Klein answered, ". . . such a tactic would have been naïve—you don't raise unnecessary issues in the middle of a presidential campaign."

1976: Carter and Ford. Governor Jimmy Carter defeated appointed incumbent Gerald Ford by the narrowest electoral vote margin in recent times. The prolonged campaign, despite a series of three televised debates between the presidential candidates and one between the vice-presidential candidates, was virtually devoid, in the opinion of most observers, of serious issue concerns. In its October 20, 1976, issue *The New York Times* complained at the height of the campaign, ". . . even by the standards of this country, 1976 is proving to be unusually barren of serious dialogue on the issues." In the absence of serious policy debate, the focus of the campaign was confined mainly to trivial yet embarrassing miscues by each of the candidates: Carter's *Playboy* magazine interview in which he admitted to lustful thoughts and Ford's comments playing down Soviet domination of eastern Europe. While there is little evidence to suggest that Jimmy Carter was more "lustful" than other presidential candidates, or that Jerry Ford was "soft" on communism, these miscues were inflated to major campaign issues in the absence of competing and more serious issues. As one Democratic senator acidly characterized the presidential contest, "It had all the issue content of a student council race" (*The New York Times*, October 20, 1976).

1980: Carter and Reagan. The victory of the Republicans over the Democrats in 1980 represents one of the most decisive landslides in American history. In the presidential race, incumbent president Jimmy Carter could garner only 41.2 percent of the popular vote and a paltry 9.1 percent of the electoral vote, while the challenger Ronald Reagan managed to attract 55.3 percent of the popular vote and a staggering 90.9 percent of the electoral vote. The conservative Reagan-led tide also enabled the Republicans to win twelve seats from the Democrats in the senatorial contest and thirty-three in the House, giving Republicans control of the upper house for the first time since 1954 and working control in the lower chamber by virtue of a revived Republican–conservative Democrat coalition. It seemed to be an election in which a strongly ideological conservative party vanquished a strongly ideological liberal party. Was this the case? Does this election break all of the rules of party politics set out above? Was the 1980 election built around clear policy and ideological choices? Did the American people choose a president on the basis of a liberal-conservative polarization? Did Americans give the new administration a mandate to make a fundamental shift from liberal to conservative policies?

In sorting out an answer to such questions, it is perhaps best to start with a consideration of the available information on why Americans voted as they did. Looking at that information, it is fairly clear that a substantial portion of the vote was motivated by anti-Carter and not pro-Reagan, or proconservative sentiments. A detailed election day survey by CBS News and *The New York Times* of over 12,000 people as they left the polls showed that 38 percent of all Reagan voters cast their ballots for reasons that were related in one way or another to dissatisfaction with Carter and the nature of the times. The prevailing sentiment seems to have been the desire for change without any particular programmatic or ideological definition of change.[33] Only 11 percent said they voted for Reagan because "he's a real conservative." To get Carter and the Democrats out of office, no matter what the nature of the alternative, was clearly the predominant motivation. Frustration with issues like the disintegration in the economy, the disarray in foreign policy, the apparent bungling of the Iran hostage crisis, as well as a widespread dislike for Carter, all seem to have been at work in the election. There is no evidence, in other words, that the electorate made its choice on consistent policy or ideological grounds.

A particularly cogent reason that the electorate did not act in 1980 on programmatic/ideological grounds is that the two parties did not pose the election alternatives in that way. While the Republican party was markedly more conservative in 1980 than it had been in previous elections, so too was the Democratic party. The anti-Soviet and anti-Cuban hysteria of the Reagan regime, it should be called, was initiated by actions of the Carter administration in the year before the election. The same must be said for the arms buildup and interventions in Central America. It was the Carter administration that pushed for the MX missile, broke off the Strategic Arms Limitation talks with the Russians, and initiated destabilizing and provocative retargeting of nuclear weapons. Under Carter, both black organizations and labor, in many ways the core of the Democratic party, complained of being almost totally ignored in the councils of government. Carter's 1976 campaign promises about tax and welfare reforms, full employment policies, and national health insurance were jettisoned in a move to balance the budget and hold the line on taxes. Under Carter, Democrats worked harder at halting inflation (primarily by means of conservative monetarist policies driving up interest rates) than at fighting unemployment. Carter's economic policies, in short, were essentially classic Republican party policies leading Edward Kennedy to label him "Ronald Reagan's clone" during his own desperate struggle for the nomination. Journalists Alexander Cockburn and James Ridgeway described Jimmy Carter as "a spiritless conservative without even the passions of a true Republican creed."[34] The campaign, in short, was one fought between two vaguely conservative political parties. The election in 1980, therefore, cannot be seen as

Ronald Reagan on the campaign trail

one in which two programmatically opposed parties faced each other across an ideological abyss.

1984: Reagan and Mondale. The landslide election of 1984 in which Ronald Reagan won 59 percent of the popular vote, all but a single state (tying a record), and a record 525 electoral votes seemed to signify, as in 1980, the victory of a strongly conservative party over a strongly liberal one. Once again, appearances were highly deceptive. Conservatism did indeed vanquish liberalism in 1984 but it forged its massive victory not in a contest between the political parties but within them, particularly within the Democratic party. The final result was a presidential election waged by two ideologically similar parties and candidates. By the time of the 1984 presidential campaign, the Democratic party had followed the Republicans into conservatism. First, the Democrats rejected the candidacy of Jesse Jackson in no uncertain terms and visibly declined to make any serious efforts to incorporate elements of his "rainbow coalition" into the affairs of the party or the presidential campaign itself. In so doing, the Democrats lost or rejected (depending on your point of view) an opportunity to define themselves as the voice of progressive populism and internationalism in contradistinction to the Republicans. Second, the party, with surprisingly little rancor (surprising, given the recent history of the Democrats), adopted a party platform that included planks committed to a continued military build-up; a strongly anti-Soviet, anticommunist stance in the Caribbean and Central America; a lightening of the tax and regulatory burden on the nation's corporations; and more "even-handedness" in civil rights and affirmative action enforcement. It also managed to hand out praises to the free market, the family, and religion. While Walter Mondale may be credited with the selection of Geraldine Ferraro as his running mate (though she ran, as well, on the party's conservative platform), he later came over to Ronald Reagan and the Republicans when he praised the invasion of Grenada and called for the quarantine of Nicaragua. The 1984 election, then, was hardly a contest between clearly posed policy alternatives and ideologies; it was a contest between a confident conservative party and its pale shadow.

The broad areas of agreement between the parties is not only widely recognized by scholars and political practitioners but also is very often praised as the source of the "genius of American politics" (a phrase penned by historian Daniel Boorstein). Why? Because the absence of conflict over the fundamentals of American political, economic, and social life in elections tends to encourage moderate candidates and policy proposals and to discourage radical alternatives. What proponents of this line of argument fail to recognize, however, is that the broad area of consensus is one largely defined by the already advantaged and powerful and supportive of their basic interests.

Promise and Performance

We are interested in this section of the chapter in the accountability of elected officials. We have learned so far that one of the basic conditions for political accountability—that elections be competitive and nontrivial—is *not* met in the United States. Let us put this fact aside, however, purely for the sake of argument, and imagine that elections are competitive and concern themselves with nontrivial matters. We would then want to learn whether American elections meet the second condition for political accountability: that once elected, officials feel duty bound to try to carry out the promises articulated during the campaign.

The noncommitment of elected officials to their campaign promises is, of course, one of the commonplaces of American folklore. There are all too many examples in recent elections. Lyndon Johnson promised no extension of the war in Vietnam and then dramatically escalated the war within months of his election. Richard Nixon compaigned on traditional conservative economic positions and then imposed wage-price controls. Gerald Ford promised at his confirmation hearings (a stand-in for election, perhaps) to allow the system of justice to run its course with Richard Nixon and Watergate, and then granted him an unconditional pardon in one of his first acts as president. Jimmy Carter promised tax and welfare reform, as well as a national health care system, but failed to deliver. Ronald Reagan promised that the major tax cuts he proposed in his supply-side economic doctrine would generate so much tax revenue by virtue of renewed economic activity that no significant reductions would be required in the federal social programs.

The incongruence of official performance and campaign promise, though in part the product of unforeseen circumstances, is so common and normal that Americans do not expect consistency from politicians. While this chasm between promise and performance seems fairly obvious to the average citizen—Gallup and Harris polls show consistently high percentages of the American people holding extremely skeptical views of politicians—the opposite assumption remains the very bedrock of the democratic theory held by most practicing political scientists. Recall the widely held view that politicians exercise care in their official behavior because of their fear of the electorate, a form of interactive relationship known as the "law of anticipated reactions." This bedrock assumption is strange because of the virtual *non*existence of supporting evidence. In fact, considerable evidence suggests that the public is more sophisticated on this subject than the academics.

In one of the few studies explicitly designed to determine whether members of Congress feel bound to their constituency in their policy-making behavior in office, political scientist Charles O. Jones concluded that little if any such commitment is evident. He found that members of Congress tend to view an election as a simple *yes* or *no* answer by the electorate to the question of continuation in office, not a mandate for or against policy. The question of promise and performance rarely becomes an issue for the member of Congress, for he or she does not interpret the election in such terms in the first place.[35]

In an ingenious and by now quasi-classic research study comparing the opinions of the voters in each congressional district with the actual voting behavior of the members of Congress, political scientists Warren Miller and Donald Stokes found little consistency.[36] With the single exception of the area of civil rights, the voting behavior of members of Congress and the policy preferences of their constituents rarely and only randomly coincided. This is easily explained by two additional and intriguing pieces of information that Miller and Stokes uncovered. First, it seems that members of Congress do not have accurate information about their constituents' policy preferences; and second, voters are only dimly aware of the voting behavior of their representatives.

On the other side of the ledger, political scientist Jeff Fishel argues that most presidents, most of the time, make valiant *efforts* to translate campaign promises into government policy. In his book *Presidents and Promises*, he carefully matches the specific programmatic statements made by presidents during their run for office with their behavior once assuming their official duties and finds surprisingly positive results.

> In light of the enormous advantages of remaining ambiguous or contradictory during elections, it is remarkable that candidates do make a substantial number of reasonably precise promises. It is even more remarkable that, once elected, every president, from Kennedy through Reagan, has demonstrated considerable

good faith, seeking through legislation or executive order to follow through on a majority of his campaign pledges.[37]

The evidence about promise and performance is mixed and somewhat ambiguous. In the popular conception, the promises of politicians are to be taken with a grain of salt; in the research literature, most but not all of the findings confirm popular conceptions. There is some reason to believe that promise and performance are at least partially matched at the presidential level;[38] there is little reason to believe that it is matched elsewhere. At best, then, the link between campaign pledge and official performance is tenuous.

From Mandate to Policy

Let us assume, again for the sake of argument, that elected leaders try to translate their promises into public policy. Are they able to do so? Do elected officials have the means, given their desire to do so, to transform the contract reached with the electorate into concrete statutes?

Given the nature of the party system, the possibilities for translating electoral mandate into policy are extremely slim, though sometimes possible. The unorganized, diffuse, and decentralized nature of American political parties, already described at length, stands in the way of any such translation. Since each of the fragments of the party may go literally anywhere it chooses, free from central direction, coordination of policy efforts is difficult, rarely attempted, and even more rarely successful. The first successes of the Reagan economic program, for instance, were dependent on the close cooperation of southern and conservative Democrats who acted in defiance of the Democratic leadership in the House of Representatives. Such extreme fragmentation, evident in both organization and policy, makes it next to impossible to transcend the decentralized tendencies of American political life inherent in a system of federalism and separated powers.

The writers of the Constitution deliberately constructed a system of governance in which the making of legislation would be a difficult and tortuous process. A potential national statute must wind its way through two houses of Congress, the White House, and very often weather a court challenge. More than anything else, the Founding Fathers feared an attack on property by the nonpropertied majority, so they designed a system that placed many obstacles in the path of majority sentiment. They devised a system to prevent the easy translation of electoral mandates into policy. Left to itself, this system acts today very much as it was intended.

Theoretically, one of the few institutions potentially capable of overcoming the inherent static nature of the American system of governance and its insulation from the public will is a party system composed of what political scientists call responsible parties.[39] A responsible party may be loosely defined as one that stands for something in its policy and program; goes to the electorate for its judgment on that policy and program; and once elected, is sufficiently well organized to command the obedience of all of its party members in the government to its mandated program. Such a party, assured of the unity of its members, is capable of translating that program into public policy upon assuming office. With such responsible parties, the translation of popular will into policy becomes likely, for party unity acts as the bridge that overcomes the otherwise inescapable fragmentation and decentralization of the system.

While some parties in the western world have on occasion fit such a description, American political parties rarely have, and they generally remain as fragmented and disorganized as the system within which they operate. Our parties are largely devoid of the means to construct and maintain a unified position. We are all too often faced with government paralysis, not only when the presidency and the Congress are in the hands of two different parties but even when control of both is lodged in a single party! No American president can be assured of the passage of his program, for he is often forced to negotiate and compromise with uncontrolled, often hostile members of his own party in Congress, particularly when they are powerful committee chairmen. This holds even when he comes to office in a landslide electoral victory. The *irresponsibility* of the American parties weakens the only potential tool for transcending the inherent status quo bias built into the constitutional system and frustrates the translation of popular will into public policy. This is, of course, not always true as demonstrated by the legislative success of Franklin Roosevelt in 1933, Lyndon Johnson in 1965, and Ronald Reagan in 1981 and 1982. The generalization holds, however, most of the time.

Elections and Elites

If elections are to be instruments by which the mass public shapes and determines public policy, it is obvious that such elections must directly influence the behavior of those persons holding positions of power who make policy decisions. If elections are to form the bedrock of the "law of anticipated reactions" by which decision makers are kept responsive and responsible, then elections must touch decision makers in such a way that their future depends on their performance.

If we narrowly define policy as the set of actions and decisions that churn out of the vast machinery of government, then elections are indeed important. Even a passing familiarity with the ballot in any national, state, or local election indicates the large number of officials who are subject to election. It is important, however, not to overstate the extent of electoral accountability, especially in light of the huge and growing number of officials who are never forced to face the electorate. Indeed, as government policy making becomes increasingly more administrative in character, the electoral mandate and sanction affects fewer and fewer decision makers. The vast federal bereaucracy remains largely untouched by elections. Protected by civil service regulations, most bureaucrats, even high-ranking ones responsible for policy decisions, enjoy longer tenure and assured position than the elected officials nominally at their head. Presidents find that even when they place their own people at the helm, important federal departments and agencies remain beyond executive control. Many other federal government agencies are even farther removed from the influence of the electorate: the Corps of Engineers, the Forest Service, the Federal Trade Commission, the Interstate Commerce Commission, the Federal Reserve Board, and so on. Indeed, most of these agencies were explicitly designed to be insulated from "politics" and thus from the public will.

If we define policy more broadly, however, as that *set of decisions that shapes the overall direction of social, economic, political, and cultural life in the United States*, then elections are almost irrelevant, for they barely and only indirectly touch even a fraction of key decision makers. If we visualize the universe of such policy decisions, it becomes obvious that the decisions made by all government officials, to say nothing of those government officials directly responsible to the voters, encompass only a small sliver of the pie (see Figure 9.1). Elections hardly affect decisions related to the location of businesses, the growth of cities, the development of technology, the center of work, the shape of educational experience, or the distribution of the American social product. Elections only barely affect the managers of corporations, the owners of capital, newspaper editors, television executives, the heads of scientific research laboratories, university presidents, or the heads of philanthropic foundations, all of whom make decisions that have profound implications for the public. The election in its present context in the United States is an exceedingly weak instrument for democratic control of public policy and of the people who construct such policy.

THE MEANING OF ELECTIONS

Elections form the base of most modern theories of democratic politics. They are, theoretically, the means by which the mass public monitors and directs the actions of those persons responsible for policy making, but under current conditions in the United States, and given the peculiar characteristics of American political parties, elections are limited and ineffectual. We have seen the following:

1. Elections barely touch nongovernment policy makers.
2. Only a portion of government policy makers are directly responsible to the voters.
3. Among those government policy makers who are elected, the election is not as powerful a sanction as has been widely believed.
4. Among government policy makers there exists little unity of direction, given the nature of the party system, and therefore little probability of translating mandates into policy.
5. Elections provide only very limited means for articulating the preferences of the voters because, given the nature of the party system, voters have no way to rationally choose between alternatives.
6. Candidate selection and formation of the political agenda are profoundly and perhaps decisively determined by those individuals, groups, and institutions which control the economic resources of the nation.

Elections and Legitimacy.   If all this is true, why have elections? Why spend scarce resources of time, energy, and personnel in such seemingly futile exercises? Be-

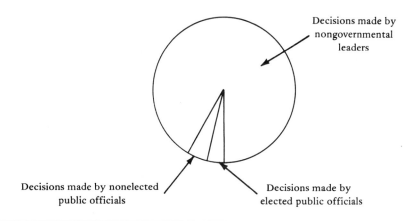

Decisions made by
nongovernmental
leaders

Decisions made by nonelected
public officials

Decisions made by
elected public officials

FIGURE 9.1   The universe of policy decisions

cause elections play an important function in the overall maintenance of the American system and the capitalist order at its base. Elections do so even though— indeed precisely because—they perform largely ceremonial and symbolic functions. Political scientist Murray Edelman suggests some of these.[40] First, participation in elections gives the citizen a sense of belonging and of being part of a common enterprise and therefore acts as a powerful mechanism in emotionally tying the individual to the system. Second, elections are cathartic, thereby allowing the citizen to blow off steam and express discontents or enthusiasms, all within safe and nonthreatening channels. Finally, elections encourage public acceptance of government policy, even those policies that have adverse consequences for many people, because voters believe that they themselves are at least partly responsible for the content of public policy. Though elections have little or no direct influence on policy, the widespread belief that elections are determinative contributes to the acceptance and legitimacy of policy. Thus the attempt to reinvigorate the economy by means of drastic cuts in public support of social services and the protection of environmental quality, while formulated by and in the service of the most privileged and powerful sectors of American society, took on a popular aura through the electoral process in 1980. The fact that little choice existed in that election or that the range of debate on issues was largely determined by the needs of the major actors in the economy is not at issue. As Edelman points out, elections are "rituals of symbolic reassurance which serve to quiet resentments and doubts about particular political acts, [and] reaffirm belief in the fundamental rationality and democratic character of the system."[41] From this view, the myth of the election and the myth of the voter are crucial devices in maintaining the status quo.

The Disappearing Voter. Elections are less, then, than they seem. Elections, that is to say, fail to serve as devices by which ordinary citizens transcend the great inequalities that characterize our economic and social systems. They are not notably effective in equalizing power, in offering clear alternatives for public policy, or in encouraging consideration of the most pressing issues and concerns of the day. I suspect that the American people know all of this for they stay away from elections in droves. Consider the low levels of participation compared to the other western democracies (Table 9.1) and the steady erosion of participation over the years (Table 9.2). In a ranking of the top 100 nations in voting turnout published a few years ago, the United States ranked eighty-eighth![42] The decline in turnout in the presidential vote, as serious as it is, is masked by the increases in the percentage turnout in the south as blacks entered political life in the 1970s. Outside the south, the turnout of eligible voters declined from 73 percent in 1960 to 57 percent in 1980.[43] The figures are even more depressed when we look at turnout in off-year congressional elections (elections in years when there is no presidential election). On the average, since 1952 only 45 percent of eligible voters have cast a ballot in such elections with the percentage declining with each new election, though there was a slight turnaround in 1982.

Since electoral participation has always been low in the United States, a more interesting indicator of declining support for the myth of elections is the very much lowered expectations that Americans have about them. In a CBS News/ *The New York Times* poll conducted during the 1980 campaign, only 40 percent of voters said that the outcome of the election mattered. Less than one-third could perceive any difference between the parties.[44]

Voting requires relatively little effort. In other forms of political activity, however, participation among Americans virtually disappears. Note the following relative participation rates for different political activities (calculated as rough averages from scores of academic studies):

☐ About 40 percent do not vote in presidential elections.
☐ About 60 percent do not vote in congressional elections.

TABLE 9.1   Average electoral turnout in national elections,
1960–1978

COUNTRY	% OF ELIGIBLE VOTERS CASTING BALLOTS
Italy	94%
The Netherlands	90
Australia	86
W. Germany	84
Great Britain	74
Canada	71
France	70
United States	59

SOURCE: G. Bingham Powell, Jr., *Contemporary Democracy*, Harvard University Press, Cambridge, Mass., 1982, p. 14.

TABLE 9.2   Voter turnout in presidential and off-year
congressional elections

YEAR	VOTE FOR PRESIDENT	VOTE IN OFF-YEAR CONGRESSIONAL ELECTIONS
1960	65%	
1962		47%
1964	63	
1966		46
1968	60	
1970		45
1972	55	
1974		38
1976	54	
1978		37
1980	53	
1982		39
1984	53*	

SOURCE: *Statistical Abstracts of the United States, 1984*, U.S. Bureau of the Census.

*Estimate: *The National Journal*, November 17, 1984, p. 2217.

☐ About 70 percent do not belong to an organization that takes stands on po-
litical issues.
☐ About 70 percent to 80 percent do not vote in off-year state and local elec-
tions.
☐ About 85 percent never make financial contributions to a party or candidate.
☐ About 95 percent never work in a political campaign.
☐ Over 99 percent never run for political office at any level.

What are we to make of this lack of participation and interest in political
affairs? What is the meaning of this *political silence?* Is silence the product of
satisfaction, the explanation so often advanced by mainstream political
science—[45] the silence of satisfaction embodied in "the gourmet's quiet, his
mouth full of peach flambée?"[46] Or is political silence that of the ignorant and
confused, another favorite interpretation of political science, the torpor of "boobus
Americanus," in H. L. Mencken's phrase? Or is it the silence of people who find
no home, no comfort, and no support in the current system of normal politics
and do not know where to turn?

The last explanation has at least as much to offer as the other two. The weak-
est explanation is surely that which attributes nonparticipation to satisfaction, for
the highest incidence of nonparticipation is found among the worst-off members
of society, the ones who would have the most to gain from participation. In fact,
political scientist Lewis Lipsitz's classic work persuasively demonstrates that the
nonparticipant poor are neither satisfied with nor ignorant of the social and po-

litical world around them. Indeed, he found them to have rather elaborate and well-developed grievances about their own situation, their future prospects, the commitment of government to them as a group, and the state of the economy. He also found them to have a fairly sophisticated sense of which groups in society are the winners and losers in American political life and to be aware of the possibility that the present political parties might act as instruments for the improvement of their own situation. Silence, concludes Lipsitz, is neither a product of satisfaction nor of ignorance but of the inability of the nonparticipant poor to translate their grievances and their aspirations into political issues because of the absence of suitable political parties to help them translate. The poor and near poor have no home in the political parties. The parties do not speak to or for them. Compared to European democracies, there is a conspicuous hole in the American party system. It is a hole filled by socialist and labor parties in these other nations.[47]

The gap in the voting rates between the top and bottom of American society is both dramatic and increasing. Journalist Thomas Edsall, in noting this phenomenon, claims that "the single most important characteristic of voting in the United States is the economic bias of turnout patterns."[48] Almost 20 million voters have simply dropped out since 1972, with most of them concentrated among the least well-off. In the 1980 election, only 39.4 percent of all people making under $5,000 annual income voted (representing 4.5 percent of total voters), whereas 73.8 percent of all people making better than $25,000 did so (they represented 35.1 percent of total voters). In that same year white-collar workers sent 52 percent of their number to the polls; blue-collar workers sent only 32.9 percent and service workers but 12.5 percent. The gap is not only significant but widening. For instance, the difference in turnout rates between white-collar professionals and blue-collar workers was 24.2 percentage points in 1968 and 33 percentage points in 1980. The drop in turnout rates for blacks has been twice as high as that for whites in recent years. It is hard to avoid agreeing with Edsall when he concludes that the evidence "shows a progressive intensification of the class bias of voting patterns."[49]

CONCLUDING REMARKS

In the last chapter, we addressed the question of whether the pluralistic interest group system served democracy by counteracting the great inequalities of benefit and power characteristic of American life. We were forced to conclude in the negative. In this chapter, we addressed the question of whether elections served democracy by equalizing power among the American people and by forcing political leaders to be responsive and responsible to popular interests, aspirations, and needs. Again, we are forced to conclude in the negative. In the next chapter we consider mass movements and unconventional politics and ask of them the very same question: Do they serve democracy?

NOTES

1. Gerald Pomper, *Elections in America: Control and Influence in Democratic Politics* (New York: Dodd, Mead, 1968), p. x. See this book for further bibliographic references to the election literature.
2. Robert D. Cantor, *Voting Behavior and Presidential Elections* (Itasca, Ill.: Peacock, 1975), p. 1.
3. Thomas Byrne Edsall, *The New Politics of Inequality* (New York: W. W. Norton, 1984), p. 96.
4. Adam Clymer, *The New York Times* (Feb. 4, 1980), p. 14.
5. Congress conveniently left itself outside most of the provisions of the Campaign Finance Act.
6. Kathleen Hall Jamieson, *Packaging the Presidency* (New York: Oxford University Press, 1984), pp. 419–427.
7. Edsall, *The New Politics of Inequality*, pp. 98–99.
8. *Ibid.*, p. 98
9. On PACs, see Elizabeth Drew, *Political Money: The Road to Corruption* (New York: Macmillan, 1983); and Amatai Etzioni, *Capital Corruption* (New York: Harcourt, Brace, Jovanovich, 1984).
10. From *What Price PACs?* quoted in Mark Green, "When Money Talks, Is It Democracy?" *The Nation*, Sept. 15, 1984, p. 203.
11. Edsall, *The New Politics of Inequality*, p. 82.
12. To be sure, they are not always successful in such efforts.
13. Twenty newspaper chains control more than a half of all newspapers sold in the United States; only 2 percent of newspapers in the U.S. are in competitive markets. See Ben H. Bagdikian, *The Media Monopoly* (Boston: Beacon Press, 1983). Most television viewing in America is controlled by three networks: controlling interest in the three national networks is held by a consortium that includes Chase Manhattan Bank, Citibank, Bankers Trust, Morgan Guarantee Trust, and the Bank of New York. The same financial group has large holdings in *The New York Times, Time* magazine, Columbia Pictures, and Twentieth Century Fox. See Peter Brosnan, "Who Owns the Networks," *Nation* (Nov. 25, 1978), pp. 577–79.
14. Walter Dean Burnham, "The 1980 Earthquake," in Thomas Ferguson and Joel Rogers (eds.), *The Hidden Elections* (New York: Pantheon, 1981), p. 119.
15. Charles E. Lindblom, *Politics and Markets* (New York: Basic, 1977).
16. See especially Benjamin I. Page and Robert Y. Shapiro, "Effects of Public Opinion on Policy," *American Political Science Review*, Vol. 77, No. 1 (1983): 175–190.
17. These are cited in Michael Parenti, *Democracy for the Few* (New York: St. Martin's, 1983), p. 203.
18. Everett Ladd, Jr., *Where Have All the Voters Gone?* (New York: Norton, 1978), p. 17.
19. William Winpisinger, President of the International Association of Machinists, *Guardian*, Fall 1981.
20. Robert Heilbroner has observed that "with rare exception . . . political office holders do not, no matter their particular party or philosophic label, pose basic challenges to the corporate system," quoted in Ralph Miliband, *The State in Capitalist Society* (New York: Basic, 1969), p. 214.

21. In their wisdom, the American people decided to take the real thing.
22. Pomper, *Elections in America*, p. 53.
23. William C. Mitchell, *Why Vote?* (Chicago: Markham, 1971).
24. This is even more the case with state and local elections, which tend to focus less on issues than on personality, and where popular participation is extremely low.
25. See Theodore T. Lowi, *American Government: Incomplete Conquest* (New York: Dryden Press, 1977), p. 313.
26. Walter Dean Burnham, *Critical Elections and the Mainsprings of American Politics* (New York: Norton), p. 177.
27. Ted Lowi, "Critical Election Misfires," *The Nation*, December 18, 1972.
28. The definition of "trivial" is a value-loaded question and ultimately rests on the values of each observer.
29. It may seem strange to suggest that the mass public was *not* the source of the anti-communist hysteria of the early 1950s, but the evidence to support that view is persuasive. See Michael Rogin, *The Intellectuals and McCarthy* (Cambridge: MIT Press, 1967).
30. Even in this, the most issue oriented of recent American elections, the "extremist" candidate moved to the center of the political spectrum during the course of the campaign. See Page, *Choice and Echoes in Presidential Elections*, ch. 5.
31. For an inside look at the 1968 Nixon media campaign, see Joe McGinniss, *The Selling of the President, 1968* (New York: Trident Press, 1969). Also see Kathleen Hall Jamieson, *Packaging the Presidency* (New York: Oxford, 1984).
32. *The New York Times*, November 9, 1968.
33. See the data as reported in "Voters Send Carter a Message," *The National Journal*, November 8, 1980, pp. 1876–1878. Voters were not necessarily acting on an unfounded basis in light of the fact that in 1980 the so-called misery index—the rate of inflation added to the rate of unemployment—reached the highest level since the Great Depression year of 1932.
34. "The World of Appearance: The Public Campaign," in Ferguson and Rogers, *The Hidden Election*, p. 71. Jeff Fishel presents an almost convincing case saving Carter's liberal reputation in his provocative book, *Presidents and Promises* (Washington, D.C.: CQ Press, 1985).
35. "The Role of the Campaign in Congressional Politics," in M. Kent Jennings and L. Harmon Zeigler, eds., *The Electoral Process* (Englewood Cliffs, N.J.: Prentice-Hall, 1966).
36. Warren E. Miller and Donald E. Stokes, "Constituency Influence in Congress," *American Political Science Review* 57 (March 1963).
37. Fishel, *Presidents and Promises*, p. 150.
38. On the other hand, Robert Goodin argues in "Voting through the Looking Glass," *American Political Science Review*, Vol. 77, No. 2 (1983) that presidents have so much flexibility in moving to positions opposite to that articulated in campaigns that a rational voter *might* choose a candidate exactly opposite from his/her own preferences.
39. The earliest "official" recognition of responsible parties is that of the American Political Science Association, *Toward a More Responsible Two-Party System* (New York: Rinehart, 1950).
40. Murray Edelman, *The Symbolic Uses of Politics* (Urbana: University of Illinios Press, 1964). Also see Benjamin Ginsberg, *The Consequences of Consent: Elections, Citizen Control, and Popular Acquiescence* (Reading, Mass.: Addison Wesley, 1982), who ar-

gues that voting serves to channel potentially popular and disruptive passions into safe channels approved by state officials.

41. *Ibid.*, p. 17.
42. James MacGregor Burns, Jack Peltason, and Thomas E. Cronin, *Government by the People* (Englewood Cliffs, N.J.: Prentice-Hall, 1984), p. 195.
43. Burnham, "The 1980 Earthquake," p. 101.
44. Those data are reported in Everett C. Ladd, "The Brittle Mandate: Electoral Realignment and the 1980 Presidential Election," *Political Science Quarterly* 96:1 (Spring, 1981), p. 4.
45. To the question of whether we ought to be concerned about low voter turnout, the leading political science book in the United States points out the following: "It is not a low rate of voting that signals a danger for a democratic system . . . but a high rate." A measure of nonvoting, it is argued, "is a sign of widespread satisfaction, indicating that many people accept the status quo. . . ." James MacGregor Burns and J. W. Peltason, *Government by the People* (Englewood Cliffs, N.J.: Prentice-Hall, 1972), p. 216.
46. This question is raised by Lewis Lipsitz in "On Political Belief: The Grievances of the Poor," in Philip Green and Sanford Levinson, eds., *Power and Community* (New York: Pantheon, 1970).
47. Burnham, "The 1980 Earthquake," p. 102.
48. Edsall, *The New Politics of Inequality*, p. 179.
49. *Ibid.*, p. 183. The above figures are from pp. 179–185.

SUGGESTIONS FOR FURTHER READING

Angus Campbell et al. THE AMERICAN VOTER. *New York: Wiley, 1965.* The classic scientific study of the American voter.

Elizabeth Drew. POLITICAL MONEY: THE ROAD TO CORRUPTION. *New York: Macmillan, 1983.* An in-depth analysis of the rise, practices, and ill effects of Political Action Committees.

Thomas Ferguson and Joel Rogers, eds. THE HIDDEN ELECTION: POLITICS AND ECONOMICS IN THE 1980 PRESIDENTIAL CAMPAIGN. *New York: Pantheon, 1981.* A collection of essays that largely succeed in their effort to unearth the economic and social forces underneath the surface world of primaries, conventions, and elections in 1980.

Jeff Fishel. PRESIDENTS AND PROMISES. *Washington, D.C.: Congressional Quarterly Press, 1985.* A careful assessment of the relationship between presidential campaign promises and post-election presidential behavior.

Kathleen Hall Jamieson. PACKAGING THE PRESIDENT. *New York: Oxford University Press, 1984.* A history and criticism of presidential campaign advertising with special attention directed to the rise of the electronic campaign.

Everett Ladd. WHERE HAVE ALL THE VOTERS GONE? *New York: Norton, 1978.* An important analysis of the decline in American voting participation.

Norman H. Nie, Sidney Verba, and John P. Petrocik. THE CHANGING AMERICAN VOTER. *Cambridge: Harvard University Press, 1976.* An updated analysis of *The American Voter* that significantly alters many of its major findings.

Benjamin I. Page. CHOICES AND ECHOES IN PRESIDENTIAL ELECTIONS. *Chicago: University of Chicago Press, 1978.* A rare book in political science that actually looks at what is said and done during the course of presidential campaigns.

Gerald Pomper. ELECTIONS IN AMERICA. *New York: Dodd, Mead, 1968.* An in-depth look at elections and their implications for American life.

Theodore H. White. THE MAKING OF THE PRESIDENT, 1960. *New York: Atheneum, 1961.* Still the best of the "making of the president" books, and a sophisticated look at a modern presidential campaign.

10

Protest and Disruption: The Politics of Outsiders

We have seen that the conventional institutions of American democracy are distorted by the great inequalities of wealth and power that exist in the nation. We have seen that the "normal" way of doing things in the great game of American politics heavily favors those who control and enjoy the fruits of the economic system. As in all capitalist societies, this class sets the rules, controls the pieces, and wins the game more often than not. This class not only receives most of the largesse of the economic system but also finds that its needs and interests are the decisive factors in determining the directions of political life. In the fact of such a static system, the "normal" or "conventional" methods of political life—methods that range from talking about politics with others, to voting, to contributing time or money to an election campaign, to writing one's representative in Congress—seem not only ineffetual but even futile and ridiculous as democratic instruments tying government policy and political decision makers to the needs, interests, and aspirations of the mass public.

It is precisely the futility and ineffectuality of normal conventional politics in the face of this static and class-biased political system that has led many groups of people throughout American history to rely on "unconventional" disruptive methods to force a hearing from policy makers and to move the government from its fixed positions. Indeed, we might profitably look at American history as a recurring series of struggles by the nonpowerful and the nonprivileged to wrest concessions from the reigning plutocracy of the day. We shall discover, in fact, that most of the advances made in humanizing and democratizing American society through the years have neither been inherent in the American system nor been bestowed by a benevolent elite, but have been forced by turmoil from below.[1] In this chapter, I shall consider the place of unconventional politics in American life, politics that encompass activities as diverse as protest, disobedience, and violence. Why have certain groups felt it necessary and proper to engage in such activities? How are such activities justified? How is the government likely to respond to them? What are the prospects and limitations of these unconventional forms of politics?

POLITICS AS BARGAINING

Political scientists generally believe that politics in the United States, given an environment where power is dispersed and pluralistic, is essentially about bargaining. Since, in this view, no single class or group in society enjoys a monopoly of decision-making power, and since by virtue of that fact no single class or group is capable of imposing its will on all of the others, it follows that political actors have no choice but to bargain with other actors and to moderate their demands and requirements in light of the countervailing power of others. Political scientists imply that in such a bargaining process, no single group can always prevail, and, perhaps more importantly, no group is completely and forever closed out or denied a hearing. The implication in modern pluralist theory (see Chapters 2 and 8) is that literally any group that so desires can get into the bargaining game at some point.

Bargaining, however, requires *resources* of some kind, something to exchange with other parties in return for political concessions. If some group is without resources, without something to trade with other persons or groups, there is no reason why others should want to enter into a bargaining relationship. Any examination of bargaining politics would logically want to consider the relative distribution of resources in the population. Only such a determination will indicate the relative probability that certain groups will be included in the political game.

In the main, the most important resources in American politics are wealth and the control of votes. Wealth, as we have seen, can be translated into a wide variety of bargaining chips. Wealth can buy high social status, for instance, which can be parlayed into political influence because of the deference paid to the socially prominent. Wealth can buy the organizational and communication skills acquired and honed in elite educational institutions. It can gain control of television networks, newspapers, and magazines. It can fund favorable think-tanks, friendly universities, and compatible political candidates. Wealth can sprinkle the political landscape with its interest groups and political action committees and dominate the media airwaves with its messages.

By definition, wealth is neither randomly nor equally distributed. It is a political resource unavailable to the vast majority of the American people. The vote, on the other hand, is available to all on a relatively equal basis. It may be used by the poor as well as by the rich. To most political scientists, it is this one-person-one-vote quality of free elections that represents the great equalizer in American political life. It is the wide availability of the vote to the aggrieved, the discontented, and the disadvantaged that opens the bargaining game of American politics beyond the privileged few, and thereby democratizes it. The needs and interests of nondominant groups can and will be attended to, it is argued, because the vote is a weapon both understood and feared by all politicians who wish to stay in office. Thus, blacks, migrant workers, blue-collar workers, women, and others can use the vote and become important actors in the give and take of political life. By using the vote, such groups gain access to a resource that allows them to enter the bargaining arena as relative equals. We learned in Chapter 9, however, that few of the claims made in behalf of the democratic qualities of free elections are supportable in light of the great disproportionalities of wealth in the United States. Economic power, we learned, spills over into the electoral process and undermines its egalitarian aspects.

DISRUPTION AS BARGAINING

The vote, then, does not seem to be a very powerful tool with which discontented, disadvantaged, and ignored groups might pry open the political process and become significant participants in the bargaining that leads to the formation of government policy. Political bargaining remains a serious game played only by a small club of privileged participants. It is not a club that happily invites into membership those groups that it can safely and quietly ignore. Some nonmember groups, however, finding that the vote does not gain them entry, have felt the need to turn to disruptive tactics as a way to gain attention and consideration. Unconventional politics, from simple non-violent civil disobedience to violent disruption, can be seen, in an important sense, as an addition to the bargaining process. It is the only resource available to some groups for which other significant actors are willing to make political concessions. In the absence of other resources, disruption and violence (or the threat of their use) can become excellent bargaining chips.[2]

Those who "belong" by virtue of their ties to property and dominant institutions, and who, as a matter of course, have easy access to all the other key political resources, almost always deplore the turn to unconventional politics by "out groups." Having no need for such tactics themselves, they find it difficult to see why other groups such as women, labor, and blacks might be forced by circumstances to resort to unconventional politics. Customarily, they point simultaneously to various peaceful and civil routes of redress, and call for the restoration of order. Order, however, always serves those in power, who both determine the outlines of that order and enjoy its fruits. Violence and disruption are often useful means for gaining concessions precisely because they threaten that order and put the comfort of more privileged groups into jeopardy. As the great black abolitionist Frederick Douglass once said, "Power concedes nothing without a demand. It never did. It never will."

Many groups of Americans have understood this truth about the nature of the political process. In the 1930s, the unemployed and the poor resorted to mass protest marches, seizures of welfare offices, rent strikes, and acts of violence against stores, landlords, and political officials as a means of prying relief monies from local, state, and federal governments. American women, in their struggle for the vote and for equal treatment, turned to actions as diverse as polite petitions, hunger strikes, and selected acts of property destruction. Working people, in their own struggle for the right to form labor unions and to be guaranteed dignity and safety at the workplace, have resorted to mass picketing, boycotts, sit-down strikes, and even violence.

This story of the severe limitations of the vote for advancing the interests of outsiders and the uses of disruption by such groups as an additional bargaining chip in the game of American politics is nowhere better seen than in the history of black Americans. For most of our history as a nation, black Americans played by the normal rules of the game, placed their hopes in the vote, and turned to the politics of disruption only after great patience, much provocation, and with more than a little trepidation. The following section, which focuses on this history, demonstrates the failure of the vote as an instrument for the protection of vital black interests and examines the creative uses of nonelectoral, disruptive politics.

THE VOTE IN THE HISTORY OF BLACK AMERICANS

Dixie in reality means all that territory south of the Canadian border.

Malcolm X

The vote has many functions in any formally democratic system. At one level, as we saw in Chapter 9, the vote plays an important symbolic function, tying citizens to the larger political community and making them feel emotionally bound to their fellow citizens. And yet, most Americans expect more from the vote than symbols and ritual. They expect it to have some impact on the course of affairs in general, and on their own interests as members of some group in particular. Expectations about the vote have generally fallen into two general categories: the *protective* and the *ameliorative*. That is, the vote has traditionally been viewed both as an instrument of protection against the acts of public officials and other citizens that might intrude on and diminish the rights and strategic interests of some group of people and as an instrument for improving group conditions by convincing officials to attend more closely to the needs and desires of those casting ballots.[3] What is so striking and ultimately depressing about the situation of black Americans is that the vote, while playing important and supportive symbolic functions, has been *neither protective nor ameliorative*. The vote has not served very well to protect them against the racism of the majority community, nor has it effectively improved their material condition as a group. We can see these two themes at work at literally every stage in American history.

Black Americans and Jacksonian Democracy

Historians generally regard the Jacksonian period as a great period of democratization in American life, primarily because of the vast expansion of the right to vote. This expansion was accomplished by abolishing property qualifications and special taxes as a condition for voting and holding public office, a process that was virtually complete by 1860 and the start of the Civil War. By 1860, in fact, the United States was the only nation in the world that enjoyed universal (*white manhood*) suffrage.

Paradoxically, the movement to enfranchise the white male population was accompanied by a simultaneous and often closely connected movement to disenfranchise the black population. From the American Revolution into the early decades of the nineteenth century, blacks outside of the slaveholding states were generally free to vote; they were considered full-fledged citizens of the various states. While the economic and social conditions of northern blacks in this period were generally dismal, in the eyes of the law (though often not so in fact) they were endowed with the dignity of citizenship. From the admission of Maine into the Union in 1819 through 1865, however, every new state denied blacks the right to vote and severely restricted other political and civil rights. In that same period, most of the older states rewrote their constitutions to expand white male suffrage and to eliminate black suffrage. Pennsylvania ended the right of blacks to vote in 1838. Indiana did the same in 1851, and Oregon followed suit in 1857. New York State, as did others, instituted special tax requirements for blacks as a condition for voting. Illinois decided to bar further black migration into the state. In the Indiana constitution, all contracts made by blacks before entering the state, including the marriage contract, were declared null and void. The Ohio constitution required blacks to post a bond of $500 guaranteeing good behavior. By the time of the Civil War, ironically, only the states of Massachusetts, Rhode Island, New Hampshire, and Vermont considered blacks to be full and equal citizens; 93 percent of all nonslave blacks thus lived in states that denied them the right to vote. The general mood in the nonslave states was so hostile to blacks, in fact, that the black vote all but disappeared after 1830.[4]

A dramatic example of the general situation of blacks during this period is provided by Roger Taney. Taney, as Chief Justice, would later help render the Supreme Court's decision in the famous Dred Scott case (1857), which declared blacks noncitizens and therefore devoid of civil and political rights. Several years prior to his service on the Court, Taney had the following to say about the black condition, citing as supporting evidence prevailing national opinion and the actions of state and federal governments:

> The African race in the United States, even when free, are everywhere a degraded class, and exercise no political influence. The privileges they are allowed to enjoy are accorded to them as a matter of kindness and benevolence, rather than of right . . . and where they are nominally admitted by law to the privileges of

citizenship, they have no effectual power to defend them, and are permitted to be citizens by the suffrance of the white population and hold whatever rights they enjoy at their mercy.

Roger Taney makes our point for us. The vote during this period did not serve as a protective instrument to defend the rights of blacks against the intrusions of officials or other Americans. The black vote, often vigorously exercised, represented a rather weak and ineffectual weapon against the racist policies of a determined and overwhelming majority. The vote afforded black people little protection. It was not an ameliorative instrument to better their position politically, economically, or socially.

Reconstruction and Jim Crow

Radical reconstruction ushered in a period of vigorous black political participation in the states of the former Confederacy.[5] The constitutional conventions called into session in all of the Confederate states under the Reconstruction Act of 1867 contained black members who were often instrumental in drafting these new documents (though they were nowhere a majority except in South Carolina). In the opinion of most historians, the resulting constitutions were the most progressive the southern states had ever known and, by and large, they form the constitutional base for most of the southern states to this day. During Reconstruction, blacks held public office throughout the former Confederacy, and their number included legislators, lieutenant-governors, judges, and an occasional sheriff. At one point, twenty black representatives were sent to Congress from the south; a black senator from Mississippi was elected as well. As the reader might guess, voter turnout among black citizens was substantial, even surpassing that of black voter turnout in the nonsouthern states. Ironically, between 1860 and the passage of the Fifteenth Amendment guaranteeing blacks the right to vote, seven non-Confederate states *voted anew* to reject black suffrage.

Imposing Economic and Social Isolation. After the Compromise of 1876, by which the Republican party terminated Reconstruction in exchange for the presidency, and freed from the civilizing effects of the presence of federal troops, dominant elements in the south moved to reimpose a virtual slave system on the black population, a movement of such scale that black votes were ineffectual as a counterweight. On the economic front, blacks were consigned to the lowest rungs by the full-scale development of tenant and sharecrop farming, by laws channeling many of them to the convict labor system, and by prohibitions against black practice of certain professions and skilled trades.

In the latter part of the nineteenth century and in the first decade of the twentieth, all southern states instituted an official system of social isolation of blacks through what are known as Jim Crow laws. These laws mandated separation of the races in all public accommodations, public conveyances, places of work (in practice, there were exceptions made here), entertainment establishments, educational institutions, and the like, often to the point of repetition, extra expense, and absurdity: separate drinking fountains, park benches, stairways, doors, eating utensils, toilets, ticket windows. During this period, "whites only" and "colored only" signs came to be as characteristic of the south as the renowned magnolias. The Supreme Court upheld the legal validity of racial segregation in the case of *Plessy* v. *Ferguson* (1896), and the legal framework of segregation constructed by that decision held firm until *Brown* v. *Board of Education*, rendered by the Court in 1954.

Disenfranchising the Black Population. To complete this assault on the black population, and spurred by the fear of a black/white working class alliance in the Populist movement, elites in the southern states created a series of ingenious devices to disenfranchise blacks. One such device included various literacy tests generally administered at the discretion of local officials responsive to the dominant whites. In order to enable whites to bypass this restrictive device, various loopholes were instituted solely for the benefit of white voters. These loopholes included *good character* clauses whereby leading citizens of the community (white) could attest to the character of the applicant; and *grandfather* clauses, whereby those persons whose fathers or grandfathers had been registered to vote (a category that obviously did not include former slaves) could waive the literacy test requirement. Other devices included disqualification for conviction of petty crimes, the poll tax, and property qualifications for voting. The most successful of the many devices was the white primary, whereby the Democratic party was defined, in effect, as a private club closed to blacks, who were thus barred from participation in its primary elections. Since the south was a one-party, Democratic-dominant region for a century following the Civil War, blacks were excluded from the only elections that mattered.

All these devices served to eliminate blacks from southern political life. Between 1896 and 1910, black voter registration dropped 96 percent. In Louisiana, registration fell from 130,000 in 1896 to 5,000 in 1900; in Alabama, from 180,000 to 3,000.[6] The south had accomplished the goal perhaps best articulated later by Senator Carter Glass on the floor of the Virginia constitutional convention. "Our goal," he declared, is "to discriminate to the very extremity of permissible action under the limitations of the Federal Constitution, with a view to the elimination of every Negro voter who can be gotten rid of, legally, without materially impairing the numerical strength of the white electorate."

The Uses of Terror. There was, of course, a less peaceful and genteel method to drive the former slave population into social, economic, and political subordination: terror. Note Table 10.1, which roughly estimates the number of lynchings from the years 1885 to 1916.

Lest the reader think of lynching as the surgically clean procedure shown in Western films, the following account describes a *not* atypical incident in Waco, Texas:

TABLE 10.1   Colored men lynched, by years, 1885–1916

1885	78		1901	107
1886	71		1902	86
1887	80		1903	86
1888	95		1904	83
1889	95		1905	61
1890	90		1906	64
1891	121		1907	60
1892	155		1908	93
1893	154		1909	73
1894	134		1910	65
1895	112		1911	63
1896	80		1912	63
1897	122		1913	79
1898	102		1914	69
1899	84		1915	80
1900	107		1916 (5 mo.)	31
			Total	2,843

SOURCE: "The Waco Horror," *The Crisis* 10 (July 1916), p. 8.

They dragged the boy down the stairs, put a chain around his body and hitched it to an automobile. The chain broke. The big fellow took the chain off the Negro under the cover of the crowd and wound it around his own wrist, so that the crowd jerking at the chain was jerking at the man's wrist and he was holding the boy. The boy shrieked and struggled.

The mob ripped the boy's clothes off, cut them in bits and even cut the boy. Someone cut his ear off, someone else unsexed him. A little girl working for the firm of Goldstein and Mingle told me that she saw this done.

I went over the route the boy had been taken and saw that they dragged him between a quarter and a half a mile from the Court House to the bridge and then dragged him up two blocks and another block over to the City Hall. After they had gotten him up to the bridge, someone said that a fire was already going up at City Hall, and they turned around and went back. Several people denied that this fire was going, but the photograph shows that it was. They got a little boy to light the fire.

While a fire was being prepared of boxes, the naked boy was stabbed and the chain put over the tree. He tried to get away, but could not. He reached up to grab the chain and they cut off his fingers. The big man struck the boy on the back of the neck with a knife just as they were pulling him up on the tree. Mr. Lester thought that was practically the death blow. He was lowered into the fire several times by means of the chain around his neck. Someone said they would estimate the boy had about twenty-five stab wounds, none of them death-dealing.

About a quarter past one a fiend got the torso, lassoed it, hung a rope over the pommel of a saddle, and dragged it around through the streets of Waco.

Very little drinking was done.

A lynch party (Indiana, 1930): an all too common occurrence

The tree where the lynching occurred was right under the Mayor's window. Mayor Dollins was standing in the window, not concerned about what they were doing to the boy, but that the tree would be destroyed. The Chief of Police also witnessed the lynching. The names of five of the leaders of the mob are known to this Association, and can be had on application by responsible parties.

Women and children saw the lynching. One man held up his little boy above the heads of the crowd so that he could see, and a little boy was in the top of the very tree to which the colored boy was hung, where he stayed until the fire became too hot.[7]

In these series of tragic events, the vote proved to be a rather weak protector against the onslaughts, both violent and nonviolent, of the white majority. Real protection would have to await the fashioning of other weapons by blacks.

Some Modern Cases

The Jacksonian and post-Reconstruction periods—perhaps because they are dated or because of the special circumstances surrounding each era—may not be fair tests of the utility of the vote for blacks. It might be reasonable to assume that since blacks have advanced broadly on all fronts during the decades since the end of World War II, the vote may now be a useful instrument of protection and amelioration and may play a role more congruent with the assumptions of democratic theory. Such a supposition seems more than reasonable, considering how fiercely black people fought for the right to vote in the south during the 1960s and the vigor with which they have exercised the franchise since the passage of the Voting Rights Act of 1965.

The Case of Durham, North Carolina. Unfortunately, the evidence does not support the common wisdom. By and large, the vote has proved to be only a slightly more powerful protector and supporter of the black community in the modern era than in the nineteenth century. In the south today, to be sure, where black electoral strength has dramatically increased and where many blacks hold offices from mayor to county sheriff, outright antiblack terrorism has virtually ceased to exist. Nevertheless, broad policies that might improve the overall lot of black citizens have been slow to materialize.

Take the case of Durham, North Carolina, the site of a truly remarkable black electorate, and a community where political scientist William Keech carefully analyzed the impact of the black vote on the behavior of the public officials during the 1950s.[8] If black votes matter, Keech argues, one ought to have been able to see this most clearly in a place like Durham, a relatively liberal community (the home of Duke University), where the black electorate was *sizable* (35 percent to 40 percent of the total electorate), *cohesive* (normally 80 percent of the black electorate voted the same way), and *deliverable* (almost all black votes followed the endorsements of the Durham Committee on Negro Affairs). For those who believe that the vote is a powerful group protector and helper, Durham should represent the perfect case, for few political blocs in the United States have been as potent, sizable, and organized as this one.

Keech's conclusions about the impact of the vote are sobering. He found that *voting had little impact on*:

1. The effects of past discrimination such as poverty, unequal education, and poor health.
2. Discrimination in the private sector, such as in the areas of housing and jobs.
3. Public officials not directly elected by the voters.
4. Policy areas highly visible to the white community. (Or, conversely, the vote was most effective in areas of little public attention which, by definition, tend to be trivial.)

Keech concludes that "Votes are not useful to secure what a majority is unwilling to concede. Neither are they useful to secure what none of the candidates with a realistic chance of winning consider legitimate concessions."[9] Votes would seem to be, therefore, relatively weak instruments for a disadvantaged minority in its quest for social justice. While some incremental improvements in public services were discovered by Keech, the overall results were not impressive. "The formal mechanisms of democracy [Keech argues] do not assure much more than that elites will have incentives to meet demands that do not conflict with the values of the elites and of the majority of the voters."[10]

Blacks and the Chicago "Machine." Again, the example might be imperfect, since it involves a southern city prior to the full impact of the civil rights movement. North of the Mason-Dixon line, however, the story has not been much more encouraging. Take, for instance, the city of Chicago, where blacks have played an important and visible political role for a longer period of time than in any other American city. From the outset of the mass migration of blacks from the rural south to the industrialized cities of the northeastern and the north central states in the years just prior to World War I, blacks were welcomed enthusiastically into the political life of Chicago, first by "Big Bill" Thompson's Republican machine, and then by every subsequent political machine after Thompson. The black southside component of the Chicago machine became so potent, in fact, that it was able to elect the first black man to the U.S. Congress since Reconstruction, Oscar De Priest. De Priest's southside organization was later taken over by Congressman William Dawson, who became one of the most powerful politicians of the city of Chicago, the state of Illinois, and, by virtue of his seniority, the U.S. House of Representatives. Even today, the black vote, concentrated now on the city's west side as well as in the traditional southside bastion, represents one of the major components of the Cook County Democratic party machine (formerly under the leadership of Richard Daley).

If black votes mean anything at all, surely one ought to be able to see it in Chicago. If votes make a difference in the material situation of a group, one ought to be able to see it most clearly in a city like Chicago where blacks have been more politically active than in other cities and where they recently helped to elect a black mayor, Harold Washington. The evidence, however, does not lend support to such a reasonable supposition. There is no evidence to suggest that blacks are any better off in Chicago in terms of income, employment, health, housing, education, or opportunity than in any other major city. Nor has black political participation translated into the recruitment of blacks into the main policy-making positions in Chicago. One study (see Table 10.2) has demonstrated that the representation of blacks among institutional policy makers in a city in which blacks make up 28 percent of the population has been almost nonexistent.[11]

In Chicago there is no persuasive evidence that links the vote to unambiguous protective or ameliorative functions. What about those cities where black electoral majorities (or near majorities) exist, and where these majorities have been translated into the elction of black mayors?

The Impact of the Black Mayors. The ultimate test of the utility of the vote for a traditional "out group" is one in which that group and its allies mobilize enough votes to capture the top political posts in some governmental jurisdiction. It would then be possible to examine how political incumbency relates to the material ad-

TABLE 10.2   Black representation in policy-making positions in Chicago

INSTITUTIONAL TYPE	PERCENTAGE
Business corporations	0%
Major corporate law firms	0
Universities	1
Voluntary associations	6
Labor unions	13

SOURCE: Harold Baron et al., "Black Powerlessness in Chicago," *Transaction* 6:1 (November 1968), pp. 17–33. Published by permission of Transaction, Inc. Copyright © 1968 by Transaction, Inc.

vancement of the interests and quality of life in that group. With black Americans, we have a series of such test cases over the years involving a handful of major cities where a black has been elected to the office of mayor: Carl Stokes in Cleveland, Richard Hatcher in Gary, Kenneth Gibson in Newark, Tom Bradley in Los Angeles, Harold Washington in Chicago, Wilson Goode in Philadelphia, and Maynard Jackson and Andrew Young in Atlanta. Strangely and unfortunately, political scientists have not turned their attention to this question, having merely assumed some direct relationship between capture of political office and the reorientation of government institutions into directions more favorable to blacks. There does not appear to be any appreciable difference, however, in the material lives of the black population in those cities governed by a black mayor compared with those cities governed by whites.[12] That is, black populations in cities with black mayors do not seem to enjoy higher standards of living in the areas of housing, health care, education, and jobs. In short, once one gets beyond the obvious psychic and symbolic payoffs, it does not seem to matter one way or another to the material situation of the black population whether a mayor is black or white.

Such a conclusion, while certainly disappointing to friends of black advancement, is not unexpected, for the office of the mayor, whether held by a black or a white, is extremely limited and circumscribed. Even in those cases where mayors are committed to bettering the material lot of the black population, they can take little positive action, given the many limitations to action in the urban environment. It is an inescapable fact, for instance, that all major cities, particularly those with a majority or near-majority black population, are experiencing serious erosion of their tax base as affluent white populations and, increasingly, business and industry flee to the suburban fringes. The cities are left with a population at the same time more in need of public services and less able to pay for them, a problem that is exacerbated in those cities where major industries are grossly underassessed and undertaxed. (U.S. Steel in Gary, Indiana, is a prime example.)

Furthermore, mayors who seek fundamental redistributions of benefits in urban areas must secure the cooperation of other major urban institutions, whether they be public (the city council, the bureaucracy, the party organization, and so on) or private (major banks, downtown businesses, principal industries). No black mayor has been able to elicit such cooperation precisely because such a program could be executed only at the expense of these very same institutions. A black mayor single-mindedly committed to the material advancement of the black, urban poor would be dependent, as well—particularly in the face of a declining tax base—on the generosity of either the state legislature (often heavily oriented toward rural and suburban interests) or the federal government, which has instituted draconian cuts during the Reagan years in programs directed toward the cities and their poor.

Black mayors (as well as most white mayors) are also constrained by what can only be called intractable and entrenched bureaucracies. Protected by civil service regulations and professional codes, many bureaucratic agencies are beyond the control of any popularly elected mayor. One scholar found that when Richard Hatcher became mayor of Gary, Indiana, he not only learned that he had no effective power to control policy directions in the schools, the welfare department, the police department, or the administrative agencies in charge of parks, public housing, and public health but also that many elements of the bureaucracy were actively engaged in a campaign to sabotage him.[13] The day after his inauguration, the Hatcher administration "found itself without the keys to offices, with many vital records missing (for example, the file on the United States Steel Corporation in the controller's office) and with a large part of the city government's moveable equipment stolen."[14] When Hatcher attempted to vigorously enforce the city's housing codes, he found that the city's legal department tabled almost all cases on technical grounds. The result was that a central plank in the new mayor's campaign platform was rendered inoperative in spite of his own continued support of it.

The dilemma of black mayors is truly an intractable one, because they can either attempt to secure the cooperation of other private and public institutions through judicious compromise and reasonableness, thereby removing fundamental change from the agenda, or they can attempt fundamental change against these institutions and be left without the resource base and the allies necessary for any such change. The dilemma is made even worse because no mayor, or any other public official for that matter, has any appreciable control over the decisive institutions that determine the relative quality of life of different groups in the population: the systems of production and social class. As pointed out in an earlier chapter, the subordinate economic and social position of blacks in the United States largely results from their limited representation in the capitalist class, and the generally low price their labor receives in the marketplace. Black mayors, whatever their intentions, cannot in reality expect to accomplish very much for the black urban population. While some changes in government operation must redound to the benefit of blacks, the changes can be no more than marginal and cosmetic.[15]

It is no wonder, then, that the structural position of the black population, the concentration of economic and social power in the hands of white institutions, and the limited powers of their office have forced black mayors in major American cities to act not much differently than white mayors. To be sure, a minor reorientation of services might occur, or the police and firefighters might recruit and promote a few more blacks than they might otherwise have done, or a city contract or two might even find its way to a black-owned business, but the general policies of the city and, more important, the distribution of life chances, remain largely untouched. We can see all these things poignantly and tragically highlighted by the actions of former Atlanta Mayor Maynard Jackson, a black long active in the civil rights struggle, who in 1978 ruthlessly broke the strike of the pathetically low-paid city garbage workers, almost all of whom are black. Jackson cited the fiscal health and reputation of the city in defense of his actions. As an ironic footnote to these events, recall that Martin Luther King was murdered in Memphis, Tennessee, where he had gone to support the strike activities of city garbage collectors.

BEYOND THE BALLOT

The history of the use of the vote by black Americans is not an encouraging one. Whether we look at cases from the Jacksonian period, or at the observable effects of the black vote in contemporary times, we must come to a depressing yet unavoidable conclusion. The vote has not been significantly effective for blacks as an instrument either of protection or of amelioration. It has not, in general, served the functions assigned to it by democratic theory, even though black people have been deeply committed to its use.

The realization of the limited potential of the vote led many blacks over the years to turn, often reluctantly, to other political methods. During the late 1950s and through most of the 1960s, black citizens demonstrated an ability to forge an unconventional and brilliant strategy of political struggle designed to force the government and the people of the United States to conform to their oft-claimed ideals. This political struggle, which we generally know as the civil rights movement, was constructed out of a myriad of traditional, borrowed, and newly created, often ingenious methods. Among the many methods, the following were the most prominent and effective.

Boycott

This nonviolent method was conceived as a strategy to bring economic pressure to bear through the withdrawal of patronage from targeted private businesses or public utilities. The most notable example from the civil rights movement, though by no means isolated, is the Montgomery bus boycott of 1957, a boycott triggered by a black woman (Rosa Parks) who refused to relinquish her seat to a white as was required under the law, because, according to legend, her feet hurt from a long day of work. The Montgomery boycott was also significant because it brought the leader of the boycott to national attention—a young minister named Martin Luther King, Jr.

March and Demonstration

Marches and demonstrations were other familiar weapons of the civil rights struggle. They were especially useful because they served several simultaneous functions. First, marches and demonstrations, by nature dramatic events, attracted
media coverage and helped dramatize the grievances of the black population, thus
highlighting the many racial injustices in American life. Moreover, marches and
demonstrations proved to be an important mechanism for the psychological liberation of many black people and a boon to their self-esteem and confidence, since
they were visible proof of collective power and dignity.[16] They thus became an
effective tool for mobilizing the black population throughout the nation and
helped create the base for further successful political and social struggle. Finally,
marches and demonstrations disrupted normal patterns of life, adversely affecting
the conduct of business, the deliberations of government, the movement of traffic,
and the like. They generated strong pressure on officials to restore the status quo,
either through repression, which became increasingly problematic in light of national attention, or through partially meeting the grievances of the demonstrators.

The massive 1963 March on Washington by more than 400,000 peaceful demonstrators was one of the most dramatic utilizations of this tactic during the civil
rights era. It helped push a reluctant federal government into passing the Civil
Rights Act of 1964. Official repression of a peaceful march, especially when the
protest is directed against obvious injustices, is also useful to the cause of the
demonstrators. A brutal and widely publicized attack by Alabama state troopers
on marchers demanding nothing more than the constitutional right to vote helped
trigger scores of additional demonstrations (for example, a march on the capital
of Alabama by 50,000 people, including Nobel prize winners Ralph Bunche and
Martin Luther King) as well as the Voting Rights Act of 1965, which effectively
reintroduced the black electorate into southern politics for the first time since
Reconstruction.

Civil Disobedience

Nonviolent civil disobedience—the deliberate breaking of some law considered
unjust, combined with the willingness to accept the legal consequences of that
action—was probably the most powerful and popularly recognizable weapon of
the civil rights struggle. Modeled after the tactics of Gandhi in the Indian struggle
for independence from the British, the aim of organizations such as Martin Luther
King's Southern Christian Leadership Conference (SCLC), the Congress of Racial
Equality (CORE), and the Student Nonviolent Coordinating Committee (SNCC)
was to provoke official and nonofficial retaliation and violence against peaceful,
nonaggressive demonstrators pressing for reasonable demands. The hope was that
such action would gain a wide and sympathetic audience for the demonstrators
and force the federal government to be more responsive to their cause.

The theory of nonviolent civil disobedience was best articulated by its leading

Marching for the right to vote in Selma, Alabama

practitioner, Martin Luther King, in his famous "Letter from Birmingham Jail, April 16, 1963":

> You may well ask: "Why direct action? Why sit-ins, marches and so forth? Isn't negotiation a better path?" You are quite right in calling for negotiation. Indeed, this is the very purpose of direct action. Nonviolent direct action seeks to create such a crisis and foster such a tension that a community which has constantly refused to negotiate is forced to confront the issue. It seeks so to dramatize the issue that it can no longer be ignored. . . .
>
> I must make two honest confessions to you, my Christian and Jewish brothers. First, I must confess that over the past few years I have been gravely disappointed with the white moderate. I have almost reached the regrettable conclusion that the Negro's great stumbling block in his stride toward freedom is not the White Citizen's Councilor or the Ku Klux Klanner, but the white moderate, who is more devoted to "order" than to justice; who prefers a negative peace which is the absence of tension to a positive peace which is the presence of justice; who constantly says: "I agree with you in the goal you seek, but I cannot agree with your methods of direct action"; who paternalistically believes he can set the timetable for another man's freedom; who lives by a mythical concept of time and who constantly advises the Negro to wait for a "more convenient season." Shallow understanding from people of good will is more frustrating than absolute

misunderstanding from people of ill will. Lukewarm acceptance is much more bewildering than outright rejection.

I had hoped that the white moderate would understand that law and order exist for the purpose of establishing justice and that when they fail in this purpose they become the dangerously structured dams that block the flow of social progress. I had hoped that the white moderate would understand that the present tension in the South is a necessary phase of the transition from an obnoxious negative peace, in which the Negro passively accepted his unjust plight, to a substantive and positive peace, in which all men will respect the dignity and worth of human personality. Actually, we who engage in nonviolent direct action are not the creators of tension. We merely bring to the surface the hidden tension that is already alive. We bring it out in the open, where it can be seen and dealt with. Like a boil that can never be cured so long as it is covered up but must be opened with all its ugliness to the natural medicines of air and light, injustice must be exposed, with all the tension its exposure creates, to the light of human conscience and the air of national opinion before it can be cured.[17]

While the tactic had been used extensively by the Congress of Racial Equality (CORE) prior to the 1960s, the real opening shot in the civil disobedience campaign was initiated by four young college students from North Carolina College of Agriculture and Technology who ordered coffee at an all-white lunch counter in Greensboro, North Carolina, on February 1, 1960. They refused to leave when they were denied service. The courage of these students in the face of the often abusive and sadistic behavior of elements of the town population helped launch a massive sit-in movement that swept through the south, affecting restaurants, hotels, public buildings, public transportation, beaches, and pools. These peaceful though disruptive sit-ins almost always provoked abuse, harassment, violence, and arrest. Almost as often, they produced widespread public sympathy across the nation, because the demonstrators were asking nothing more than the opportunity to practice the rights formally guaranteed them as citizens. Only four years after the first civil rights sit-in, the Civil Rights Act of 1964 became law, outlawing segregation in public accommodations. The sit-in movement was a key component in the wave of sentiment that led to that legislation. What peaceful petition and the vote had failed to deliver was forced from the government in the streets.

Violence

In the limited sphere in which the nonviolent civil rights movement operated, its methods proved to be spectacularly effective and successful. The movement helped mobilize the black population and gave black people a new and more positive image of themselves and their potential power. Combined with the concrete results of the various federal, state, and local civil rights acts, the movement helped dramatically and probably permanently alter the social status and role of the black population in the south by destroying the legal and moral structure of official segregation. More specifically, the general political mobilization of American blacks exemplified by the disruptive tactics of the civil rights movement had some important, lasting, and positive effects on the material situation of some segments of the black population. Most important, the legislation forced by the mobilization ended the structure of legal segregation not only in the south but also in the remainder of the nation as well. The legal support of the right to vote enabled blacks to significantly shift the balance of political power in the south, which not only led to the election of more moderate white candidates but also to the rapid increase in the number of black officeholders in that region.[18] The shift in political power has meant greater job opportunities in public employment; more even-handed distribution of federal, state, and local funds; more educational opportunity; and perhaps most important, the end of terrorism as a weapon of white domination. The movement was successful, in no small part, because its energies were directed against the most flagrant abuses of fundamental rights and liberties guaranteed in the Constitution. To oppose the civil rights movement from 1960 to 1965 was to appear to be against the American political tradition itself.

While the focus on black access to constitutional rights and liberties was a significant source of its strength, the movement could not touch upon the deeper problems of class, deprivation, and poverty and was thus limited as a vehicle of liberation. Martin Luther King seems to have sensed this limitation, and in the days before his assassination he began to link the problems of racial segregation, an inherently unjust economic system, and an imperialist foreign policy. The limited goals and thus the limited effects of the civil rights movement are also suggested by the perhaps ironic fact that the movement in the south was struggling for a set of rights and liberties (including the right to vote) long enjoyed and practiced by northern blacks, a group whose objective economic and social situation was hardly exemplary.

By the middle 1960s, the mood among many blacks had changed. The commitment to nonviolence, while retained by the Rev. King's Southern Christian Leadership Conference, was renounced by SNCC,[19] the Black Muslims and their popular spokesman Malcolm X,[20] and the new Black Panther party for Self-Defense. The civil rights movement had little to say to northern urban blacks, since it had a set of goals largely irrelevant to them, and strategies more in keeping with the culture of southern black religion. Once the civil rights movement mobilized the subordinate black population as a whole, grievances against de facto segregation, poverty, unemployment, bad schools, police abuses, and other discriminatory items came to be expressed in a series of violent outbreaks. From the first outburst in the Watts section of Los Angeles in August 1965, through the massive destruction in Detroit and Newark in 1967, to the near conflagration after the assassination of Martin Luther King in 1968, violence and disruption swept most American large and medium-sized cities. By and large, most of the violence was directed against symbols of civil authority, such as the police, and against those white business establishments with a long history of exploitive relationships with ghetto residents, targets that suggest the pointed, nonrandom, and ultimately political nature of the disturbances.[21]

One often hears the claim that violence neither works nor is justifiable in a democratic system in which alternatives to violence exist. The National Advisory Commission on Civil Disorders claimed in its report to the American people, "Violence is counter-productive. Violence cannot build a better society. Disruption and disorder nourish repression, not justice."[22] And yet, Americans have no slaves, women have the vote, and labor enjoys collective bargaining—results accomplished mainly through the use of disruption. Not only is the commission's sermon inaccurate in the general case, but it is also amiss with regard to the black situation. Largely as a result of the urban violence of 1965–1968, blacks saw the formation of prestigious panels and commissions charged with studying their grievances; the general loosening of welfare standards and the expansion of welfare rolls; the escalation in ghetto-bound funds from various government agencies and private foundations; and some further advancement of opportunity for blacks in higher education, the building trades, and in some corporations.[23] As historian Arthur Schlesinger has pointed out, ". . . collective violence, including the recent riots in black ghettos, has often quickened the disposition of those in power to redress just grievances. Violence, for better or worse, does settle some questions, and for the better."[24]

Disruption and Change

What is true for black Americans is true for all nonprivileged and nonpowerful groups. The vote remains a very poor instrument, in the absence of other resources, for any "out group" to substantially change its position in society. Indeed, in the face of the static United States political system, change is generally possible only through energy unleashed by a social movement, usually acting outside of the electoral arena. In the words of political scientist Theodore Lowi:

> Any political theory in the United States—moral or empirical—must begin with the recognition that our political system is almost perfectly designed to maintain an existing state of affairs—any existing state of affairs. . . . As one observer put it, our system is so designed that only a determined and undoubted majority could make it move. This is why our history is replete with social movements. It takes that kind of energy to get anything close to a majority.
>
> Our system is uniquely designed for maintenance. But if the constitutional system and the established support groups explain the amazing persistence and adaptability of our politics, quite evidently the other half of the explanation, that which explains change, lies outside the system, outside established institutions and organized arrangements. Such a relationship between the whole system and those elements that form in opposition to it can on occasion be violent, but this violence is fall-out and not essence. The essence lies in the relationship itself, between elements of the organized system and an evanescent but momentarily brilliant movement. Change comes, therefore, neither from the genius of the system nor from the liberality or wisdom of its supporters and of the organized groups. It comes from new groups or nascent groups—social movements—when the situation is most dramatic.[25]

It is perhaps ironic that many of the social reforms to which we point with pride today were constructed not out of the mix of normal politics, but out of the turmoil, disruption, and even violence generated by social movements. One immediately thinks of the freeing of the slaves, the movement to regulate the corporations before the turn of the century, the social reforms of the New Deal, and, of course, the extension of civil rights to black Americans. The passage of the Nineteenth Amendment in 1920 by which women won the right to vote came to fruition only after the prolonged and often disruptive political activities of the suffragettes. A life of decency for migrant farm workers became possible only after the efforts of the United Farm Workers almost brought the California farm industry to a standstill. The terrible war in Vietnam was likely shortened by the efforts of the antiwar movement at home.

The Social Security Act was introduced by Franklin Roosevelt and approved by Congress only because of the agitation and turmoil that was sweeping the country in the wake of the growing realization that the New Deal was unable to solve the problems of the Great Depression. The year 1934 saw widespread strikes and other turmoil in the ranks of labor; agitation by the radical Unemployed Councils and Unemployed Leagues; and the emergence of important movements seeking basic economic redistribution, the most notable being those led by Huey Long (the "Share Our Wealth" movement), Father Coughlin (the "Radio Priest"), and Dr. Francis Townsend of California.

The Wagner Labor Relations Act, which finally gave government sanction and backing to the right of working people to organize and bargain collectively, was possible only because of the effects of some of the most serious labor violence in American history. In Toledo, an entire city was brought to a halt as the strike of workers at an auto parts supplier spread, a development supported by the Unemployed League and the Marxist American Workers Party. In Minneapolis, a general strike materialized as labor armed itself to fight the Citizens' Alliance, an employers organization that had for years prevented widespread unionization by using propaganda, violence, espionage, jury tampering, and so on. In San Francisco, the violent response by employers and police to a waterfront strike led to a crippling general strike. In the great Cotton-Textile strike—perhaps the greatest strike in American history—the entire eastern seacoast and a half million workers were idled. By the end of 1934, with the wildfire spread of labor agitation and strike action, it seemed to many that the nation was on the verge of class warfare. It is reported that Secretary of State Cordell Hull worried publicly about the threat of a general strike that would topple the government. The Wagner Act was a move to head off the threat of escalating disorder.

It is at least conceivable, in light of this discussion, that the effort to ratify the Equal Rights Amendment grounded to a halt in the early 1980s because the women's rights movement proved to be too polite, playing within a set of rules that was largely stacked against it. By moving its efforts to the hallways and hearing rooms of the various state legislatures, ERA leaders may have severed their connections to the vigorous grass-roots women's movement and sapped the energy and morale of a social movement once rooted in the politics of disruption.

THE PROSPECTS AND LIMITS OF THE POLITICS OF DISRUPTION

The great social movements of American history by which "outsiders" have sought a place at the bargaining table with the powerful and the privileged have left a residue of public policy which has made the United States more democratic and just than it would have been in their absence. The gains achieved by the agrarian Populists, women, labor, and black Americans have been more than symbolic. Throughout the course of American history, but especially during the twentieth century, these outsiders have sometimes been able to elbow their way to the table, take part in forming the political agenda, and play a role in determining what government does.

It cannot be said, therefore, that the American political system is completely fixed and static. It often responds to the less powerful when threats to order, security, and tranquility arise from disruptive and agitational politics. Nevertheless, while the system often responds to the grievances expressed in "out group" turmoil (that is, when it does not choose to repress it forcefully, either directly or indirectly) it rarely does so in a manner that seriously addresses the source of those grievances. To do so would require challenging the basic foundations of the social order itself. For government to attempt seriously to ameliorate the condition of disadvantaged groups would require an attack on the overall social class system, the distribution of social rewards, and the privileges of the wealthy and of large-scale business enterprise. Government generally responds to grievances only to the degree necessary to deflate turmoil and remove its disquieting influences. When turmoil subsides, government may even roll back some of the gains achieved by protest movements.

Meeting Grievances Less Than Half Way

We can see this dynamic at work at many places in our political history. Progressive reforms during the first two decades of this century, while meeting some of the grievances that prevailed among the population, by and large further entrenched the giant corporations at the apex of the economic order, all the time utilizing the symbolism and rhetoric of the anticorporation reform movement. When the Roosevelt administration responded to the agitation and turmoil of 1934 and 1935 with the Social Security Act, it partially met the grievances of the elderly and the unemployed. In the main, however, it appropriated the language of the Townsend movement in the service of one of the most *regressive* programs in the federal government. The Wagner Act, which granted working people the right to organize, also helped structure labor-management relations such that it permanently and peacefully integrated organized labor as a "junior partner" to the corporation within the system of monopoly capitalism. As many business leaders had been predicting since at least the turn of the century, government-sponsored collective bargaining became one of the foundation stones of the corporate planning system.

Political leadership enjoys significant latitude and flexibility in its response to turmoil. Typically, political leadership meets the protest movement in *symbolic* ways, without seriously touching on the substantive issues. Political scientist Michael Lipsky has demonstrated how the rent strike movement led by Jesse Grey in New York City in the early 1960s was defeated by public officials who, through a series of visible and widely publicized actions, met the problem on the surface but did nothing about the root causes of the protest.[26] A group of black ghetto residents initiated the rent strike to protest against slum landlords who were not maintaining their properties to meet city codes and statutes; the strike was a weapon to pressure city officials to enforce the law. City officials responded not with a broad attack on the problem of slums and absentee landlords, but with a vigorous and visible enforcement of city codes in a half-dozen particularly loathsome buildings. Thinking that the law was now enforced, with dramatic newspaper and television news reports to that effect, white liberal allies of the rent strike (in universities, foundations, the media, and political parties) turned their attention to other causes and issues. Though the basic problem leading to the original protest remained unsolved, the rent strike collapsed in the face of the symbolic response by the city and the subsequent loss of its supporters and allies outside of the ghetto.

Officials can also respond to agitation and turmoil without significantly altering the basic, traditional patterns of social life by allowing the passage of some strongly worded statute, and then lightly and indifferently enforcing its provisions. It might be instructive to mention but a few examples of such official behavior:

☐ Though the statute books list seemingly tough federal mine safety laws, mining companies are left relatively free to ignore them because of the shortage of federal mine safety inspectors, the reluctance of the Department of the Interior to force companies to obey the law by closing unsafe mines, and the standing policy of the department not to impose maximum penalties (see Chapter 1).

☐ Though the United States has probably the most far-reaching and stringent antitrust statutes of any nation in the western world, the concentration of the economic life of the nation into the hands of a relative handful of giant corporations goes on unabated.

☐ Most states have strongly worded laws against discrimination in housing and employment, but few states back up the law with the financial and human resources required to enforce them. A strongly worded legal pronouncement is typically joined to a weak and ineffectual compliance apparatus. The Michigan constitution includes, for instance, the following clause: "It shall be the duty of the [Michigan Civil Rights] Commission . . . to investigate alleged discrimination against any person because of religion, race, color or national origin in the enjoyment of the civil rights guaranteed by law and by this constitution, and to secure the equal protection of such civil rights without such discrimination.'' For that enormous and complex task, the Michigan legislature normally appropriates less than $1 million per year.

Some political scientists claim that such actions are not accidental but are a conscious strategy for meeting protest without challenging the prevailing structure of power and privilege. For example, Eley and Casstevens conclude their investigation of fair housing laws across the United States with the following observation:

> The ironic political fact of fair-housing legislation at this time seems to be that the price of its passage is assurance of token implementation. . . . Its function has therefore come to be mainly symbolic and ritualistic. Its existence holds aloft the explicit standard of equal opportunity in housing, confirming the American creed for all of us; but tacitly those who pass the law know that its provisions will not be enforced in a way which basically threatens white neighborhoods. *Proponents of fair housing have the public policy they desire, and opponents have the practice they want to preserve.* [emphasis added.][27]

Rolling Back the Gains

The gains of protest movements are not chiseled in Washington in granite and marble. Even the relatively modest gains forced by the mobilization of previously silent groups in American society are often partially rescinded as turmoil subsides and the membership at the political bargaining table once again takes on its exclusive coloration. Thus the gains made by labor during the New Deal were significantly diminished by the Taft-Hartley Act passed by a conservative, antiunion Congress in 1947 and further whittled away by a pro-business National Labor Relations Board during the Reagan years. The gains made by women over the course of the century look more problematic today in the face of the severe cuts in federal social programs and the consequent and spectacular increase in the number of women living in poverty in the 1980s (some are now calling the process the "feminization of poverty"). Black Americans in the 1980s find themselves not much better off than they were in the 1950s. Black unemployment, infant mortality, and poverty rates remain roughly double that of whites. Black shares of income and wealth have declined significantly since the early 1970s. Black wants and demands make little impression on the political parties—the Republicans have largely "written off" blacks, while Democrats continue to make symbolic gestures without substantive content. The executive branch of the federal government, once an advocate for the needs of black Americans, now sides with those who oppose busing, favor tax-exempt status for private, racist academies, and oppose special hiring programs for minorities in the public sector (especially among police and firefighters). In 1984, the staff director of the U.S. Civil Rights Commission announced a major change in the commission's policy by which it would focus on the "possible adverse effects of affirmative action, racial quotas, court ordered busing, and bilingual education."[28]

Why the Gains of Protest Movements Are Limited and Vulnerable

The nonpowerful and the nonprivileged may sometimes force gains from government by turning to the politics of protest and disruption; as we have seen, these gains, however, are not what they seem on the surface. The reasons for their limitations and vulnerability are fairly obvious:

1. Because the politics of mobilized protest demands so much of its participants in terms of time, financial sacrifice, and risk (of jail, injury, etc.), it is difficult to sustain the mass support for such movements over the long haul. At best, a social movement may be able to sustain itself until legislation is passed or administrative action is taken to meet some of its grievances. Once the social movement slows or unravels, it reduces the pressure on the powerful and the privileged who may then go back to "business as usual."

2. The gains of protest movements will almost always spark a reaction from groups that oppose such gains. These reaction groups are often more powerful than the protest movement itself. The civil rights movement, for instance, sparked an antiblack, antifederal government backlash among white southerners during the 1970s and 1980s which contributed to the rise of politicians like George Wallace, the rapid formation of the New Right, and ultimately the election of Ronald Reagan.[29] The contemporary women's movement, while making some substantial gains, also sparked a powerful backlash among fundamentalist and evangelical religious groups and among other women committed to traditional female roles within the family. The many successes of the consumer and environmental movements during the 1970s energized a powerful, well-funded, and well-organized counteroffensive by America's leading corporations and business organizations.[30] This counteroffensive helped change the political agenda in America and contributed significantly to the election of a president opposed to "excessive" government interference with business.

3. Protest movements almost always become organizations. The grass-roots labor insurgency during the 1930s became a set of powerful labor unions. The grass-roots women's movement became the National Organization for Women. The civil rights movement became the Southern Christian Leadership Conference and the National Urban League. Such organizations have the characteristic of being conservative and cautious institutions compared to broad-based social movements. The latter focus on risk, mobilization of the grass-roots, significant disruption of the routines of daily life, and continuous and often unreasonable pressure on the powerful. The former are concerned about the health of the organization, fund raising, the protection of organizational leaders, and access to the powerful. The former are also interested in stability;

the latter in instability. As an example, note how grass-roots "wildcat" strikes in industry are opposed not only by management but also by the labor union hierarchy, for to lose control of the strike weapon is to diminish the power and bargaining ability of the labor union as an organization. The transition from movement to organization dampens and tames the wild and unpredictable energies of the grassroots. In the end, the effect is to reduce much of the pressure on the powerful for it is the unpredictability of mass turmoil which is the greatest political asset of "outsiders."[31]

CONCLUDING REMARKS

While the use of unconventional and disruptive political methods by "outsiders" often compels government to respond and remains far superior to normal election politics for this purpose, the results are almost always limited, short-term, and ultimately disappointing, because government is necessarily committed to the interests of the capitalist class. Even militant disruption and turmoil, as long as they aim only at joining the ongoing bargaining process and as long as "outsider" groups remain isolated from each other and committed only to their own particular needs, are seriously deficient as tools of liberation for oppressed groups. Militant tactics tied to reformist ends and conducted outside the framework of an "outsiders' " coalition, while often psychologically satisfying, cannot lead to significant changes in the material situation of nonprivileged groups. Progressive politics must transcend the effort to enter the prevailing bargaining arena and demand the end of a system built on dominant and subordinate classes. The final chapter of the book addresses this subject. At this point let me simply conclude that the politics of protest and disruption are but limited tools of democratic politics. They do not, that is to say, overcome the severe biases found in the interest group and electoral systems.

NOTES

1. On the "salutary" effects of turmoil from below see Theodore J. Lowi, *The Politics of Disorder* (New York: Basic Books, 1971); and Frances Fox Piven and Richard A. Cloward, *Poor People's Movements* (New York: Vintage, 1979).
2. For the best discussion of the uses of disruption and violence as political bargaining see H. L. Nieburg, *Political Violence: The Behavioral Process* (New York: St. Martin's Press, 1969). Much of the following analysis is based on this book.
3. See Gerald Pomper, *Elections in America* (New York: Dodd Mead, 1971) for treatment of these issues.
4. The preceding section on Jacksonian democracy is based on John Hope Franklin, *From Slavery to Freedom: A History of Negro Americans* (New York: Knopf, 1967); and Leon Litwack, *North of Slavery* (Chicago: University of Chicago Press, 1961).
5. This section depends largely on the classic work by C. Vann Woodward, *The Strange Career of Jim Crow* (New York: Oxford University Press, 1974).

6. Ibid., p. 85.
7. "The Waco Horror," *The Crisis* 10 (July 1916), p. 4.
8. William Keech, *The Impact of Negro Voting* (Chicago: Rand McNally, 1968).
9. Ibid., p. 104.
10. Ibid., p. 108.
11. To be sure, political involvement by black Americans in urban areas has significantly increased the number of elected and appointed black public officials. See Rufus P. Browning, Dale Rogers Marshall, and David H. Tabb, *Protest Is Not Enough: The Struggle of Blacks and Hispanics for Equality in Urban Areas* (Berkeley: University of California Press, 1984).
12. Symbolic advances should not be overlooked, however, for in the short run they often add to the self-esteem and sense of dignity of some groups of people, which seems to have been the case for blacks. See Edward S. Greenberg, "Black Children, Self-Esteem and the Liberation Movement," *Politics and Society* 2:3 (Spring, 1972), pp. 293–308.
13. On the story of Mayor Richard Hatcher and his troubles in Gary, Indiana, see Edward Greer, "The 'Liberation' of Gary, Indiana," *Trans Action* (January 1971), pp. 30–39.
14. Ibid., p. 36.
15. This judgment, of course, depends on one's own definition of what constitutes *significant* change. I do not claim that no changes at all took place, or that things do not get better to some extent, only that they do not seem to amount to much.
16. Greenberg, "Black Children, Self-Esteem and the Liberation Movement."
17. From pp. 81, 87–88, *Why We Can't Wait*, by Martin Luther King, Jr. (N.Y.: Harper & Row, 1968).
18. The increase in the number of black elected officials has been nothing short of astounding, increasing from 1,472 in 1970 to over 5,654 in 1984 (see *Statistical Abstracts of the United States, 1985*, p. 504, U.S. Bureau of the Census). Nevertheless, even at this rate of phenomenal increase, black elected officials will account for only 3 percent of elected officials by the year 2000.
19. As one SNCC activist so articulately expressed it: "Nonviolence might do something to the moral conscience of a nation, but a bullet didn't have morals and it was beginning to occur to more and more organizers that white folks had had plenty more bullets than they did conscience." Julius Lester, "The Angry Children of Malcolm X," *Sing Out!* 16 (October–November 1966), p. 22.
20. Just prior to his assassination, Malcolm X split with the Black Muslims to form his own militant organization.
21. For a discussion of the political nature of urban violence see David J. Olson, "Black Violence as Political Protest," in Edward S. Greenberg, Neal Milner, and David J. Olson, eds., *Black Politics: The Inevitability of Conflict* (New York: Holt, Rinehart & Winston, 1971).
22. *Report of the National Advisory Commission on Civil Disorders* (New York: Bantam, 1968), p. 2.
23. See Frances Fox Piven and Richard A. Cloward, *Regulating the Poor* (New York: Pantheon, 1971) for a treatment of the aftereffects of urban violence.
24. Arthur Schlesinger, "The Dark Heart of American History," *Saturday Review*, October 19, 1968, p. 22.
25. Theodore Lowi, *The Politics of Disorder* (New York: Basic Books, 1971), pp. 53–54. Also see Frances Fox Piven and Richard Cloward, *Poor People's Movements* (New York: Vintage, 1979) for a similar view.

26. Michael Lipskey, *Protest in City Politics* (Chicago: Rand McNally, 1969).
27. *The Politics of Fair Housing Legislation* (San Francisco: Chandler, 1968). A similar case is made for the "cooling out" function of official race riot commissions in Michael Lipsky and David J. Olson, *Commission Politics* (New Brunswick, N.J.: Transaction Books, 1977).
28. Robert Pear, "New Director of U.S. Rights Panel Calls for Major Change of Course," *The New York Times* (Jan. 5, 1984), p. 1.
29. For a compelling analysis of the rise of the New Right, see Kevin P. Phillips, *Post-Conservative America* (New York: Random House, 1982).
30. For this story, see Thomas Byrne Edsall, *The New Politics of Inequality* (New York: W. W. Norton, 1984).
31. This position is powerfully articulated by Piven and Cloward in *Poor People's Movements*.

SUGGESTIONS FOR FURTHER READING

John Hope Franklin. FROM SLAVERY TO FREEDOM. *New York: Knopf, 1967.* The standard history of black Americans.

Jo Freeman. THE POLITICS OF WOMEN'S LIBERATION. *New York: McKay, 1975.* Though somewhat dated, it remains the best available discussion of the reemergence of the women's movement and the internal debate over movement goals.

Edward S. Greenberg, Neal Milner, and David Olsen. BLACK POLITICS: THE INEVITABILITY OF CONFLICT. *New York: Holt, Rinehart & Winston, 1971.* A collection of readings on the black political situation and the place of disruptive and violent tactics in the liberation struggle.

Ethel Klein. GENDER POLITICS. *Cambridge, Mass.: Harvard University Press, 1984.* An analytically sophisticated and empirically detailed examination of the emergence of feminist politics.

H. L. Nieburg. POLITICAL VIOLENCE. *New York: St. Martin's Press, 1969.* A provocative discussion of violence as an addition to the bargaining process.

Frances Fox Piven and Richard Cloward. POOR PEOPLE'S MOVEMENTS. *New York: Vintage, 1979.* This controversial work argues that social movements, not social organizations, are the principal tools by which the poor may occasionally move the social order. The theory is buttressed by four compelling and detailed case studies.

Michael B. Preston, Lenneal Henderson, Jr., and Paul Puryear (eds.). THE NEW BLACK POLITICS. *New York: Longman, 1982.* A solid collection of research on the forms and effects of black participation in conventional politics.

Thomas Sowell. ETHNIC AMERICA: A HISTORY. *New York: Basic Books, 1981.* A discussion of blacks and other ethnic groups in America written from a neoconservative point of view.

C. Vann Woodward. THE STRANGE CAREER OF JIM CROW. *New York: Oxford University Press, 1966.* An analysis of the genesis and mechanics of the southern Jim Crow system at the turn of the century.

Part

IV

The Institutions

of Government

In this section of the text, we turn our attention to the principal institutions of the federal government responsible for the formulation and execution of public policy. We shall see that both the form and modes of operation of these institutions are intimately connected to the operations of a capitalist economy.

11

The Presidency
and American Capitalism

THE AGGRANDIZEMENT
OF PRESIDENTIAL POWER

The presidency is today the preeminent institution in the national government of the United States. While the Founding Fathers had no intention that it be so, the office has become the central energizer of government policy over the years, the articulator of the national purpose, the principal symbol at home and abroad of the American political system, and the focus of the hopes (and fears) of countless individuals and groups. For better or worse, we tend to think about American history in four- or eight-year chunks corresponding to the term in office of a particular incumbent. We invariably turn to the president when the times are out of kilter, demand remedial action from him, blame him if improvements are not immediately forthcoming, or praise him unduly if the burden of problems is eased. We depend on the president to set the legislative agenda for Congress, to define national objectives in time of war and conflict, and to represent the United States before the world.

In these and in countless other ways, both symbolic and actual, the presidency embodies the headship of the government, surely not a monarch, but just as surely more than "first among equals." I shall argue that the office has reached this position over the course of our history not because of random events or usurpations of power but because of certain developments in American capitalism. As capitalism in the United States gradually came to assume a concentrated corporate form, it became apparent to political and economic leaders that the laissez-faire approach to the role of government had to give way to a more activist form of government in order to support, coordinate, protect, subsidize, and sustain its main economic institutions and processes.[1] Because of certain political, social, and constitutional factors (which shall be explored in the following pages), it also became apparent that the most appropiate helmsman to guide this new form of government was the president.

To argue that the presidency has reached this preeminent position is not to say, at the same time, that all presidents are equally powerful, influential, or effective. Indeed, the presidencies of Gerald Ford and Jimmy Carter amply demonstrate that while the office has become increasingly important over the course of American history, there are certain times when either the nature of the conditons in which a president must operate or the particular character of a president's talents (or lack of same) cause the office to diminish. Nevertheless, this waxing and waning of importance and power in the office takes place along a trend line that, in a historical sense, has been steadily rising. Thus, Presidents Ford and Carter, despite their ineffectuality in office and their paltry public stature, remained more central to the formulation of national policy and purpose than nearly every nineteenth-century president (with the obvious exceptions of Jefferson, Jackson, and Lincoln).

To argue that the presidency has reached this preeminent position is not to say, however, that the office is omnipotent or free to act as it desires. In fact, to an extent not matched in any other nation, political power in the United States is widely dispensed into the hands of other persons, groups, institutions, and political jurisdictions over which the president has no authority. For enactment of his legislative program, he requires the cooperation of Congress whose members are each independently elected from constituencies different than his own. For implementation and continuous monitoring of his program as well as assistance in the conduct of the business of government, the president is dependent on a vast bureaucracy, most of whose members are protected from direct presidential authority by civil service laws and the knowledge that their own tenure in office is likely to outlast his. In attempting to mold the domestic and international policy environment, any president must also be mindful of the important and independent power wielded by the courts, state governors and legislatures, powerful interest groups, and ultimately the electorate. The president cannot command any of them; success as a national leader comes down, in the end, to his ability to persuade them that what he wants is appropriate and worth their active support (or, at the least, their passive acceptance).[2] The difference between the ability to command and the ability to persuade was articulated by Harry Truman as he was about to turn over his office to former General of Allied Forces Dwight Eisenhower: "He'll sit here and he'll say, Do this! Do that! And nothing will happen. Poor Ike—it won't be like the army. He'll find it very frustrating."[3]

Yet, in spite of all these factors, the presidency has become the most important single institution in the national government, the driving engine of the policy process, and the articulator of the national purpose. As presidential scholar Wilfred

Binkley has put it, "The history of the presidency is [the] history of aggrandizement." This and the following chapter will examine the roots of this aggrandizement of function, responsibility, power, and prestige and provide an appreciation for the role of the presidency in the overall American system.

THE PRESIDENTIAL MYSTIQUE

The aggrandizement of the presidency takes several concrete forms, not least important of which is the growing mystique and imperial symbolism that surround the office, a development quite at odds with custom and practice in the early days of the Republic. It is instructive and a bit sobering to note that President Jefferson was in the habit of retiring to his Washington boarding house after a day of work, and would stand in line there with the other boarders patiently waiting for his dinner. Such behavior would be unthinkable today not only because of the ever-present threat of assassination but also because of the aura that now attaches to the office. Think of the trappings that surround the modern presidency: several imposing official residences as well as elaborate unofficial ones, a special presidential theme played at most ceremonial functions, bands and security forces deployed at every minor stop-over during presidential travels, a sizable personal staff to serve every conceivable need of the president and his family,[4] the monopolization of television time for press conferences or addresses, the presidential portrait hanging prominently in every post office, the hushed tones and reverential attitudes assumed in the presence of the president (it is reported, for instance, that Robert Kennedy, even in private, always addressed his brother John F. Kennedy as "Mr. President"), and the constant press attention to the lives and opinions of all members of the presidential family. The contrast to George Washington staying at common inns during his travels, or to Abraham Lincoln shining his own shoes, is truly staggering.[5]

The mystique that surrounds the institution is nowhere better expressed than in journalist Theodore White's description of the way even men of power behave in the presence of the greater power of the president (or a potential president). The scene that White describes below took place immediately after the nomination of John F. Kennedy in 1960, as leaders of the Democratic party, including mayors, governors, and members of Congress, awaited his arrival.

> Far off in the distance they could see a winking row of red lights, pricking a serpentine across Los Angeles Boulevard. All of them recognized the blinking, winking, ominously tantalizing, flashing train of light; for they were bosses, mayors, governors, masters of police themselves. This they recognized: it was a police cavalcade, bearing the possible next President of the United States from his hideaway to this cottage.
>
> Kennedy loped into the cottage with his light, dancing step, as young and lithe as springtime, and called a greeting to those who stood in his way. Then he seemed to slip from them as he descended the steps of the split-level cottage to a corner where his brother Bobby and brother-in-law Sargent Shriver were

chatting, waiting for him. The others in the room surged forward on impulse to join him. Then they halted. A distance of perhaps thirty feet separated them from him, but it was impassable. They stood apart, these older men of long-established power, and watched him. He turned after a few minutes, saw them watching him, and whispered to his brother-in-law. Shriver now crossed the separating space to invite them over. First Averell Harriman; then Dick Daley; then Mike DiSalle; then, one by one, in an order determined by the candidate's own instinct and judgment, he let them all congratulate him. Yet no one could pass the little open distance between him and them uninvited, because there was this thin separation about him, and the knowledge they were there not as his patrons but as his clients. They could come by invitation only, for this might be a President of the United States.[6]

Is it any wonder that even the most ordinary of men, even men with little ambition or pretention (even those who publicly admit to making their own breakfast, like Gerald Ford, or who wear cardigan sweaters and blue jeans on occasion, like Jimmy Carter), quickly come to appreciate and to insist on the prerogatives, privileges, and honors of the office? Is it any wonder that less humble men, men of driving ambition such as Lyndon Johnson and Richard Nixon, insisted on pushing the prerogatives of the office to its farthest limits, enhancing both the deference demanded by other people and the ceremonials surrounding the office? Perhaps few presidents took matters as far as Richard Nixon (insisting, as he did after a trip to European capitals, that White House guards be dressed in gaudy, fancy-dress costumes appropriate to the majesty of the president's office), but few incumbents have been immune to the *hubris* that develops from the trappings of majesty.[7]

From Symbolic Aggrandizement to the Use of Power

Such ambitions rarely remain confined to empty ceremonials. There seems to be a strong drive among presidents to "live up to" the requirements, traditions, and majesty of the institution and either to leave the office undiminished and unimpaired for future incumbents, or better still, to expand the boundaries of the permissible and the possible. Former presidential advisor and Secretary of State Dean Acheson stated in his memoirs that President Truman refused to seek congressional authority for military action in Korea because of his desire "to pass on [the presidency] unimpaired by the slightest loss of power or prestige."[8] Richard Nixon constantly used this notion as the basis for his refusal to cooperate with the various Watergate investigations. Especially prominent in this regard was his constant invocation of the doctrine of executive privilege.

Many twentieth-century presidents have justified this institutional ambition and aggrandizement on the grounds that they represent not only the single government institution capable of decisive action but also the only office that is directly elected by the whole people. Congress merely represents separate interests,

President Reagan and Chancellor Kohl at Bitburg, West Germany

in this view, while the presidency represents the national interest. The president is not simply the holder of one among several governmental offices but the executive of the whole people. While many presidents have articulated these two themes, no president expressed it as cogently as did Woodrow Wilson in 1908:

> The nation as a whole has chosen him, and is conscious that it has no other political spokesman. His is the only national voice in affairs. Let him once win the admiration and confidence of the country, and no other single force can withstand him, no combination of forces will easily overpower him. His position takes the imagination of the country. He is the representative of no constituency, but of the whole people. When he speaks in his true character, he speaks for no special interest. If he rightly interprets the national thought and boldly insists upon it, he is irresistible; and the country never feels the zest for action so much as when its President is of such insight and calibre.[9]

Among presidents, the Wilsonian conception of the presidency has triumphed. It has gained expression from Teddy Roosevelt's notion of the president as ''steward of the people'' to Richard Nixon's notion of the president as the stern but loving father guiding the affairs of his children, the American people.

It should be added that presidents have not been alone in their desire to expand the majesty and power of the institution and to find expression for their personal and institutional ambitions. They have been avidly encouraged by leading journalists, scholars, and businesspeople, to say nothing of the American people. A strong president is needed, it has generally been believed, because his leadership is the only tool for decisive action in a dangerous world, the only route around congressional stalemate, and the best hope for the coordination of policy.[10] Having gone into temporary abeyance after the bitter experiences with the abuse of power under Presidents Johnson and Nixon, the view that presidents must be granted power commensurate with their awesome responsibilities has once again gained the highest intellectual respectability. As Senator Daniel Moynihan floridly put the case, "I am of those who believe that America is the hope of the world and for that time given him, the President is the hope of America."[11] For many Americans, if public opinion polls and election returns are to be believed, Ronald Reagan seems to have lived up to this exalted expectation.

To both the popular and the scholarly mind, the great presidents of the twentieth century have been those who have exercised power, mobilized the government and the public to great deeds, permanently placed the office on a higher plane of competency, and made of it an institution better able to meet the needs of the nation. When historians and journalists play the game of ranking the great presidents of the twentieth century, they have customarily included Teddy Roosevelt, Woodrow Wilson, and Franklin Roosevelt at the top, with Harry Truman narrowly missing. In late 1984, *Newsweek* magazine wondered aloud whether it was not time to place Ronald Reagan on this list. The "mediocre" category (by definition, those who have held a more modest conception of the office) has generally included Harding, Coolidge, Hoover, and Eisenhower. Even though the Watergate and Vietnam experiences tempered enthusiasm for presidential power for a short time, the office retains the central symbolic place in the American pantheon, whether the president is kicking off the March of Dimes campaign, lighting the national Christmas tree, delivering a message to the nation, meeting visiting dignitaries as representative of the American people, launching air strikes against some unfortunate (and pathetically weak) adversary like Grenada, or announcing a trade boycott of the Soviet Union. The stylistic changes of the Ford and Carter administrations, their less magisterial poses, were temporary in nature and have not fundamentally altered the status of the presidency as the main ritual icon of the American system.

The Basis of Presidential Symbolic Power

The symbolic aggrandizement of the presidency probably results from three important factors. First, in the United States we combine the functions of *head of state* and *head of government* in a single office. In most European nations, in comparison, the various ceremonials that symbolize national life and unity are embodied in an office that has little or no responsibility for governance—the monarchy or the presidency of the republic. The operating head of the government is lodged in a separate office, usually that of the prime minister or premier.

In Great Britain, for instance, the queen or members of the royal family cut ribbons, christen warships, and present awards and medals. In the United States, we insist that the president perform these duties at the same time that he shapes national policy. Interestingly enough, while this might add considerably to his burdens, it also enhances the prestige, aura, and mystique of the office and serves as a useful corollary instrument for the exercise of his political power in other arenas. As President Taft put it, "The president is the personal embodiment and representative of the people's dignity and majesty."[12]

Second, and perhaps more important, the symbolic centrality of the presidency is tied to its emergence as the single most important policy-making institution in American government, a subject to which much of the remainder of this chapter is devoted. The exercise of power always has appended to it some sense of awe on the part of those who witness it. As the presidency has become the preeminent power among competing political institutions, it takes on increasing symbolic and mythical qualities. When one adds this to the president's ceremonial role as the embodiment of the American people, the combined symbolic stature becomes impressive indeed.

Finally, the powerful combination of head of state and head of government becomes more accessible to the mass public because of the twentieth-century revolution in mass communications. While nineteenth-century Americans were in contact with the president only through newspaper accounts, secondhand reports, or intermittent campaign forays, twentieth-century Americans can hardly escape some daily contact with the president or his family. Because of the wonders of modern mass communications and the priorities of the mass media, everything a president does becomes news, whether the act is of enormous magnitude (bombing Cambodia, imposing wage-price controls, arming counterrevolutionary terrorists in Nicaragua, requesting voluntary curtailments in energy use, and so on) or of overpowering triviality (putting ketchup on cottage cheese, picking up a dog by its ears, falling on the ski slopes, opening Christmas presents, teaching a Sunday school bible class, or riding a horse on his ranch). Through the mass media, the president is an almost omnipresent reality, so visible in his daily activities that he becomes the center of a veritable "cult of personality." Political scientist Thomas Cronin has suggested that "So much media news time is devoted to presidential elections that people might expect an election to produce a savior rather than a president."[13] While the state and government functions of the presidency are the basic elements in its symbolic aggrandizement, the mass media represent the preserver and the transmitter of this powerful mix to the population.[14]

Presidential Aggrandizement and Capitalist Development

In many ways, however, this symbolic aggrandizement merely reflects the enormous aggrandizement of responsibility and power that has flowed to the presidency during the course of the twentieth century, a development concurrent with and intimately related to the rise and maturation of corporate capitalism. In the face of the leadership incapacities of Congress and other federal institutions, the president has become the figure in the government best able to direct that broad range of government functions required by modern capitalism (see Chapters 13–14)—overseas expansion and management of the economic environment. It is no accident that as the corporate economy has required expert, decisive, unified, and often rapid policy making by the government, the presidency has gained ascendency over more contentious, slow-moving, and pluralist-bargaining institutions such as Congress. As the corporation itself has required firm leadership at its helm, so too has corporate capitalism required strong executive leadership. Given the inherent dangers and uncertainties of overseas expansion, economic policy planning, and economic fine tuning (government functions absolutely essential to the health of corporate capitalism), anything less than unified, expert, and decisive leadership would have seemed like folly to dominant groups.

The aggrandizement of presidential responsibility and power derives from two closely related developments in the organization of economic life, both of which are derived from the transformation from laissez-faire to monopoly capitalism. They are:

1. the overseas expansion of the United States and its development into an imperial power
2. the rise of the ''positive'' or ''welfare'' state, a form of political society in which government becomes the main instrument for regulating, coordinating, and rationalizing economy and society.

The remainder of the chapter will examine each of these statements in detail, demonstrating how each is related to the aggrandizement of the presidency.

THE PRESIDENT AND
THE CONDUCT OF FOREIGN AFFAIRS

The most decisive factor in the transformation of the presidency has been the transformation of the United States from an insular and isolated nation to one with worldwide interests and concerns, constructed primarily out of the search for new markets and sources of raw materials by a handful of giant corporations. Since the authors of the Constitution believed that relations with other nations were best conducted by a single executive, and wrote provisions to that effect in the 1789 document, the expansion of the overseas activities of the United States has automatically enhanced the role of the president. Let us look at some of these consitutional provisions in light of their interpretation by various presidents and see how their meanings have changed under the pressures of American overseas expansion.

Diplomatic Recognition

Article II, Section 2 of the Constitution grants to the president the power to "appoint Ambassadors, other public Ministers and Consuls," with the advice and consent of the Senate. Section 3 grants to the president the power to "receive Ambassadors and other Public Ministers." While such provisions may not seem at first glance to add much to the sum total of presidential power, they do, in fact, afford additional instruments for the presidential conduct of foreign affairs. The simple responsibility of naming and receiving ambassadors, from the first days of the Republic, has implied the authority to recognize (or not to recognize) foreign regimes. While *recognition* may appear to be a mere technicality, most presidents have used this authority as an instrument of foreign policy. President Washington, for instance, expressed his distaste for what he considered the excesses of the French Revolution by refusing to receive the French ambassador, Edmond Genêt, in 1793. Woodrow Wilson attempted to use nonrecognition of the 1913 Huerta government in Mexico as a tool to destabilize a government more friendly to European than to American investments. (When that failed to work, he sent in American troops.) Several American presidents, from Wilson through Hoover, refused to recognize the Bolshevik regime of the Soviet Union by the simple act of refusing to send or receive ambassadors. The same policy was followed with respect to the popular communist regime in China from its inception in 1949 until President Nixon's partial turnabout in 1971 and President Carter's formal recognition in 1979.

The transformation of over two decades of American policy toward China, as welcome and as overdue as it was, is particularly instructive. As columnist Tom Wicker pointed out, "President Nixon's approach to Peking . . . was planned in secrecy, decided by presidential fiat, carried out clandestinely and finally announced only as an accomplished fact."[15] If anything, Carter's decision was made with even less consultation or public preparation. And yet, all of this discretionary power is built on what seems a relatively trivial constitutional grant, that of receiving and appointing ambassadors. While most presidents consult with many other members of the government concerning the question of recognition, they need not do so, and very often have acted in isolation.

Treaties

The presidency derives even greater latitude in conducting foreign affairs from the constitutional provision in Article XI, Section 2 "to make Treaties." Such a provision confers significant powers on the president, for "to make Treaties" certainly implies the ability to initiate and to negotiate treaties with the representatives of foreign governments. While the Constitution requires the final "advice and consent of the Senate," the president holds the initiative. The Senate, by and large, reacts to the action taken by the president and is usually presented with a *fait accompli*. Once a treaty is negotiated and signed by American officials, it is often difficult or embarrassing to vote it down. Thus only about 1 percent of all such treaties have been rejected by the Senate.

The advice and consent process in the Senate is a time-consuming, drawn-out process, and occasionally a dangerous one. Many important treaties have been *denied* advice and consent, the most famous one being the Versailles treaty negotiated by President Wilson at the end of the first World War. Carter's Panama Canal treaty almost met the same fate. The SALT II treaty with the Soviet Union was strewn with pitfalls and withdrawn after it became apparent that the Senate would refuse consent. As a way around the uncertainties of the treaty process, presidents have increasingly turned to the use of what are called *executive agreements*, which are internationally valid compacts entered into by the president in the name of the United States, but they require no participation from the Senate. To enter into such compacts, presidents have drawn on what they consider to be the *implied powers* of the treaty-making provision in the Constitution, a justification supported on numerous occasions by the courts. Not surprisingly, given the freedom of action this route provides the president in foreign policy making, the executive agreement has become the preferred, even normal, process (see Table 11.1).

At first, executive agreements dealt only with relatively unimportant or highly technical matters, the treaty power being reserved for more significant matters of policy. Gradually, however, the relative priorities have been reversed, with the executive agreement gaining prominence not only in numbers but also in the significance of the issues in the agreements. Roosevelt's "Destroyers-for-Bases" agreement with Great Britain in 1940, an agreement that tacitly aligned the United States in the European war, was entered into through an executive agreement, as were the commitments at Yalta and Potsdam in 1945. In recent years, executive agreements have been used for the Marshall Plan to reconstruct capitalist Europe; for secret military agreements, obligations and commitments to Spain, Thailand, Ethiopia, South Korea, Israel, Cambodia, and South Vietnam; for the conduct of a secret war in Laos; and for secret aid agreements with many other less developed nations.

One should not underestimate these developments, for what they ultimately mean is that presidents have generally arrogated to themselves most of the au-

TABLE 11.1   Treaties and executive agreements

PERIOD	TREATIES	EXECUTIVE AGREEMENTS	NUMBER OF EXECUTIVE AGREEMENTS PER ANNUM	EXECUTIVE AGREEMENTS AS PERCENT OF ALL INTERNATIONAL AGREEMENTS
1789–1839	60	27	0.5	31%
1839–1889	215	238	4.8	53
1889–1939	524	917	18.3	64
1940–1973	364	6,395	194.8	95
1974–1979	102	2,233	446.6	96

SOURCE: Congressional Research Service, Library of Congress, 1980.

thority in reaching international agreements that they had traditionally shared with the Senate. In a very real sense, recent presidents have felt that it was a prerogative of the office to commit the United States to significant international obligations without public or congressional debate, which is especially striking and disturbing in the many recent cases involving secret, bilateral military commitments. Former Senator William Fulbright once complained that "We get treaties dealing with postal affairs and so on. Recently, we had an extraordinary treaty dealing with the protection of stolen art objects. These are treaties. But when we put troops and take on commitments in Spain, it is an executive agreement."[16]

The War Power

By far the most awesome aggrandizement of presidential power is derived from the use and broad interpretation of what are called the *war powers*. The war powers are broad implied powers derived from the provision in Article XI, Section 2: "The President shall be Commander in Chief of the Army and Navy of the United States, and of the Militia of the several states, when called into the actual service of the United States." At a very early stage, Alexander Hamilton saw the potential for the aggrandizement of power inherent in this provision. He prophetically pointed out in *The Federalist* that "Of all the cases of concerns of government, the direction of war most peculiarly demands those qualities which distinguish the exercise of power by a single head." Surveying developments with respect to presidents and the conduct of war, one scholar has gone so far as to claim that, "By the early 1970s, the American president had become on issues of war and peace the most absolute monarch . . . among the great powers of the world."[17] While recent presidents have had their wings clipped in regard to these powers, they remain awesome. Let us look briefly at developments in this area, and the relative balance of power between the president and Congress.

The Constitution grants to Congress what seems an important role in the conduct of foreign and military affairs, though not equal to that of the president. The Constitution requires the advice and consent of the Senate in ratifying treaties; it grants Congress the responsibility for regulating commerce between the United States and foreign nations; it gives Congress the power to raise an army and a navy; and it grants Congress the sole right to declare war. Furthermore, Congress retains a decisive, constitutionally granted role in the appropriations process and thus potentially retains a great deal of influence even in those foreign policy matters conducted solely by the president if they require some funding. (Only a very few matters are free from the necessity of some funding.) Congress retains, then, an important constitutional role in the formulation and conduct of foreign affairs, including that of war.

As Hamilton so rightly pointed out, however, the conduct of war is an inherently executive one, and the more the United States finds itself in the midst of war, whether total, quasi, counterinsurgency, or "cold," power and prerogative tend to flow into the presidential office. This perhaps inevitable trend has been accentuated by the very strong claims on this war power by several of our presidents.

From Defensive War to Offensive War. It appears that the main goal of the Constitutional Convention with respect to this issue was to prevent the executive from waging offensive war on his own (thus the provision for the congressional declaration of war), while at the same time allowing him to meet sudden attacks and to wage defensive war.[18] To fulfill this defensive role, the framers of the Constitution envisaged full presidential power to move and to deploy the armed forces of the United States. The distinction between offensive and defensive war, however, is a difficult one to draw, though it seems that most of our early presidents were particularly conscious of the problem and felt a strong sense of limitation with respect to it. As Jefferson put it: "The line of demarcation between cases may be difficult; but the good officer is bound to draw it at his own peril, and throw himself on the justice of his country and the rectitude of his motives."[19]

The Constitution thus grants to Congress the power to initiate offensive war, and to the president the power to initiate defensive war and to move and deploy troops to that end. The history of this relationship, particularly in the twentieth century, has been the extraordinary expansion of the definition of defensive war and the almost limitless deployment of armed forces. The expansion has been of such scale that the concept of offensive war has dropped by the wayside, leaving the president, to a very large degree, with the predominant power in waging war of any kind. This development has been slow but inexorable, as precedent has piled upon precedent. President Polk, for instance, provoked war with Mexico by moving American troops into disputed land between Mexican and Texan forces (under his prerogative as commander in chief), knowing full well that they would come under fire. It is interesting to note the remarks of a young congressman named Abraham Lincoln reacting to this presidential initiative. The words are hauntingly prophetic:

> Allow the President to invade a neighboring nation whenever *he* shall deem it necessary to repel an invasion . . . and you allow him to make war at pleasure. Study to see if you can fix *any* limit to his power in this respect.[20]

For his own part during the dark days of the Civil War, Lincoln assumed the broadest interpretation of the war powers of any nineteenth-century president, wedding his power as commander in chief to his constitutional duty "to take care that the laws be faithfully executed." On his own accord, he assembled an army and a navy, imposed a naval blockade on the south, spent unauthorized monies, suspended the right of habeas corpus, declared martial law, seized Confederate property, emancipated the slaves in the rebellious states, censored newspapers, and formulated a plan of reconstruction for the south, all without specific congressional authorization or declaration of war. Historian Arthur Schlesinger argues, and it is not without merit, that such actions were justifiable on the grounds that

Lincoln was confronted with the most critical emergency any nation-state can endure, that of civil war. In Lincoln's own words, "Was it possible to lose the nation and yet preserve the constitution?" Furthermore, it is clear that Lincoln considered the assumption of these war powers temporary, strictly limited to the duration of the emergency.

Teddy Roosevelt, true to his dictum, "Speak softly and carry a big stick," won a dispute with Congress over the wisdom of his plan to show American might to the remainder of the world merely by using his power as commander in chief to send the navy halfway around the world. He left it to Congress to decide whether to appropriate the funds to get the fleet back into home waters. Needless to say, Congress had no choice but to comply with presidential policy. Roosevelt also used troops without specific congressional authorization (but certainly with their silent approval, as well as that of American businessmen) to keep the Caribbean safe for American investments and to help carve a place in China for the United States. Similar movement of troops as an instrument in the conduct of foreign relations was vigorously pursued by Presidents Wilson (who ordered the seizure of Vera Cruz, the pursuit of Pancho Villa, intervention in Russia against the Bolsheviks, and the occupation of Haiti and the Dominican Republic) and Franklin Roosevelt (whose naval deployment and convoy policies helped ease America into World War II).

The Cold War and Presidential Powers. With the coming of the Cold War in the late 1940s, the dominant capitalist class's fear of socialist revolution caused tension in the United States. Most limitations on the expansion of the presidential war powers were laid aside. As it became apparent to dominant groups in the United States that the protection of overseas markets, investment opportunities, and sources of raw materials depended on a vigorous, strong, and perpetual American military presence in the world, presidents felt confident in asserting and expanding their conception of the powers of their office. Since socialism was rightly perceived as a threat to the continuation of capitalist hegemony, the Cold War came to be defined as the ultimate defensive war, a defensive war that had to be fought everywhere on the globe (even at home), and since it was defensive, a war to be directed, managed, and planned by the executive. In these developments toward presidential domination in making foreign policy and waging war, Congress, with some notable exceptions, was generally cooperative and supportive. It is only with the Vietnam debacle that Congress and private elites began to trim the sails of executive discretion.

President Truman took perhaps the most decisive steps in the bloating of presidential war powers. His actions, the most serious moves toward presidential aggrandizement since Lincoln, were doubly significant because he perceived them to be not temporary, but powers inherent in his office. Though we are more accustomed to it since the Vietnam war, Truman took the step, startling at the time, of conducting a major land war in Korea not only without a congressional declaration, but based on a claim that, aside from appropriations, Congress had no official role in the policy decisions. The decision to wage war in Korea, claimed Truman, was inherent in his powers as commander in chief. To take another case much in the style of Teddy Roosevelt, Truman ended the heated debate over the propriety of stationing troops in Europe, surely an important matter of national policy, simply by shipping them there. Again, Truman claimed the right to do so because of his constitutional authority to deploy troops as commander in chief.

While President Eisenhower seems in retrospect a rather cautious, conservative, and relatively honest and forthright incumbent, he also added considerably to the arsenal of the presidential fortress. To the Eisenhower years we owe, to a very large extent, not only the most extreme claim (until Nixon) of the right of the president to deny foreign policy and national defense information to Congress,[21] but also the first widespread and wholesale use of secret agencies such as the CIA to conduct covert operations around the globe. While his Secretary of State, John Foster Dulles, was most proud of the role of covert agencies in the overthrow of legitimate but anti-American regimes in Iran and Guatemala, they were active in scores of other countries as well, though not very successfully in Cuba, Laos, and in spy flights over the Soviet Union.

President Johnson and General Westmoreland plan war in Vietnam

Vietnam and the Presidency. With the tragedy of Vietnam came the most extreme, even arrogant claims for the president's powers as commander in chief, and some concrete examples of the dangers inherent in the unchecked aggrandizement of the office in military and foreign affairs, dangers seen even by those groups in American society who most directly benefit from a vigorous, imperial world policy. The escalation of presidential claims in this period reached an extreme level. President Kennedy, for his part, first committed ground forces to military action in Southeast Asia in his capacity as commander in chief; stepped up the clandestine war in Laos; and surreptitiously channeled funds to anticommunist forces in the region. When President Kennedy announced the deployment of additional forces to Thailand in 1962, he labeled it a *defensive act.* Lyndon Johnson irretrievably made the war in Southeast Asia an American one. In the crisis atmosphere after the North Vietnamese staged a rather mild retaliatory raid on American destroyers that had undertaken hostile actions against the North Vietnamese mainland (such hostile actions, from shelling to the landing of saboteurs, had been going on secretly for years, a fact that did not become generally known until the publication of the Pentagon Papers), Johnson convinced Congress to pass the Gulf of Tonkin Resolution in August 1964, declaring congressional support for the president's "determination to take all necessary measures" to repel attacks on American forces and to prevent aggression. Based on its nebulous, broad, and ambiguous language, Johnson proceeded to conduct a presidential war in Vietnam. In 1965, he greatly expanded American forces in South Vietnam, ordered them into combat, and sent fighter bombers over North Vietnam. All this was done without a declaration of war (though Congress did vote appropriations), or threat of invasion, or dangers to American citizens or property. In fact, the Johnson administration claimed that the Tonkin Resolution was helpful but not necessary, because the president, in his capacity as commander in chief, had the inherent power to repel any threat to "national security" wherever it might occur. Under the cloak of national security, the concept of defensive war had reached its absurd, though logical, conclusion.

Under President Richard Nixon, the presidency ran amok. In his conduct of the war, Nixon refused to adhere to any sense of limitation, precedent, or counsel from other elites, private or public. When Congress repealed the Tonkin Resolution, he claimed he did not need it anyway. When it became clear that no justification for the war existed under the SEATO treaty, he disclaimed any necessity for it. In a starkly Orwellian manner, he launched a ferocious attack on the sovereign nation of Cambodia in order to, as he put it, protect American troops. He sharply escalated the secret CIA war in Laos without congressional authorization. When the Congress several times passed resolutions forbidding the president from conducting operations in Cambodia and Laos, Nixon claimed the resolutions to be nonbinding, superseded by his own prerogatives as commander in chief.[22] When Congress passed the Mansfield Amendment to the Military Selective Service Act, which declared it the policy of the United States to terminate military operations at the earliest practicable date, the president signed the bill but announced his decision to ignore the amendment. This total arrogance, this claim to absolute power in the conduct of war,[23] would be one of the contributing factors in the forced resignation of Richard Nixon, a story that will appear later in this chapter.

Post-Vietnam Assertiveness. After the rather modest assertion of presidential war powers during the Ford and Carter administrations, President Reagan revived war powers with a vengeance and helped reinvigorate American imperial policy. Faced with a threat to U.S. political and economic interests in Central America and the Caribbean from popular liberation movements, Reagan put into play the full range of powers inherent in his role as commander in chief. In waging an undeclared war against Nicaragua, he authorized the secret mining of harbors, supplied ships for raids on port facilities, and provided helicopters and pilots to carry "contras" deep into Nicaragua. Contrary to explicit promises made to Congress, Reagan used a series of maneuvers in Honduras (Big Pine I, II, and III) to build a permanent military infrastructure (bases, airstrips, radar installations, supply depots) for the waging of counterinsurgency war in Central America. The number of military advisers in Central America, again contrary to explicit promises, escalated from 150 in 1983 to almost 2,600 in 1984. By 1984, U.S. military personnel were flying tactical support missions over El Salvador, manning radar posts, and training the military forces of Honduras, El Salvador, and Guatemala. The CIA, for its part, was arming, training, supplying, and funding about 15,000 anti-Nicaraguan guerrillas.[24] Not content to confine itself to strictly military matters, the CIA became deeply involved in ensuring an outcome in the Salvadorian "democratic" elections favorable to U.S. foreign policy objectives.[25] The American invasion of Grenada was carried out in complete secrecy, without congressional authorization, and with strict press censorship and news management.[26] With these actions and the strong popular support they elicited—the invasion of Grenada was, arguably, the simply most important factor in the rebound of Reagan's popularity during his first term—Reagan managed to transcend most of the political and psychological limitations upon the "war powers" imposed during the immediate post-Vietnam war years.

Defensive War on the Home Front. Another indicator of the enormous aggrandizement of the presidency based on the broad interpretation of war powers is that several presidents have claimed the right to suspend basic constitutional rights and liberties during war emergencies. Lincoln, for instance, censored the press, suspended habeas corpus, and tried civilians in military courts. Wilson censored the press even more than had Lincoln, assumed near-dictatorial powers over the domestic economy, and launched a vigorous campaign against radicals and their organizations. Franklin Roosevelt authorized the forced removal of Japanese-Americans from the West Coast into "internment" camps in the western deserts. Truman instituted an elaborate system of security checks for government employees. Kennedy and Johnson gave the FBI and CIA, as well as the military intelligence services, leave to spy on the activities of American citizens. And Richard Nixon, as always carrying excesses to the extreme, created in the White House what can only be called his own secret police to spy on and harass political opponents and dissident groups. Ronald Reagan tightened controls over the granting of passports to American citizens and visas to foreign visitors with potentially dangerous ideas. Thus the precedents set by Lincoln in the midst of an unprecedented crisis became translated over the years into normal practice, primarily because the concept of defensive war became broadened into the concept of national security.

The twentieth century has witnessed an enormous aggrandizement of presidential power in the conduct of foreign and military affairs. This aggrandizement has been constructed on a constitutional base—an extremely broad interpretation of implied and inherent powers by modern presidents—and on the very real requirements for an expansionist foreign policy to fill certain needs of modern corporate capitalism (for development of this point see Chapter 13). Under Nixon, some of the dangers of an all-powerful president became apparent to other public and private elites as he pursued his own policies not only without consulting other elites but also at their expense. As a result, a wide variety of attempts to limit unchecked presidential power and discretion in military and foreign policy were legislated in the 1970s by Congress. Nevertheless, while Congress has gained a greater role in these matters (by passing the War Powers Act, in particular),[27] the president remains the key actor in these policy areas. And as the generally enthusiastic public reaction to President Ford's action to rescue the supply ship Mayagüez and to President Reagan's "rescue" of American medical students in Grenada suggest, the president has almost unlimited power to act in emergencies, whether they be real, imagined, or manufactured.

THE PRESIDENT AS SOCIAL AND ECONOMIC MANAGER

We have seen the broadening of the responsibilities and powers of the presidential office as America expanded the reach of its interests and presence around the world. Such expansion is inherent in modern capitalism (as we shall see in Chapter 13) as the search for market outlets, investment opportunities, and safe sources of raw materials become continuing, government-supported activities. There are other sources of presidential aggrandizement tied to the transformation of capitalism as a system, however. The consolidation of the American economy into a relative handful of giant industrial and financial corporations has led to a set of problems (economic instability, excess competition, diseconomies like air and water pollution, social disorganization and crime, and so on) that business has not been able to deal with on a private, voluntary basis, thus causing it to turn gradually to the federal government as the institution best able to provide an environment of stability and predictability. As a result, the twentieth century has witnessed an explosive expansion of government activities ranging from economic management to business regulation, to mediation, to subsidization, to the provision of social services, and much more. As the chief executive and the main executor of government policy, the president has necessarily accumulated expanded responsibilities and powers.

Article II, Section I of the Constitution states that "The executive Power shall be vested in a President of the United States of America," a clause that implies that the business of government is to be executed and administered by the president and his appointees. As it became evident that the requirements of managing society and economy in the twentieth century were either too complicated for Congress or called for a type of initiative and unity of action not available in that branch, the constitutional grant of power became accentuated in practice. The presidency, therefore, increasingly assumed many of the domestic policy-making and managerial functions traditionally left to Congress. Although Congress retains a major role in the formulation of domestic policy and causes the degree of independent action available to the president to be less than that in the conduct of war and foreign affairs, the trends toward the aggrandizement of presidential power and influence are unmistakable.

The President as Chief Legislator

While the Constitution grants both Congress and the president a role in the formulation of policy, it is clear from the constitutional debates that the center of policy making was envisioned to be Congress, with the president acting as the executor and administrator of these policies. Article I says that "all legislative powers herein granted" shall be the responsibility of Congress. Over the years, however, the president has become not only the chief executive of the written Constitution but also the chief legislator of the unwritten one. Let us briefly examine this transformation.

President and Congress in the Early Republic. Conflict over the respective roles of the two branches has been with us since the very beginning of the Republic. The first decades in the life of the new nation saw many tests of the conflicting conceptions of the appropriate relationship between president and Congress. The results of this testing period were anything but decisive, since the first two political parties, the Federalists and the Republicans, remained fundamentally divided on the issue.

The Federalist position, best exemplified in the words and deeds of Alexander Hamilton, embodied an implicit conception of a parliamentary form of government. Hamilton is known to have worked closely with Congress in a manner quite similar to a British cabinet minister, who formulates and introduces policy recommendations. He also conceived of the office of president becoming as powerful as that of a prime minister, and playing a similar legislative role.

This interpretation was firmly rejected by the Jeffersonians, who conceived the primary focus of government initiative to be in the legislative branch. They made their philosophy an operative reality when they attempted to gain strong internal control of Congress by devising standing committees as a counter to the executive during the Federalist ascendency.

The Jeffersonians were faced with a complex and slightly embarrassing dilemma when Thomas Jefferson became president, for despite his anounced philosophy, he became a very active president, initiating policy actions overseas and purchasing the Louisiana Territory. Jefferson, however, was not disturbed by inconsistency, for as he put it once, "What is practical must often control what is pure theory."[28] Jefferson was also the first president to mobilize partisan support for his legislative initiatives.[29]

After 1808, however, the Jeffersonians lacked the strong leadership afforded by their preceptor. The party caucus, which under Jefferson had been an instrument for executive control of Congress, became reversed after his tenure, and "It started on its career of the control of the Executive."[30] Historian Wilfred Binkley claims that in the first quarter of that century, "Congress, by direct election or through the caucus, had chosen every President,"[31] and thus controlled his activities.

Andrew Jackson became the first president since Washington to be nominated and elected outside the confines of Congress, and this represented a decisive development. In 1832 the more democratic convention had replaced the congressional caucus as the presidential nominating instrument. Prior to this, given one-party dominance in the nation, nomination by congressional caucus guaranteed election. With the expansion of suffrage, the responsibility of nomination was removed from congressional control. This marked the transformation of the presidency from a congressional to a popular institution, and for the first time the office became the focus for the aspirations and hopes of the mass population. As a legislative leader, Jackson was the first to make widespread use of the veto and to use the veto message to gain public support for his policies.

While Congress dominated the domestic policy-making process in the nineteenth century, one also sees during that period the seeds of future presidential aggrandizement. For one thing, the precedent of Andrew Jackson proved too powerful to ignore. President James Polk is reported to have said that "The President represents in the executive department the whole people of the United States as each representative of the legislative department represents portions of them." This view has been at the base of most presidential assertions of power to the present day.

The demands of the Civil War enabled Lincoln to assume unprecedented powers, which set guidelines for actions of several future wartime presidents. His actions challenged the Whig philosophy of his own party (e.g., a conception of government in which the legislative branch plays the leading role in formulating national policy, and the executive acts primarily as the executor of that policy) because he claimed that his first duty was to preserve the Union, not the niceties of constitutional law.

> My oath to preserve the constitution imposed on me the duty of preserving by every indispensible means that government, that nation, of which the consti-

tution was the organic law. Was it possible to lose the nation and yet preserve the constitution? . . . I felt that measures, otherwise unconstitutional, might become lawful by becoming indispensible to the preservation of the constitution through the preservation of the nation.[32]

Even during this wartime emergency, however, Congress proved a powerful and assertive coequal branch. The relationship of president and Congress was tense and sometimes hostile. The attempt to deny Lincoln the nomination in 1864 was led by Republican members of Congress. The struggle over which branch of the federal government was to direct Reconstruction led to the formulation of the Republican-sponsored Wade-Davis Manifesto, which made the boldest claim for congressional policy dominance heard in many a year and which became the prevailing philosophy for the remainder of the nineteenth century. The Manifesto stated that the president must "confine himself to his executive duties, to obey and execute, not to make the laws." The strength of this viewpoint was made brutally clear when Congress took the unprecedented step of impeaching a sitting president who tried to defy the will of Congress. Though Congress failed to convict the president, its domination was assured for the remainder of the nineteenth century. As political scientist and later President Woodrow Wilson put it in his classic work *Congressional Government*, "The business of the President, occasionally great, is usually not much above routine. Most of the time it is *mere* administration, mere obedience of directions from the masters of policy, the Standing Committees."[33] The precedents of Jackson, Polk, and Lincoln lay dormant for later use as Congress became the center of national policy making. To an extent not seen before in American history, the period from 1865 to 1902 was largely one in which Congress legislated and the president executed and administered. This procedure was perfectly consistent with the general ideology of the American people and with the requirements of the business community at this stage of its development.

President and Congress in the Twentieth Century. The beginning of the transformation in the legislative relationships of the two branches was affected by the ascendency of Teddy Roosevelt to the presidential office at the very time when America was launched into its imperialist adventure and when the corporations were beginning to turn to government for assistance. With Roosevelt, the presidential personality and the times were congruent, the perfect ingredients to effect the transformation. Roosevelt was a true disciple of Jackson. He strongly believed that he carried a mandate from the people that was broader and more profound than the one carried by Congress, divided as it was among narrow special interests. In a bold expansion of the concept of the presidency, Roosevelt felt that the executive power was limited only by specific restrictions and prohibitions appearing in the Constitution. Most important, Roosevelt believed that the president carried primary responsibility for legislation, since he was the instrument through which the will of the people was expressed.

After another brief lapse of presidential initiative, Woodrow Wilson solidified

FDR: the first great manager of corporate capitalism

the legislative-activist concept of the office. He came to see his office as a unifying force in a highly complex society and economy. He believed that without strong presidential leadership, the system would falter and stagnate. True to his concept of president as prime minister, Wilson worked closely with Congress, initiated policy recommendations, and exerted strong influence over the legislative process in his perceived roles as party leader and elected tribune of the people. He was also the first president to personally deliver the "State of the Union Message."

The Republican ascendency of the 1920s briefly and partially returned the office to the passivity so consistent with the Republican tradition. It took the trauma of the "Great Crash" and Franklin Roosevelt to enshrine permanently the Jacksonian concept of the office in the institutions of American government. The crisis of the Great Depression, the smashing electoral victory of 1932, and the legislative skill of Franklin Roosevelt resulted in the famous "100 days," the high-water mark of presidential leadership in legislation until Lyndon Johnson's first years. Roosevelt's behavior during this period of legislative productivity permanently influenced the office. Other presidents before Roosevelt had drafted bills and sent them to Congress, but Roosevelt made such an impact on the popular mind that today the public knows the president primarily as chief legislator. He was prepared to recommend any measures that a stricken nation in the midst of a crippling depression might require. The precedent he set of sending a message to Congress, accompanied by detailed legislative proposals, prevails to this day. Roosevelt, in fact, sent more messages and draft proposals to Congress than any previous president.

The incumbency of Harry Truman is significant in the growth of the president's role as legislative leader, for he was the first to submit a full-range legislative program to Congress for its consideration. Richard Neustadt defines the full-range program as ''. . . the elaborate paraphernalia of a comprehensive and specific inventory, contents settled and defined as regards substance no less than finance, presented in detailed fashion and packaged form at the opening of each session of Congress.''[34]

This revolution in presidential relations with Congress can be traced to several factors. In 1944, Franklin Roosevelt announced his ''Economic Bill of Rights,'' which promised a broad program of governmental involvement in solving economic ills. The Employment Act of 1946 further obligated future presidents to this type of action. It stated that ''The President shall transmit to Congress at the beginning of each session . . . a program to carry out . . . policy.'' Intensifying this movement to submit full-range legislative programs were the rush of public needs and expectations arising from postwar reconversion and the crisis in Cold War foreign policy. Finally, as is often the case with government programs, the recurrent use of the presidential legislative program created a momentum and survival power of its own, which became built into the institutional arrangements and expectations of Congress, the executive agencies, and the presidential staff.

It is significant that even Dwight Eisenhower, a firm believer in the Whig philosophy, was expected by most sectors of government and the public to submit a full-range legislative program to Congress. When he failed to do so in 1954, he created a furor. One legislator explained the facts of life to an Eisenhower senior official like this: ''Don't expect us to start from scratch on what you people want. . . . That's not the way we do things here. You draft the bills and we work them over.''[35] Eisenhower never made the same mistake again. After 1954, his administration conformed to legislative expectations. Today, the presentation of such a legislative program by the president, though a rather recent innovation, is an accepted and expected part of the American political tradition. A president who would fail to formulate such a program and present it to Congress would be considered derelict in the performance of his duties. The role of Congress has become primarily that of modifying, approving, or rejecting the legislative program of the president.

While the historical trends suggest a general enhancement of the presidential role in legislation, it is not the case that each and every president is as successful or accomplished in this activity as every other president. Indeed, both the legislative skill of the incumbent as well as a national mood demanding decisive action on the part of the president seems to be central to the legislative legacy of the office. One is reminded of the early New Deal of Franklin Roosevelt, the Great Society programs of the Johnson years, and the budget and tax initiatives of the first Reagan administration. What we have then is a picture in which the presidential legislative role waxes and wanes along a trend line in which the office's general role in this area steadily increases. Jimmy Carter showed himself to be a poor constitutional scholar yet a perceptive analyst of contemporary American politics when he observed that " . . . Congress is not capable of leadership. Our Founding Fathers never felt the Congress would lead this country."[36]

Delegation of Powers

The president's growing responsibility for the conduct of the nation's business has been further accelerated by Congress's own recognition that it is incapable of providing specific policy direction in many areas of government activity and thus tends to delegate to the president a great deal of discretionary power. Increasingly, as new problem areas in American life become visible, Congress usually constructs very broad and vague guidelines within which it allows the president and his appointees to make policy. Increasingly, Congress provides the guidelines and leaves it to the executive departments to fill in the details, but the details are often more important than the guidelines.

Examples of such delegations are almost too numerous to mention. During World War I Congress granted President Woodrow Wilson extraordinary powers to manage the economy, an action political scientist Rexford Tugwell has called "the most fantastic expansion of the executive power known to the American experience." Tariffs on imported goods since 1922 have been generally set by the president within limits authorized by Congress. The president has been granted the power to vary the rate of the *interest equalization tax* to regulate foreign investments and the balance of payments. Since 1931, Congress has granted to the president the right to reorganize the executive branch in order to effect budgetary savings. The Federal Salary Act of 1967 authorized the president to adjust salaries to close the gap between public and private pay scales. In 1921, Congress transferred the responsibility (and the power) for formulating the federal budget to the president. In the Employment Act of 1946, Congress authorized the president to make a report on the economic health of the United States and to formulate a plan to ensure economic stability, economic prosperity, and full employment. In the midst of the economic crisis of the early 1970s, the Economic Stabilization Act of 1970 gave the president the power to impose controls on wages and prices at his discretion. During the energy crisis of 1972, at a time when the administration of Richard Nixon was beginning to disintegrate under the blows of the Watergate revelations and had lost most of its legitimacy, Congress nevertheless delegated broad powers over oil imports and duties to the president. In 1976, Congress passed the National Emergency Act which grants the president broad powers in the face of a national emergency. Congress left to the president alone the power to declare an emergency and to exercise extraordinary power for a period of six months.[37]

The Spending Power

Evolving at the same time as the president's role as legislative leader and policy maker through delegated powers, and intimately related to both, is the president's growing *spending power*, his control over the spending of federal monies. While most Americans are aware of the prominent role of the presidential office in the appropriations process (primarily as maker of the budget, though Congress has the final word on the appropriations side), few are aware of the powerful policy-making developments inherent in his control of the spending process. As political scientist Louis Fisher points out, "Billions of dollars are impounded, transferred, reprogrammed, or shifted in one way or another by the president and his assistants. Billions more are used in confidential and covert ways, without the knowledge of Congress and the public. In many cases, the decisive commitment to spend funds is made not by Congress but by executive officials."[38] While much of the president's independent discretion was pared by the Budget and Impoundment Act of 1974, passed in the wake of the Nixon excesses, the presidential spending powers remain formidable.

THE PRESIDENCY AND THE CAPITALIST CLASS

The rise of the presidency is tied to the transformation of the American economy from one characterized by small competitive and domestically oriented enterprises to one characterized by an economy of concentrated multinational giants. This new form of capitalist economy requires a stable, predictable environment for the conduct of its far-flung business activities, an environment made possible only through the intervention, support, and cooperation of the federal government. (See Chapters 13–14 for an in-depth consideration of these points.) Only the government is capable of providing the framework of legitimacy, the instruments of social control, and the fiscal and monetary mechanisms necessary for the continued health and prosperity of the corporate-dominated economy. Finally, because of certain structural and representational problems in Congress (see Chapter 12) as well as certain inherent qualities in the constitutional design of the executive branch, the role of the presidency has become increasingly dominant as the responsibilities and activities of the federal government have themselves expanded. Because the executive is the most unified and energetic branch, the explosive expansion in the role of the government, almost as a matter of course, has redounded to the benefit of the president.

All the qualities of the office, as well as the forces in the economy and society that originally led to the aggrandizement of the presidency, remain intact and operative today. Indeed, Ronald Reagan has managed to renew the process of aggrandizement temporarily halted during the Ford and Carter administrations, a development encouraged and welcomed by most business and financial leaders.

Corporate capitalism continues to require a government that ensures social stability, stimulates a sense of popular legitimacy, and guarantees growth and profits. The office of the president, because of its special qualities and because of the deficiencies of Congress, remains the institution best able to provide the leadership for a government capable of providing such services.

No president is a free agent able to act entirely as he wishes. Invariably his actions are constrained by his need to satisfy the demands of the most powerful groups and institutions in the nation. As presidential scholar Thomas Cronin has suggested, "Ours is a system decidedly weighted against radical leadership, a system that encourages most presidents, most of the time, to respond to the powerful, organized, and already represented interests at the expense of the unrepresented."[39] What this statement means is that presidents are most responsive to the wishes, needs, and demands of powerfully organized business interests, particularly the major corporations and financial institutions. While few presidents have made their commitments as explicit as Calvin Coolidge when he uttered his famous quote, "The business of America is business," most operate on the assumption "that harmony and confidence between government and business are profitable to both."[40] Why is this so? First, as indicated in detail in Chapter 8, presidents must act in such a way that they maintain the confidence of business leaders and ensure an economic environment conducive to profitable investment. The president's popularity and thus much of his ability to effect a domestic program and foreign policy objectives is dependent upon state of the economy and the sense of well-being felt by the American people. Since businesspeople cannot be forced to make productive, job-creating investments in the American economy, government must induce them to do so. They are induced, in the main, by public policies that encourage and ensure profitability, especially among the most powerful economic actors and enterprises in the system. Thus, while no president can afford to respond to every whim of important business leaders, all his actions are bounded by the need to maintain "business confidence." Even liberal presidents have discovered that programs purportedly aimed to relieve the suffering of the poor and the weak are less likely to be opposed if such programs provide benefits to the business community.

There are many examples of liberal presidents conforming, in the end, to corporate needs.[41] John F. Kennedy's angry public attack on the U.S. Steel Corporation for raising prices in 1962 led to the greatest one-day loss in stock value in the history of the New York Stock Exchange ($21 billion in losses) and sharp declines in indicators of corporate investment. Both developments portended the coming of a serious recession. Much of the remainder of Kennedy's presidency was spent courting business leadership and making amends. Most importantly, JFK overruled the advice of many of his key advisers and decided to make tax cuts for corporations and upper income individuals and cuts in domestic programs the centerpieces of his expansionary economic policy.[42]

Lyndon Johnson, for his part, coupled the domestic reforms of his Great Society to a series of actions designed to maintain business confidence. He appointed

Henry Fowler, legal counsel to the powerful Business Council, to head the Department of the Treasury. He sought the advice of the Business Council itself during numerous meetings held in the White House throughout 1964 and 1965 (a typical meeting might include Watson of IBM, Rockefeller of Chase Manhattan Bank, Donner of GM, and Cook of Merrill Lynch). Johnson's Attorney General Nicholas Katzenbach assured business leaders that vigorous antitrust actions were not on the president's agenda. As one big business leader said in an anonymous interview with *Newsweek*, "What the hell, business is making money. We've solved every damn problem except unemployment. We've got a President who listens to us, and one of our own men is Secretary of Commerce. It's no wonder you see people smiling."[43]

Jimmy Carter—the last of the liberal presidents and a man elected on a platform advocating national health insurance, more generous social welfare programs, and labor law reforms—began to court big business almost immediately after his election. He undertook active policy consultation with business leaders, especially Shapiro of DuPont, Jones of General Electric, Murphy of GM, and DeButts of AT&T. While offering stronger human rights policies in foreign affairs and stricter enforcement of environmental laws, he also supported corporate tax cuts, cuts in social spending, deficit reductions, and deregulation of business favored by corporate leaders. His efforts in support of the creation of a Consumer Protection Agency and the reform of the nation's labor laws, an effort strongly supported by organized labor, were desultory. Finally, in the campaign to slay the dragon of "stagflation," Carter chose to pursue a strict monetarist policy (when he appointed Paul Volker to head the Federal Reserve Board), an approach long favored by business and the Republican party.

Second, we can see the close linkages between the requirements of corporate capitalism and presidential behavior in the typical pattern of appointments to policy-making positions in the executive branch. To put it simply, representatives of major corporations dominate policy-making positions. Since the executive branch has become the most important policy-making branch of the federal government, this fact is of considerable importance. One must conclude that the pattern of appointments of federal executive positions is not random but reflects the close interlock and collusion between executive branch and the dominant economic class.

This linkage is so close that even presidents with a strong reformist image act very much the same way as other presidents when it comes to key appointments. Jimmy Carter, to take a case in point, campaigned as an "outsider" who would bring fresh ideas and faces to Washington, yet he populated his upper level appointments with people from the same elite institutions. As White House correspondent James Wooten described matters,

> Like so many Presidents before him, he is populating the Cabinet and upper federal echelons with a gallery of lawyers, bankers, professors, economists, consultants and blue-chip executives who share overlapping relationships with such

institutional pillars as the International Business Machines Corporation, Harvard, the General Motors Corporation, Princeton, the Chase Manhattan Bank, Yale, the Coca-Cola Company and Columbia.[44]

Ronald Reagan, being an unabashed friend and supporter of dominant economic interests, did not depart from the conventional pattern except that he tended to give greater prominence in his appointments to sun-belt corporations.

Third, and perhaps most important, we can see the close linkages between the president and corporate capital in the vital role played by the latter in determining who shall be president. Standing dominant at critical points in the long, complicated, and even tortuous process by which the American people designate those few persons out of millions who are of presidential caliber, leaders of the main economic institutions of American life help determine the boundaries of political life in the United States. Let us look at this process in greater detail.

Few Americans realize that nominating a president and defining the pool of eligibles is a far more important process in terms of public policy than the election itself. The former takes a universe of perhaps 100 million people who are constitutionally eligible for the office (in terms of age, birthplace, lack of criminal record, and so forth) and winnows it down to two. The election is merely a selection between two candidates who are customarily indistinguishable from each other in terms of ideology or program (see Chapter 9). The process of "winnowing," the process that undergirds nomination itself, determines the not more than a score of men who are actually eligible. The role of dominant elites is crucial in this process.

There are, first of all, some traditional screening devices for shrinking the pool. Candidates are normally from states with large blocs of electoral votes, though this is becoming less the case today. Candidates for the top office are almost always men. While constitutionally eligible, women have never been seriously considered a part of the pool of eligibles. Candidates have almost always been Protestant, and few Horatio Algers dot their ranks. Finally, candidates are not of the "Cincinnatus" variety, drawn reluctantly from private life by the wishes of their fellow citizens. Rather, they are almost always professional politicians who actively seek the office. We can already see, if we are guided by these informal yet operative criteria, that our original pool of approximately 100 million is now no more than several thousand.

The several thousand are narrowed to a relative handful by the judgment of dominant elites that a very few of their number are "presidential" in character. It is only by such designation that a potential candidate is taken seriously. It is only after endorsement of some kind by members of Congress, other politicians, financial leaders, heads of foundations, or educators and intellectuals that a person is considered presidential and treated as such by the mass media and the contributors of campaign funds. Potential candidates enter the pool of actual candidates only if and when they are acceptable to other political, business, and media leaders. While an aberrant character such as George Wallace may occasionally slip through, the process effectively screens out extremist candidates, particularly of an anticapitalist variety.

The ability to attract money is both an important part of the definition of a serious candidate and a byproduct of such a designation. That is, the ability to attract big money is one of the indicators by which opinion leaders differentiate those who are serious candidates from those who are not. Once designated as a person of presidential timber, the candidate more easily attracts contributions. Money is a critical aspect—probably the most important aspect, given the costs of modern campaigns—in determining presidential candidates.

While ceilings on total campaign spending and contributions now exist because of campaign finance reforms, the linkage between money and presidential politics remains a strong one as we saw in Chapter 9. Given the way income and wealth is distributed in the United States, it should occasion no surprise to learn that in one way or another all campaign money comes from people connected to powerful business enterprises. This historic linkage is made even tighter by the phenomenon of the rapidly proliferating corporate political action committees that can spend unlimited amounts of money in political campaigns so long as the money does not go directly into the coffer of a candidate's official electoral organization.

The availability of money to finance a nomination campaign is the key factor in determining who will be a serious candidate for the presidency, and the source of that money is almost exclusively the dominant corporate class. It would be naive to suppose that this money is given in a random, disinterested way. While few give money as a quid pro quo for future favors, most contribute to ensure the availability of safe, accessible presidents, sympathetic to the business point of view. There is little question that such contributors have enjoyed a good return on their investment.

CONCLUDING REMARKS

The history of the presidency is a history of aggrandizement of power and responsibility. During that history, the institution has been fundamentally transformed from the office intended by the Founders. This transformation is explained not by the whims of presidents or random historical events but by the transformation of capitalism into its modern, concentrated corporate form, a form that requires an interventionist government with vigorous leadership at the top. It is true, of course, that "gliches" have occasionally appeared in the presidential aggrandizement trend line—the administrations of Ford and Carter being the most recent examples—yet the upward tilt of the line has been inexorable. This development has had profound implications for the other branches of the federal government, a subject we shall explore in the next chapter.

NOTES

1. The important relationship between transformations in the American economy and government policy is examined in depth in chapters 13–14.
2. The observation that presidential power ultimately rests on the ability to persuade is best articulated by Richard Neustadt in his modern classic *Presidential Power* (New York: Columbia University Press, 1963).
3. Quoted in Neustadt, *Presidential Power.*
4. The White House staff includes more than six hundred persons ranging from close advisors to speechwriters, public relations experts, cooks, valets, butlers, gardeners, caretakers for pets, and even joke writers.
5. The common touch of Jimmy Carter—walking up Pennsylvania Avenue at his inauguration, staying with local families during his travels, taking phone calls from ordinary citizens, selling the presidential yacht *Sequoia*—was soon overwhelmed by the kingly trappings of the office. Ronald Reagan was never tempted by the "folksy" touch and began his term with an inaugural ball that rivaled the celebrations of European royalty.
6. Theodore White, *The Making of the President,* 1960 (New York: Atheneum, 1961), pp. 170–71.
7. Joseph Califano, advisor to Lyndon Johnson and later HEW secretary under Jimmy Carter, tells of the time when, after a speech at a military base, LBJ was walking toward the wrong plane for his departure. An airman directed him toward another plane, saying, "Mr. President, your plane is over there." Johnson responded by saying, "Son, all of them are my planes."
8. Dean Acheson, *Present at the Creation* (New York: Signet, 1970), p. 539.
9. From Woodrow Wilson's *Constitutional Government in the United States,* quoted in James M. Burns, *Presidential Government* (Boston: Houghton Mifflin, 1965), p. 96.
10. Political scientist Michael Nelson demonstrates how pervasive is the idea of the need for a strong and decisive presidency among scholars, journalists, members of Congress, federal bureaucrats, and the American people. See his essay "Evaluating the Presidency," in Michael Nelson (ed.), *The Presidency and the Political System* (Washington, D.C.: CQ Press, 1984).
11. Quoted in Thomas E. Cronin, *The State of the Presidency* (Boston: Little, Brown, 1980), p. 103.
12. Quoted in Robert Denton, Jr., *The Symbolic Dimensions of the American Presidency* (Prospect Heights, Ill.: Waveland, 1982), p. 119.
13. Cronin, *The State of the Presidency*, p. 96. The unravelling of the presidencies of Nixon, Ford, and Carter demonstrates that the reverential expectations of the office are often very hard to meet and that both elites and the public are capable of venting their disappointment against the incumbent. The failures of our icons, that is to say, can be as spectacular as their successes.
14. All presidents are, of course, anxious to encourage media coverage and devote much of their staff capability toward that end. In the Nixon White House, a staff of over one hundred was involved in some form of news dissemination and/or public relations. It is important to note, of course, that in the end it did Nixon little good, which should alert us to the fact that television might also act to magnify faults as well as virtues in a president and thereby occasionally hinder as much as help him.
15. *The New York Times*, July 29, 1971, p. 25.

16. Quoted in Arthur Schlesinger, Jr., "Congress and the Making of Foreign Policy," in Thomas Cronin and Rexford Tugwell, eds., *The Presidency Reappraised*, 2nd ed. (New York: Praeger, 1977), p. 216.

17. Arthur Schlesinger, Jr., *The Imperial Presidency* (New York: Popular Library, Atlantic Monthly Press, 1973), p. 11.

18. Much of this discussion of "defensive war" is based on the discussion in Schlesinger, *The Imperial Presidency.*

19. Quoted in ibid, p. 36.

20. Quoted in ibid, p. 54.

21. Eisenhower made more claims of executive privilege in his first term as president than all other presidents combined in the first one hundred years of the Republic.

22. Future Watergate hero Elliot Richardson had the following to say to the Senate Appropriations Committee in 1973 when told that funding would be suspended for the Cambodian operations: "We will consider that we have the authority to do it anyway. We can find the money to do it anyway. . . . "

23. These assertions of presidential prerogative were by no means limited to Vietnam, as the American complicity in the overthrow of the legitimate government of Allende of Chile so clearly indicates. For that tragic story, see chapter 13.

24. Hedrick Smith, "U.S. Latin Forces in Place," *The New York Times* (April 23, 1984), p. 1.

25. Phillip Taubman, "CIA Said to Have Given Money to 2 Salvador Parties," *The New York Times* (May 12, 1984), p. 1.

26. Next to the Korean Airline incident, the invasion of Grenada represents perhaps the most sophisticated "disinformation" campaign in recent American history (See "K.A.L. 007: What the U.S. Knew and When It Knew It," *The Nation* (August 18–25, 1984) pp. 105–124). The invasion itself had been well prepared during a series of maneuvers in Puerto Rico during the previous year. U.S. forces were in readiness well in advance of the invasion and were awaiting the proper incident. Medical school officials were approached prior to the invasion and invited to declare their students to be in danger and in need of rescue. News of Grenadian government guarantees of student safety and the free flow of civilian air traffic in and out of Grenada was suppressed until well after the invasion itself.

27. The War Powers Act was passed on November 7, 1973, over the veto of President Nixon. The act limits a president's ability to wage an undeclared war to a period of sixty days and requires him to report to Congress any commitment of combat forces abroad within forty-eight hours of their use. Needless to say, much can be done in sixty days that is difficult to render undone, given the nature of modern warfare. Moreover, in the crisis atmosphere that would invariably be generated by the use of American troops, it is unlikely that Congress would do anything to hinder a president's conduct of hostilities even with a report in its hands.

28. This quote and most of the remaining quotes in this section are from Wilfred E. Binkley, *The Powers of the President* (Garden City, N.J.: Doubleday, 1937).

29. Stephen J. Wayne, *The Legislative Presidency* (New York: Harper and Row, 1978), p. 9.

30. Binkley, *The Powers of the President*, p. 54.

31. *Ibid.,* p. 64.

32. Lincoln to Hendon, February 15, 1848. Abraham Lincoln, *Collected Works,* Vol. 1, R. P. Basler, ed. (New Brunswick, N.J.: Rutgers University Press), pp. 451–452.

33. (New York: New American Library, 1956), p. 170.
34. Richard E. Neustadt, "Presidency and Legislation: Planning the President's Program," *American Political Science Review* 49 (December 1955), p. 981.
35. Quoted in Wayne, *The Legislative Presidency,* p. 19.
36. Quoted in the *National Journal* XX11 (May 29, 1976), p. 739.
37. Aaron S. Liemen, "Preparing for the Hour of Need: The National Emergencies Act," *Presidential Studies Quarterly* 60 (Winter 1978), pp. 47–64.
38. Louis Fisher, *Presidential Spending Power* (Princeton, N.J.: Princeton University Press, 1975), p. 3. The discussion in this section is based largely on Fisher's work.
39. Cronin, *The State of the Presidency,* p. 144.
40. Louis W. Koenig, *The Chief Executive* (New York: Harcourt, Brace, Jovanovich, 4th ed., 1981). Note that Ronald Reagan, on more than one occasion, has articulated his admiration for Coolidge.
41. See Kim McQuaid, *Big Business and Presidential Power* (New York: William Morrow, 1982) for details.
42. Ronald Reagan borrowed the strategy in 1981 and made continual references to the memory of JFK while doing so.
43. Quoted in McQuaid, *Big Business and Presidential Power,* p. 236.
44. *The New York Times,* February 4, 1977.

SUGGESTIONS FOR FURTHER READING

James David Barber. THE PRESIDENTIAL CHARACTER. *Englewood Cliffs, N.J.: Prentice-Hall, 1972.* A compelling psychological analysis of the people who have filled the presidential office.

Thomas E. Cronin. THE STATE OF THE PRESIDENCY, 2nd ed. *Boston: Little, Brown 1980.* A solid and comprehensive treatment of the presidential office in the post-Watergate period.

George Edwards III. THE PUBLIC PRESIDENCY. *New York: St. Martin's Press, 1983.* This book examines the many ways presidents pursue public support for their programs and some of the obstacles they meet along the way.

Kim McQuaid. BIG BUSINESS AND PRESIDENTIAL POWER. *New York: William Morrow, 1982.* The most complete treatment in the literature on the relationship between the presidency and the capitalist class.

Michael Nelson, (ed.). THE PRESIDENCY AND THE POLITICAL SYSTEM. *Washington, D.C.: Congressional Quarterly Press, 1984.* A comprehensive collection of essays representing the very best of recent scholarship on the American presidency.

Richard Neustadt. PRESIDENTIAL POWER. *New York: Columbia University Press, 1963.* An early and influential work calling for the further concentration of presidential power.

Richard M. Pious. THE AMERICAN PRESIDENCY. *New York: Basic Books, 1979.* The most exhaustive treatment of the development and performance of the office, presented with a strong constitutional emphasis.

Arthur Schlesinger. THE IMPERIAL PRESIDENCY. *New York: Atlantic Monthly Press, 1973.* A comprehensive analysis of the drift toward presidential government in the United States.

12

President,
Congress,
and the Bureaucracy

As the president attempts to provide coherent leadership for the American system, he finds, more often than not, that the main obstacles standing in his way are his purported partners in the governing process in Washington: Congress and the bureaucracy. There are any number of reasons why this tends to be the prevailing situation—constitutional, political, personal—yet no reason is as powerful as that which locates governmental structure and processes in the capitalist system itself. I have argued at various points in this book that American political institutions can only be understood in relationship to the capitalist system in which they are imbedded and by which they are shaped. This is true, we have seen, for the electoral, interest group, and social protest systems. It is also true, as we discovered in the last chapter, with regard to the presidency. In this chapter, we shall see how capitalism helps define the overall structure and mission of Congress and the federal bureaucracy as well as the relationship of each of them to the presidency.

The key to understanding these institutions, in my view, is the distinction that must be made between *particular* and *general* interests in capitalism. Because capitalism is a system in which enterprises are always, in some sense, in competition with each other in the marketplace, the interests of each enterprise are, to a significant degree, in opposition to the interests of other enterprises. Each is self-interested; each has a *particular* interest which it attempts to maximize in relationship to other enterprises. Each may sometimes turn to government to advance its own interests. Because capitalism is also a system in which the capitalist class as a whole stands in opposition to the working class as a whole (see Chapter

251

3), and in which enterprises share the desire for an overall environment conducive to economic growth and profitability, dominant economic actors hold many fundamental interests in common. They share, that is to say, many *general* interests as a class which they often attempt to advance through government. Much of the drama of American politics derives from this inescapable tension between particular and general interests and the attempt by government to reconcile and ease this tension.

I take the position in this chapter that Congress and the federal bureaucracy are the main respositories at the national level for the representation of narrow and particularistic interests while the presidency is the main repository for the representation of general interests. Much of the tension and perpetual political struggle between the presidency and the other two, I further argue, is derived from these differences in forms of representation and uncertainty about which form shall prevail in the determination of public policy. Finally, I suggest that the dominant trend since at least World War II has been a significant strengthening of the resources of the presidency relative to Congress and the bureaucracy in an attempt to better protect and advance the common interests of the dominant capitalist class.

PRESIDENT AND CONGRESS

If the history of the presidency is a history of the aggrandizement of power, as suggested in the last chapter, then the history of Congress is one of declining influence, competency, and policy leadership. The end result of these twin developments is that Congress is, today, less than a coequal branch of the federal government, lost in the shadows of the more powerful executive even in an era of post-Watergate legislative assertiveness. Congress finds itself, in particular, unable to act as a formulator of coherent policy for the American system as a whole. It has increasingly ceded that power and responsibility to the president and is now content with a secondary though not unimportant role as representative of narrow interests.

These developments represent a major historical and constitutional transformation in the relative positions of the two branches. It is abundantly clear that the founding fathers conceived of Congress as the main national policy-making branch of the federal government, with the president conceived primarily as the executor and administrator of policy determined in the legislative branch. Indeed, with the notable exceptions of the Jefferson, Polk, and Lincoln administrations, Congress played the leading policy-making role for most of the nineteenth century. Speakers of the House of Representatives during that century were the equals of presidents. Speaker Henry Clay was at least as important in the affairs of governance as were Presidents Madison, Monroe, and Adams. President John Quincy Adams returned to the House of Representatives at the expiration of his term, an act unimaginable in the present era of the imperial presidency. That Americans are not generally cognizant of the preeminent position of Congress in the last century reflects our tendency to read back into our past history the general presidential dominance of our own day.

It should be pointed out, however, that while Congress has suffered a historical loss of power as a policy-making institution, it is not powerless. Indeed, compared with the legislative bodies of other western nations, Congress is exceptional in the degree to which it plays a continuous and vital role relative to the executive. Because of its constitutional role in legislation and the independent bases of political power of its members, Congress is necessarily central to the formulation of public policy and its voice must be attended to by every president. While it cannot itself formulate national policy, it has the capacity to undermine the president's ability to do the same. While its power is primarily negative in that it can be exercised to block presidential initiatives, it is power nevertheless, and not to be trifled with or ignored. Presidents do so at their own peril.

Representation in Congress

While members of Congress represent in a formal sense the people of their districts or states, in reality they represent those groups and persons that can most directly influence their continued tenure in office: e.g., those that can either mobilize people to vote in the context of low turnout elections (which is true of most congressional elections) and/or those that control the flow of contributions to the campaign treasury. Members of Congress, for very rational reasons, are most attuned either to interest groups that are well organized and financed nationally (such as the gun lobby and organized medicine) or to those powerful business

President Reagan meets with congressional leaders

groups and organizations in their constituencies who can directly affect their political future. It is not at all surprising or uncommon to find senators from oil-producing states supporting depletion allowances and tax breaks for the oil industry; representatives from farming districts supporting the wishes of the Farm Bureau or various agricultural commodity organizations; senators from the south supporting growers of cotton, peanuts, or tobacco; those from the Rocky Mountain region supporting the interests of mining companies; or representatives from areas where a single company dominates supporting the legislative desires of that company (U.S. Steel in Gary, Indiana; Anaconda Copper in Montana; Boeing Aircraft in Seattle; Lockheed in Sunnyvale, California; and so on). While Congress may occasionally respond to popular mobilization and mass protest (see Chapter 10), it does so only rarely and episodically for it is an institution that is not very hospitable to the unorganized and the powerless. In this respect, Congress is no different than the other institutions of American political life.

We can best conceptualize Congress as a collection of representatives for special, well-organized, well-financed, and narrow interests. It is the sum total of scattered local interest groups, industries, and other business elites. In candidly explaining his job to a group of businesspeople in his home state, one turn-of-the-century senator said the following:

> I believe in a division of labor. You send us to Congress; we pass laws under
> . . . which you make money, . . . and out of your profits you further contribute
> to our campaign funds to send us back again to pass more laws to enable you to
> make more money.[1]

While Congress primarily represents the most powerful and privileged, it represents them in their fragments. It becomes an arena in which individual or groups of corporations compete with each other, strike bargains, and make compromises. It is a place where the general policies formulated by the chief executive are amended and altered in light of the needs of a wide range of narrow interests. It is in Congress, for instance, where efforts to create a national energy policy pay attention to the needs of powerful utilities and energy corporations.

This representation of very narrow business interests has been greatly enhanced, ironically, by reforms in the campaign finance laws and subsequent interpretations of these laws. By placing limits on contributions to presidential candidates, but remaining silent on candidates for House and Senate seats, the 1974 and 1976 election laws helped redirect special interest money, mainly from business groups, into congressional races. The election laws and interpretations of those laws by the courts and by the Federal Election Commission (enabling corporations to freely raise money from both their stockholders and employees) have also helped encourage the rapid formation of corporate political action committees (PACs) with great leeway for raising and spending money in campaigns.[2]

The narrow interest representation is one of the key factors in the historical decline of Congress as a national policy-making institution, for such a form of representation makes it difficult for Congress as an institution to formulate coherent policy for the nation and the corporate system as a whole. A senator or representative is inescapably a spokesperson for a narrow set of particularistic interests. Although Congress is an effective institution for the representation of the interests of individual business enterprises or particular industries, it is generally unable to bring these interests together and make policy for the capitalist class as a whole. Thus bills to assist individual companies or particular wealthy individuals flow easily through the complex machinery of Congress ("private member bills"), while policies relevant to the problems of capitalism as a whole, like those related to energy or the economy, are left by default to the initiative of the president.

Why Congress Cannot Be a National or Class Policy Leader

I have suggested that the presidency has become the center of policy initiative and policy coherence in the national government and that this development may be partially explained by the fragmented and narrow interest representation in Congress. The difficulties faced by Congress as a policy maker derived from its narrow interest representation is further exacerbated by the way Congress fragments power and makes leadership difficult to attain. The organization and operations of Congress, in fact, make it a nearly perfect haven for the protection and nourishment of narrow and particularistic interests.

Constitutional Organization. As described in Chapter 4, the Founders, fearful of a vital national government open to popular pressures, designed a government of "checks and balances." One of the most important of these checks on popularly fueled coherent public policy (which might threaten private property, in the view of James Madison) was the organization of Congress, the most popular branch, into two separate houses, each capable of checking the actions of the other. Not only was Congress created as a *bicameral* legislature, but it was divided into two bodies of radically different size and constituency base. The House of Representatives, designed by the Founding Fathers as the more popular chamber, today contains 435 members, each of whom represents (with some exceptions) some subsection of one of the states. Each of these congressional districts is based on population size, with their boundaries redrawn by each state legislature every decade (based on census reports). The Senate, on the other hand, designed to serve as a check on the possibly precipitous and dangerous action of the more popular branch, is composed of members elected from a statewide constituency. While the evolution of the two houses has not been entirely consistent with the expectations of the writers of the Constitution, the bicameral nature of Congress and its contrasting constituency bases not only serve to slow down the pace of legislation but also significantly decrease the probability that any general purpose legislation will manage to wind its way to completion. These elements of the constitutional organization of Congress make it halting, conservative, and indecisive. The Constitution further contributes to these characteristics by specifying that only one-third of the Senate shall be up for election at any one time, helping to insulate that body from the tides of popular sentiment. By its constitutional organization, then, Congress faces barriers to decisive, popular, and unified action. When groups in the population have wanted such decisive action (meaning both popular and corporate groups), they have generally turned to the other, more energetic institution—the presidency.

Careerism and Incumbency. When viewed in broad historical perspective, another development that serves to fragment and decentralize Congress and make it deficient as a national policy-making institution is the prevalence of *careerism* among its members. Although there has been a small reversal in recent elections, the tendency for nearly two centuries has been the increased importance of age and tenure in Congress.[3] In the twentieth century there has been relatively low turnover in congressional seats when compared with the ninetenth century. In 1900, only 9 percent of all representatives had been in the House more than ten years, while in the modern era the figure approaches 40 percent. In a similar vein, there has been a significantly declining percentage of first-term representatives from the early Republic to modern times.

During the course of American history, moreover, tenure has become increasingly important as the prime prerequisite to positions of power in Congress. Henry Clay was elected Speaker of the House, a position as important as that of the president in the early Republic, during his very first term in office. In modern times such a thing would be unthinkable. The speakership, the chairmanship of major committees, and party leadership posts are open only to those who have served long apprenticeships.

While trends toward incumbency and careerism are now universally recognized, much disagreement about the reasons for these historical trends still exists among observers of congressional life. Political scientist Morris Fiorina argues that incumbency may be most reasonably traced to the rise of a powerful national government. This development has led to the alteration of the main congressional role from lawmaker to supplier of government favors and ombudsman for constituents before the vast federal bureaucracy. Fiorina points out that concentrating on the role of national lawmaker is irrational for a member of the House or Senate, because making laws is inherently controversial; it is likely that some constituents will be upset no matter what position the legislator takes. Supplying "pork barrel" to the district in the way of dams, military installations, federal buildings, sewage treatment plants, and research installations, on the other hand, is generally applauded in the constituency, especially by those who are most likely to contribute to campaign war chests. As the federal government escalates its activities and its annual expenditures, the level of "pork" available to each legislator is enhanced. Furthermore, as government does more every year, as it subsidizes, regulates, and mandates, constituents find that members of Congress are useful as agents to "affect a decision in a favorable way, to reverse an adverse decision, or simply to speed up the glacial bureaucratic process."[4] The longer a member of Congress is in office, the more effective he or she is in such a role. Incumbency is thus an attractive quality when the concerns of a very large part of the public involve gaining favors and dispensations from government agencies.

The changing legislative role from that of lawmaker to that of deliverer of federal dollars and constituent ombudsman to the federal bureaucracy considerably enhances the ability of incumbents to remain in office, if they choose to do so, for it enables them to generally claim credit for government largesse and to listen sympathetically and assist constituents when government seemingly goes awry. A whole range of additional advantages available to incumbents accentuate the electoral advantages gained from this role transformation. Members of Congress, for instance, enjoy the "franking privilege" that allows them to mail information to constituents and media outlets free of charge. They enjoy, furthermore, sizable paid staffs to operate offices both in Washington and the local district. Sizable travel allowances better enable them to return regularly to their districts to "press the flesh." Most important, perhaps, since they are already in positions of influence, incumbents are better able to attract contributions for electoral contests because they are better able to press the claims of important constituents in the myriad halls and offices of the federal government. The great bulk of money from the corporate-sponsored political action committees, for instance, has gone disproportionately to incumbents in recent elections.

Whatever the cause, the increasing importance of incumbency and careerism in Congress is inescapable. The implications of such developments are worth pondering. If members of Congress need not generally fear defeat at the polls, the only mechanism by which votes serve as democratic tools for the control of elected officials is rendered useless. As long as members of Congress deliver federal dollars to their state or district and help important constituents with their bureaucratic problems, they need not worry about whether their voting behavior conforms to constituent positions on the great issues of the day.

Incumbency and careerism have also helped contribute to Congress's ever-greater fragmentation of power and its loss of position as a general policy maker for the nation. From a sense of self-importance, given their long tenure, and from their need to provide services and favors for their districts, members of Congress have sought control of various points of power within the institution, while resisting the lure of centralization and coordination theoretically available in party discipline.

The Committee System. To understand the committee system is, in very large part, to understand Congress as a whole. First created as a way to enhance the policy expertise of Congress and increase its power relative to the president, the committee system has become the perfect environment for protecting and nourishing narrow interests. Power in Congress is scattered in twenty-two standing committees in the House, fifteen in the Senate, and seven major joint committees (on which members of both the House and Senate sit), and further dispersed into a proliferating network of subcommittees (today, well over two hundred). Each major standing committee enjoys jurisdiction over a particular subject matter (these usually parallel the executive departments: justice, interior, commerce, labor, etc.); a sizable professional staff to help it in its work; and a history of general deference from other congressional committees in its area of jurisdiction. The committees have traditionally been organized internally into vertical hierarchies of power based primarily on seniority, with the committee chairman at its head.

Congress does its real business not on the floors of the Senate or the House of Representatives but in the scattered committee chambers. To a very large extent, legislation is not the outcome of a general debate of the entire membership but rather a general assent to the decision of a single committee (which often merely ratifies the decision of one or more of its subcommittees) or to the agreements struck among several committees.

If legislative power has been centered in the committees, power within the committees has traditionally been centered in the various committee chairmen. Indeed, from the 1910 revolt in the House until the early 1970s when the Democratic Caucus imposed a series of reforms, committee chairmen were virtual autocrats, able to wield almost total power within their committees, especially in the House of Representatives. Committee chairmen enjoyed the authority to assign professional staff as they wished, to create or to abolish subcommittees, to chair whatever subcommittee they chose or to assign any other committee member from the majority party to that post, to schedule meetings, to set the agenda, to report legislation to the full House or Senate, and to act as floor manager of committee legislation. This centering of power in the committee chairmen became an especially difficult problem when formulating broad national policy, because the most senior members of Congress were invariably from southern, rural districts and states devoid of interparty competition. Committee chairmen were thus largely cut off both from the mainstream of the population (which was urban and nonsouthern) and from the corporate centers of American life. The power of southern conservative committee chairmen like Judge Howard Smith of Virginia and James Eastland of Mississippi helps explain why Congress was so slow to act on the issue of civil rights for black Americans, even when a majority of Americans, business leaders, and members of Congress themselves favored such advances.

The spread of incumbency from the south to the remainder of the country, however, broke the nearly exclusive lock held by southern Congressmen on chairmanships. Seniority is now distributed on a more neutral geographical and ideological basis, although the general problem of decentralization and fragmentation remains. We shall see that it has been made worse by the enhanced role of the subcommittees.

The implications of such a distribution of power were and are serious. For a bill to become law, it has always been necessary to first gain the approval of powerful and strategically located chairmen scattered in various committees. A single legislative proposal, for instance, might have to clear at least three committees in its own chamber,[5] to say nothing of the other chamber, as well as the "conference committee" to work out any disparities between versions of bills coming out of each house of Congress. Needless to say, the survival rate of legislation that must find its way through this labyrinth is small indeed, especially if it is legislation to which one or more committee chairmen are opposed. The ability of Congress to formulate and successfully complete legislative work on important pieces of national policy, whether related to energy, the environment, the economy, or foreign policy, is thus limited, but the same is not necessarily the case for legislation related to congressional "pork barrel," by which virtually all members of Congress have something to gain. As one scholar has put it, "The House will allow a civil rights or defense procurement or environmental bill to languish in the Rules Committee, but it takes special precautions to insure that nothing slows down the approval of dams and irrigation projects."[6]

The Rise of Subcommittee Government. Some students of the congressional process were initially encouraged by a series of reforms legislated in the 1970s regarding the committee system. It was hoped that these reforms would enhance the ability of Congress to act as a coequal branch of the federal government, since almost all these reforms were directed at breaking the autocratic power of the chairmen of standing committees. In 1970, for instance, Democratic senators decided that no senator could chair more than one committee or sit as a member of more than one of the major standing committees (Appropriations, Armed Services, Finance, Foreign Relations, and Judiciary). This reform opened up previously closed slots and even allowed several freshman senators to serve on the powerful Appropriations Committee for the first time in living memory. In the House of Representatives, the Democratic Caucus introduced a series of committee reforms in 1971, 1973, and 1974 designed to further disperse power in the House. These included removal of committee appointment power from the Democratic members of the Ways and Means Committee and its transfer to the more democratically organized Steering and Policy Committee; the introduction of secret ballots for chairmanship elections; and a reinvigorated role for the Speaker of the House in chairmanship appointments (as chairman of the Committee on Committees). Most important, the reforms enhanced the power of subcommittees and diminished that of standing committees and their chairmen by establishing permanent subcommittees with fixed jurisdiction, adequate budgets, professional staff, and the right of each member of the House to at least one "choice" subcommittee assignment.

The consequent decline of the power of committee chairs and the rise in legislative prominence of the vast array of subcommittees and their chairs represent the most significant development in the contemporary Congress. Unlike the past, when most legislative decisions were made in committee, today it is in the subcommittees where testimony is heard, bills rewritten, and decisions taken that are considered virtually binding by the parent committees and chamber. While the formulation of coherent national policy was surely obstructed in the past by the need to placate a handful of committee chairmen, such persons were at least able to deliver the vote of the entire committee once their agreement was secured by the House or Senate leadership. It was *difficult yet possible* for congressional leadership to aggregate the range of agreements that was necessary to act legislatively. It could do so on any particular piece of legislation by reaching agreement with no more than five or six powerful committee chairmen. With the dispersal of power into a vast array of subcommittees and the diminution of the power of committee chairmen, the essential task of compromise and agreement has become nearly impossible. Basic responsibility for legislation in the House has expanded from 20 or so committees in the past to over 160 committees and subcommittees today. The net result of this increase is that the tools of obstructionism for general interest legislation have been made more widely available in Congress than in the past, while the environment for narrow interest legislation has been greatly improved. Private interest groups, mostly representing business, have been better able to penetrate and form cozy relatonships with subsections of Congress. Thus the ability to arrive at policies conducive to general class interests (as opposed to particular, parochial interests) has further deteriorated.

The traditional problems of Congress that have exercised reformers over the years are therefore no longer at issue. It no longer matters whether committee chairmen are liberal or conservative, young or old, northern or southern. Rather, the heart of the congressional crisis has to do with its decentralization, its lack of coordination, and the absence of strong, unified leadership. Its crisis relative to the presidency is that it cannot act decisively with power so fragmented and decentralized. It remains a wonderful mechanism for slowing and blocking action (true to the intentions of the Founders) but not a center of policy initiative. The committee "reforms" of recent years, while greatly diminishing the power of autocratic committee chairmen, have catalyzed further fragmentation and decentralization of power in both houses and have spawned great possibilities for obstruction, inaction, and special interest representation.

Mechanisms of Leadership and Coordination

With all of this said, it is important to point out that Congress is not entirely devoid of ways to at least partially overcome this fragmentation and particularization. While not terribly effective, some mechanisms of coordination and leadership exist.[7] Among the most important of them are the following:

1. *Political Parties.* The principal institution of coordination in each house is the political party, particularly the majority political party (almost exclusively the Democratic party since 1945 but the Republicans in the Senate after the 1980 election). Devoid as it is of much constitutionally mandated formal organization, Congress derives virtually its only organizing principle from the political parties.

While the political parties provide some necessary coordination and leadership, they are distinctly limited in this capacity. The parties are mainly active at the opening of each two-year session of Congress when they designate the leadership in each chamber as well as distribute members to the various committees.

The parties also act as a weak ideological glue sometimes holding their members together, but this is becoming less important all of the time. As the political party has declined in significance nationally, as the protective qualities of incumbency become evident, and as the role of narrow interest groups has increased both with Congress and in the electoral process, party cues have become less important than in the past as a guide to individual legislative behavior.[8] The passage of the Reagan budget and tax programs in 1981 was heavily dependent not only on Democratic votes in the House but also on the cooperation of several Democratic committee and subcommittee chairmen. One of them even acted as cosponsor of the Republican budget measure. The reformulation of the Reagan budget in 1985, even after his landslide election, was fashioned with the assistance of many members of the president's own party.

2. *The Speaker of the House of Representatives.* As we have seen, the dispersal of power into the committees, and increasingly into the subcommittees, cripples Congress in general, and the House of Representatives in particular, as national policy-making institutions. Partial recognition of this truth has led House Democrats to restore limited powers to the Speaker, though these powers hardly look formidable in historical perspective. A Democratic Speaker of the House now has a greater say in the appointment of committee members (in his role as chairman of the Democratic Committee on Committees), in the activities of the Rules Committee (where he chooses the Democratic members), and in policy formation (as chairman of the Democratic Steering and Policy Committee). To help in these activities, the Democratic party in the House has provided the Speaker with an expanded whip system and budget for staff. Nevertheless, despite what appears to be a dramatic turnaround in the powers of the Speaker, close observers of the House generally agree that the policy-coordinating abilities of the office do not adequately counteract the tremendous fragmentation in the House generated by the expansion of the number and formal powers of the subcommittees or the heightened influence of special interest groups.

3. *The Senate Majority Leader.* The principal elected leader for legislative coordination in the Senate is not endowed with an impressive array of powers. At most, the Senate majority leader has some influence in committee assignments, office assignments, and control of access to the floor of the Senate. Other than that, whatever influence majority leaders may have is based purely on their skills of personal persuasion and their role as the center of many of the various communications networks (conversations, disputes, negotiations) in that body. The power of the position is therefore personal and not institutional. Some have failed to use the office as an effective instrument of coordination for the Senate (Mike Mansfield) and some have been moderately successful (Robert Byrd), while only a handful have developed the office to the limits of its potential (Lyndon Johnson). The Senate remains a body of one hundred independent, relatively equal members tied together very loosely by the thin threads of party loyalty and their mutual concern for the next election. The majority leader is rarely able to use the limited powers of that office to forge the upper chamber into a coherent, policy-

making body capable of tackling national problems as a coequal partner to the president.

4. *The Budget Committee.* Many reformers held high hopes for the coordinating possibilities of the budgetary process created by the Budget and Impoundment Control Act of 1974. The Act created new House and Senate budget committees and a precise budgetary calendar. The purpose of the legislation was to allow Congress to better coordinate the budgetary process of setting target figures for overall spending and taxing to serve as a guide to the individual committees in their actions. The legislation included a provision called "reconciliation," which could be invoked as a method to force the individual committees to conform to the overall targets. The act also established a Congressional Budget Office so that in its deliberations, Congress would have its own source of budgetary analysis and not be dependent on the executive branch as it had been in the past. Its sponsors saw the act as a way to allow Congress to regain some control over national fiscal policy. By 1984, however, most observers were forced to admit that the bright promises of 1974 had been virtually extinguished. In 1983, Congress passed a budget resolution but then ignored its specific provisions. The next year, Congress could not agree to a resolution at all and temporarily suspended the provisions of the Budget Act so that it could proceed with its business.

The Unequal Branches

The last several chapters have traced some of the more important factors in the general decline of Congress as a coequal branch of the federal government. They have focused on the changing needs of corporate capitalism at home and abroad and the qualities and advantages of the presidency that make it the logical institution to lead, coordinate, and energize new government tasks and functions. They have also briefly analyzed some of the inherent representational and organizational problems of Congress, which contribute to such shifting power. There remains, however, an additional explanation for the decline of Congress and the ascendency of the presidency: Congress's own belief that it can no longer play anything but a subordinate national policy role. This argument is circular but nevertheless true. As the presidency gains in power and influence over Congress, all participants begin to believe that this is as it should be, further contributing to the imbalance. Within Congress, this leads to what can only be called an *institutional inferiority complex*. While Congress attempts to control the executive and reassert its own position, its continual ineffectuality leads to more and more halfhearted and rhetorical attempts. In effect, Congress has itself accepted the myth of the modern presidency and thus adds to the fund of power enjoyed by that branch. The late Representative Carl Vinson once expressed this view rather pointedly in the following observation:

> The role of Congress has come to be that of a sometimes querulous but essentially kindly uncle who complains while furiously puffing on his pipe but who finally, as everyone expects, gives in and hands over the allowance, grants the permission,

or raises his hand in blessing, and then returns to his rocking chair for another year of somnolence broken only by an occasional anxious glance down the avenue and a muttered doubt as to whether he had done the right thing.[9]

There are many concrete ways to see this sense of inferiority at work. One might point to the increasing tendency for Congress to delegate policy-making authority to the president, providing only barely controlling congressional guidelines. As one journalist aptly put it, delegation "usually consists of a hopeful mandate for the president to do good things" about some problems.[10] Or one might point to Congress's refusal to intervene in cases where presidents have overstepped the bounds of propriety and tradition. As journalist Elizabeth Drew asks, "Where [was] Congress when the [Nixon] administration waged a secret war and established a secret police?"[11] Where was Congress when the Reagan administration was using passport and visa controls to regulate which political ideas American citizens might encounter? Where was Congress when the Reagan administration was conducting a campaign of noncompliance with the Freedom of Information Act?

There are also the many cases in which Congress has been so deferential in its efforts to reassert its prerogatives that the resulting actions have been all but ineffectual. Take the case of the congressional cutoff of the Cambodian bombing during the Vietnam conflict. That bombing had been in progress for years against a neutral country; a peace treaty had been signed; American troops had been withdrawn (hence, the original rationale for bombing—to protect the troops— was no longer operative); and the bombing had been financed by illegal, secret budget transfers. And yet congressional legislation granted the president permission to bomb for an additional ninety-two days, thus legitimating bombing it had never approved in the first place. In attempting to regulate the president's ability to conduct unilateral war, Congress passed the War Powers Act of 1973. The act states that "The President in every possible instance shall consult with Congress before introducing United States Armed Forces into hostilities. . . ." and then goes on to grant him the right to conduct hostilities for sixty days before he must ask permission of Congress to continue.[12] Of course, much damage can be done in sixty days. Ironically, as several members of Congress pointed out during the debate, the act gives permission to the president to conduct war on his own without securing constitutionally required *prior* congressional approval.[13] The Reagan administration completely ignored the War Powers Act when it sent U.S. marines to Lebanon claiming that its "peacekeeping" mission lay outside of the provisions of the Act.

A similar irony is contained in the Budget and Impoundment Control Act of 1974, which, in the course of attempting to control some constitutionally questionable conduct by the president, actually served to legitimate and cement it. The preamble to the act, written by former senator Sam Ervin of North Carolina, states that the practice of policy impoundment is unconstitutional. The act then proceeds to grant the president the right to do it as long as he notifies Congress within ten days and gains congressional approval within sixty days. Ironically the act not only legitimates the practice of policy impoundment but also gives the president a two-month free ride in the use of an unconstitutional practice. While it surprised Congress, the legislation "was interpreted by the Administration as a new source of authority for withholding funds,"[14] which resulted in a significant increase in the number of impoundments under President Ford.

There is also the example of the use of the Budget and Impoundment Control Act by President Reagan in 1981 to literally run roughshod over the legislative branch. Backed by an overwhelming victory in the presidential election, a Republican and conservative resurgence in the House and Senate, and a public opinion that seemed to demand a reduced government role, Reagan was able to use the reconciliation provision of the act to sharply constrain the possibilities of independent congressional action. For the first time since its passage in 1974, under considerable presidential pressure to pass his budget program, binding spending ceilings were voted at the beginning of the budget process with precise spending-cut figures (conveniently supplied by budget director David Stockman) allotted to each authorizing committee with a fixed date for enactment. The result was "nothing less than the exercise of a kind of executive power not seen in Washington since the administration of Lyndon B. Johnson."[15]

There is also Ronald Reagan's whitewashing of the human rights record of our brutal ally in El Salvador as a prerequisite for economic and military aid to that country. Though its legislative intent was cynically transformed by Reagan's annual certification of human rights improvements in El Salvador throughout his term of office, Congress failed to do anything about it. Though openly and continually lied to in the most active presidential "disinformation" campaign in recent American history, Congress failed to make a serious effort to investigate and expose the truth about the shooting down of Korean Airlines 007.[16] It winked at or shied away from exposing the distortions, half-truths, and falsehoods surrounding the "rescue" of American medical students in Grenada. It refused to call the Reagan administration to task in Nicaragua against whom the United States has been waging a not-so-secret war, even though no one believed the administration's justifications for being there—interdicting arms shipments to Salvadorian rebels. The Reagan administration used the CIA (illegally) to secretly fund the 1984 Salvadorian elections, but Congress failed to significantly react. Nor did it do anything besides complain when it discovered that aid earmarked for economic development was being used for military purposes in Central America. The examples could be multiplied; the point would remain unchanged. With rare exception, Congress has ceded the policy initiative, agenda setting, and policy implementation to the president, and in so doing, has acknowledged its overall inferiority as a national policy leader.

Much has been made in recent years about the resurgence of congressional power as embodied in its willingness to stand up to presidents on impoundment, foreign interventions, the budget, and the like. Such interpretations are exaggerated, however, because, as we have already seen, many of the reforms designed to buttress congressional power have not had the intended effects and have often had the paradoxical effect of enhancing the role of the president. Moreover, reassertions of congressional prerogatives and independent role in the 1970s were still necessarily exercised as negative instruments with an eye toward checking the actions of overzealous or ambitious presidents. None served to elevate Congress to the role of independent national or class policy maker. Finally, the various factors that have served to reverse the positions of the presidency and Congress in the twentieth century (see Chapter 11) have not disappeared nor are they likely to do so. In this regard, any minor trimming of the sails of the imperial presidency that took place during the 1970s was short-lived,[17] as the ascendency of Ronald Reagan has demonstrated.

One is tempted, in the end, to agree with journalist Taylor Branch's tongue-in-cheek proposal that in order to conform with contemporary developments, Article I of the Constitution must be rewritten to state "The Powers and Duties of the Congress shall be to cheer the President, and to Complain About Him." To be sure, Congress is not totally without influence, nor is it any longer powerless before the ascendent president, and it has on more than one occasion acted vigorously to prevent unilateral action by the executive. It has also proven to be an effective investigator of executive conduct (and misconduct) for many years now, showing this ability most pointedly during the 1970s, in exposing some of the most reprehensible conduct of the intelligence community—the CIA, the FBI, the National Security Agency, and the military intelligence branches. Congress does not seek to be nor is it capable of being, however, the policy leader for the nation or for corporate capitalism.

PRESIDENT AND BUREAUCRACY

The president's leadership tasks are further complicated by the existence of a vast federal bureaucracy whose ostensible purpose is to help the president execute policy but whose actual behavior is often in the service of narrow, particularistic interests. In this section of the chapter, we explore the shape of this bureaucracy, the ways in which narrow interests are serviced within it, and how the presidency has gradually fashioned tools of coordination and leadership over it.

The Shape of the Federal Bureaucracy

Even with the leveling off of federal government employment in recent decades, what is apparent from a broad historical perspective is the sheer growth in the size of government and the expansion in the scope of its functions. Consider that during the administration of George Washington the federal government met its responsibilities with only 780 people who worked for only three departments (War, State, and Treasury) and a handful of minor agencies. Today, the business of government is executed by thirteen departments, a White House minibureaucracy, and literally hundreds upon hundreds of bureaus, agencies, commissions, boards, and the like. While organization charts do not generally explain how a

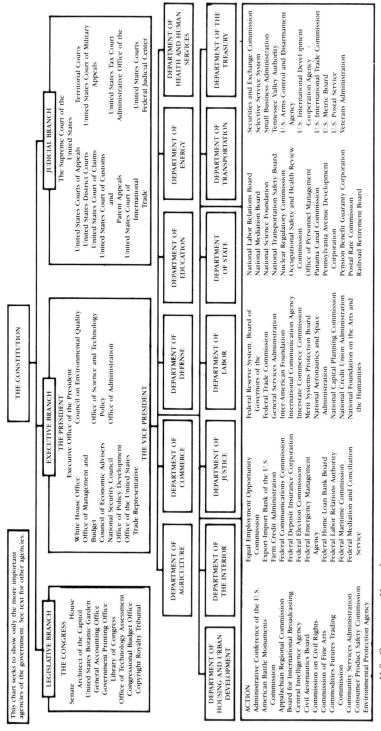

This chart seeks to show only the more important agencies of the government. See text for other agencies.

THE CONSTITUTION

LEGISLATIVE BRANCH

THE CONGRESS
Senate   House

Architect of the Capitol
United States Botanic Garden
General Accounting Office
Government Printing Office
Library of Congress
Office of Technology Assessment
Congressional Budget Office
Copyright Royalty Tribunal

EXECUTIVE BRANCH

THE PRESIDENT
Executive Office of the President

White House Office   Council on Environmental Quality
Office of Management and   Office of Science and Technology
Budget   Policy
Council of Economic Advisers   Office of Administration
National Security Council
Office of Policy Development
Office of the United States
Trade Representative

THE VICE PRESIDENT

JUDICIAL BRANCH

The Supreme Court of the
United States

United States Courts of Appeals   Territorial Courts
United States District Courts   United States Court of Military
United States Court of Claims   Appeals
United States Court of Customs
    and   United States Tax Court
Patent Appeals   Administrative Office of the
United States Court of   United States Courts
International   Federal Judicial Center
Trade

DEPARTMENT OF
AGRICULTURE

DEPARTMENT OF
COMMERCE

DEPARTMENT OF
DEFENSE

DEPARTMENT OF
EDUCATION

DEPARTMENT OF
ENERGY

DEPARTMENT OF
HEALTH AND HUMAN
SERVICES

DEPARTMENT OF
THE INTERIOR

DEPARTMENT OF
JUSTICE

DEPARTMENT OF
LABOR

DEPARTMENT
OF STATE

DEPARTMENT OF
TRANSPORTATION

DEPARTMENT OF THE
TREASURY

DEPARTMENT OF
HOUSING AND URBAN
DEVELOPMENT

ACTION
Administrative Conference of the U.S.
American Battle Monuments
    Commission
Appalachian Regional Commission
Board for International Broadcasting
Central Intelligence Agency
Civil Aeronautics Board
Commission on Civil Rights
Commodities Futures Trading
    Commission
Community Services Administration
Consumer Product Safety Commission
Environmental Protection Agency

Equal Employment Opportunity
    Commission
Export-Import Bank of the U.S.
Farm Credit Administration
Federal Communications Commission
Federal Deposit Insurance Corporation
Federal Election Commission
Federal Emergency Management
    Agency
Federal Home Loan Bank Board
Federal Labor Relations Authority
Federal Maritime Commission
Federal Mediation and Conciliation
    Service

Federal Reserve System, Board of
    Governors of the
Federal Trade Commission
General Services Administration
Inter-American Foundation
International Communication Agency
Interstate Commerce Commission
Merit Systems Protection Board
National Aeronautics and Space
    Administration
National Capital Planning Commission
National Credit Union Administration
National Foundation on the Arts and
    the Humanities

National Labor Relations Board
National Mediation Board
National Science Foundation
National Transportation Safety Board
Nuclear Regulatory Commission
Occupational Safety and Health Review
    Commission
Office of Personnel Management
Panama Canal Commission
Pennsylvania Avenue Development
    Corporation
Pension Benefit Guaranty Corporation
Postal Rate Commission
Railroad Retirement Board

Securities and Exchange Commission
Selective Service System
Small Business Administration
Tennessee Valley Authority
U.S. Arms Control and Disarmament
    Agency
U.S. International Development
    Cooperation Agency
U.S. International Trade Commission
U.S. Metric Board
U.S. Postal Service
Veterans Administration

SOURCE: *U.S. Government Manual*, 1983.

FIGURE 12.1   The government of the United States

system operates, Figure 12.1, which depicts the overall organization of the federal government, gives a fairly clear-cut view of the complexity of functions performed by the bureaucracy and the scope of its everyday activities. It is worthwhile to note that each of the departments and many of the major agencies are themselves enormous bureaucracies, employing tens of thousands of people and composed of scores of subdivisions.

Note Figure 12.2, which depicts the vast bureaucratic machinery of a single department, Health and Human Services. Since HHS employs almost 150,000 persons, the chart does more than depict empty boxes. Nor is it alone or unique. The Veterans Administration employs about 240,000, the Department of the Treasury over 115,000, and the Department of Agriculture about 122,000. The largest of them all is the Department of Defense, which manages to support almost one million civilian employees in addition to the two million persons in the uniformed services.[18]

The organizational chart also indicates the several forms that executive branch agencies take. There are thirteen *departments*, for instance, each headed by a cabinet level secretary, appointed by the president and approved by the Senate. An *Executive Office of the President* helps the president formulate policy and attempt to maintain control of the far-flung bureaucracy. Government *corporations* are agencies that operate in a market setting very much like a private company (e.g., Conrail, Amtrak, Tennessee Valley Authority, Federal Deposit Insurance Corporation, etc.). *Independent regulatory commissions* like the Securities and Exchange Commission or the Interstate Commerce Commission are bodies designed to regulate in the public interest those sectors of the economy with potential monopoly or other adverse effects. The rest of the agencies, those that do not fit any of the above categories, are simply referred to as *independent executive agencies*. Among the most prominent are the General Services Administration (in charge of all government buildings, equipment and supplies) and the Veterans Administration (which, while vast in size, is not represented in the Cabinet).

Organizational charts and information about the number of employees in each agency still fail to convey the full impact of the federal bureaucracy. They fail to capture the vast array of activities performed by these bureaucratic units, activities that range from education, to medical research, to the regulation of business, to the support of the aged, to deep sea and outer space exploration. Perhaps one way to gain an appreciation of the range and complexity of bureaucratic activities is to note the perhaps startling fact that bureaucratic agencies are active in all three major areas of governmental responsibility: administrative, legislative, and judicial. That the federal bureaucracy administers programs should occasion no surprise, since that is generally regarded as the chief responsibility of the executive branch of the government. The judicial and legislative functions are another matter, however. Many bureaucratic agencies, particularly the independent regulatory agencies (like the Interstate Commerce Commission, the Civil Aeronautics Board, the Federal Communications Commission, and so on), are empowered to hear contested administrative rulings and to reach judicial deci-

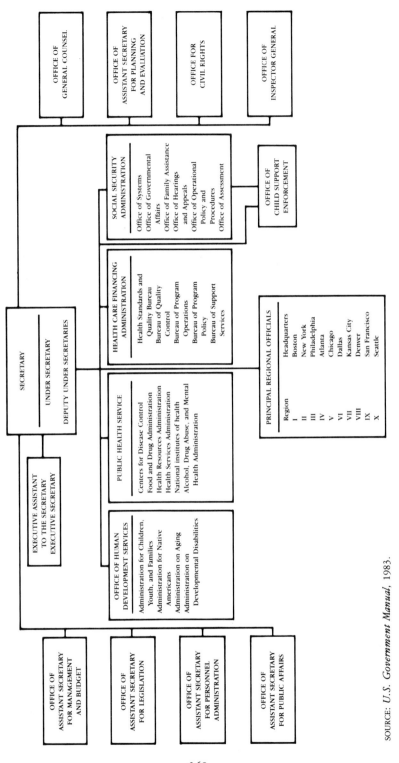

FIGURE 12.2   Department of Health and Human Services

SOURCE: *U.S. Government Manual*, 1983.

sions. Even more surprising is the extent to which many bureaucratic agencies engage in lawmaking through the promulgation of seemingly countless rules and regulations. The Environmental Protection Agency issues rules and regulations to help industry meet federal pollution standards. The Occupational Safety and Health Administration produces a body of binding law directed toward enhancement of the safety of the work environment. The Internal Revenue Service annually produces a vast array of rules that are legally binding, unless and until such time as they are overruled by the tax courts. The list of administrative rules and regulations is so vast that we can only hint at its dimension. The *Federal Register,* which annually publishes all such executive branch rules and regulations, runs over 61,000 pages of very fine print. As Senator James G. Abourezk once described the situation:

> Last year the Congress enacted 647 public laws while approximately 6,000 administrative rules were adopted by 67 Federal agencies, departments, and bureaus. More law, in the sense of rules governing our society, is produced by the executive branch and independent agencies than is produced by the national legislature. Administrative agencies, the headless "fourth branch" of Government, have grown up virtually unsupervised. Administrative rule-making has filled the gaps between the broad principles embodied in acts of Congress, yet this process has not been subjected to effective congressional control and direction.[19]

That this multitude of activity is based on but two minor references in the Constitution to an executive branch is truly astounding. Other than Article I, Section 8 (Congress shall have the power "to make rules for the government") and Article II, Section 2 (the president "may require the opinion, in writing, of the principal officer of each of the Executive Departments"), surely rather vague references in themselves, not a single mention of a federal administrative branch may be found.

Accounting for the Federal Bureaucracy

Scholars have attempted to explain the growth in size and complexity of the federal bureaucracy over the course of our history in many ways. Explanations range from the imperatives of technology to the perfidies of politicians, with the most popular being the tendency of all bureaucratic agencies to seek expansion. Yet it seems that the phenomenon of bureaucratic expansion is easily understood. The bureaucracy is simply the operative arm of the government, the administrative structure requisite to the execution of policy. As government has been called upon to perform an ever-expanding range of services and chores for a corporate capitalist society (see Chapters 13 and 14), the bureaucracy has expanded accordingly. With almost every action it takes, Congress necessarily creates an administrative structure to effect the goals it articulates in legislation. The Constitution allows and mandates Congress to create such governmental machinery by empowering it to make all laws "necessary and proper" in performing its constitutional duty. Congress is unable, in fact and in law, to execute policy on its own behalf. For his own part, in pursuing his constitutional duty to "take care that the laws be faithfully executed," the president either attempts to transmit his will through preexisting bureaucracies or creates new administrative structures in an effort to bypass or neutralize recalcitrant or uncooperative officials, agencies, or departments. There exists, then, a strong and inexorable impetus toward bureaucratic growth. As government takes on more tasks, it finds that additional administrative mechanisms are required. This is not to say that some expansion may not be traced to the tendency of bureaucrats to seek increased budgets, personnel, and functions. Nevertheless, this is a secondary and subsidiary explanation, though it remains immensely popular.

The federal bureaucracy is thus a kind of mirror reflection of the tasks that the federal government has been called upon to perform over the past half century or so, a form of administrative residue of past political action. Since these residues tend to strongly resist elimination, both because of the inherently slow processes of change in bureaucracies and because of the vested interests that clientele groups build in them, the federal bureaucracy comes to look as complex, contradictory, and one-sided (in that politics is dominated by the powerful and the privileged) as past political action itself. Each agency, bureau, and department not only has its own complex history but also its own set of private and public allies and enemies. Not surprisingly, many bureaucratic elements even work at cross purposes and in contradiction to one another making the formulation and execution of coherent national policy highly problematic.

The Bureaucratic Representation of Narrow Interests

To a degree that would no doubt surprise many Americans, our government has become the playground of a multitude of narrowly based interest groups. The federal bureaucracy is permeated by networks of government—private interest group alliances. In most cases (though not universally), the private groups represented are particular businesses and industries, with government bureaus and agencies acting as their supporters and protectors against other government bodies, other interests, and the general public. Very often, in fact, the symbiotic relationship becomes so pronounced that the private interest group comes to make its own policies and regulations, with the federal agency serving to legitimate its actions. Thus bankers closely advise the Department of the Treasury on bank policy, often setting the parameters of that policy. The same is true of the major oil firms with respect to Department of State international oil policy. In a very real sense, then, private interest groups come to seize and virtually to own pieces of the bureaucratic machinery, which they use to protect and to advance their positions.[20] As political scientist Grant McConnell described the customary state of affairs:

The existence of an array of narrow-interest-centered power structures within the open framework of American political life is no secret. It is not a hidden government, it is highly visible to anyone who spends time in Washington or who reads news beyond the headlines. It is obscure, certainly, but its obscurity is the result of dullness, routine, and the general acceptance of a largely unarticulated orthodoxy. It is apparent in the press only when, from time to time, weak public servants adrift on the beaconless sea of their own discretion are discovered to be corrupt. Even in these recurrent scandals, the venality of the weaklings usually proves petty, and the scandals quickly lose their interest and are soon forgotten. The underestimation of the significance of this pattern of power, however, is also partly a product of the cautious language used to describe it by scholars who are familiar with it. "Clientele relationships" (or, even less happily, "clientelism"), the term usually applied to the phenomenon, not only confers an aura of professional respectability on the participants in these relationships; it also obscures the fact that they are power relationships and misses the most important facts about them.[21]

Needless to say, not all private groups and associations are equal in this comfortable game; not all are invited to play. We find ourselves here in that heaven where the angels sing with a decidedly upper class and corporate accent. It could not be otherwise in a political system where, as we discovered in Chapters 8, 9, and 10, the already powerful and privileged hold decisive advantages. This is not to say that an occasional labor union, or welfare rights organization, or consumer's group is not represented in the federal bureaucracy; it *is* to say that they are but a faint shadow of the representation of producer groups, especially the giants among them.

The Implications of Narrow Interest Group Representation

According to political scientist Ted Lowi, this private group–bureaucratic symbiosis has increasingly come to serve as a practical strategy for administering government programs and as a method to legitimate expansions in the reach and function of the federal government.[22] As to the first, policy makers often find it convenient to have programs administered for them by the private groups themselves. Doctors and lawyers, for instance, through medical and bar associations, are empowered to regulate and virtually to police their professions; local commodity organizations formulate and administer government farm programs within the Department of Agriculture; and oil industry spokespersons help determine government energy policy within the Department of the Interior. Moreover, by using such private associations both to make and administer policy, policy makers help allay fears among the powerful that the federal government is overreaching its traditional prerogatives and functions.[23] As to the second, if government parcels out its sovereignty to affected groups and interests, it becomes, for many Americans, less dangerous. For these reasons, Lowi argues, contemporary government policy is built on the assumptions that organized groups must be accommodated not only because of their power, but also because by accommodating itself to the existing social arrangements of power, government acts democratically. That is, by accommodating existing social groups, government structure, process, and policy become mere reflections of the society around it, and government is thereby rendered nonthreatening. It is obvious, of course, that there is nothing democratic about accommodating the administration of national policy to powerful interests.

Examples of these private interest group–government bureaucratic-agency friendships are common. Independent regulatory commissions, to a remarkable degree, are the captives, voices, and guardians of the industries they are charged with regulating. The Department of Commerce, a particularly dramatic case, is filled with scores of business advisory committees representing particular industries and business enterprises. The Rivers and Harbors Commission, a private trade association, is closely aligned with the Corps of Engineers, the government agency most often charged with executing public works projects. The views of the American Legion are carefully solicited by the Veterans Administration. The American Farm Bureau Federation is often the decisive voice in formulating and executing policy in the Department of Agriculture. The National Petroleum Council is closely consulted in regard to Department of the Interior oil policies. Regulation of federal land and water usage in the western states is given over to and exercised by local "home rule" boards dominated by the largest landowners and ranchers.

These few examples merely touch the tip of an enormous and little-understood iceberg. Literally every federal bureau and agency is locked into a clientele relationship with some private association, industry, or company. The linkage is usually strengthened by the addition of a sympathetic congressional committee or subcommittee, which creates a pervasive system of three-sided special interest government, called by some a government of "iron triangles."[24] Thus special interests do not merely have their voices heard but become islands of government power, and the fact that this phenomenon is not created by statute does not make it any the less real.

Despite claims made by more than a few political scientists that such a system is representative and democratic, there are obvious problems with such a proposition. While private interests are accommodated, it is questionable whether such arrangements may reasonably be termed *democratic*. Only a tiny and privileged sector of the population has available to it the financial, organizational, and legal skills required to sustain a permanent presence within the government. More important, however, is that by so subdividing the government bureaucracy into advocates and champions of narrow interests, the inherent problems of coordinating the capitalist system become more pronounced. In championing specific narrow interests, segments of the government very often find themselves in conflict with other bureaucratic-congressional–private interest alliances. In such an incongruent and contradictory governmental environment, problems of immobility and drift become dangerously heightened for the system as a whole.

Only in this light can we understand the persistent complaints from both academic political scientists and sitting presidents about the problem of gaining control of the executive branch. While clearly the center of policy making in the federal government, the presidency remains an office unable to fully control or direct the vast administrative apparatus upon which it formally rests. To be sure, there are many convincing reasons why presidents cannot dominate their own branch. Certainly sheer size is a problem, since no single federal officer, even with strong staff assistance, can possibly keep track of, let alone directly control, the activities of almost three million federal employees. Furthermore, most civil servants have more secure job tenure than elected presidents and their high-level administrative appointees, thus making the bureaucracy less responsive to central direction than it might be. Granted all this, however, the principal obstacle to the formation of coherent policy in the national administration is the minute division of that administration into narrow islands of special interest domination, of close alliances among administrative agencies, congressional committees and subcommittees, and powerful private interests.

How Presidents Attempt to Gain Control

If, as suggested in Chapter 11, the major governmental responsibility for pulling together, coordinating, and rationalizing the diverse and often contradictory strands of modern capitalist society is lodged in the office of the president, the tools to carry out this responsibility are often less than what are required. Most presidents, in attempting to formulate coherent national policy, have been repeatedly frustrated by their inability to move the vast bureaucratic machinery and to overcome the islands of special interest power embodied in the "iron triangles."

> Everybody believes in democracy until he gets to the White House and then you begin to believe in dictatorship, because it's so hard to get things done. Every time you turn around, people resist you. . . . (An aide to John F. Kennedy)

> There is a tendency before you get to the White House or when you're just observing it from the outside to say, "Gee, that's a powerful position that person has." The fact of the matter is that while you're here trying to do things, you are far more aware of the constraints than you are of the power. You spend most of your time trying to overcome obstacles getting what the President wants done. (Richard Cheney, Chief of Staff to President Gerald Ford)

> It's a terrible problem and it's getting worse. . . . At State they try to humor the president but hope he will not interfere. . . . Personally, I think you can't expect too much from the bureaucracy. It is too much to expect that they will see things the president's way. (A senior Johnson administration counselor)

> The problem is that there is no fear of the White House. People out there are just doing whatever they want to do (an aide to President Jimmy Carter).[25]

It may well be impossible to overcome this fragmentation. Nevertheless, attempts have been made during the past several decades to enhance the managerial and public policy leadership tools available to the president. These efforts have involved the invention of some new administrative machinery for the president, the reconstruction of some traditional machinery, and the redefinition of the principal missions and responsibilities of yet other machinery. The result has been the evolution of a new bureaucracy, or more accurately, a new set of bureaucracies, designed to enhance the managerial capabilities of the presidency and make the office better able to reconcile and transcend the system of narrow interest representation found in the traditional federal bureaucracy. While the resulting machinery has not always worked as originally anticipated, it represents a major attempt to reorient the upper reaches of the federal bureaucracy, under the tutelage of the president, *toward a class rather than an interest group point of view*.

This is apparent in the sheer growth of the bureaucracy that surrounds the presidency, a growth so significant that it has transformed the office itself into a vast bureaucracy. In fact, as one scholar points out, it no longer makes any sense to view the executive branch of the federal government in the traditional way, neatly divided into departments, topped by a cabinet made up of the department secretaries.[26] An organization chart of the executive branch drawn today would have to include at the top, closest to the president, the various advisors, staff assistants, and thousands of other employees of the Executive Office of the President who spill from the White House into the Executive Office Building next door as well as into several nearby high-rise office buildings. Between five thousand and six thousand people work directly for the president, all of whom in one way or another assist him in the task of keeping the far-flung activities of the federal government under some modicum of control. To put this in perspective, only a little more than one thousand such persons served Eisenhower during the early years of his administration.

One mark of the prominence of this new bureaucracy is the decline in the power and prestige of the president's cabinet. (The cabinet, as such, is not mentioned in the Constitution.) It has become an informal consultative body made up of the heads of the major executive branch departments and other officials designated at the discretion of the president (the ambassador to the United Nations is usually included, for instance) that exists because of custom and informal precedent. Since the cabinet has no statutory or constitutional basis, it tends to be used or not used as presidents choose. For a number of reasons, recent presidents have not turned to the cabinet for either consultation or managerial coordination. Cabinet members are usually appointed to either heal wounds in the president's political party caused by the nomination struggle or to placate powerful interest groups and, as such, appointees are rarely the president's men, willing to easily follow his programmatic direction. Moreover, each of these appointed department heads is usually a powerful figure from the world of private corporations, universities, or foundations, and they are, again, not likely to meekly follow the lead of the president. Finally, as the department heads begin to work with the career bureaucrats in their departments and with their attached interest groups, there is a tendency for the secretaries to become "captives" of their departments, each of which has its own priorities.

It is for these reasons that most recent presidents have decided they could do without cabinet-oriented government. They have rarely consulted it as a body, and scheduled meetings serve mainly as public relations devices. As Duane Lockard bluntly states the issue, the growth of the presidency and his personal bureaucracy "has rendered (the cabinet) a very marginal institution."[27] Or, note the observations of two other students of the executive branch:

> Cabinet meetings in the United States, despite occasional efforts to make them into significant decision-making occasions, have, at least in this century, been characterized as vapid non-events in which there has been a deliberate nonexchange of information as part of a process of mutual nonconsultation.[28]

Except for those few who might be long-time political intimates of the president, cabinet members often find that they have no direct access to the president, but are intercepted by his close advisors and assistants. One telling mark of these developments was Secretary of the Interior Walter Hickel's public and rather pathetic call for President Nixon to consult occasionally with his cabinet members. Hickel was forced to resign for his efforts. In a perhaps equally pathetic case, there is the story of Secretary of State William Rogers "insisting that he *did* have a role in making foreign policy," a statement that convinced few observers, given Henry Kissinger's national security apparatus in the basement of the White House, and was itself strong evidence of his impotence.

The Tools of Presidential Management

The new bureaucracy of presidential coordination and management defies easy placement into neat organizational boxes. The instruments of centralized management are scattered throughout the bureaucracy; they involve many offices and agencies and are not located in any single, identifiable place. The organizational picture is further confused because presidents do what they feel they must in these areas, creating, discarding, and reorienting administrative structures as required. In spite of the confusion, however, the trends toward enhanced managerial capabilities at the center are unmistakable. The growth and reorganization in the upper reaches of the bureaucracy over the past several decades have been designed so that when the president says, "Do this! Do that," some reasonable probability exists that it will get done. While the new machinery has not always been successful in this effort, the management capacities of the president have been immeasurably enhanced over the years.

The White House Office. Of the most direct assistance to the president in his efforts to control the far-flung activities of the federal government is the White House Office, which consists of his most immediate assistants, advisors, and their staffs. As presidents have been increasingly called upon to act as central managers, staff instruments for that management task have grown so that the internal White House bureaucracy employs well over two thousand people, compared with the several dozen who worked for Franklin Roosevelt.

The highest-ranking assistants usually become powerful in their own right, wielding political power greater than that of most elected representatives or appointed department heads. This development generally follows from the intimate contact they enjoy with the president, contact that inevitably transfers some of the mystique and aura of the presidency to them.[29] While few presidents have allowed the latitude Nixon granted to aides John Ehrlichman and H. R. Haldeman, or that Reagan granted to James Baker, Michael Deaver, and Donald Regan, every administration has had its handful of powerful staff members who are decisive in shaping government policy, but who are neither elected by the people nor confirmed by Congress. Sherman Adams was virtually Dwight Eisenhower's alter ego. In the Kennedy administration, McGeorge Bundy (Special Assistant to the President for National Security Affairs) played a more important role in forming and executing foreign policy than the Secretary of State, Dean Rusk. Rusk played a similar second fiddle to Johnson's advisor, Walt Rostow. Henry Kissinger was the major voice in foreign policy during the first Nixon administration, easily eclipsing Secretary of State William Rogers. Hamilton Jordan played a greater role in formulating domestic policy in the Carter administration than cabinet secretaries, as did Reagan's triumverate of Edwin Meese, James Baker, and Michael Deaver during Reagan's first administration.

The role of the presidential staff relative to the cabinet is vividly illustrated by the following observations of Senator Ernest Hollings of South Carolina:

> It used to be that if I had a problem with food stamps, I went to see the Secretary of Agriculture, whose department has jurisdiction over that problem. Not anymore. Now, if I want to learn the policy, I must go to the White House to consult John Price [a special assistant]. If I want the latest on textiles, I won't get it from the Secretary of Commerce, who has the authority and responsibility. No, I am forced to go to the White House and see Mr. Peter Flanigan. I shouldn't feel too badly. Secretary Stans has to do the same thing.[30]

The Office of Management and Budget. As we have seen, trends in presidential policy making have been toward evolving a capacity for formulating comprehensive and coordinated legislative programs and for gaining control of the executive branch departments, bureaus, and agencies that administer these programs. The presentation of legislative programs to Congress, for instance, has evolved from the simple practice of sending it discrete and independent pieces of legislation to the presentation of comprehensive and elaborately coordinated legislative programs. The budget is the most important instrument for the coordination of all these programs and for the exercise of central control over the federal bureaucracy. The Office of Management and Budget (OMB) is the executive branch agency responsible for formulating and administering the federal budget and is therefore essential to presidential efforts to coordinate policy. The old Bureau of the Budget was traditionally considered the most powerful single agency in the federal bureaucracy, because it received all requests for legislation and/or money from Congress and the executive branch. Thus the Bureau of the Budget (and through it, the president) gained some control over the vast bureaucratic machinery. The new OMB, organized in 1970, incorporates the Bureau of the Budget's traditional prerogatives as formulator of the budget and clearinghouse for legislation with new responsibilities for following, evaluating, and intervening (when necessary) in the execution of government programs. The OMB thus affords the president tighter control over the bureaucracy, and while it is tiny by today's standards (556 people), it is one of the most powerful bureaucratic units in the federal government. During the Reagan administration, the OMB, under director David Stockman, came to exercise the greatest control over departmental legislative proposals, administrative practices, and budgets ever seen in Washington and, as such, became the president's main instrument in his program to reduce federal social expenditures and to deregulate the economy. Stockman's office constantly intervened, for instance, in the code writing of OSHA and the Environmental Protection Agency.

Counterpart Units. Presidential control of the bureaucracy, and hence of policy in general, has also been enhanced by the evolution of what one scholar has designated *counterpart units* in the White House.[31] These units consist of individual advisors or assistants (with their own staffs) who are responsible for overseeing some specific area of government policy for the president—among them consumer affairs, science and technology, national security, international affairs, and so on— and for coordinating the numerous executive branch units involved.

In 1970, Richard Nixon attempted to further coordinate federal domestic policy by the creation of the Domestic Affairs Council, a kind of supracabinet position charged with overseeing the other cabinet-level departments and subcabinet agencies. While the Watergate affair made this reform stillborn under Nixon, and while President Ford made little use of the office, Jimmy Carter revived it with the appointment of special assistant Stuart Eizenstat and a staff of twenty professionals. Ronald Reagan carried this process forward by organizing his administration around seven "cabinet councils" made up of selected cabinet officers with common areas of concern (economic affairs, human services, food and agriculture, commerce and trade, natural resources and the environment, legal policy, and management and administration) and representatives from OMB.

The Council of Economic Advisors. The president has also become the focus of responsibility for the nation's economic health. Toward that end, he has several instruments available for formulating and executing economic policy. Of greatest importance is his general influence, through the OMB, on the size and disposition of the federal budget. Again, the role of the OMB was most dramatically evident in this regard during the first years of the Reagan administration. In determining overall econcomic policy, the president is assisted by a three-member Council of Economic Advisors (created by the Employment Act of 1946) who are charged with preparing the annual economic report, monitoring national economic developments, and advising the president on economic matters. The influence of the CEA dramatically declined under Reagan because of the president's distaste for the "doom and gloom" forecasts of its chief Martin Feldstein.

The Presidential Personnel Office. More than any other recent President, Ronald Reagan has inserted ideological appointees deep into the federal bureaucracy as a means for gaining control over bureaucratic activities. His principal instrument for this "conservatization" of the federal bureaucracy has been the Presidential Personnel Office under the leadership of John Herrington which has relied heavily on lists of acceptable appointees provided by such conservative organizations as the Committee on the Present Danger and the Heritage Foundation (Edwin Feulner, president of Heritage, justifies such a strategy on the grounds that "personnel is policy"). Rather than approach the appointment process in a haphazard manner or as a way to distribute "spoils" to the various wings and groupings in the Republican party, the traditional mode of operation in American politics, "this Administration has taken the appointment process more seriously than any other Administration as a device for imprinting their ideological stamp on the government. Ideology has been a much more dominant criterion than in other Administrations."[32] There is every evidence that the strategy has been broadly successful and that the Reagan administration has managed to shift the priorities of bureaucratic agencies like OSHA, the Environmental Protection Agency, the Civil Rights Commission, Health and Human Services, and the Nuclear Regulatory Commission, among others.

The National Security Apparatus. Chapter 11 developed the theme that as the United States became a major world power during the twentieth century, the presidency simultaneously, and largely because of that development, became the dominant political institution in this country. This process followed almost as a matter of course from the constitutional position of the office and the commonly assumed requirement for unitary and decisive action in foreign affairs. Not surprisingly, an elaborate and sizable national security bureaucracy evolved at the same time (particularly from the end of World War II), which enabled the president to take over foreign policy making and to manage more successfully the diverse and scattered foreign and military affairs activities of the United States.[33]

The national security bureaucracy is difficult to describe in structural terms because each president has felt it his due to shift functions, to reassign responsibilities, and to create temporary structures of coordination. No two presidents have utilized this bureaucracy in the same way, or even allowed the structure to remain unchanged. Because of the complex mix of presidential personality and preferences, individual foibles, and shifting foreign policy needs, the national security bureaucracy is more like a can of squirming and tangled earthworms than a neat organizational chart of interconnected boxes.

There remain some general observations to be made about the structural compostion of this bureaucracy, however. The first major set of components are the old line departments traditionally active in foreign and military affairs, mainly

State and Defense, but including as well, elements of Treasury and Commerce. As American foreign policy has necessarily become more militarized, however, because of the expansive qualities of American corporate capitalism (given the need to protect markets, sources of raw materials, and export platforms from the threat of indigenous national liberation struggles), the Department of Defense and its ranking policy makers have gained prominence within the national security bureaucracy at the expense of the other departments. From the death of John Foster Dulles in the late 1950s, secretaries of state have been in virtual eclipse in the higher councils of the government (with the exception of Henry Kissinger's tenure at the Department of State) as presidents turned for advice, information, and the execution of policy to the Department of Defense, the uniformed services, and advisors like Robert McNamara, Clark Clifford, Melvin Laird, Elliot Richardson, James Schlesinger and Zbigniew Brzezinski. It seemed to many that U.S. foreign policy was being run from the Defense Department by Casper Weinberger during the Reagan years.

Also important in the national security bureaucracy are those administrative structures created in the first few years of the Cold War that enhanced the capabilities of the presidency in managing foreign and military policy. During the space of but a few years in the late 1940s, the separate military services were consolidated into a new Department of Defense under the unified command of a secretary appointed by the president; the National Security Council (NSC), headed by a special assistant to the president, was created for the purpose of integrating "domestic, foreign, and military policies relating to the national security"; and the Central Intelligence Agency was established as an extension of the wartime Office of Strategic Services, responsible to the NSC, and charged publicly with coordinating intelligence gathering but privately with conducting presidentially assigned covert activities. Both the timing of their creation and the missions assigned to these new organizations demonstrate American policy makers' visible recognition of the organizational and administrative requirements of the new American imperial role and the strategic role of the president in the new order. While the structures have been used in various ways depending on the preferences of the president—the NSC was used extensively by Eisenhower and Nixon, for instance, but virtually ignored by Kennedy and Reagan—each of them remains in place as a potential instrument the president can use in coordinating national security affairs. Thus his bureaucratic capabilities (though not necessarily his wisdom or judgment) are considerably enhanced in his conduct of American military and diplomatic affairs in the world.[34]

The National Security Bureaucracy and Corporate Capitalism. It is exceedingly difficult to delineate the exact nature of the relationships among these various bureaucratic elements, given the shifting preferences and practices of individual presidents. Yet what is most striking about the principal policy makers in the national security bureaucracy is their close and intimate connection to the dominant institutions of corporate capitalism. Chapter 8 indicated the extent to which the secretaries of defense, state, treasury, and commerce are traditionally recruited almost exclusively from the ranks of the major industrial and financial corporations, investment houses, and corporate law firms. The same seems to hold for the national security bureaucracy in general. In this regard, let us note the summary observation by Richard Barnet, a long-time student of the subject:

> Between 1940 and 1967 . . . all the first and second level posts . . . were held by fewer than four hundred individuals who rotate through a variety of key posts. The temporary civilian managers who come to Washington to run America's wars and preparations for wars . . . were so like one another in occupation, religion, style, and social status that, apart from a few Washington lawyers, Texans, and mavericks, it was possible to locate the offices of all of them within fifteen blocks in New York, Boston, and Detroit. Most of their biographies in *Who's Who* read like minor variations on a single theme—wealthy parents, Ivy League education, leading law firm or bank, introduction to government in World War II.[35]

While mainstream political science is prone to find pluralism in American policy making, some close students of the national security bureaucracy argue that the similarities in family background, education, occupation, institutional affiliations, and patterns of recruitment to government service translate into similarities in political outlook and policy preferences.[36] As Barnet so cogently points out, this highly mobile and interchangeable national security elite is bound together by a common imperial creed cloaked in humanitarian terms. The creed articulates America's unselfish role in the world, the absence of any desire to seize or to hold territories in the form of colonies, the good intentions of American expansion, the benevolent effects of American investment and corporate entry for other countries, and the necessity of blocking socialist expansion in the interests of world peace and order. All this is cemented together by a strong sense of America's mission, a mission made both possible and imperative by our wealth and power. Note the articulation of these views by a number of prominent policy makers:

> The interests of the United States are global and that is good fortune for all the world's people and most of their leaders. (Harlan Cleveland, former Assistant Secretary of State)

> World responsibility may in today's world be possible . . . only for nations such as the United States which command resources on a scale adequate to the requirements of leadership in the twentieth century. (George Ball, former Undersecretary of State)

> History and our own achievements have thrust upon us the principal responsibility for the protection of freedom on earth. (Lyndon Baines Johnson)[37]

The president has available to him, then, a group of highly trained, talented, and ideologically committed people from the highest reaches of the private economy and academic life who control the complex machinery of the national security apparatus and who add to the president's capabilities in managing the foreign and military activities of the American government.

CONCLUDING REMARKS

Dominant groups in capitalism are always being torn between the particularistic and the general. The major economic actors in the system, that is to say, sometimes feel compelled to pursue their own interests without concern for the interests of others; and yet at other times, they find it prudent to cooperate with others among the privileged and powerful in order to protect and advance their common interests. In the formation of public policy, dominant actors consider it important to attend to both kinds of interests and find that mechanisms of compromise and accommodation exist when the two are in conflict. These purposes are neatly fulfilled by the institutional division of labor between the president, Congress, and the bureaucracy. The president generally acts with a broad national and social class perspective while Congress and the bureaucracy devote their time and energies to the representation of more parochial perspectives. In the perpetual struggle, compromises and agreements reached between the president, Congress, and the bureaucracy may be found the complex processes by which the general and particularistic are reconciled in modern capitalism.

Contrary to conventional wisdom and Fourth of July oratory, there is not much room for democracy in all of this. It is a game in which the powerful and privileged are the main contestants, and make most of the rules and enjoy most of the rewards. This is not to say that democracy is entirely absent. It is to say, however, that the voices of the nonpowerful and the nonprivileged are faint; attended to when occasionally raised to a shout, yet treated as part of the background in normal times.

NOTES

1. Quoted in Mark Green et al., *Who Runs Congress?* (New York: Bantam, 1972).
2. See chapter 8 for a more detailed discussion of political action committees.
3. See Morris P. Fiorina, *Congress: Keystone of the Washington Establishment* (New Haven: Yale University Press, 1977), for the best single analysis of congressional incumbency and its effects. Also see David Mayhew, "Congressional Elections: The Case of the Vanishing Marginals," *Polity* 6 (1974), pp. 295–317.
4. Fiorina, *Congress*, p. 42.
5. A bill in the House of Representatives might include enabling features that require the attention of a subject matter committee, financial aspects that require the attention of the Appropriations Committee or the Ways and Means Committee, and a place on the House calendar that requires approval of the Rules Committee.
6. Fiorina, *Congress,* p. 42.

7. For a view that argues quite persuasively for the robustness and importance of these mechanisms see Arthur Maass, *Congress and the Common Good* (New York: Basic Books, 1983).

8. Two students of Congress have pointed out that "the United States House of Representatives stands out from other western parliamentary bodies because of its low levels of party voting." David W. Brady and Charles S. Bulloch III, "Coalition Politics in the House of Representatives," in Lawrence C. Dodd and Bruce I. Oppenheimer, eds., *Congress Reconsidered*, 2nd ed. (Washington, D.C.: The Congressional Quarterly, 1981), p. 186. While it is true that the Republicans in the Ninety-seventh and Ninety-eighth Congresses unified behind the Reagan programs to a remarkable degree, it remains to be seen whether this was anything other than a temporary aberration.

9. Quoted in Arthur Schlesinger, Jr., *The Imperial Presidency* (New York: Popular Library, Atlantic Monthly Press, 1973), p. 204.

10. Branch, "Profiles in Caution," p. 50.

11. Elizabeth Drew, "Why Congress Won't Fight," in David C. Saffell, ed., *Watergate: Its Effects on the American Political System* (Cambridge, Mass.: Winthrop Publishers, 1974), p. 45.

12. This form of legislation in which Congress allows certain activities unless vetoed by Congress was declared unconstitutional by the Supreme Court on June 23, 1984. It is too early yet to tell what the effects of this decision will be, though most commentators predict a further erosion of congressional power vis-a-vis the president.

13. To show how cautious Congress tends to be in the face of a "national emergency," President Ford's actions in the Mayagüez affair, which directly and unambiguously broke the law of the War Powers Act, were not only quietly allowed by the Congress but also applauded by most of its members, including the sponsors of the War Powers Act! It is interesting to note that forty-one casualties were sustained in a bid to recover thirty-nine persons who were already being released by the Cambodian government.

14. Louis Fisher, *Presidential Spending Power* (Princeton, N.J.: Princeton University Press, 1975), p. 200.

15. "Reconciliation's Long-Term Consequences," *The Congressional Quarterly*, August 15, 1981, p. 1465.

16. For the most complete and detailed account of this incident see David Pearson, "KAL 007: What the U.S. Knew and When We Knew It," *The Nation* (Aug. 18–25, 1984), 105–124.

17. A point made by Lawrence Dodd in his provocative article "Congress, the Constitution, and the Crisis of Legitimacy," in Dodd and Oppenheimer, eds., *Congress Reconsidered*.

18. *Statistical Abstracts of the United States*, 1984, U.S. Bureau of the Census.

19. *Congressional Record*, S7587–88, May 7, 1975.

20. These pieces may be very small agencies, parts of agencies, or entire departments, as in the case of Agriculture and Labor.

21. Grant McConnell, *Private Power and American Democracy* (New York: Knopf, 1967), p. 339.

22. See his important work, *The End of Liberalism* (New York: Norton, 1969).

23. It is interesting and important to note that expressions of concern about government interference have grown only with increased demands that business demonstrate its commitment to the public interest in the areas of the environment, occupational safety,

and affirmative action. Favorable, supportive government intervention, on the other hand, has not only been welcomed but actively encouraged by the major corporations.

24. Randell Ripley and Grace Franklin, *Congress, the Bureaucracy and Public Policy* (Homewood, Ill.: Dorsey Press, 1976), ch. 4.
25. All the above quotations are from interviews conducted by Thomas Cronin and reported in his work, *The State of the Presidency* (Boston: Little, Brown, 1980), ch. 7.
26. Thomas E. Cronin, "The Swelling of the Presidency," *Saturday Review/Society,* February 1973.
27. Duane Lockard, *The Perverted Priorities of American Politics* (New York: Macmillan, 1976), p. 272. This is not to say, of course, that presidents do not meet with individual department secretaries or with several of them together as needs arise.
28. Edward Weisband and Thomas M. Frank, *Resignation in Protest* (Baltimore: Penguin, 1975), p. 139.
29. As Senator Daniel Patrick Moynihan has observed, "Never underestimate the power of proximity." Quoted in Cronin, *The State of the Presidency,* p. 269.
30. Related in Cronin, "The Swelling of the Presidency."
31. Theodore J. Lowi, *American Government: Incomplete Conquest* (Hinsdale, Ill.: Dryden Press, 1977), p. 377.
32. G. Calvin MacKenzie, quoted in Ronald Brownstein, "Jobs Are the Currency of Politics, and the White House Is on Spending Spree," *National Journal* (Dec. 15, 1984), p. 2386.
33. I use the words "national security" because of the general usage of the term, though I am not convinced that the activities described here have anything whatever to do with actual national security.
34. Again, a devastating series of foreign policy failures stretching from Vietnam to Iran to Nicaragua suggests that bureaucratic machinery, while necessary to coordination of policy, is surely not sufficient.
35. Richard Barnet, *The Roots of War* (Baltimore: Penguin Books, 1972), pp. 48–49.
36. See in particular Barnet, *The Roots of War;* and Gabriel Kolko, *The Roots of American Foreign Policy* (Boston: Beacon Press, 1969).
37. All these quotations are from Barnet, *The Roots of War,* p. 19.

SUGGESTIONS FOR FURTHER READING

Richard Barnet. THE ROOTS OF WAR. *Baltimore: Penguin, 1972.* Still the most complete discussion of the national security bureaucracy.

Morris P. Fiorina. CONGRESS: KEYSTONE OF THE WASHINGTON ESTABLISHMENT. *New Haven: Yale University Press, 1977.* A provocative essay that examines the problem of incumbency in Congress, its causes and implications.

Hugh Heclo. A GOVERNMENT OF STRANGERS. *Washington, D.C.: Brookings, 1977.* An analysis of the life and work of senior appointed federal executives.

Theodore J. Lowi. THE END OF LIBERALISM. *New York: Norton, 1969.* An important examination of the symbiotic relationship among private interest groups, executive branch agencies, and congressional committees.

Arthur Maass. CONGRESS AND THE COMMON GOOD. *New York: Basic Books, 1983.* An uncommon argument in which Congress is conceptualized not as the preserve of special interests but of a broad national vision.

Donald R. Mathews. U.S. SENATORS AND THEIR WORLD. *New York: Vintage Books, 1960.* A classic analysis of the informal folkways of the Senate.

Michael Nelson (ed.). THE PRESIDENCY AND THE POLITICAL SYSTEM. *Washington, D.C.: Congressional Quarterly Press, 1984.* This collection of scholarly articles on the presidency has particularly compelling treatments on presidential relations with Congress (Davidson) and the bureaucracy (Rourke).

James Sundquist. THE DECLINE AND RESURGENCE OF CONGRESS. *Washington, D.C.: Brookings, 1981.* A historical analysis of the shifting power balance between Congress and the president with a particular focus on the purported resurgence of the former.

Part

V

What Does

Government Do?

In this section of the book, we ask what government does with its vast resources and with what effects. We shall see that public policy is shaped in a fundamental way by the fact that government acts in an environment that is largely defined by capitalism and the needs of the major corporations.

13

What Does Government Do?
Managing Economic Growth
and Corporate Profitability

The principal task of the federal government is to preserve, protect, and guarantee the future of American capitalism. Such a task is inevitable given the distribution of political power in the American system. Such a task is inescapable given the fact that modern corporate capitalism is not self-correcting. Modern corporate capitalism, that is to say, not only creates unprecedented prosperity but also a wide range of significant and inescapable problems, tensions, and contradictions which are not automatically solved by the market mechananism. Operating at peak efficiency, corporate capitalism produces a cornucopia of goods and services but it also produces personal disorders, social disharmony and disintegration, environmental degradation, and economic instability (see Chapter 5). These problems, tensions, and contradictions are so serious and inescapable, in fact, that the system may be said to be in a perpetual state of jeopardy. For the system to continue, government intervention is essential.

I shall argue in these pages that contemporary government policy in the United States is neither random nor accidental but is the outcome of a set of important, indeed imperative, services which government must perform for capitalism. Public policy in the United States is a reflection of government's role as the coordinator and manager of the complex machinery of capitalist production, and the first-aid administrator to the social ills capitalism generates as a byproduct of its operations. To that end, it must perform two essential sets of tasks. First, it must help create and preserve conditions under which the major corporations, the most important economic actors in the system, can expand their operations, plan for contingencies, and guarantee for themselves substantial, stable, and predictable profits. Thus, one objective of public policy is to ensure the process of capital accumulation. Second, in the face of the social inequalities, social and environmental disruptions, and diseconomies so characteristic of the operations of capitalism (see Chapter 5), government must struggle to maintain conditions of social harmony and social stability, which are necessary to the function of capital accumulation. Most importantly, government must manage the potentially explosive relations between social classes, which are inherent in capitalism, and do it in such a way that the privileged position of dominant groups is ensured.[1] Government policy in the United States is thus the product of two powerful vector forces, both of which are directly tied to the development of capitalism. Dynamic, concentrated capitalism and a large-scale interventionist government, rather than being polar opposites as the popular imagination has it, are inseparable and mutually reinforcing.

Let me suggest two important caveats in regard to these twin tasks. First, the need to provide conditions conducive to capital accumulation and social harmony are often contradictory. Various governmental efforts to help guarantee the process of accumulation in the economy are often in conflict with its efforts to maintain social harmony in the population. A delicate process of balancing is always in order and a proper balance is not easily attained. To take a case in point, the massive increase in federal government spending on welfare and social services in the late sixties and seventies, made necessary by the need to manage the social turmoil of the former decade, had, by the beginning of the eighties, contributed to problems of economic stagnation in the overall American economy. In an effort to reverse this trend and to reinvigorate the process of capitalist accumulation, the Reagan administration has made substantial and unprecedented reductions in the welfare/social service role of the federal government. While it remains to be seen whether rates of productive private investment will be enhanced by the subsequent tax reductions for the corporations and for the very wealthy, and whether it will have the desired effect on the growth of the economy and corporate profitability, cuts in domestic programs raise the likelihood that social upheaval and dislocation will again reappear.

Second, it often happens that in the course of effectively dealing with one or the other of its essential tasks, the very act of government intervention creates other equally serious problems. Although government intervention may sometimes serve to lessen the severity of some of the normal problems of the capitalist economy, the very act of intervention creates problems of bloated government budgets, bureaucratization, inefficiencies, and inflation. In this and the next chapter, I shall examine all of these issues in more detail.

To understand what government does in the United States, one must appreciate the revolution in the economy caused by the emergence and preeminence of the great corporations, a subject examined at length in Chapter 7. While the goals of these business enterprises remain growth and substantial profits, the means of reaching these goals have significantly altered from those of traditional, free-market capitalism. Modern corporations require a stable and predictable environment for their operations. Given their enormous investment in plant and equipment, their staggering cash flow, their vast workforces, and the very long lead time and mobilization effort required for new product lines, the giant corporations seek the stability conducive to long-range, rational planning. Such an environment is possible only through the efforts of an active, interventionist, and cooperative government. Much of what government does in the United States has to do with constructing this nurturant environment for these enterprises.

Specifically, government attempts to provide supportive services for corporate capitalism in the following ways.

1. It encourages and protects corporate concentration and cooperation.
2. It manages the business cycle.
3. It provides infrastructural services.
4. It protects overseas markets and sources of raw materials for American-based multinational corporations.

ENCOURAGEMENT AND PROTECTION OF CORPORATE CONCENTRATION

The drive of business leaders from the beginning of market society, free-market, free-enterprise rhetoric not withstanding, has been to dampen competition, mainly through cooperative efforts among businesspeople to limit production and set prices. Prior to the Industrial Revolution, the evolution of national markets, and the appearance of a national communications network, the economy of the United States comprised a complex mixture of local and regional markets. Within these markets, the leading enterprises usually agreed to ease or to eliminate cutthroat competition. Agreements most often took the form of price and marketing arrangements designed to provide the major firms within each region and within each industry a relatively stable, guaranteed rate of return. The combined waves of the Industrial Revolution, massive population increases, the appearance of railroad and telegraph lines, the rapid development of the west destroyed these localized markets and local anticompetitive agreements.[2]

These breathtaking changes in the late nineteenth century had the paradoxical effects of both substantially increasing the size of enterprises (the fabrication of steel, for instance, requires substantial investments in plant and equipment) and, because new technologies, new markets, and readily available capital encouraged the entry of numerous competitors, making it more difficult for the largest firms to maintain their market shares and profit levels. In the years immediately following the discovery of Pennsylvania oil in 1861, to take one case, oil sold for $20 per barrel from John D. Rockefeller's Socony Oil Company. By 1865, seventy-seven firms had entered the industry, and prices fell to a business-wrecking 10 cents per barrel.[3]

Under such conditions of expanding markets, new technologies, ample investment capital, and easy market entry, the tacit anticompetitive agreements entered into by major firms to protect their market shares were abandoned in favor of more formal arrangements. These arrangements included buying and selling pools, price regulation associations, and syndicates. When such arrangements proved too easily broken, the leading businesses turned to other arrangements more conducive to the integration of competing firms: the *trust* and the *holding company*.

The final step in the process of dampening competition through merger of competing companies was made possible by the states of New Jersey and Delaware. In the last decade of the nineteenth century, each introduced liberal incorporation laws under which corporations could buy the stock of competing enterprises and merge with them into a single legal and economic entity. So momentous were these combined economic and legal developments that in the relatively short span of the time between the end of the Civil War and the beginning of World War I, the economy of the United States was transformed from one of farms and small businesses to one dominated by a handful of industrial and financial companies.

Thus the incorporated form of business culminated decades of voluntary efforts by large businesses to form cooperative arrangements designed to limit production, apportion markets, and set prices. The development of giant trusts, holding companies, and corporations, however, along with the multitude of cooperative arrangements among them, proved insufficient. It soon became apparent that even these advances in business organization were not adequate to protect the major firms within each industry from intense competition, falling prices, and declining profits. Standard Oil's share of the market, for instance, fell from 90 percent to 50 percent between 1900 and 1921. Similar developments faced the major firms in steel, autos, agricultural machinery, telephones, copper, and meat packing.[4] The most farsighted corporate leaders realized that the sponsorship of the federal government could help build the most formidable cartels. Such sponsorship would legitimate intercorporate cooperation as being in the "public interest," put new competitors at a disadvantage, and protect corporate prerogatives from the hostile inroads of state legislatures.

In the opening years of the twentieth century, under the sponsorship of some of the leaders of the nation's largest corporations and financial institutions, there began a movement that lauded the economic and social benefits of concentrated corporate size and cooperation—efficiency, economies of scale, technological advances, peaceful industrial relations, and the like—and that demanded that the federal government support and nurture this new "cooperative capitalism." Out of this movement came such landmarks as the Federal Trade Commission Act, the Federal Reserve System, the War Industries Board of World War I, the trade association movement of the 1920s, the National Industrial Recovery and Wagner Labor Relations Acts of Roosevelt's New Deal, and a host of other regulatory and subsidy programs whose overall effect was to "cartelize" the American economy under federal government sponsorship.[5]

From the early years of the twentieth century, then, the leaders of the largest corporations realized that a stable, ordered economy was possible only through the cooperative intervention of government. Those years also witnessed the beginning of the rather successful efforts by business leaders to encourage a structure of federal legislation that would form a protective umbrella under which the dominant corporations could legally cooperate with one another, stabilize and regularize their relationship through trade associations, standardize practices and products within an industry, and receive assistance and subsidies from the government when the situation required.

This protective umbrella consists of a multitude of practices, all of which serve the same end: the encouragement of cartel-like intercorporation practices. I shall review a few of these below.

Trade Associations and Regulation of Businesses

The federal government sponsors cartel-like arrangements by allowing giant business enterprises to set their own rules of behavior in many areas of public regulation. The operating philosophy of business regulation in the United States is to encourage the formation of trade associations (''an administrative structure whose . . . mission is regularizing relations among participants in the same industry, trade, or sector''),[6] and to allow them to determine the content of government policy within their own industry. Government legitimacy is thus granted to trade association efforts to eliminate cutthroat competition and to regularize intercompany cooperation. In public works, for instance, the private Rivers and Harbors Congress (a trade association) screens all proposed government projects. The Federal Housing Administration is run under standards and guidelines set by the National Association of Real Estate Boards. The National Petroleum Council, an arm of the American Petroleum Institute, is an integral partner with the Department of the Interior in forming oil policy. The Civil Aeronautics Board grants the American Transit Association (an airlines trade association) the authority to regulate many aspects of the travel industry, including the licensing of travel agents. The Interstate Commerce Commission, the Civil Aeronautics Board, and other agencies depend on industry trade associations to establish *rate conferences* to determine the schedule of prices for the entire industry. The Department of the Interior allows the oil industry, through the inaptly named Texas Railroad Commission, to determine state-by-state and company-by-company production quotas for domestic crude, thereby assuring the industry that production will not outrun demand.[7] Over one thousand business advisory councils are formally a part of the decision-making process throughout the executive branch of the federal government.

The examples easily could be multiplied, but they would not substantially add to the picture painted above. To a striking extent, business regulates *itself* under the sponsorship of the federal government, a phenomenon that pervades literally every agency that has anything to do with business activities in the United States.

Capture of Independent Regulatory Agencies

Government regulatory agencies protect the largest firms within their respective industries from the intrusions of the public, Congress, and potential competitors. Independent regulatory agencies are composed of persons appointed by the president for fixed terms of office, whose main purpose is to bring industries with monopolistic tendencies under public scrutiny and control. Such agencies are charged with regulating these economic sectors by various means, among them determining rates, controlling market entry of new competitors, and approving mergers. The origins of the regulatory agencies differ substantially. Some are the products of genuine grass-roots demands and protest (the Interstate Commerce Commission of 1887 and the Securities and Exchange Commission of 1934); others are the result of direct pressure from the major corporations (the Federal Power Commission of 1920 and the Federal Communications Commission of 1934). The result, however, is identical—support and solidification of the positions of the major firms within each industry.

The capture of independent regulatory agencies by those who are supposed to be regulated by them is now widely accepted as a fact of life by both scholars and politicians.[8] These developments were discerned early in the history of the regulatory commissions. One U.S. attorney general predicted as early as 1892 in a statement to a concerned railroad president that:

> The Commission . . . can be of great use to the railroads. It satisfies the popular clamor for a government supervision of railroads, at the same time that the supervision is almost entirely nominal. Further, the older such a commission gets to be, the more inclined it will be found to take the business and railroad view of things.[9]

Their capture is usually based on several inescapable realities facing a regulatory commission: the necessity of meeting on a regular basis with the representatives of the organized industry; the dependence on the industry for necessary information; the absence of other, countervailing organized groups, particularly consumer groups; the dependence on industry expertise that leads over time to the domination of the commission by appointees from the industry; and the availability of lucrative positions in the regulated industry for cooperative commission staff people after their term of service.

There are numerous examples of such developments. The appointment of commissioners by the president, for instance, is almost always cleared with the dominant trade association in the regulated industry. The flow of excommissioners and staff members into the industry is as common today as ever. "Over half the former FCC commissioners leaving in recent years are high executives in the communications industry, [while] all but two of the ICC commissioners leaving that agency in the 1960s have either gone into the transportation industry or become ICC practitioners lawyering for the industry.''[10] One leading student of the subject has concluded that ''the outstanding political fact about the independent regulatory commissions is that they have in general become promoters and protectors of the industries they have been established to regulate.''[11] Most of these institutional arrangements have survived the deregulation fever of recent years.

Nonenforcement of Antitrust Laws

The federal government also encourages concentration through the nonenforcement of antitrust laws. As pointed out in an earlier chapter, these laws are rarely invoked by the antitrust division of the Department of Justice; actions are rarely directed against the largest corporations and are rarely successful, even when pressed; and in the few successful cases, dissolution rarely has its intended effects.[12] Despite occasional widely heralded antitrust cases, the trend toward corporate concentration and interlock has not been sufficiently affected by government activities in this area of public policy. During the presidencies of Jimmy Carter and Ronald Reagan, government policy makers explicitly acknowledged for the first time that bigness and even monopoly were not necessarily bad and that the federal government would be more accommodating to large-scale mergers. The Reagan Justice Department signaled these changes by dropping the IBM antitrust suit and approving mergers between such giants as GM and Toyota, and Republic Steel and LTV Corporation.

Federal Subsidies to Corporations

The federal government encourages concentration through its use of subsidies. The top corporations are so large, affect so many people, account for such a substantial portion of economic activity, and are so closely tied to other corporations and financial institutions that there is a great temptation to ensure that none of the major firms goes out of business. The most obvious recent examples involve the federal government's bail-out of the nearly bankrupt Lockheed Corporation in 1971, the Chrysler Corporation in 1981, and the Continental Illinois Bank (to the tune of $4.5 billion) in1984, but they are only the tip of a vast iceberg. In fact, by 1980 the federal government had outstanding some $163 billion in direct loans, as well as $298 billion in loan guarantees, or a total of $461 billion. The heaviest loans and loan guarantees find their way to firms in aerospace, shipbuilding, grain export, and national defense. In the last area, government subsidies provide a substantial portion of basic capital costs and almost all research and development monies. Given the reasons for subsidies in the first place, the stream of dollars is generally directed toward the largest firms in each industry.

A Short Note on Deregulation

It seems that the role of the federal government as guarantor of corporate concentration was reversed in the last days of the Carter administration and during the free-market–oriented Reagan administration through their mutual commitment to deregulation. The most dramatic example of this commitment was the loosening of the federal government controls in the transportation industry, particularly in trucking, airlines, and banking. Nevertheless, despite the talk of deregulation by politicians in both parties and the handful of dramatic cases in which this rhetoric was put into effect, deregulation has had an uneven history over the past few years. In general, that history can be summarized as follows: deregulation has largely taken place with respect to those activities that have hurt the profit position of the major corporations and has been conspicuously absent where government control and regulation contribute to their market dominance and profitability.[13] When faced with the music of its free-market rhetoric with the impending collapse of the Continental Illinois Bank, Ronald Reagan "blinked." As U.S. Representative Fernand St. Germaine put it, the lesson of the bail-out was "the concept that the large shall not fail."[14] I shall say more about regulation and deregulation in the next chapter.

GOVERNMENT
AND THE BUSINESS CYCLE

The objective of macroeconomic policy is to ensure the health, safety, and profitability of America's most important economic institutions based on the dictum that "what is good for General Motors (or Chase Manhattan, or IBM, or Standard Oil) is good for America." While specific macroeconomic policies may shift over time from Keynesianism, to monetarism, to supply-sidism, overall macroeconomic policy is formulated, nevertheless, within the boundaries of the guiding objective. Means change, that is to say; ends do not.

Why macroeconomic policy at all? Why not simply let the free market run its course without the benefit of a government role? The answer is readily apparent.

Without the intervention of the federal government into the management of the business cycle, advanced capitalist countries would continually face collapse. Without using the full arsenal of fiscal and monetary devices available to modern governments, capitalist economic systems would face ever more severe cycles of inflation alternating with mass unemployment and underutilization of plant and equipment. In no small measure, modern capitalism owes its survival to the set of government taxing and spending strategies directed toward control of the business cycle.[15]

This role as manager for the entire economic system of capitalism is light-years away from the traditional American concept of the proper role of government. The laissez-faire view stresses the necessity of limited government, one confined to "night watchman" functions and essentially noninterventionist in the private economy. Nothing better demonstrates the distance modern capitalist governments have traveled from this traditional concept than the words of the Employment Act of 1946, which unequivocally articulated the modern view: "The Congress declares that it is the continuing responsibility of the federal government to . . . promote maximum employment, production and purchasing power.'' While mouthing the rhetoric of laissez-faire theory, government under Ronald Reagan continued to use its fiscal and monetary tools in an attempt to create an environment conducive to capital accumulation.

The Keynesian Revolution

This revolution in the relationship of government to the economy was literally forced on political and economic decision makers by the general recognition of the inherently unstable nature of capitalism. In fact, from the end of the Civil War to the start of the Great Depression in 1929, the American economy suffered sixteen major recessions or depressions.[16] These periodic collapses culminated in the Great Depression of the 1930s, a depression so severe that none of the supposed "self-correcting" features of the free market was sufficient to bring the nation out of the doldrums. It took the combined impact of the 1937 economic collapse (brought on by a "balanced" federal government budget), the prosperity of the World War II years (bolstered by massive deficits in federal government spending), and the theoretical work of the great economist John Maynard Keynes to demonstrate the necessary role of government in the management of the business cycle.

The key to understanding the capitalist business cycle is the relationship between what economists call aggregate demand and productive capacity. A stable economy requires a close fit between the level of overall demand—money spent for goods and services by consumers, businesspeople (through investments), and government—and the total goods and services produced by the economic system when operating near its maximum potential. The business cycle is determined by the fluctuation of aggregate demand, which almost never rests at the equilibrium point required for a stable economy. At most times, aggregate demand falls well below full capacity (leading to idle plant and equipment, declining profits, and unemployment) and causes recession. At other times, aggregate demand, the total value of the money spent for goods and services, exceeds the value of the goods and services the system is able to produce, leading invariably to price inflation.[17]

Keynes demonstrated that the only way to stabilize alterations in the business cycle was for government to control the level of aggregate demand in the economy. He argued that during times of lagging demand, when consumer spending and private investment are insufficient, government should boost demand by significantly increasing its own spending, by decreasing taxes on individuals and business, or by lowering interest rates to encourage borrowing (or any combination of these strategies). In times of excess demand, Keynes argued that government should deflate the overall level of spending by slashing its own expenditures, increasing taxes, or raising interest rates (or any combination). It is to this complex mix of fiscal and monetary mechanisms that all western capitalist governments have subscribed in the years since World War II, and with much success. This management of the level of aggregate demand through Keynesian devices caused the relative prosperity of the 1960s, a prosperity free of serious recession or infla-

The Great Depression: living at the bottom of the business cycle

tion that moved even a nominal conservative like Richard Nixon to declare "We are all Keynesians now."[18]

In the formation of macroeconomic policy from the 1950s through the 1970s, virtually all of the western capitalist nations were guided by one variant or another of Keynesianism. One is struck by the great similarities among the western nations, despite some policy differences, in their approaches to macroeconomic policy. The great exception is the United States. In our own nation, Keynesianism took on a unique coloration, first, because of important compromises with "monetarism" and second, because of the militarization of macroeconomic policy.

Keynesianism and Monetarism. The main concern of Keynesian theory is economic growth and employment. The main concern of monetarism is price stability and a strong dollar. The main instruments of the former have been federal tax policy and the federal budget (cutting taxes or increasing spending to spur the economy). The main instrument of the latter has been control of the money supply, and in particular, the availability and price of credit (increasing interest rates, in the main, to dampen inflation). In one way or another, most administrations in the United States in the post-war period have tried to loosely integrate these two forms of macroeconomic policy, priming the economic pump through deficit spending and trying to control inflation by maintaining high interest rates.

As political scientist David Cameron demonstrates, the United States is unique among the western nations to the extent that its macroeconomic policy has been at least as interested in price stability as in growth and employment.[19] While political and economic leaders in the United States have been traditionally concerned with ensuring a sound dollar—note the effects of the cheap money policies of the Rhode Island legislature and Shay's Rebellion (Chapter 4) on the Founders' desire for a new constitution—Cameron suggests that this traditional preference has been exaggerated over the past several decades by the increasing power and prominence of finance capital (banks) and multinational corporations who want price stability and a strong dollar,[20] and by the erosion of the position of American labor unions who are most interested in growth and employment.

The United States is also different from other capitalist countries, according to Cameron, in its widespread usage of monetary instruments to create "managed recessions" so that wage rates might be dampened and corporate profitability reestablished after periods of sluggish corporate performance. The unique relations between the social classes in the United States—especially the power of capital and the weakness of labor compared to the typical western European situation—is thus reflected in a rather unique approach to macroeconomic policy. While Keynesian growth and employment concerns motivate American political leaders, they are neatly counterbalanced by concerns for price stability and a strong dollar.

Military Keynesianism. Keynesian economic theory is concerned with the level of aggregate demand in the economy; the level of overall spending by individuals, businesses, and government; and the mechanisms by which government manages the level of economic activity. It is an economic theory in which government becomes the coordinator of the system. Keynesian theory does *not* offer advice, however, about the objectives and priorities of government taxing, spending, and interest rate policies. In times of insufficient demand, it does not matter whether government spends its money on roads, hospitals, bullets, or empty holes, so long as it spends a sufficient amount of money to increase economic activity and employment. In times of excess demand, it does not matter whether taxes are levied against the present consumption of blue-collar workers, white-collar workers, or the very wealthy, as long as total spending is reduced by the appropriate amount. With all these potential options, the overriding spending commitment of the federal government for at least three decades has been on the military.

It would be no exaggeration to say that the United States has been on a *permanent war footing* since 1941. Well over one-half of all budget expenditures since that date have been devoted to military activities (to say nothing of the millions of men and women in the armed forces, the bases scattered around the globe, and entire industries devoted to the production of war materials). While there was a significant decrease in military budgets in the wake of the U.S. military's humiliating defeat in Vietnam, they have been rapidly expanding since the late 1970s. Under Ronald Reagan, the military budget expanded faster than in any other period in peace-time American history. Military expenditures stood at $192 billion and 25 percent of the federal budget when he came to office in 1981. If the projections of his own Office of Management and Budget are to be believed, he will leave office in 1988 with a military budget of $370 billion, representing 35 percent of total federal outlays (8 percent of GNP, up from 5.5 percent).

Why does the federal government spend so much on the military? Why is it that out of the universe of possibilities open to it, political leaders have depended so heavily on military outlays to bolster aggregate demand? The answer is fairly straightforward. Military spending represents a brilliant solution to the main problem facing capitalism: how can one spend massive amounts of public money without adversely affecting the private domination of the economy by the major corporations?

While we have focused on both the upward (inflation) and downward (recession or depression) aspects of the business cycle, the principal problem that has confronted capitalism in the twentieth century has been the *crisis of overproduction*. While there is some debate about whether overproduction is the product of insufficient buying power among consumers or of overinvestment by business, the final outcome remains unambiguous—the underutilization of productive capacity with resulting high unemployment. Government is involved in a perpetual race to constantly bolster demand as a method to forestall collapse. In this herculean effort, the federal government is forced to spend ever-increasing amounts of public money.

The military sector is a particularly attractive outlet for such spending. In the military sector, one can spend prodigious amounts of money (given the arms race and the perpetual obsolescence of weapons systems) without direct challenge to the privately dominant sector. To invest on a large scale in mass transportation, housing, public health, and the like, would be to challenge and compete directly with private corporations. In spending for tanks, aircraft carriers, and missile systems, the major corporations are enriched and face no serious threat to their own market position.

It is an established fact, moreover, that the wealthy have been willing to have their savings taxed for military but not for massive social purposes. The rapid turnaround of business sentiment on the subject of government deficit spending as America moved from "Doctor New Deal" to what Roosevelt called "Doctor Win-the-War" in the early 1940s is only the most dramatic example of a commonly witnessed phenomenon.

Military spending, furthermore, tends to be concentrated in the capital goods industry (representing about 20 percent of the sales of the engine and turbine industries, 39 percent of machine tools, 17 percent of electronics, and so on), the sector which is, according to economists, the key to the business cycle. In the words of Paul Samuelson, ". . . there is good reason to believe that the movement of durable goods represents key causes [of the business cycle]."[21] Military spending acts as a prop and a support to a key industrial sector in the movement of the business cycle.

It is also the case that military spending is enormously profitable for American corporations. Various studies confirm that military contract dollars go disproportionately to the largest corporations and to the richer regions of the country. Profits are guaranteed by noncompetitive bidding, cost-plus contracts, rent-free use of government property, subsidized research and development, toleration of massive cost overruns, and protection from bankruptcy (see the case of Lockheed). Finally, political leaders have found military spending to be an attractive option for "priming" the economic pump because a strong military is essential for protecting the worldwide interests of the American based multinational corporation,[22] a subject to which I shall return later in this chapter.

Reagan Macroeconomic Policy.   It is interesting to see how these various strands of traditional macroeconomic policy came together with a vengeance during Ronald Reagan's first administration and led to significant improvements in American economic performance. In order to control inflation, the Reagan administration deferred (as it must under the law) to the draconian tight-money policies of the Federal Reserve Board under the leadership of Paul Volcker. In order to "prime" the economic pump, the Reagan administration turned to two Keynesian methods used with great success by John F. Kennedy in the early 1960s: a massive tax cut for corporations and upper income groups, and the creation of unprecedented deficits fueled by the explosive expansion of the military budget.

GOVERNMENT AND THE CORPORATE INFRASTRUCTURE

Under conditions of competitive capitalism (which no longer exist), business people were able to generate increased profits only by decreasing their costs of production relative to their competitors'. Since capital and raw material costs remained virtually identical for all of the competing firms within an industry, the only alternative was to squeeze labor costs, cutting the cost of labor per unit of production. The route to profits was through extracting increasing amounts of work from existing workers by such means as longer hours, the speed-up, closer supervision, work specialization, and so on. All that was required from the owner of an enterprise, other than ownership of plant and equipment and thus of available jobs, was an army of work supervisors, industrial engineers, and a private police force to work within the factory. All the requirements for the extraction of profits were available, in large part, to each individual owner.

In the era of concentrated corporate capitalism, the generation of profits is no longer exclusively tied to these crude forms of squeezing the workforce. Rather, the output and earnings of the corporate sector depend on improvements in the tools of production; advances in technology; the quality of the environment; the skill, education, and health of the workforce; the efficiency and convenience of the transportation system; and so on. Advances on all these fronts exist *outside* the scope and capacities of any company or set of companies. Advancing the quality of technology, the workforce, and transportation requires a larger agency, an agency with greater scope and resources than any group of enterprises—namely government. Rather than manage such social improvements by itself or pay for them out of profits, the corporate sector allows government to "socialize [the] costs of retirement pensions, health plans, manpower training, research and development and other outlays" it cannot profitably absorb.[23]

I won't bore you with a full litany of the thousands of ways in which government lifts a potential burden from the corporate sector through the socialization of the costs of production. It is worth pointing out, however, that the public, through its taxes, pays for almost all of the costs of research and development in American industry; of the construction, maintenance, and subsidization of transportation systems; of cleaning up the pollution generated by private businesses; and of personnel training through its system of public education. The public, not the corporate sector, bears all these costs of improving the climate in which the system of production operates and from which it benefits.

This discussion leads us to a further consideration of what economists call *diseconomies*. While production in the United States is almost totally in private hands, much of the production of private business has serious adverse side effects that private owners do not expect to rectify. The overdependence on the automobile has the now familiar effect of making the air in many parts of the United States both unpalatable and unhealthy. Many industrial processes produce toxic chemicals that pollute rivers and streams. Other processes act to deplete precious natural resources. In almost no case, however, are business enterprises expected by political leaders to bear the costs of these adverse costs of production. A significant portion of government expenditure is directed toward minimizing these social costs of private production. It is for that reason that increasing subsidies and tax breaks are directed toward the corporations to encourage them to rectify sets of problems for which they themselves are responsible (e.g., pollution, auto safety, and industrial safety).

The adverse effects of economic development are not confined to the mass public, however, but often seriously affect other important industries. The operations of one industry may increase the problem of profit extraction for another industry, and government is often called upon to ease the impact. The very poor performance of the auto industry in the field of safety, for instance, is a matter of serious concern to the major insurance companies who must pay ever-increasing costs as a result of court judgments in auto accident litigations. The insurance industry has been a leader, not surprisingly, in the effort to convince government to push the auto firms on the safety issue, to finance research in that area, and to place a ceiling on insurance payments.

There are also many cases in which the operations of a corporation not only create problems for third parties, but threaten its very own resource base. The traditional practice in mature capitalism is to increase government regulation in affected areas, but it is also to subsidize, either directly or through tax incentives, the efforts of corporations to maintain their *own* resource base. To take a case in point, it is the federal government that, in the main, pays for the reforestation of timber lands that private corporations have themselves denuded.

During the second Reagan administration, many of these programs were cut back in the face of the deficit crisis created by Reagan's tax cuts and military buildup. The corporate requirements for these programs have not disappeared, however, so we are certain to see their resurrection.

THE OVERSEAS INTERESTS
OF CORPORATIONS AND U.S. FOREIGN POLICY
The Case of Allende's Chile

In November 1970, after a popular electoral victory, Marxist Salvador Allende assumed the office of president of Chile.[24] Allende's platform called for Chile's gradual and peaceful transformation to socialism and for the expropriation of the major American firms in Chile (primarily ITT and the copper giants, Anaconda and Kennecott). It was reasonable that Allende should run and win on such a platform; between 1945 and 1972, American firms sent home $7.2 billion in profits from Chile but reinvested only $1 billion in the local economy. In the sixty years prior to the election of Allende, Anaconda and Kennecott took home in profits the equivalent of one-half of Chile's total assets.[25] Clearly, American business operating in Chile, and, as will be seen, the United States government, were more than a little concerned about this potential drift of events toward expropriation and the end of privileged American investment in that country.

When Allende expropriated the copper companies with the unanimous vote of the opposition-dominated congress, arguing that the profits enjoyed by the companies over the previous sixty years had more than adequately compensated the companies, American corporate and political officials launched a campaign of economic warfare designed to wreck the Chilean economy, generate internal opposition to Allende, and prepare the ground for a military coup. As Secretary of State William Rogers told a group of business leaders who had substantial interests in Chile, "The Nixon Administration is a business Administration. Its mission is to protect American business."[26]

The game plan, while less direct than the military interventions ("gunboat diplomacy") characteristic of the early decades of the twentieth century, was nevertheless deadly effective. American corporations cooperated in the effort to bring down Allende by refusing to sell spare parts to Chile; cutting back production in nonnationalized plants, thereby increasing unemployment; cutting private loans from American-dominated banks operating in Chile; speculating against Chilean currency in international markets; and subsidizing dissident groups and newspapers within Chile. The U.S. government did its part by cutting off Export-Import Bank credits; pressuring the American-dominated international financial agencies (the International Monetary Fund, the World Bank) to end all loans to Chile; organizing a world boycott of Chilean copper; ending all foreign aid assistance (with the notable exception of military aid, which jumped from $800,000 in the year before Allende's election to $12 million two years later!); covertly financing opposition parties, unions, and newspapers; and producing the funds necessary to sustain the middle class–dominated antigovernment strikes.

The conclusion of the socialist experiment in Chile developed much as corporate and government policy makers had hoped, though the ferocity unleashed by the military coup caused some embarrassment to the U.S. government, with about twenty thousand people dying at the hands of the junta within a few short weeks. By the time of Allende's overthrow and brutal murder on September 11, 1973, the Chilean economy was in almost total collapse while Chilean society was virtually paralyzed by the violence and strike activity unleashed by the anti-Allende forces. It was only a matter of time, given this state of affairs, before the American-trained and financed armed forces made their move, precipitated by the reassuring presence of American naval vessels stationed off the coast, involved at the time in joint maneuvers with Chilean forces.

Since the coup, Chile, under Augusto Pinochet, has been governed by one of the most brutal and repressive regimes on the globe, but it is friendly to American business investment and continued American presence. A clue to the orientations of the ruling military junta is that in its *very first statement of policy,* it "restored many prerogatives of private business and offered to reopen negotiations with foreign companies with the goal of making Chile once again attractive to foreign capital."[27] Needless to say, the years since the coup have witnessed the resumption of aid, more favorable loan terms from the IMF and World Bank, and the resumption of American private business investment. While this relationship was temporarily strained by the assassination of former Allende minister Orlando Letelier (and colleague Ronnie Moffat) by elements of DINA (the Chilean secret police) in the streets of Washington, D.C., it has not altered the major contours of that policy. Indeed, the Reagan administration has often emphasized its policy of good relations with Chile as part of its anticommunist crusade in the hemisphere.

The Contours of American Foreign Policy

While the Chilean tragedy is more dramatic than most cases because of the brutality of the military repression and the open and obvious supportive role of the United States, the tight fit between the goals of American foreign policy and business interests is all too typical. The very foundation of American foreign policy, its defining purposes, are embedded in the interests of the giant American corporations.

Why is this so? Why is it that such a close fit exists between government and business in foreign policy? Why is it that American business tends to expand into the world, followed closely by the protective arm of the government? Why is it that America consistently supports authoritarian, often brutal, yet pro-business

U.S. adviser instructs a Salvadorean cadet

regimes such as those in South Africa, Iran (under the now deposed Shah), South Korea, Argentina, Brazil, Nicaragua (until the popular overthrow of the hated Somoza regime), Indonesia, Taiwan, and the Dominican Republic? Why does it consistently wage war (covert and overt) against popular yet anti-American regimes as in Nicaragua under the Sandinistas, Brazil under Goulart, Guatemala under Arbenz, the Dominican Republic under Bosch, and Jamaica under Manley?

Such a close fit between corporation and government is inevitable and unavoidable. Capitalism is inherently expansive, and government has no alternative, if it remains concerned with the health of the American economy, but to support the activities of these firms in their overseas operations. Let us examine these issues in more depth.

The Dynamics of Imperialism

Capitalism is a system that presses outward from national boundaries in a never-ending search for sources of profit, raw materials, and markets, and over the centuries it has managed to tie together, through an elaborate system of unequal market relations, all of the nonsocialist world.[28] This elaborate system, which I shall call *imperialism*,[29] ties together *core* capitalist states (the centers of capital accumulation) and less developed *periphery* states (the centers from which economic surplus is extracted) and adapts the latter to fit the needs of the former through economic, political, and military means.

In the earlier stages of capitalism, imperialism took a form very much different from the contemporary one. While modern imperialism maintains its system of domination through elaborate, indirect, and barely visible methods, early capitalism extracted surplus in rather crude ways. Direct plunder formed the basis for the earliest capitalist accumulation process and provided the motive force for capitalist development. The plunder generated by the wave of crusades from the eleventh through the fifteenth centuries provided the capital for the rise of the Italian city states. In the fifteenth and sixteenth centuries, plunder from the New World (transferred from Spain because of its horrendously adverse balance of trade) formed the basis for capitalist development in England, Holland, and Germany. The naked theft and sale of human beings (the slave trade) was an important factor in the rise of England and Holland as important merchant and financial powers. Marx described these processes as follows:

> The discovery of gold and silver in America, the extirpation, enslavement and entombment in mines of the aboriginal population, the beginning of the conquest and looting of the East Indies, the turning of Africa into a warren for the commercial hunting of blackskins, signalized the rosy dawn of the era of capitalist production. These idyllic proceedings are the chief momenta of primitive accumulation.
>
> The treasures captured outside Europe by undisguised looting, enslavement, and murder floated back to the mother country and were there turned into capital.[30]

After the era of primitive accumulation through plunder had sparked the industrial development of the core capitalist states (England, Holland, Germany, and France), the relationship among these states and the subordinate periphery underwent an important transformation. The need for goods acquired through direct and brutal plunder gave way to the need for assured supplies of raw materials for their factories and markets for finished products. The need for regularized if unequal trade (a more benign form of plunder), led to the fashioning of more stable and predictable linkages between core and periphery. Thus by the late nineteenth and twentieth centuries a worldwide system of colonialism had come into being in which the core capitalist states established direct political-military rule over less developed societies and in which each colonial power attempted to establish areas of privileged trade and investment closed to other core capitalist states. As a result, this period was witness to an intense competition among the major European powers to carve Africa, Asia, and the Pacific into colonial spheres of influence.

Except in a very minor way, the United States never became seriously involved in colonialism. Discounting the short-lived colonial adventures in the Caribbean after the Spanish-American War, American imperialism has always taken anti-colonial forms. That is to say, its unequal relations with the less developed world has not depended on direct political rule and administration of these areas but on more indirect means. There has been much speculation about why American imperialism has taken anticolonial forms. Some have argued that America's own colonial past made it ideologically difficult to impose such relations on other peoples. Others have suggested that America had no need of external colonial expansion because it had its own internal empire, the vast areas stretching to the Pacific Ocean available to it after the extermination of the Indians and the victory in the Mexican War. Still others have suggested that by the time the United States was overcome with the external expansionary impulse at the turn of the century, the known world had already been parceled out among the major European powers. Finally, others have pointed out that the emergence of the United States as the industrial and financial leader of the capitalist world after 1900 gave it an economic power in international trade that would allow it to become predominant if it were allowed to trade freely with all parts of the world. A country in such a position required not so much its own colonies as the right to penetrate the colonies of the European states. The Open Door policy articulated by Secretary of State John Hay (calling for the opening of the China market to all capitalist countries, irrespective of already established European spheres of influence) is the best single example of this world posture, and it became the hallmark of American policy in general.

Whatever reason one chooses to explain the phenomenon, the fact is that American imperialism has been and remains anticolonial. Nevertheless, it remains imperialism. It continues to be a system in which the well-being of the United States is dependent on the extraction of wealth from less developed areas. In modern capitalism, this extraction is accomplished through a complex international economic network of trade, finance, and direct investment under the direction of American multinational corporations.

Increasingly, the capitalist world is tied together in relationships of superordination and subordination by the direct investment activities of the multinationals, the outright purchase and establishment of mines, factories, communications systems, and transportation, and their integration into a worldwide division of labor. In most of the less developed world, as a result, the control of domestic mineral, agricultural, and manufacturing assets is lodged in the hands of the multinations. In this division of labor, periphery countries are becoming the suppliers of some single component (whether a raw material such as copper or bauxite, or an industrial product such as auto engines or frames) that is processed or assembled into a finished product elsewhere on the globe under the managerial direction of corporate headquarters, normally in the United States. The inherent weakness of the periphery societies in such a system in which each performs some specialized economic task under core capitalist managerial and financial direction is obvious.

Imperialism is also held together by the financial networks of the core capitalist countries. The conduct of international business requires an infrastructure of finance, currency transaction, and credit, so it is not surprising that a world capitalist banking structure, mainly under the direction of the United States, has grown enormously over the past three decades. The world banking structure enhances the capacity of multinational companies to float short-term loans, to convert currencies almost instantaneously, and to gain access to international bond and equity capital. It also enables the United States in particular to dominate domestic banking in the less developed countries. Such domination not only gives operational control of local currencies and credit policies to an outside nation but also makes local savings (in U.S. branch banks) available to international companies.

Theories of Imperialism

The United States stands at the head of a system of world imperialism that ties together core capitalist states and peripheral, less developed states through the mechanisms of financial domination, unequal exchange, and the direct ownership of resource and industrial capacities and that transfers wealth from the periphery to the core as a matter of course. What needs to be explored further, at this point in the analysis, are the reasons why imperialism is a "way of life" in the United States.

Convincing theories of imperialism all begin with a consideration of the inner logic of mature capitalism and the requirements of its major component part, the corporate sector. One theoretical position holds that in concentrated capitalist societies firms continuously increase productivity and productive capacity in the race with other firms for profits. The result is that society is pushed toward the abyss of overproduction (since consumers, in a system of highly unequal income distribution, are never able to purchase all that the system is capable of producing) and there arises the concurrent problem of unused capacity, unemployment, and unrealized profits. In the United States, the overcapacity problem has become increasingly more serious through the years. The Federal Reserve Board has reported, for instance, that the manufacturing utilization rate was only 77.2 percent in the 1970–1975 period as compared with a 91.9 percent rate in the 1950–1954 period and continues to decline.[31] As historian Gabriel Kolko has pointed out, "The capitalist economy's traditional nemesis of inadequate demand and overexpansion [has] reappeared in almost classic form despite all the vast means that [have] been employed to counteract them and leads to the search for outlets for surplus."[32] Imperialism, in this view, is an inevitable phase in the development of the capitalist mode of production, a way to temporarily escape some of its basic contradictions.[33]

Added to overproduction as a motive force for overseas expansion is the dependency of the United States on raw material sources in the less developed world. While the fact of petroleum dependency is by now obvious, what would no doubt surprise most Americans is the degree to which the United States has become, in general, a dependent society in terms of most of its resource requirements, the degree to which it is a raw material have-not nation. Almost every raw material needed to keep the industrial system in operation depends on raw materials found only in the Third World.

One could make an equally persuasive case for the inherently expansionary nature of mature capitalism by examining the business practices and needs of individual corporations. Most importantly and most simply, overseas operations translate into higher profits, and the rational firms with the resources to make it possible (mainly giant corporations) invariably focus escalating proportions of their operations beyond the constricting business boundaries of the United States. The available data demonstrate two points conclusively. First, profits from overseas operations are at least twice as high as those from domestic operations. Second, overseas investment, production, and profit taking are concentrated among the largest firms in the American economy. The bases for the generation of super-profits by the largest firms are not too difficult to discern. With high costs in fixed capital already in place at home and market saturation a recurrent problem, the easiest way to increase sales without the necessity of cutting prices is to find new markets. Overseas markets remain the only loci where saturation is not yet a reality, and they are therefore open to the sales effort. Profitability is also the outcome of conducting most foreign operations in environments characterized by minimal taxation and few consumer or environmental protection requirements. Finally, in those increasingly common operations where production and assembly are being transferred overseas so as to cut tariff and transportation costs, multinational enterprises are blessed with an abundance of cheap labor in places like Korea, Taiwan, and Singapore, labor that works for wages often less than one-tenth that paid to American workers. The temptations of shifting operations overseas are great indeed.

The multinational firms are also expansionary because of their dependency on unsubstitutable raw materials for their operations. Direct ownership and control of raw material supplies is one way that the giant corporation attempts to add stability and predictability to its operations. Steel companies, therefore, seek not only additional markets but control of assured supplies of iron ore. Aluminum companies seek dependable supplies of bauxite. To have such supplies in the hands of either industrial competitors or hostile social systems are situations to be avoided at all costs. It must be added that the effort to control raw materials is not simply one of supplying needed materials for the industrial machine but of ensuring the stability of market shares by denying resources to potential new rivals. The major oil companies, to take a case in point, traditionally searched for new oil reserves even during those periods characterized by a world oil glut so as to keep the "independents" from challenging their domination of the industry.

Whichever theoretical explanation one chooses, and I am of the opinion that all of them must be taken together, it is abundantly clear that capitalism requires expansion into the far corners of the globe and the subordination of the less developed countries to its needs as an economic system. No other set of theoretical explanations has yet been able to adequately describe the inexorable drive of capitalism toward expansion and a world structure of unequal relations between core and periphery.

Government Foreign Policy Services

The American-based multinational corporations do not venture into the world naked and exposed but go with the assistance and protection of the American government. As historian Gabriel Kolko has pointed out, "In the aggregate it is a fact that the final intended result of the whole course of United States foreign policy after the Civil War was to optimize the power and profit of American capitalism in the global economy, striving for the political and military preconditions essential to the attainment of that end."[34] Since global corporations are the most important components of the American economy, the federal government cannot help but be concerned with their stability and profitability. To act otherwise would undermine the very economy that allows the government to maintain its legitimacy in the eyes of the public. It is this close cooperation between the government and American business in its overseas operations that forms the foundation and framework of American foreign policy. Foreign policy is neither motivated by the effort to expand "human rights" nor designed to establish the United States as a "good neighbor." Rather, it is based firmly on the needs and interests of the major corporations operating in the world economy.

Government supports the American-based corporations in many ways, some obvious, some more subtle. Most important, the government attempts to ensure that American private capital enjoys free access to new markets on favorable terms. It may do so by ensuring that IMF and World Bank loans are extended only on condition of the maintenance of a favorable investment climate. It may also do so by tying foreign aid to the signing of investment guarantee treaties by the recipient country. The federal government, faced with a regime in a developing nation unfavorable to American investment, may initiate more coercive actions. These moves can range from cutting off foreign aid, to manipulating the lending policies of world monetary organizations, to fostering disruption and internal subversion (the continual harassment of Cuba after the Castro revolution by the Central Intelligence Agency is a good example), all the way to the assassination of foreign leaders, and direct military intervention (as in the unsuccessful invasion of Cuba, the overthrow of popular leftist regimes in Iran, Guatemala, Chile, and the Congo, the invasion of tiny Grenada, and sponsorship of the war against Nicaragua by hired mercenary armies).

In addition to guaranteeing an environment favorable to the penetration of

American business, the federal government pursues certain policies that directly benefit the largest U.S. firms. Aid programs, for instance, customarily require the recipient country to spend aid funds on American products (even if the products can be found elsewhere at a lower price) and to ship such products on American flag vessels. Also, the government customarily uses tariff policy to try to prevent developing nations from being anything other than raw material sources, to ensure that they do not compete with American firms in producing finished products. Coffee beans enter the United States free of duty, for instance, yet a high tariff wall faces finished products such as ground or instant coffee. The same is true of bauxite and aluminum, iron ore and steel, and so on down the list.

While each and every foreign policy decision is not directly related to the interests of a specific American corporation, the broad outlines of foreign policy are indeed related to the interests of American-based multinational corporations in general. American world policy, since at least the presidency of Woodrow Wilson, has been directed toward allowing American corporations to operate freely and profitably in as many countries as possible, to construct and to maintain an "open door" around the globe for business enterprise.[35] Such a task, of course, requires a vigorous, assertive, and interventionist foreign policy as well as substantial military capacity. To the extent that the corporate sector of American capitalism depends on global operations for its health and vitality, the federal government performs perhaps its most important service for it by encouraging, maintaining, and protecting that global presence.

CONCLUDING REMARKS

It is generally assumed, at least by the public and by the media, that the so-called "Reagan Revolution" has fundamentally altered the role of the federal government in the United States. We shall see in the next chapter that something approximating a revolution has indeed been achieved in that aspect of American public policy having to do with the relations between social classes. With respect to that aspect of public policy having to do with capital accumulation, however, the "Reagan Revolution" has acted within the accepted post-war American tradition although Ronald Reagan and his people have acted more skillfully, coherently, and energetically than previous administrations. Public policy under Reagan has further encouraged corporate concentration, produced economic expansion through military Keynesianism, and reinvigorated American imperial expansion and the suppression of popular movements in the Third World. He has been more single-minded[36] and successful in the pursuit of these goals than his predecessors. He has not strayed, however, from the goals themselves.

NOTES

1. For a discussion of the twin tasks of capital accumulation and legitimation (the management of class relations), see James O'Connor, *The Fiscal Crisis of the State* (New York: St. Martin's Press, 1973).

2. For the best discussions of these changes see Samuel P. Hays, *The Response to Industrialization: 1885–1914* (Chicago: University of Chicago Press, 1957); Gabriel Kolko, *The Triumph of Conservatism: A Reinterpretation of American History, 1900–1916* (Chicago: Quadrangle Books, 1967); and Robert H. Wiebe, *The Search for Order: 1879–1920* (New York: Hill & Wang, 1967).

3. See Kolko, *The Triumph of Conservatism*, p. 40.

4. Ibid.

5. For a summary of this history see Edward S. Greenberg, *Capitalism and the American Political Ideal* (Armonk, N.Y.: M. E. Sharpe, 1985).

6. The definition is from Ted Lowi, *The End of Liberalism* (New York: Norton, 1969), p. 36.

7. On these issues see Lowi, *The End of Liberalism:* Mark Green, ed., *The Monopoly Makers: Ralph Nader's Study Group Report on Regulation and Competition* (New York: Grossman, 1973); and Grant McConnell, *Private Power and American Democracy* (New York: Knopf, 1967).

8. On the politics of regulatory agencies see Marver Bernstein, *Regulating Business by Independent Commission* (Princeton, N.J: Princeton University Press, 1955); Murray Edelman, *The Symbolic Uses of Politics* (Champaign: University of Illinois Press, 1964); Green, *The Monopoly Makers;* Lowi, *The End of Liberalism;* McConnell, *Private Power and American Democracy.*

9. Quoted in McConnell, *Private Power*, p. 284.

10. Green, *The Monopoly Makers,* p. 16.

11. McConnell, *Private Power*, p. 287. Active and determined regulation of these industries by commissions staffed by appointees from various public interest groups during the Carter years partially undermined this traditional generalization about "capture." The reversal, however, was short-lived as the Reagan appointees took over, bringing the commissions back into bed with the regulated industries.

12. Financial analysts are in general agreement that the "landmark" AT&T divestiture in 1981 has resulted in a more profitable and powerful company since it rid itself only of its regulated, unprofitable units (local phone companies).

13. For details see Alan Stone, "State and Market: Economic Regulation and the Great Productivity Debate," in Thomas Ferguson and Joel Rogers, eds., *The Hidden Election* (New York: Pantheon, 1981).

14. *The New York Times* (July 27, 1984), p. 42.

15. Sidney Ulmer, *The Welfare State* (Boston: Houghton Mifflin, 1969), p. 27.

16. Ibid.

17. As pointed out in chapter 6, administered pricing by oligopolistic firms make an equally important contribution to inflation.

18. What Keynes failed to appreciate, however, was the political difficulty in slashing government expenditures once groups in the population came to understand receipt of such federal monies as a right.

19. David R. Cameron, "The Politics and Economics of the Business Cycle," in Thomas Ferguson and Joel Rogers (eds.), *The Political Economy* (Armonk, N.Y.: M. E. Sharpe, 1984), pp. 237–262.

20. The former want a strong dollar in order to protect the value of their assets and loans. The latter want it because much of their production is overseas and a strong dollar allows them to produce cheaply abroad and to penetrate the American market.

21. Paul Samuelson, *Economics,* 8th ed. (New York: McGraw-Hill, 1970), p. 240.

22. If this analysis is correct, it would suggest that the incredible military buildup of the late Carter presidency and of the Reagan administration had less to do with the Soviet threat than with a faltering economy and a desperate search for solutions as well as a disintegration of the American empire and the need to protect it.

23. James O'Connor, *The Corporation and the State* (New York: Harper & Row, 1974), p. 40.

24. In the 1964 election in Chile, the United States pumped over $20 million into the electoral campaign to support Frei against Allende (see the *Washington Post,* April 6, 1973). In the 1970 campaign, it poured $400,000 into an anti-Allende media campaign alone (see U.S. Subcommittee on Intelligence, 1975).

25. Steven J. Rosen, "Rightist Regimes and American Interests," *Society* 11:6 (September–October 1974), p. 56.

26. Quoted in Richard J. Barnet and Ronald E. Müller, *Global Reach* (New York: Simon & Schuster, 1974).

27. Rosen, "Rightist Regimes and American Interests," p. 57.

28. It is interesting to note that at earlier stages in American history, at a time when empire was generally admired and the civilizing potential of Christian and European culture was considered axiomatic, discussions linking American liberty and an expanding empire were very much in evidence. James Madison, in particular, may be cited in this regard for his famous argument about the necessity of "expanding the sphere in defense of the Constitution," a position standing in contradistinction to arguments like those of Thomas Jefferson who saw republican government and a small territorial state as synonymous.

29. I shall use the term *imperialism* to characterize this relationship because of the traditional usage of that term and with the full knowledge that capitalism is neither the first nor will it be the last example of imperialism. Nor is it the first or the last example of expansionism or militarism. Nevertheless, unequal relations, expansionism, and militarism take on particular forms under modern capitalism that distinguish it from previous forms and that heighten its impact on subject societies.

30. Karl Marx, *Capital* (Moscow: Foreign Languages Publishing House, 1954) Vol. 1, Part VIII, ch. 31.

31. Gabriel Kolko, *Main Currents in American History* (New York: Harper & Row, 1976), p. 339.

32. Ibid.

33. For renderings of this view see Paul Baran and Paul Sweezy, *Monopoly Capital* (New York: Monthly Review Press, 1966); V. I. Lenin, *Imperialism: The Highest Stage of Capitalism* (New York: International Publishers, 1939); Harry Magdoff, *The Age of Imperialism* (New York: Monthly Review Press, 1966); James O'Connor, "The Meaning of Economic Imperialism," *The Corporations and the State,* James O'Connor, ed. (New York: Harper Colophon Books, 1974); and Kolko, *Main Currents,* ch. 9.

34. Kolko, *Main Currents,* pp. 49–50.

35. For the classic exposition of the relationship between the "open door" and the expansion of American business, see William A. Williams, *The Tragedy of American Diplomacy* (New York: Delta, 1959).

36. While Jimmy Carter attempted to maintain the health of the American empire, he was also genuinely interested in the status of human rights in our client states. Ronald Reagan erased that concern from the foreign policy agenda after he came to office.

SUGGESTIONS FOR FURTHER READING

Murray Edelman. THE SYMBOLIC USES OF POLITICS. *Champaign: University of Illinois Press, 1964.* A careful look at myth and symbol in political life, with a compelling section on government regulation and the encouragement of economic concentration.

Norman Furniss and Timothy Tilton. THE CASE FOR THE WELFARE STATE. *Bloomington: Indiana University Press, 1977.* A careful comparison of the growth and operations of modern government in the western capitalist countries, with an elaboration of how and why they differ so greatly.

Edward S. Greenberg. CAPITALISM AND THE AMERICAN POLITICAL IDEAL. *Armonk, N.Y.: M. E. Sharpe, Inc., 1985.* An attempt to explain the emergence of modern large-scale government in the United States as a direct result of capitalist development and transformation.

Theodore Lowi. THE END OF LIBERALISM. *New York: Norton, 1969.* An analysis of the tightly interlocked nature of interest groups and government agencies.

Grant McConnell. PRIVATE POWER AND AMERICAN DEMOCRACY. *New York: Knopf, 1967.* A modern classic that focuses on the relationship of governments to institutions of private power.

James O'Connor. THE FISCAL CRISIS OF THE STATE. *New York: St. Martin's Press, 1973.* A sophisticated and complex argument from the Marxist view directed toward an understanding of modern capitalist governments.

L. S. Stavrianos. GLOBAL RIFT: THE THIRD WORLD COMES OF AGE. *New York: William Morrow, 1981.* A brilliant synthesis of the literature on the history of the expansion of capitalism and the consequent transformation of the Third World.

Eric R. Wolf. EUROPE AND THE PEOPLE WITHOUT HISTORY. *Berkeley, California: University of California Press, 1982.* The best single treatment in the literature on the rise of capitalism, its penetration into the Third World, and the transformation of both core and periphery societies.

14

What Does Government Do?
The Welfare State and
the Management
of Discontent

Contrary to popular conception, capitalism does not operate automatically. Concentrated corporate capitalism, the prevailing form of capitalism in the United States today, requires, as we saw in the last chapter, the continual intervention of government to provide and ensure a proper environment for capital accumulation. Much of what government does in the United States is determined by this imperative: without the gyroscope of government, American capitalism would have long ago succumbed to perpetual economic crisis. While this responsibility explains much of what government does, it by no means explains it all. To understand American government, we must also take note of the disruptive impact of capitalist production, the responses called forth among adversely affected members of the population, and the efforts by political leaders to reestablish social stability and a sense of legitimate authority. These issues are examined in greater detail as we turn our attention to the American welfare state.

CAPITALISM AND SOCIAL DISRUPTION

I have suggested at several points in this book that capitalist economies, being incredibly dynamic and change-oriented, are disruptive of traditional values and institutions, conducive to personal disintegration and interpersonal tensions, and dangerous to social harmony and stability. Working at peak efficiency, capitalism continually creates the new and discards the old: new technologies replace old ones; new communities rise while old communities die; new occupations appear

314

while old ones disappear. In the midst of inequality and poverty, wealth is created in prodigious quantities. The business cycle alternates periods of economic growth with stagnation and unemployment. Pollution and alienation are generated as quickly as useful products.

The list could go on, but the point is clear. Capitalist economies, even admitting their great ability to produce goods and services, are highly problematic for the people living within them. Most of the time, most people simply put up with the radical transformations, tensions, and disruptions in their lives caused by this dynamo. Sometimes, however, some people refuse to remain idle, immobile, and apathetic. From the earliest days of market capitalism, in fact, people have periodically devised ways to check the advance of market logic and its harsh consequences.[1]

Social Disruption
and Government Policy

Thus, the history of the advance of corporate capitalism in the United States is also the history of ordinary people organizing to protect themselves against its harsh consequences. In that effort, they have often turned to government for the redress of grievances. Thus we see added to the modern state not only programs directly favorable to and proposed by large-scale business enterprises but also programs at least partially beneficial to the mass of the population, programs forced into public policy by the efforts of ordinary people. I am referring to programs such as old age assistance, unemployment insurance, guarantees of collective bargaining, welfare, pollution controls, product safety laws, public health measures, antitrust actions, and hundreds of additional interventions by government into previously private economic affairs for the general protection of the public.

Several things must be said about these numerous and varied programs. For the most part, they are not necessarily consistent with specific popular desires but are, rather, partial and halting responses by social, economic, and political elites fearful of mass discontent, turmoil, and possible dangerous voting behavior. Note that the first large-scale social insurance programs in the western world were inaugurated by the archreactionary German premier Otto von Bismarck in an effort to decrease the attractiveness of socialism and the Social Democratic Party to the German masses. In our own country, many reforms were incomplete responses to mass pressures for change. The Federal Trade Commission Act, for instance, was introduced by business leadership to forestall more radical anticorporation activities by state legislatures. The highly regressive Social Security Act was Franklin Roosevelt's response to the threats represented by widespread factory takeovers, the "share the wealth" plan of Huey Long, and the popular Townsend movement. The array of civil rights initiatives passed in the mid-1960s was a response by government to the turmoil in America's streets. A similar litany could probably be composed for nearly all government programs ostensibly designed to meet the needs of the mass public (see Chapter 10).

Most important, while popular pressure has forced government to respond to capitalist disruptions, government has done so only in ways that do not seriously undermine the basic class relationship of capitalism, particularly corporate prerogatives. Government concessions to aroused mass publics have been substantial in sheer numbers but extremely limited in their effect on the basic operations of capitalism. The greatest limitation is that problems are dealt with only *after* they have become serious, when social disruptions are fully developed. Most of the activities of the modern capitalist state are merely a set of programs that react to social disaster and prevent full catastrophe. They fail to substantially alter the system of production that causes the deterioration and disruption of social life in the first place.

Social Disruption and Government Repression

In our nominally democratic system, government deals with potential social disruption by at least partially responding to the demands of people and groups in some way hurt by the processes of capitalist development. It generally does so reluctantly, however, and in limited ways. Even this limited response is forthcoming only when demands are made on government that are themselves limited and consistent with (or not opposed to) the overall logic of capitalism and the needs

Restoring "order" in one of America's black ghettos

of the major corporatons. For persons and groups who advance beyond these boundaries and offer fundamental challenges to the present system, government has a wide range of coercive instruments available for use. While Americans are often loath to acknowledge such matters, government has served as a coercive instrument for the repression of dissident groups throughout our history. As suggested in Chapter 4, its armed forces, its courts, and its jails have been brought to bear against various radical (though formally legal) organizations that include unions (like Industrial Workers of the World), political parties (the Socialist party, the Communist party, the Socialist Workers' party), black liberation organizations (the Black Panthers), and antiwar groups (Vietnam Veterans Against the War, the church sanctuary movement to provide aid to refugees from war zones in Central America). Suffice it to say that along with its many benevolent responses to social disruption and turmoil, government helps ensure social stability by the occasional use of repression.

Cultural Integration

It might also be pointed out that the deep discontents created by the normal operations of capitalism in the United States rarely take political form so that the ultimate weapon of repression is rarely required. This situation exists primarily because of the cultural hegemony of capitalism and of liberal representative democracy, the wide dissemination of the belief that the economic and political arrangements that characterize the American system are both inevitable and the best that could possibly exist in the real world.

The sources of these beliefs are diverse and most have already been previously examined in this book (see Chapter 3 in particular). They are sufficiently important, however, that they should at least be mentioned in passing before we proceed to the main subject matter of this chapter: the welfare state. The most central set of cultural beliefs contributing to capitalist predominance is derived from classical liberalism with its affirmations of possessive individualism, the sacredness of private property holdings and their free usage, the need for strict delimitations on government activities, and the efficient and just qualities inherent in the market economy. Not to be outdone in its power as a cultural mechanism is the belief that each citizen, through the vote and the right to associate with others to petition the government, plays an important role in the process by which public policy is formulated, legislated, and administered. Since, in this view, we are all responsible for what government does, we cannot, in good conscience, direct our discontent against the system itself. The same might be said for the law, because the belief that all citizens, no matter their race, religion, or economic status, are equal before the law makes illegitimate any attempt to circumvent the law by disaffected groups or persons. Rarely mentioned, though inescapable as a powerful weapon of social integration, is what I would call *patriotic chauvinism,* the belief that American institutions are somehow divinely inspired and vastly and uniformly superior to those of any other society. Alternatives to current economic, social, and political arrangements come to be defined in this light as un-American and foreign, to be shunned by patriotic citizens.

THE ELEMENTS
OF THE WELFARE STATE

With all of that said, it is self-evident that cultural mechanisms are not always sufficient for the protection of capitalist institutions. It is further obvious that repression, while always available as a last resort, is a blunt instrument whose overuse can sometimes undermine the widespread sense of legitimate authority so essential to social stability. More central to the task of managing social discontent are the many programs that together form what is commonly known as the welfare state: those diverse domestic government programs that seemingly redistribute resources to the poor, the weak, and the elderly; grant a role in political life to organized labor; and regulate the activities of business enterprises so that they might better serve the public interest. The remainder of the chapter will address these issues with an eye toward understanding the role that such programs play not only in sometimes enhancing the lives of many Americans but also in the maintenance of corporate hegemony.

Welfare Programs as a Response
to the Problems of the Underclass

The unmistakable trends toward economic concentration, the transfer of operations to overseas locations, and the delimitation of areas of the economy open to small and medium-sized business, lead inexorably to the problems of surplus and exploited labor. This set of relationships, which is inherent in all forms of capitalism, is exaggerated in the modern form of corporate capitalism in the United States.

In its normal course of development, capitalism is always in the process of discarding unwanted labor. Driven by competition, capitalist-sponsored technological advance and work reorganization have always had the result of decreasing the amount of labor required to produce a given output of goods and services. Capitalism is always in a race, then, to expand production fast enough to keep pace with productivity gains, the alternative being serious unemployment and underconsumption crises. The problems are heightened in modern corporate capitalism because of the staggering increase in the rate of scientific discovery and technological development, which exacerbates the productivity-unemployment problem.

As a result, unemployment has become one of the most striking features of modern capitalism, a problem that is made even graver by the flight of corporate business overseas, as well as the incredible rate of small business failure in the economy. In the early 1960s, economists generally considered the nation to be at "full employment" when about 3 percent of the workforce was out of work.

Today, economists generally consider 5 percent to 6 percent to be normal full employment, while the American economy seems stuck between the 7 percent and 9 percent figures. If one counts *hidden* unemployment, that is, people who either work part time but want full-time work, and people who are so discouraged that they have quit seeking work, then real unemployment is probably about double the official figure.

Political scientist David Cameron empirically demonstrates what most economic observers have long understood: that a full-employment economy threatens corporate profitability because of upward pressures on wages. He demonstrates, furthermore, that government often attempts to induce mild recessions (and thus increase unemployment) in order to reestablish the "proper" relationship between wages and prices.[2]

Modern capitalism is also characterized by the intense exploitation of competitive sector workers who find themselves trapped in a sector of the economy where wages are low, benefits are almost nonexistent, job security is a distant hope, and union protection is nowhere to be found. An explanation for this state of affairs is quite straightforward. The competitive sector is a part of the national economy comprised of small and meduim-sized businesses that are so marginal

Unemployment: irresolvable problem of modern capitalism

that the effort to keep costs to a minimum, particularly labor costs, is a require-ment for survival. Jobs in this sector, in retail trade, services, and the like, are filled primarily by women and minorities who are unable to penetrate into the unionized bastions of the corporate sector, as well as former corporate sector work-ers displaced by technological advance and work rationalization. The outcomes of massive unemployment and endemic labor power exploitation are not difficult to discern: inequality, marginality, and poverty.

Such a massive pool of unemployed, underemployed, and exploited labor represents a potentially disruptive and explosive mixture. The problem of social control and management inherent in any society is made more difficult in capi-talism because its normal operations constantly add to that pool, while at the same time it raises the expectations for mass consumption so necessary for further economic advance. Control and management of this troublesome problem can take many forms ranging from the benign to the repressive. The principal in-strument for the treatment of this explosive mixture under modern capitalism is the system of welfare.

The welfare commitment of the federal government began in a serious way with the Social Security Act of 1935. Under one provision of the act, the federal government agreed to contribute to state and locally administered programs of aid to the aged, the blind, the disabled, and dependent children. It was thought, at the time, that these welfare measures were a response to a specific and tem-porary emergency and that especially with the old age insurance provisions of that same Social Security Act coming into effect, the welfare program would gradually wither away.[3]

Expectations were not met. What has happened over the years has been a significant increase in the size of relief rolls, a phenomenon most often called the "welfare explosion." The expansion since 1965 has been especially significant (though Ronald Reagan reversed the trend), with aid to families of dependent children (AFDC) being the most prominent component. Nevertheless, while there has been an enormous increase in the number of people receiving welfare benefits, such programs in no way threaten the structure of income inequality (see Chapter 6).[4] Neither the total amount of money involved nor the average payment per recipient is anywhere near a level that would have *significant* redistributive effects. Since 1950, for instance, total welfare expenditures by all levels of government have not exceeded 4 percent of total personal income. Moreover, total welfare expenditures as a percentage of total personal income have actually declined since the Great Depression. Finally, despite the increase in the number of recipients, an expansion in the number of people served and an increase in the size of pay-ments, the average payment to each recipient has actually declined over the past two decades when compared with the national median income (see Table 14.1).

Obviously, a family dependent only on its welfare check is doomed to per-manent poverty. In no single year since 1950 has the average annual AFDC family payment exceeded 70 percent of the government's own niggardly poverty line, nor has it passed 50 percent of the Bureau of Labor Statistics' minimum family

TABLE 14.1   Aid to families with dependent children

YEAR	AVERAGE MONTHLY PAYMENT PER FAMILY	AVERAGE ANNUAL PAYMENT PER FAMILY	ANNUAL AFDC FAMILY PAYMENT AS A PERCENTAGE OF MEDIAN FAMILY INCOME
1960	$108	$1,296	
1965	137	1,644	23
1970	190	2,280	23
1972	192	2,304	21
1973	195	2,348	19
1976	236	2,832	19
1979	271	3,252	17
1981	310	3,720	15

SOURCE: Calculated from *Statistical Abstracts of the United States, 1980*, p. 351, U.S. Bureau of the Census.

budget. President Reagan's "social safety net" approach left more than one-half of the officially designated poor out in the cold. Even "in-kind" payments to the poor, such as food stamps, Medicaid, rent supplements, and the like, do not lift very many recipient families above the poverty line.[5] These "in-kind" programs, while redistributive in their effects, are limited by the meagre size of program budgets. All such programs taken together have never exceeded 1 percent of the federal budget.[6]

By no stretch of the imagination, then, can public assistance to the poor be interpreted as a bottomless pit draining the American system of its resources and vitality. Despite the admittedly rapid expansion of welfare spending and the increase in the number of recipients—a trend that is now being significantly reversed—[7]the program pales beside other federal budgetary commitments.

The Functions of Welfare. Why welfare at all? According to Piven and Cloward, leading students of the welfare system in the United States, public assistance has always been a tool used to control the poor population and to help provide a pool of cheap labor for capitalists.[8] Every modern capitalist society has come to realize that some minimal level of support for the poor is required in the interests of pubic peace and safety. A poor, disenfranchised population—without any stake in the system, without anything to lose in effect, and concentrated in the nation's largest cities—is nothing less than social dynamite. A welfare system, particularly one that so closely monitors the behavior of its recipients, can go a long way toward creating out of this dangerous mass a dependent, controlled population for a relatively small outlay of funds. It is surely less expensive than a system of coercion and permanent policing.

What is most interesting in the Piven and Cloward analysis is their claim (buttressed by very convincing evidence) that the number of people on the welfare rolls and the size of welfare budgets in the United States have always been highly sensitive to the rhythms of social protest and disruption. Both expand when social protest and disruption are present and contract when they are absent. The great expansion in welfare programs which began in the mid-1960s had nothing whatsoever to do with "soft-hearted" liberals but was forced from government by popular pressures from the very bottom of American society. The massive cutbacks in these same programs effected by Ronald Reagan—the 1984 budget lopped 14.3 percent off of Carter budget baseline projections for AFDC, 13.8 percent from food stamps, 28 percent from child nutrition, 8.3 percent from low-income energy assistance, and 23.5 percent from Social Services Block grants—[9] were made possible by the absence of the poor and the near-poor from both the voting booths and the streets.

In normal times, the social control function of the welfare system cannot be allowed to intrude on the second major function of the system: to provide a cheap labor supply. Capitalist economies always require some means, short of outright coercion, by which to persuade people to take low-paying, demeaning, and/or dangerous jobs. There is a need for people to pick cotton, to pour steel, and to clean houses, and to do so at prices that allow capitalists to continue to make profits. Piven and Cloward suggest three ways in which such a labor pool is maintained by the welfare system. First, public assistance is generally denied to able-bodied workers, no matter how poor they might be, so that an incentive exists to take any available job, at whatever wage. About one-fourth of all officially designated poor families are headed by able-bodied, employed males, but public assistance is generally denied to them. The so-called midnight raids, whose purpose is to discover whether a woman on welfare is living secretly with a man, have the same rationale—to deny assistance to any family where an able-bodied male is available. Second, public assistance, while largely funded by the federal government, is organized and administered by local governments so that payments may be geared to local economies. Such an arrangement ensures that public assistance payments will nowhere approach the lowest wages paid in the local economy. Again, this maintains the incentive to find work, even if full-time work is no guarantee against poverty. Finally, Piven and Cloward suggest that the degrading, demeaning, and contemptuous treatment of welfare recipients is designed to convince many poor people that any kind of work is preferable to a life on welfare. The welfare system creates an outcast class that no rational person, given a choice, would join. The alternative is to fill the low-paying jobs that must get done if the system is to function.

Social Security

Another key building block in the edifice of the American welfare state is Social Security. To understand its overall place in the legitimation and support of modern capitalism, we must first examine the history of the passage of the Social Security Act of 1935.

The immediate impetus for this historic legislation was the existence in 1934 and 1935 of several popular movements whose aim was the radical redistribution of economic resources in the United States. Huey Long of Louisiana led a "share our wealth" movement that sought free homesteads and education, inexpensive foodstuffs, severe limitations on fortunes, and a minimum guaranteed annual income of $5,000. Long was so popular, in fact, that until his assassination, FDR feared that he would split the national Democratic party and deny him the renomination. Father Coughlin, the influential "radio priest" of the Great Depression days, garnered the support of millions of listeners for his program of currency inflation, guaranteed wages, and the nationalization of banking and natural resources.

The largest and most influential movement was led by Francis Townsend of California who advocated the disarmingly simple proposal that all citizens over the age of sixty receive a pension of $200 per month with the only conditions being that they not hold a job (thus opening up employment for others) and that they spend all their money within thirty days (thus stimulating economic recovery). By 1936 there were an estimated seven thousand Townsend clubs throughout the country and a membership of over 2 million people. Twenty-five million people signed petitions in favor of the plan. To the leading students of the legislation, it was the Townsend Plan and its widespread support that led to the Social Security Act.[10] In the words of one of the leading architects of the measure, Secretary of Labor Frances Perkins ". . . there was the Townsend plan which both drove us and confused the issue. Without the Townsend plan, it is possible that the old-age insurance system would not have received the attention which it did at the hands of Congress."[11]

There were even more radical stirrings in the population to add impetus to the new priorities of the New Deal. The Unemployed Councils and the radical Unemployed Leagues both grew rapidly in 1934, thus demanding greatly expanded relief efforts. While it is almost impossible to gauge their national strength, the membership of the latter exceeded 100,000 in Ohio and 70,000 in Pennsylvania. In Congress, there was surprising support for the Lundeen Bill that called for unemployment compensation (with no time limitations) commensurate with local wages, financed by taxes on inheritances, gifts, and high incomes, and administered by workers' and farmers' councils.

It was clearly in response to this threat to political and social order that the administration moved to incorporate the rhetoric of reform, though not its substance, in the Social Security Act. While the measure met the widespread demand for unemployment and old age benefits and thus symbolically moved to meet strongly felt grievances, in substance, the measure was highly conservative. The most important feature of the measure was to make it an *insurance* program rather than a program financed out of general revenues. In fact, the major internal battle in the Roosevelt administration concerned whether to finance the measure from payroll taxes or from taxes on upper income groups. The president, who never wavered in his desire to have an actuarially sound insurance system, chose the former and thus brought about a system in which the worker was forced to save for a rainy day by subtracting money from current wages. The system that was ultimately constructed proved to be one of the most regressive in the western world, as we shall see below.

There is abundant evidence that the initial groundwork for Social Security legislation began several decades before the New Deal under business sponsorship. As one of the leading students of the measure said, "The American Association for Labor Legislation [AALL] created and sustained the organized social insurance movement in the United States."[12] The AALL efforts in the area of social insurance began in 1910 with a series of research studies and proposals on the subject that came to largely determine the terms of the debate and the central features of the old age insurance. In fact, the direct precursor and model for the Social Security Act was the Wisconsin Plan passed in 1932, written by Professor John R. Commons and two men with close ties to the AALL, Arthur Altmeyer and Edwin Witte. It is interesting to note, given its centrality to the Social Security Act, that the AALL was an offshoot of the big business-created and -dominated National Civic Federation. The goal of the AALL was to bring together reformers, economists, and business leaders for the promotion of uniform state and national labor laws, for as its motto declared, "Social Justice is the Best Insurance Against Labor Unrest."

It is clear, then, that the Social Security Act did not represent a radical turn by the New Deal. In reality, the measure was a legislative response to what has been called "The Thunder on the Left," but it responded to it in a way that was highly conservative, consistent with reforms proposed by an important element of the business class, and supported in its final form by most prominent business leaders. The measure had the effect of supplying minimal benefits to the elderly and the unemployed, thus blunting demands for more radical change. Yet at no time did it challenge the structure of inequality. The act showed a recognition, as did Bismarck's Germany, that no modern state can survive with widespread destitution and discontent.

Social Security today remains true to its original design and intentions. It remains, in fact, one of the most regressive programs in the federal arsenal in that its taxing and spending features tend to favor the better-off members of the American population. It is a program characterized by horizontal as opposed to vertical transfers in that it transfers income from the active members of the workforce to the inactive—mainly from the young and middle-aged to the elderly. As a result of several long-standing features of the system, it is a program that forces transfers within the working class rather than between classes.

Social Security is supported not out of government general funds as are "means-tested" programs for the very poor like food stamps, Medicaid, legal services, or aid to dependent children, but by a sharply *regressive* tax. It is regressive in the following important ways:

1. It taxes a *flat rate* up to a maximum income ceiling. Income above the ceiling is not subject to the tax. The wealthy, therefore, pay the tax on only a small

proportion of their income, while most Americans find the tax applied to their entire income.

2. Only income from wages and salaries is taxed. Income from rents, dividends, interest, and capital gains is immune from taxation.
3. Because of 1 and 2 above, there exists an *inverse* relationship between income and tax rate under Social Security. That is, those persons with the lowest income pay a high proportion of their income, while those at the top pay the lowest proportion of theirs.

Social Security is regressive in payout as well:

1. Retirement income is calculated on the basis of lifetime contributions in the form of taxes. Those with the highest incomes, who paid the most in absolute dollars (but *not as* a percentage of their income), receive the highest benefits during retirement. There exists a direct relationship between income earned during working years and benefits received in retirement.
2. Retired persons who earn above a certain income after age sixty-five lose a fixed percentage of their Social Security benefits. If such income is derived from property, however, no loss in benefits occurs. The disadvantage accrues only to wage and salary income.
3. Over one-third of Social Security benefits goes to persons with outside income greater than that of their Social Security.

It is these features that make Social Security probably the most regressive program in the federal system.[13] Were this a small program, claiming few dollars, its effects would not be worth considering, but its striking regressivity involves a program larger than any other in the federal government, with the exception of the military commitment. In 1984 it accounted for 33 percent of all nondefense federal government budget outlays.

The history of Social Security is surely a strange one. Forced upon political leaders by popular pressures from below, it has become a program that distributes its benefits primarily to the middle- and upper-middle class (especially the old age assistance and Medicare parts of Social Security). As such, and in contrast to social welfare programs, it has been relatively immune to the nondefense budget–cutting frenzy of the Carter and Reagan years.

Health Care

Another important feature of the American welfare state is the large and growing government role in the field of health care. The beginning of serious federal involvement in the 1960s, after decades of successful resistance by the organized medical profession, was heralded as a breakthrough and a triumph of modern liberalism. Since the introduction of Medicaid (a program designed to pay the medical expenses of the indigent) and Medicare (a program for the medical support of the elderly) in 1965, the growth in federal budgetary involvement has been most impressive. In fact, by 1984, budget outlays for Medicaid represented

4 percent of federal nondefense outlays while Medicare accounted for 12 percent. The large cash outlay has not been for naught; millions of persons long excluded or ignored by modern medicine have been brought partially under its protective umbrella. I am prepared to argue, however, that the overall impact has, like Social Security, been regressive.

Because it is funded out of general tax revenues, Medicaid is the most progressive of the two medical assistance programs. The federal government provides matching funds to those states that choose to organize such a program for their indigent citizens (under broad federal guidelines), but the program is severely limited in scope by several factors. First, only about 50 percent of the states participate in the program, leaving the indigent in the remaining 50 percent of the states bereft of any federal medical support. Second, the states are for the most part free to construct their own eligibility requirements, and they set maximum income levels so low that most persons below the Bureau of Labor Statistics' minimum standard of living are not eligible for the Medicaid program. Third, since states must match federal funds, there is a tendency—particularly during times of economic downturns and state fiscal problems (as is the case today)—to cut back funds and thus decrease benefits and coverage. As a result, the majority of the poor find themselves outside of the Medicaid system. It is estimated that no more than one-third of the designated poor receive any form of assistance under the program.

Medicare, as it is tied to the Social Security system, shares all of its regressive features and adds some wrinkles of its own. That is not to say that many people have not been immeasurably helped by the program. Every reader must know of some elderly person, formerly without any medical assistance, who is now receiving first-class medical care under the provisions of the Medicare program. Nevertheless, the total impact of the system remains regressive for several reasons. First, Medicare is financed through the Social Security tax, which, as already pointed out, is the most regressive in the federal system. To the extent that expansions in program benefits are financed through increases in this tax, the program remains regressive. Second, Medicare, consistent with American ideology and the organization of economic power, in no ways seeks to regulate the system of medical care delivery in the United States and thereby contributes to higher costs without commensurate improvement in health care. Why is that?

In economic terms, both Medicaid and Medicare have tremendously increased the demand for medical services without significantly enhancing the supply side of the equation—the number of doctors, other health care personnel, hospital beds, and the like. As introductory economics students know, an increase in demand without a simultaneous increase in supply causes an upward movement in prices, which is precisely what has happened in the medical field. In a situation in which the government lacks the will or the power to regulate prices, doctors, hospitals, drug companies, and other sectors of the medical industry are free to raise their prices to the level that the traffic will bear. With "too many dollars chasing too few goods," inflaton is inevitable. In fact, over the past two decades, medical costs have increased many times faster than the general increase in the cost of living. Paradoxically, what government gives with one hand it takes back with the other. While government programs assist some of the needy and the elderly in meeting their medical costs, the overall effect is to inflate costs so drastically that those poor and near-poor who do not fall under either Medicare or Medicaid protection find their own medical care situation infinitely worse than before.[14]

As one might expect, the place of Medicare and Medicaid in public policy is entirely predictable given the distribution of political and economic power in the United States. Because Medicare benefits are given mainly to the middle class and Medicaid benefits to the very poor, the former is a much more substantial program whether considered as total budgets or average benefit per recipient. Because Medicare is mainly for the middle class, moreover, it has escaped relatively unscathed from the nondefense budget–cutting frenzy of recent years whereas Medicaid has been a more inviting target.[15]

Creating an Environment of Labor Peace

Another central function of the modern welfare state is to manage and stabilize the potentially explosive relations among social classes. In the United States this task is accomplished primarily under the terms of an elaborate labor law based on the Wagner Labor Relations Act of 1935. The history of the development of this legal structure is worth looking at, if only briefly. It is a story of continuous democratic pressure from below and efforts by the elite to contain and channel that pressure.

The history of labor-management relations in the United States is one of the bloodiest on record, primarily because of the intransigence of business leadership in efforts by working people to organize. Nevertheless, some far-sighted business leaders, as early as the turn of the century, recognized that a stable economic environment conducive to corporate growth and profitability was impossible without a peaceful, cooperative labor force. Some began to advocate collective bargaining as a means to regularize labor contracts, eliminate unpredictable strikes, and imbue union leaders with a sense of responsibility for industrial peace. As the Anthracite Coal Commission (made up of prominent business leaders) stated as early as 1903:

> Experience shows that the more full the recognition given to a trade union, the more business-like and responsible it becomes. Through dealing with businessmen in business matters, its more intelligent, conservative and responsible members come to the front and gain direction of its affairs.[16]

After years of educational effort by the corporate-founded and -financed National Civic Federation and the American Association of Labor Legislation, and propelled by the rise of labor militancy and the Socialist party, collective bargaining agreements had become widespread in the railroad industry by the beginning of World War I. The powerful War Industries Board that directed the American economy during the war years, composed mainly of representatives of the giant corporations and banks, first introduced generalized collective bargaining. In return for government authorization of cartel-like business arrangements during the war period, major industries were encouraged to allow their employees to organize on a voluntary basis. Testimony from some of the major business and labor leaders of the period suggests that this wartime experience in "cooperative capitalism" provided a powerful precedent and model for later developments in collective bargaining. That experience not only convinced labor leaders such as Samuel Gompers and Sidney Hillman of the attractiveness of business-union collaboration, but it convinced business and political leaders like Bernard Baruch, Gerard Swope, Herbert Hoover, and Franklin Roosevelt as well.

This sympathy toward labor-management cooperation as a means of stabilizing the corporate environment and dampening radical tendencies in the labor movement found its most important expression in Section 7(a) of the National Industrial Recovery Act passed in the first hectic days of Roosevelt's New Deal. Section 7(a) guranteed (though no enforcement machinery was provided) the right of employees to organize and to bargain collectively. Interestingly enough, 7(a) was not advocated by a single labor union leader. It was, in fact, the culmination of the efforts of those business leaders who envisioned a cooperative, regulated capitalism in which big business was guaranteed a predictable and stable environment through unionization, national collective bargaining contracts, and government regulation of the economy.[17]

During the Great Depression, the leaders of the New Deal accepted the analysis long advocated by the most progressive wing of the business class that the way out of economic crisis was the road of cooperative capitalism. The right of working people to bargain collectively was an integral part of that analysis. The analysis was given urgency by the great uprising of working people in the 1930s and the massive organizing drives of the Congress of Industrial Organizations. The Wagner Labor Relations Act of 1935 was forced by popular pressure from below. It was a force of such power that Secretary of State Cordell Hull worried aloud about the possibility of "class war."

The predictions of the Anthracite Coal Commission were prophetic. Under the umbrella of the labor laws constructed on the Wagner Act, "responsible" labor unions have become an integral part of the corporate planning process. Collective bargaining contracts serve corporate planning needs by standardizing wage costs among industrial firms, sanctioning strikes only at the expiration of a contract, and negotiating contracts that are binding on all union members. The statesmanlike union leader, embraced in the high councils of government and business, tends increasingly to restrain his own membership and to negotiate "realistic and responsible" agreements with business leaders. In contemporary labor-management relations, unions do *not*, in contrast, articulate a vision of a better society or challenge management prerogatives either within the factory or in the larger society outside the factory gates.

The federal government, therefore, through a series of elaborate legislative statutes and the operations of various administrative agencies, created a structure for regularized and cooperative relations between the major corporations and labor unions. This structure of law and services ensures that most worker-management bargaining will take place through their respective attorneys, not through disruptive and unsettling confrontations at the workplace.

It is important to note that the stabilization of labor-management relations at the top has not altered the essentially exploitative relationships at workplaces, nor eliminated the resultant conflict found there. Nor has it necessarily advanced the economic, social, and political interests of the working class as a whole. This may help explain why recent years have witnessed an unusual number of rank-and-file revolts within major unions (the mineworkers, steelworkers, and Teamsters among others), as well as a significant increase in wildcat strikes throughout the unionized sector of American industry.

It is also important to take note once again (see Chapter 8) of the combined corporate-government assault on American labor unions in the 1980s. Corporations, for their part, have launched a campaign of antiunion propaganda which, in its scope and ferocity, has not been seen since the 1920s; they have vigorously challenged collective bargaining drives, initiated union decertification procedures at an unprecedented rate, broken the labor laws with increasing boldness, used bankruptcy proceedings to abrogate union contracts, and moved business operations to nonunion or antiunion areas of the United States and the world with increased urgency. For its part, the federal government under Ronald Reagan broke the Air Traffic Controllers Union, prosecuted the leaders of public employee unions for their political activities in the 1984 elections under provisions of the Hatch Act, and made the National Labor Relations Board into a body decidedly unfriendly to organized labor.

Why the reversal of a half century of growing corporate-union cooperation under federal government sponsorship? The answer is quite simple: the loss of American economic hegemony in world trade. In the 1940s, 1950s, and most of the 1960s, when U.S. corporations faced little competition from its rivals in western Europe and Japan, the cost of cooperation with labor unions on wages and benefits could be easily and automatically passed on to the customer by the corporations in the form of higher prices. In the dangerous world economy of the 1970s and 1980s, however, higher prices lead to a steady loss of markets for American products. In this new environment, it has become rational for U.S. corporations to try to hold the line on prices. An important way to control prices, of course, is to hold down the cost of the corporate wage bill, an objective that can only be accomplished by resisting and weakening labor unions.

The Regulation of Business in the Public Interest

Another important component of the modern welfare state is that set of programs whose ostensible purpose is the regulation of the activities of business corporations so that they might better serve public purposes or at least desist from activities harmful to the public interest. The programs are many and diverse, as are the goals to be served, ranging from the prevention of monopoly practices to the protection of air and water quality. We might perhaps better comprehend these complex and diverse programs by examining them briefly in light of their historical origins. Regulation is primarily the product of three great "reform" waves spanning the last hundred years.

1. *Progressive era reform.* The period spanning the years from 1900 to the first World War witnessed a flurry of legislation designed to regulate the activities of the newly emergent giant corporations. It would be a mistake, however, to interpret this period of reform as anticorporate in spirit, an image conveyed in most American history textbooks. While there are some exceptions, most of the landmark regulatory legislation of the period not only served to assist the corporations in their efforts to maintain their market dominance but also were conceived, formulated, and drafted by prominent business leaders.[18] As historian Gabriel Kolko has so brilliantly pointed out, after the corporations were unable to dampen excessive competition and stabilize their economic position through their own voluntary efforts, their leaders turned to the federal government for protection and assistance. The results were such regulatory landmarks as the Federal Trade Commission Act, the Meat Inspection Act, the Pure Food and Drug Act, the Federal Reserve Act, and the reorientation of earlier reform efforts like the Interstate Commerce Act and the Sherman Anti-Trust Act to the big business point of view. Progressive era reform was thus primarily directed toward the protection of the most powerful economic enterprises in American society. That is to say, the range of regulatory provisions developed during this period were designed to and did serve to fulfill what has been referred to in these pages as capital accumulation functions.

2. *The New Deal.* The New Deal of Franklin Roosevelt was a semisuccessful effort to revive a collapsed capitalist economy whose main contributions to the present structure of American public policy have mostly to do with the management of the business cycle, the incorporation of organized labor into a position as junior partner in the corporate economy, and the construction of programs in income security (old age and survivors benefits, unemployment compensation, aid to families with dependent children, etc.). Not to be overlooked, however, were the many important New Deal efforts in business regulation whose purpose, despite the extensive rhetoric to the contrary,[19] was to help the major corporations recover their position of preeminence and to protect and preserve them at the topmost position in the economic structure. Regulatory programs were concentrated in the areas of banking and the stock market, not surprising perhaps in light of the immediate causes of the Great Depression. This legislation included federal bank inspection, regulation of speculative investments, federal deposit insurance, Federal Reserve credit coordination, regulation of the stock and bond markets under the Securities and Exchange Commission, business self-regulation and planning under the terms of the National Industrial Recovery Act, and a score of other programs.[20]

3. *The modern consumer environmental and public interest movement.* If the first two periods of regulatory reform were designed to allow business to essentially regulate itself, the same cannot be said for the broad regulatory initiatives that were formulated in the years spanning the late sixties and practically all of the seventies. During this period, a powerful consumer and public interest movement managed to mobilize public opinion and legislative support for the regulaton of a wide range of business activities harmful to public health and safety. Just a few examples follow: the Environmental Protection Agency was created to regulate business activities that contributed to air and water pollution; the Occupational Safety and Health Administration directed its efforts at improving the wholesomeness of the work environment; the Nuclear Regulatory Commission received a mandate to formulate tough standards for the construction of nuclear power plants, considerably slowing their rate of construction; the Consumer Product Safety Commission was given the power to ban unsafe products from the marketplace; reformers appointed to the Federal Trade Commission induced it to step up its enforcement of the antitrust laws and to scrutinize advertising claims, while fellow reformers on the Federal Communications Commission moved the commission to conduct investigations of the nature of children's television programming as well as ownership patterns in the media.

Such broad-ranging programs were an irritant to business and seriously increased its normal costs of operation. Nevertheless, in the short run, business was not unified in its various attempts to resist and roll back the regulatory tide and was unable to resist an aroused and politically sophisticated consumer/environmental/public interest movement. Thus, for a short period in American history, at least one important section of public policy in the United States was directed toward the correction of some of the worst abuses of industrial capitalism. The effect of this shift was to give the federal government an aura as benevolent steward of the public interest.

With the unseemly and hasty retreat on consumer and environmental regulation in the last year of the Carter presidency and the militantly antiregulatory policies of the Reagan administration, it is now patently evident that such a commitment on the part of the federal government was short-lived. In vivid contrast to just a few years ago, deregulation has now become the watchword of nearly every politician in Washington, whatever the party label, whatever the ideological self-designation. What has happened to effect such a rapid turnabout is the almost universally shared sense of desperation about the state of the American economy and the perceived role of government regulation in its gradual deterioration. What is now taken as gospel by virtually all public opinion leaders is that government regulation of business, because of the increased costs that it incurs and its bureaucratic irrationality, is a major contributing factor to inflation, declining productivity, the disappearance of innovation and entrepreneurship, and thus the deteriorating competitive position of the United States in the world economy.

This reversal should not be taken to mean, however, that the federal government will simply quit the job of business regulation. While such a development might prove to be appealing to conservative ideologues, business leadership tends to be much more pragmatic, attuned less to conceptual niceties than to its own profit position. As a result, deregulation has taken on the following, not very surprising pattern: regulatory programs that have proved helpful to big business will continue to go largely untouched while those that have increased the costs and damaged the profit position of such enterprises in the name of consumer, worker, and environmental protection will continue to be assaulted and diminished. Deregulation is a term, then, that is more than a little ambiguous because it conveys the general impression that the role of government is being cut back while the role of the market mechanism is being given renewed emphasis. In reality, however, government continues to serve as an important prop in the maintenance of economic concentration and privilege. Its role is being seriously diminished primarily in those areas where the American people have been partially protected against the diseconomies and irrationalities of market capitalism.[21] The pattern will remain in place until the next great upsurge in popular pressure.

CONCLUDING REMARKS

In this section of the text, I have argued that the growth in the size, reach and responsibility of government in the United States cannot be understood as the product of the demands of an agglomeration of empire-building bureaucrats, overly sensitive and soft-headed liberals, venal, self-seeking politicians, or the grasping poor, which is the belief of most modern conservatives. Nor can government be understood as a benevolent institution moved primarily by its concern for the helpless and the poor, which is the view of most modern liberals. I have argued instead that modern government is the inevitable product of capitalist development. The transformation of capitalism from a free-market to a concentrated corporate form created both a set of problems for which government intervention offered the only solution and a set of powerful economic institutions capable of bending public policies to their special needs.

I have suggested in these chapters that most public policies in the United States may be subsumed under two major headings: the first has to do with government's need to sustain the capitalist accumulation process; the second has to do with government's need to promote system stability and legitimacy. The first includes those activities designed to maintain conditions in which the major corporations can expand their operations, plan for contingencies, and guarantee substantial, stable, and predictable profits. Such activities include government programs to encourage and protect economic concentration, to manage the ups and downs of the business cycle, to provide needed infrastructural services, and to protect the overseas interests of the major corporations. The second includes those activities whose purpose is to maintain conditions of social harmony and social stability. They include occasional repression, ideological inculturation, welfare programs and other social services, Social Security, the coordination of labor-management relations, the public regulation of business, and the occasional use of repression against troublesome groups and individuals.

From one point of view, then, modern government is composed of a complicated mixture of programs derived from both corporate needs and interests and from popular pressures to deal with diseconomies. From another point of view, however, modern government appears quite simple in its form and implications. It remains the main integrator and coordinator of advanced capitalism, the highest institutional expression of what Marx termed "the mean average interest" of the entire owning class organized at a national level. Modern government looks the way it does because modern capitalism requires the services and support that only government can provide on a continuing basis. The existence of the one is impossible without the other. To return to a world of small-scale, limited government, as many suggest, would require the end of corporate capitalism itself.

NOTES

1. On the relationship between capitalist development and mass protest see Frances Fox Piven and Richard Cloward, *The New Class War* (New York: Pantheon, 1982).
2. David C. Cameron, "The Politics and Economics of the Business Cycle," in Thomas Ferguson and Joel Rogers (eds.), *The Political Economy* (Armonk, NY: M. E. Sharpe, 1984). Also see the discussion in Piven and Cloward, *The New Class War.*
3. See Gilbert Steiner, *Social Insecurity: The Politics of Welfare* (Chicago: Rand McNally, 1966).
4. For a summary of the literature on this point see Ben Page, *Who Gets What From Government* (Berkeley: University of California Press, 1983), pp. 178-195.
5. In Sweden, public assistance is almost equal to the median national income. See Ralph Husby and Eva Wetzel, "Public Assistance in Sweden and the United States." *Social Policy* 7, 5 (March/April 1977), p. 28-31.
6. D. Lee Bawden and John L. Palmer, "Social Policy," in John L. Palmer and Isabel V. Sawhill (eds.), *The Reagan Record* (Cambridge: Ballinger, 1984), p. 181.
7. The Reagan administration has not only made deep budget cuts in all the programs designed to assist the very poor but also has effected a change in fundamental policy so that the working poor have been denied coverage; thus talk of the "truly needy." Under the Reagan plan, almost one million families in this category lost all their government benefits in 1981, most of whom were blacks. See *The New York Times,* September 21, 1981, p. 1.
8. Frances Fox Piven and Richard Cloward, *Regulating the Poor* (New York: Pantheon, 1971).
9. Bawden and Palmer, "Social Policy," pp. 185-186. The authors suggest that the net effect of these actions was to cut support for social programs one-sixth below prior policy levels.
10. See Paul H. Douglas, *Social Security in the United States* (New York: McGraw-Hill, 1939); Roy C. Lubove, *The Struggle for Social Security* (Cambridge: Harvard University Press, 1968); and Edwin E. Witte, *The Development of the Social Security Act* (Madison: University of Wisconsin Press, 1962).
11. Foreword to Witte, *The Development of the Social Security Act,* p. 6.

12. Lubove, *The Struggle for Social Security*, p. 29. Confirmed by Douglas, *Social Security in the United States*, p. 12.

13. For this judgment see Milton Friedman, "The Poor Man's Welfare Payment to the Middle-Class," *Washington Monthly* 4:3 (May 1972).

14. Given budget cuts and inflation, both Medicaid and Medicare pay a lower percentage of medical costs each succeeding year. Medicare paid only a 37 percent share of the medical costs of the elderly in 1978, compared with 48 percent in 1966. Out-of-pocket medical costs for the elderly rose from $241 a year to $1,100. See *The New York Times*, November 18, 1978, p. 16.

15. However, it is important to note that cuts in Medicaid have been less severe than cuts in other social programs for the poor. This is probably the case because Medicaid benefits actually flow through the poor to a politically active and powerful medical establishment which benefits greatly from the program.

16. Quoted in G. William Domhoff, *The Higher Circles: The Governing Class in America* (New York: Random House, 1970), p. 227.

17. The Wagner Act, the basic law establishing collective bargaining, was merely a response to the turmoil unleashed by 7(a). It served to put in place the enforcement machinery necessary to enforce its provisions.

18. For this history see Edward S. Greenberg, *Capitalism and the American Political Ideal* (Armonk, NY: M. E. Sharpe, 1985); Gabriel Kolko, *The Triumph of Conservatism* (Chicago: Quadrangle, 1967); and James Weinstein, *The Corporate Ideal in the Liberal State* (Boston: Beacon Press, 1968).

19. Under the terms of the National Industrial Recovery Act, corporations were encouraged to act as cartels by cooperating on production, marketing, and pricing under the protection of so-called codes of fair competition.

20. For this history see Paul Conkin, *The New Deal* (New York: Crowell, 1967); Greenberg, *Capitalism and the American Political Ideal;* and Broadus Mitchell, *Depression Decade* (New York: Holt, 1947).

21. Because of the widespread popularity of government regulatory activities in the area of consumer, worker, and environmental protection, the Reagan administration wisely chose not to assault such programs head-on, as it were, through legislative repeal. The preferred strategy was to accomplish the same task indirectly by appointing to leadership positions with regulatory responsibilities persons with a strong business point of view, who were openly hostile to the programs they were charged with administering (Watt at Interior, Gorsuch at the Environmental Protection Agency, Bell at the Equal Employment Opportunity Commission, Burford at the Bureau of Land Management, Auchter at the Occupational Safety and Health Administration, etc.), thus slowing down the rate of regulatory enforcement and placing a hold on the writing of new regulations. In the first thirty-one months of Thorne Auchter's term as head of OSHA, the agency did not adopt a single new standard to protect workers from hazardous substances. In Auchter's first two years, inspections dropped 17 percent and dollar penalties dropped 78 percent.

SUGGESTIONS FOR FURTHER READING

Martin Anderson. WELFARE: THE POLITICAL ECONOMY OF WELFARE REFORM IN THE UNITED STATES. *Stanford, California: Hoover Institution, 1978.* A conservative analysis of the status of the welfare system.

Edward S. Greenberg. SERVING THE FEW. *New York: Wiley, 1974.* An analysis of the general bias in the conduct and effects of federal government policy in the United States.

Robert H. Havemen, ed. A DECADE OF FEDERAL ANTI-POVERTY PROGRAMS. *New York: Academic Press, 1977.* A useful compendium that gives detailed descriptions and analyses of the impact of major federal social programs.

Benjamin I. Page. WHO GETS WHAT FROM GOVERNMENT. *Berkeley: University of California Press, 1983.* A comprehensive analysis of the distribution of the benefits and burdens of government policy.

John L. Palmer and Isabel V. Sawhill, eds. THE REAGAN RECORD: AN URBAN INSTITUTE STUDY. *Cambridge: Ballinger, 1984.* A careful and detailed analysis of changes in and the impact of government programs during the first Reagan administration.

Frances Fox Piven and Richard A. Cloward. REGULATING THE POOR. *New York: Pantheon, 1971.* A controversial analysis of the welfare system that sees it as a mechanism for the management of class relations.

Frances Fox Piven and Richard Cloward. THE NEW CLASS WAR. *New York: Pantheon, 1982.* A provocative analysis of changes in social policy wrought by the ''Reagan revolution'' and how popular pressures will defeat the conservative effort.

Part

VI

Beyond Capitalism
and Representative
Democracy

This final section of the book turns from the analysis and critique of the American system to a consideration of alternatives to it. It maintains that only a radical transformation of the capitalist system will make possible the creation of a society in which justice and democracy are realized.

15

Toward Justice and
Democracy

This book has presented a comprehensive critique of the American system, arguing that social justice and democracy are difficult if not impossible to attain under capitalist economic arrangements. Since the many negative social, political, and economic consequences of capitalism are intrinsic to it and thus inescapable, moreover, any effort to attain justice and democracy in America must go beyond mere reform of the present way of doing things. This chapter addresses those questions that have probably been bothering the reader from the very first pages of the book: "What alternatives might one propose to the present system?" "What would one put in its place?" The answer is reasonably unambiguous and straightforward: corporate capitalism must be replaced by a system characterized by democratic control of the economy, participatory democracy in political life, and material equality. I would call such a system *democratic socialism* though none of the present socialist societies meet the definition. It is only in socialism, properly understood, in my view, that it becomes possible to escape the irrationalities, cruelties, and antisocial aspects of capitalist production and provide a setting in which democracy and justice become possible.

A BRIEF REVIEW OF MATERIALS

Before considering democratic socialism, it would be useful to first recapitulate some of the materials that have shown justice and democracy to be incompatible with American capitalism and that force us to seek more attractive alternatives.

The materials described here—materials that deal with subjects as diverse as the American economy (capitalism and corporate capitalism), the dominant culture (liberalism), the distribution of life chances among the population, the role and function of the national government, and the operations and commitments of governmental institutions—certainly support this proposition.

Social Justice

The reader will recall that several definitions of social justice and democracy were presented in Chapter 2 in order to facilitate our ability to judge the overall value and attractiveness of our socio-political system, or, for that matter, any other sociopolitical system. As to social justice—that standard of evaluation pertaining to the distribution of advantages and disadvantages in the population—there appears very little evidence to suggest that conditions in the United States closely conform to it, no matter which definition one uses. Needless to say, the *socialist* definition of justice, which stresses the need for *substantive* equality in social, political, and economic life, is most distant from fulfillment. This is the case not only because the normal operations of a capitalist market economy guarantee inequality of condition but also because the main tenets of the dominant American ideology—equality of opportunity and competition—justify and legitimate such outcomes. It therefore comes as something of a further surprise to find that the evidence fails to substantiate the existence in the United States of conditions that meet even the classical *liberal* concept of justice, that of equality of opportunity. In fact, the evidence overwhelmingly reveals the relative "fixedness" of the distribution of life chances in the United States, the stability of social class, the absence of significant social mobility or redistributive trends, and the prevalence of entrenched institutions of power. In such an environment, though publications such as *Fortune* magazine annually publish their lists of new millionaires, equality of opportunity is a dim and unrealized ideal. Indeed, given the fixedness of social class, the stability of wealth and income distribution, and the structured inequalities of political power, the standard of justice most closely approximated is, quite ironically, the *classical conservative* one. I say "ironically" because, as pointed out earlier, the classical conservative tradition has ostensibly never found a friendly environment in the United States. The fit is not perfect even here, however, since classical conservatism celebrates inequality based on character and breeding and not necessarily on wealth and income. While the conservative tradition advocates rulership by a natural aristocracy, it has only rarely been favorable to rulership by a plutocracy. Thus the evidence in these pages strongly supports the original contention advanced in Chapter 2: that the United States is not a just society by whatever standard one chooses to use.

Democracy

With respect to *democracy,* the performance of the United States is no more impressive than it is with respect to social justice. The *classical-participatory* concept of democracy is far from fulfillment not only because normal politics are abstract and distant to most people, but, more important, because people's participation is neither appreciated, invited, nor felt in most of the arenas of decision making that shape social life. Rather than being active participants in directing their own lives, most Americans are buffeted in one direction and then another by external forces. They adjust as best they can to the requirements of new situations.

Perhaps more surprising is the absence of convincing evidence of conditions that meet either *pluralist* or *liberal* representative formulations of democracy in the United States. There is no evidence, for instance, of widespread inter–elite group competition to protect against oligopolistic or monopolistic political decision making or of an open, accessible, responsive, and competitive leadership. More characterstic of American arrangements, as has been seen, is concentrated economic power allied with concentrated political power primarily serving the interests of the giant corporations. Furthermore, conditions in the United States, which seem at first glance to conform to liberal notions of democracy, are less than perfect on closer inspection. Earlier chapters demonstrated that the free exercise of civil liberties has but a spotty history in the United States; that judicial and legal protections are biased in their distribution and are not freely available to all; and that the power of *representation* is almost completely negated by the role of the wealth and corporate power in American electoral politics. While the outward *forms* of liberal democracy are generally observed, the *quality* of their observance is much lower than is generally assumed. The evidence seems to support the initial contention in Chapter 2 that no matter which of the three models of democracy one uses as a standard, the United States cannot make valid claim to being a healthy democratic political system.

Capitalist society, despite its prodigious powers of production and consumption, is incapable of attaining conditions conducive to either justice or democracy. Justice is impossible because property-based class divisions not only enshrine substantial inequalities in material distribution in the population but also embody a relationship of exploitation between capital and wage labor. Democracy is impossible not only because government in capitalist society is primarily the instrument of the dominant class, but also because the condition of wage labor in which most people find themselves is one in which powers of self-direction and assertion are stifled. As pointed out in Chapter 5, social rationality is unlikely in capitalist society because production is directed toward exchange, not use. That is, the guiding principle of production is not social utility but the selling of commodities and the accumulation of profits. With such a steering mechanism, capitalism only rarely avoids irrationality, waste, and private indulgence.

Capitalism thus remains a system wedded to the goal of churning out goods and services at the expense of the community and the full development of human potential. It is a system that rewards greed, waste, irrationality, and antisocial behavior. As such, capitalism is, in the end, a system that must be criticized, transcended, and replaced by a system of social organization that makes justice, democracy, and rationality possible.

GOAL: A DEMOCRATIC AND JUST SOCIETY

What to replace corporate capitalism with? What would a system look like that would maximize the probability of attaining justice, democracy, and rationality? What principles of social relations and organization are necessary for a decent society? There is such a system, in my view, at least in theory. That system is democratic socialism.

What is democratic socialism? The question is greatly confused because societies whose socioeconomic systems are organized in vastly different ways all call themselves socialist. The task of definition is even more difficult than it might be because socialism, rather than being a term of opprobrium, as it is in the United States, is a term so revered around the world that almost all societies appropriate it in one way or another in their self-conceptions and characterizations. As a start, I shall avoid describing and analyzing presently existing socialist societies and turn instead to considering the socialist tradition itself—that body of ideas, theories, past practices, and aspirations that have accumulated over the years—and extract from that tradition those general ideas and principles considered the bedrock of the "socialist idea."[1] I shall present here no blueprints, no cast-in-concrete constitutional arrangements, only the building blocks of an edifice that people, if they so desire, must perforce arrange, design, and construct for themselves.

THE GOALS OF DEMOCRATIC SOCIALISM

Let me begin with a brief consideration of the goals of democratic socialism. While it might surprise those whose familiarity with socialism is derived from the distortions of western scholarship and official propaganda, the central goal of socialism has always been *humankind* itself. In the words of Erich Fromm, socialism has always aimed at creating "a form of production and an organization of society in which man can overcome alienation from his product, from his work, from his fellow man, from himself and from nature; in which he can return to himself and grasp the world with his own powers, thus becoming one with the world."[2]

Put less abstractly, the goals of democratic socialism are essentially twofold. First, socialism is concerned with ending the exploitation inherent in any system of social class relations. Since exploitation is inescapably embedded in social class divisions, socialism aims at abolishing social classes by putting an end to systems in which the ownership and control of the productive assets of a society are concentrated into the hands of but a few people whether private owners or party commissars. Exploitation—the extraction of surplus value from working people and the use of their labors, efforts, and skills for purposes not determined by them—is to be abolished by transforming private property into social property.[3] Second, democratic socialism is concerned with transforming an economic system that takes as its goal the accumulation of private profits through the production of goods and services for a marketplace, with all of its attendant waste, irrationality, and injustice, into a system in which production is directed toward human purposes and social needs. Again, such a reorientation is possible only through the abolition of the private property-based system and its replacement by one in which production is socially directed—that is, democratically determined.

You will note the distinction between *socially* directed and *state* directed. The democratic socialist tradition has always been committed to the concept of direct, participatory, mass democracy, involvement by ordinary people in the discussions that give direction to the social order. This conception has often been pushed aside in practice in presently existing socialist societies by a tightly organized and disciplined revolutionary party, a substitution often required by the exigencies of making a revolution and protecting it in a backward society. Nevertheless, the democratic socialist tradition has always emphasized the necessity of expanding the realm of democracy from its narrow confines in the political world to all aspects of social life, including the economic and social orders. The aim of democratic socialism, that is to say, is the democratization of life in general. If we understand socialism in these terms, then it is entirely reasonable to suggest that *Soviet-style societies are not socialist.*

THE ASSUMPTIONS
OF DEMOCRATIC SOCIALISM

As with all other sociopolitical traditions, the socialist tradition makes certain assumptions about the nature of human beings and their relationships to others. It starts with those characteristics that are common to all human beings and that entitle all people to equal consideration and respect.[4] Socialists take the position that all persons share certain *needs:* that there exists some minimum requirement of food, shelter, health, and so forth, which all people share. It follows that no decent society would be organized so as to concentrate the distribution of needed goods and services into the hands of the few while the needs of their fellows go unmet. Such a society is one in which common humanity is denied.

Socialism maintains, moreover, that human beings share certain capacities and that if society is to allow human beings to realize their humanness, it must be organized in such a way that it can both allow and encourage the development of these capacities. Human beings, from the socialist view, are purposeful beings who are able, if given a chance, to make decisions intelligently, who have intentions and purposes, and who can become aware of alternatives and rationally choose among them. People are, to one degree or another, potentially self-directed and self-determining, and to be placed in settings where others direct all essential aspects of their efforts—as in the wage-labor relationship—is to be separated from one's humanness. People also possess, in the socialist view, the capacity for self-expression and creativity. They are capable of developing excellence in some area of life, whether it be "intellectual, aesthetic, or moral, theoretical or practical, personal or public."[5] While people do not have equal capability in each and every area, they "share the capacity to realize potentialities that are worthy of admiration."[6]

Much of this may sound unfamiliar to you, for it suggests that the aim of democratic socialism is the flowering of the individual human being through the meeting of basic human needs and the provision of an environment conducive to the development of individual capacities. The image of socialism in the United States is quite contrary to this, an image constructed of pictures of massed, collectivized, and regimented populations. Individualism, we have come to believe, is a monopoly of liberal-capitalist countries. Yet socialism is *more* committed to the full development of human capacities than is liberal capitalism, because individualism in the latter is confined largely to the marketplace and to the goal of accumulation. As Fromm so eloquently points out:

> Marx's aim was that of the spiritual emancipation of man, of his liberation from the chains of economic determination, of restituting him in his human wholeness, of enabling him to find unity and harmony with his fellow man and with nature. Marx's philosophy was, in secular, nontheistic language, a new and radical step forward in the tradition of prophetic Messianism; it was aimed at the full realization of individualism, the very aim which has guided western thinking from the Renaissance and the Reformation far into the nineteenth century.[7]

THE PRINCIPLES OF A JUST AND DEMOCRATIC SOCIETY

In the socialist view, then, human beings share certain needs and capacities. It follows that a society committed to human ends and purposes must be organized around principles that recognize the common humanity of all persons. What are the guiding principles of such a society?

Equality

The bedrock of the socialist ideal is the principle of equality of condition, the distribution of the assets of the community in a manner that meets the basic needs of all of its members. It is a principle of social organization that insists "that we find ways of sharing our resources that match the variety of [human] needs, interests, and capacities."[8] It is a principle of social organization which, while not insistent upon *exact* mathematical equality, nevertheless insists that all members of society share in the enjoyment of those goods and services produced by society that are requisite to a life of decency, fulfillment, and self-respect. Recognizing that production is social in nature, that production is the outcome of the shared contribution of the skills, intelligence, and labor of the many, socialism insists that the distribution of the fruits of production be social as well, and not hoarded into the hands of a few.

Socialists generally believe that only when there exists equality of condition does it become possible for people to develop fully as human beings, because only as basic needs for food, shelter, and security are provided are people freed to cultivate their talents and interests. The development of meaningful individualism for the majority of the population becomes possible only when their subordinate position to capital is erased and they gain the wherewithal to broaden their horizons. It must also be added that while the options, potentials, and freedom of the majority are expanded, the situation of the privileged few must of necessity be transgressed—their freedom is by definition limited, circumscribed, and diminished. As R. H. Tawney points out, "As freedom for the pike is death for the minnows, so is effective freedom for the minnows death for *the pike as pike.*"[9]

In the socialist tradition, equality is an idea of such pervasive appeal and import that it affects all social relations. In socialist society, equality is a principle relevant not only to the distribution of material goods and services but also to the distribution of respect, political power, and the power of self-determination.

Moreover, when equality exists in all sectors of social life, socialists believe that it translates into a tone in the social order in which people treat each other

In a market capitalist society, many of the elderly are poor.

as equals, meet in fellowship, and come to disdain attitudes of lordly superiority or fawning subservience. All such hierarchical encounters represent a rejection of the equal dignity and worth of human beings that exist by virtue of their humanness. It is a society, as George Orwell described revolutionary Spain in the 1930s, where one "breathes the air of equality . . . [where there is] no boss class, no menial class, no beggars, no prostitutes, no lawyers, no priests, no bootlicking, no cap-touching."[10]

Such a conception of equality is at once significantly more than and superior to notions of equality that are confined simply to the enjoyment of legal and political *rights*. Where inequalities of life conditions exist they must surely make a mockery of these rights, for material inequalities give to some members of society a greater probability of effectively exercising legal and political rights. "Economic realities make short work of legal abstractions."[11] Moreover, equality of condition must be distinguished from another liberal-capitalist concept, that of *equality of opportunity*, a concept that is rendered moot in any society in which wide disparities in material conditions exist. The notion of equality of opportunity in a setting of extreme inequality is, in the apt phrase of R. H. Tawney, little more than "the impertinent courtesy of an invitation offered to unwelcome guests, in the certainty that circumstances will prevent them from accepting it."[12]

Dispersal of Power

Intimately connected to the concept of *equality of condition*—indeed, logically derived from it—is the concept of the dispersal of decision-making power. If the service of human needs, interests, and capacities requires an environment of rough equality of condition, it follows that the distribution of power, the ability to shape the directions of group life, must also be distributed in some roughly proportional fashion. To organize society in any other manner would be to introduce significant inequality into the social order and to largely negate the advances made through the equalization of material conditions. The reintroduction of inequality in decision-making power would not only serve to undermine the common humanity and fellowship implicit in material equality, but also would block the development of the human capacity for self-direction, autonomy, and self-determination. To be a passive receiver of orders, to have the direction of one's life determined by decisions in which one has played no active role is, in the socialist view, to be stunted in one's growth and to be less than human.

It is important to note that the principle of direct, participatory democracy is one that is to be applied to all spheres, wherever decisions are made that significantly affect others. In this view, all decisions and policies that have social implications and consequences must be arrived at socially, a view quite contrary to the liberal-capitalist one, which gives almost free rein to the owners of property in determining the uses of their property. The goal of this democratization is to erase mass helplessness before concentrated economic and political power, to erase the sorts of situations described by Tawney in the following words: "Lord Melchett smiles, and there is sunshine in 10,000 homes. Mr. Morgan frowns and the population of two continents is plunged into gloom.''[13]

The dispersal of power must be a pervasive phenomenon in socialist society, relevant to all spheres, political as well as economic. This requirement follows from the often perceived phenomenon in which concentrated power in some single sphere of activity spills over into others, multiplying influence and power. In the capitalist countries, for instance, economic power is almost always translated into political power, as we have already seen in some detail. It is important to add, however, that something similar and as reprehensible usually happens in the contemporary Soviet bloc nations, where concentrated political power in the party is translated into power in all other spheres of social relations. It is important to keep this observation in mind, because it suggests that *socialism is not guaranteed by the abolition of private property alone, but only when it is joined to the democratization of social life in general, the appropriation by ordinary people of the direct control of their own lives.*

Production for Use

Socialist society is one in which production is guided not by the pursuit of private aggrandizement and the accumulation of profit but by social purposes determined democratically by politically active, participatory people who live in conditions of substantial equality. Since production is itself social in form and in consequence, it is to be made social in its direction in socialist society. The direction of social life and production is to be removed from the service of the few, and from that of abstract economic principles (such as profit), and reoriented toward the service of human beings. In a just society, production can never serve any other end than the betterment of the lives of human beings, to provide the means by which needs are met and capacities cultivated. For production and accumulation to become ends in themselves is to stand the world on its head, to make people the slaves of the machinery that they themselves have created.

For production to be directed by the few, whether they be owners of capital or an elite political leadership, is to reintroduce inequality, social distinctions, and passive citizenship. In the socialist view, production must be both directed toward the service of human needs and capacities and determined by the people themselves. To have a handful of persons make decisions leading to production for use is, by definition, a contradiction. Implied in social production is the concept of self-direction, autonomy, and personal growth through active participation in social decision making.

The attractions of a system of production directed toward human purposes rather than toward the satisfaction of the greed of the few ought to be immediately obvious. Production consciously directed toward the fulfillment of human needs and capacities not only puts first things first and gets priorities in their proper order but also avoids all those irrationalities, externalities, waste, and social injustices inherent in a system of commodity production. It eliminates any possibility of justifying by claims of the ''rights'' of private property those activities

Children at play amid the consumer wasteland

clearly detrimental to other human beings. Moreover, democratic participation of
the people in determining the direction of production not only opens the way to
a more rational and humane economic system but also involves people in those
decisions that shape social life, developing those capacities for rational judgment
and self-direction so central to what it means to be fully human in the socialist
view.[14]

BLUEPRINTS FOR DEMOCRATIC SOCIALISM

Socialist society is constructed out of the raw materials set out above, building on
the principles of equality, the democratization of social decision making, and production for use and human need. While the basic raw materials of democratic
socialism have been set out, there is no possibility or even good reason for pre-
senting a carefully worked out set of architectural plans for such a society. There
are two important reasons for this apparent timidity. First, people do not initiate
radical social change and construct new societies out of some guidebook of blueprints. Quite to the contrary, people tend to learn and to experiment with social

forms and relationships in the very midst of their struggles for change. To ask or to expect them to do otherwise is patently unrealistic. Second, it is entirely possible, even probable, that using the same set of building materials, different groups of people will build strikingly different edifices. Guided by the principles of equality, democracy, and production for use, people are likely to create social orders that differ radically in design and operation. To set out some particular and specific set of organizational forms, and then to label it democratic socialism, unduly and prematurely constricts the realm of possibilities. As French revolutionary Auguste Blanqui once observed, "One of our most grotesque presumptions is that we . . . pose as legislators for future generations." Democratic socialism embodies several key principles; its particular institutional arrangements are limited only by the human imagination.

That is not to say, however, that democratic socialism is simply a set of abstract and utopian concepts. In fact, bits and pieces of democratic socialism already exist in many places. In Sweden and Norway, for instance, economic investment is largely guided by democratic political processes. In most of the western European nations, worker councils exercise much control over everyday work processes. In Yugoslavia, economic enterprises are run entirely by the people who work in them. In many presently existing socialist societies, education, medical care, and nutrition have been made available to all. In the Israeli kibbutz, direct participatory democracy and material equality coexist comfortably with prosperity and economic efficiency. Democratic socialism is, in some sense, the simple amalgamation of programs and institutions that already exist, that already work, and that already contribute to the reality of democracy and justice.[15]

PRESENTLY EXISTING SOCIALISM IS NOT SOCIALISM

If the preceding describes the essence of democratic socialism, what are we to make of cases like the Soviet Union, which look nothing like our model? What are we to make of real-world examples of self-proclaimed socialist societies that range from the grim, bureaucratic Soviet Union to the market socialisms of Yugoslavia and Hungary, to the "communism with a human face" that flared briefly in Czechoslovakia before it was crushed by invading Soviet troops?

Clearly these societies share little with one another, and there are many distinctions among them. At one level, none of these societies is socialist in the sense described in the previous section, or as formulated and envisioned by Marx and others. None has managed to incorporate into its structure and operations all the basic socialist principles, though some professed socialist societies better approximate them than others. Almost all the societies that call themselves socialist have made vast strides toward equality of condition. Yet they have all been terribly deficient in democratizing social life and the control of production, which suggests that present-day socialist societies are, in fact, socialist in name only.

Indeed, a growing number of Marxist scholars and intellectuals claim that the Soviet Union is not socialist, though it has appropriated the rhetoric and symbolism of that tradition.[16] While the terminology varies among these observers, most of them define the Soviet Union as either state-capitalist or state-socialist. The term *state-capitalist* is used by those who claim that "those countries [the Soviet Union and Eastern European Soviet bloc nations] underwent the process of capitalist development in the name of socialism, whereby the state played a major role, not in creating a socialist society, but in bringing together the forces necessary for capitalist development."[17] That is, the state stimulated economic development but used capitalist-type criteria (efficiency, hierarchy at the workplace, money incentives, surplus extraction, and so on) in the organization of production. Other Marxist intellectuals, however, who are unwilling to use the term *capitalist* to describe the Soviet Union, principally because of the abolition of privately held wealth in property, tend to use the term *state-socialism* in an effort to recognize the existence of a powerful, centralized state bureaucracy that dominates the direction of social life.

Whatever approach one chooses to take, whether one defines them as quasi-socialist, state-capitalist, or state-socialist, the Soviet Union and most other socialist countries do not fare very well when measured against the democratic socialist model. At best, these societies represent intense efforts to create the material preconditions for the transition to socialism. At worst, they have nothing whatever to do with socialism.

THE UNITED STATES AND DEMOCRATIC SOCIALISM

No existing socialist society has very much to say to our own situation or to political possibilities here in the United States. Each and every revolution in the name of socialism has taken place in settings and in circumstances vastly different from our own. Most important, socialist revolutions have occurred in nonindustrialized countries and in countries dominated by outside imperialist powers. Much of the harsh discipline characteristic of many present-day societies can surely be traced to such factors. There is no reason to believe that socialist transformation in the industrialized western countries (which Marx believed would be peaceful), including the United States, would take the form that so many Americans find distasteful. In fact, there is every reason to believe—given the virtual conquest of scarcity in the western countries (that is, of essential goods and services), the absence of the necessity for passing through the throes of the primitive accumulation characteristic of early industrialization, and the tradition of civil and political liberties—that a socialist transformation could transcend the injustice, wastefulness, and irrationality of capitalist society and usher in a humane social order.

It seems more than a little odd to speak of democratic socialism in an era dominated in the United States by Reaganism and all that it entails: individualistic competition, inequality, militarism, working-class retreat, corporate asser-tivcncss, and a minimalist social safety net. Nothing lasts forever in American politics, however, and public policies and accepted approaches to national prob-lems that seem rock solid one day turn to dust the next. Reaganism shall surely pass; what will take its place is not entirely obvious.[18] If democracy and justice are to be a significant part of the American future after the passing of Reaganism, however, it is important that the American people have available a vision of a decent and humane society to guide their actions. Democratic socialism is, in my view, just such a vision. Whether this vision is transformed into reality depends entirely upon the efforts of the American people.

NOTES

1. While the socialist tradition centers most strongly in the monumental work of Karl Marx, it remains a tradition enriched by the contributions of many people both before and after his time.
2. Erich Fromm, *Marx's Concept of Man* (New York: Ungar, 1961), p. 59.
3. Let me reiterate that private property to socialists does not mean personal possessions such as clothes or appliances but, rather, a social relationship that enables some people to buy the labor power of others.
4. Much of the following section is based on Steven Lukes, "Socialism and Equality," *Dissent,* Spring, 1975, pp. 154–168.
5. Ibid., p. 157.
6. Ibid.
7. Fromm, *Marx's Concept of Man,* p. 3.
8. Michael Walzer, "In Defense of Equality," *Dissent* 20:4 (Fall, 1973), p. 347.
9. Quoted in Ross Terrill, *R. H. Tawney and His Times* (Cambridge: Harvard University Press, 1973), p. 134.
10. George Orwell, *Homage to Catalonia* (Baltimore: Penguin, 1962), p. 66.
11. Terrill, *R. H. Tawney and His Times,* p. 122.
12. Ibid., p. 123.
13. Ibid., p. 144. In the modern day we might substitute corporate names such as Exxon, General Motors, and IBM for those of Melchett and Morgan.
14. There is persuasive evidence to suggest a strong association between participation in social decision making and mental health. See Edward S. Greenberg, "The Conse-quences of Worker Participation: A Clarification of the Theoretical Literature," *Social Science Quarterly,* September 1975; and Greenberg, "Participation in Industrial Decision-Making and Work Satisfaction," *Social Science Quarterly,* March 1980.
15. For a comprehensive look at innovations in democracy and social justice in western Europe see Martin Carnoy and Derek Shearer, *Economic Democracy* (White Plains, N.Y.: M. E. Sharpe, 1980).
16. For an additional case, see Charles Bettelheim, "China Since Mao," *Monthly Review* 30:3 (July 1978) for a blistering Marxist critique of the contemporary directions of Chinese society.
17. Alan Wolfe, *The Seamy Side of Democracy* (New York: David McKay, 1973), p. 243.

18. On what is likely to come after Reaganism see Edward S. Greenberg, *Capitalism and the American Political Ideal* (Armonk, N.Y.: M. E. Sharpe, 1985).

SUGGESTIONS FOR FURTHER READING

Martin Carnoy and Derek Shearer. ECONOMIC DEMOCRACY. *White Plains, N.Y.: M. E. Sharpe, 1980.* A detailed look at concrete reforms of the workplace and the economy in the western European nations that have significantly advanced justice and democracy.

Branko Horvat. THE POLITICAL ECONOMY OF SOCIALISM. *Armonk, N.Y.: M. E. Sharpe, 1982.* A monumental work which examines the shortcomings of capitalism and presently existing socialism and then constructs the foundations for a model of democratic socialism.

David Schweickart. CAPITALISM OR WORKER CONTROL? AN ETHICAL AND ECONOMIC APPRAISAL. *New York: Praeger, 1980.* A brilliant, in-depth comparison of the models of capitalism and worker controlled socialism.

Ross Terrill. R. H. TAWNEY AND HIS TIMES. *Cambridge: Harvard University Press, 1973.* An introduction to the work of one of the most interesting and humane thinkers in western socialism.

Eric Olin Wright. CLASS, CRISIS, AND STATE. *London: New Left Books, 1977.* A provocative collection of essays on the general topics of capitalist crisis and the transition to socialism.

Appendix:
The Constitution
of the United States

We the People of the United States, in Order to form a more perfect Union, establish Justice, insure domestic Tranquility, provide for the common defense, promote the general Welfare, and secure the Blessings of Liberty to ourselves and our Posterity, do ordain and establish this Constitution for the United States of America.

Article I

Section 1. All legislative Powers herein granted shall be vested in a Congress of the United States, which shall consist of a Senate and House of Representatives.

Section 2. The House of Representatives shall be composed of Members chosen every second Year by the People of the several States, and the Electors in each State shall have the Qualifications requisite for Electors of the most numerous Branch of the State Legislature.

No Person shall be a Representative who shall not have attained to the Age of twenty-five Years, and been seven Years A Citizen of the United States, and who shall not, when elected, be an Inhabitant of that State in which he shall be chosen.

Representatives and direct Taxes shall be apportioned among the several States which may be included within this Union, according to their respective Numbers, which shall be determined by adding to the whole Number of free Persons, including those bound to Service for a Term of Years, and excluding Indians not taxed, three fifths of all other Persons. The actual Enumeration shall be made within three Years after the first Meeting of the Congress of the United States, and within every subsequent Term of ten Years, in such Manner as they shall by Law direct. The Number of Representatives shall not exceed one for every thirty Thousand, but each State shall have at Least one Representative; and until such enumeration shall be made, the State of New Hampshire shall be entitled to chuse three, Massachusetts eight, Rhode-Island and Providence Plantations one, Connecticut five, New York six, New Jersey four, Pennsylvania eight, Delaware one, Maryland six, Virginia ten, North Carolina five, South Carolina five, and Georgia three.

When vacancies happen in the Representation from any State, the Executive Authority thereof shall issue Writs of Election to fill such Vacancies.

The House of Representatives shall chuse their Speaker and other Officers; and shall have the sole Power of Impeachment.

Section 3. The Senate of the United States shall be composed of two Senators from each State, chosen by the Legislature thereof, for six Years; and each Senator shall have one Vote.

Immediately after they shall be assembled in Consequence of the first Election, they shall be divided as equally as may be into three Classes. The Seats of the Senators of the first Class shall be vacated at the Expiration of the second Year, of the second Class at the Expiration of the fourth Year, and of the third Class at the Expiration of the sixth Year, so that one third may be chosen every second Year; and if Vacancies happen by Resignation, or otherwise, during the Recess of the Legislature of any State, the Executive thereof may make temporary Appointments until the next Meeting of the Legislature, which shall then fill such Vacancies.

No Person shall be a Senator who shall not have attained to the Age of thirty Years, and been nine Years a Citizen of the United States, and who shall not, when elected, be an Inhabitant of the State for which he shall be chosen.

The Vice President of the United States shall be President of the Senate, but shall have no Vote, unless they be equally divided.

The Senate shall chuse their other Officers, and also a President pro tempore, in the absence of the Vice President, or when he shall exercise the Office of President of the United States.

The Senate shall have the sole Power to try all Impeachments. When sitting for that Purpose, they shall be on Oath or Affirmation. When the President of the United States is tried, the Chief Justice shall preside: And no Person shall be convicted without the Concurrence of two thirds of the Members present.

Judgment in Cases of Impeachment shall not extend further than to removal from Office, and disqualification to hold and enjoy any Office of honor, Trust, or Profit under the United States: but the Party convicted shall nevertheless be liable and subject to Indictment, Trial, Judgment and Punishment, according to Law.

Section 4. The Times, Places and Manner of holding Elections for Senators and Representatives, shall be prescribed in each State by the Legislature thereof; but the Congress may at any time by Law make or alter such Regulations, except as to the Places of chusing Senators.

The Congress shall assemble at least once in every Year, and such Meeting shall be on the first Monday in December, unless they shall by Law appoint a different Day.

Section 5. Each House shall be the judge of the Elections, Returns and Qualifications of its own Members, and a Majority of each shall constitute a Quorum to do Business; but a smaller Number may adjourn from day to day, and may be authorized to compel the Attendance of absent Members, in such Manner, and under such Penalties, as each House may provide.

Each House may determine the Rules of its Proceedings, punish its Members for disorderly Behaviour, and, with the Concurrence of two thirds, expel a Member.

Each House shall keep a Journal of its Proceedings, and from time to time publish the same, excepting such Parts as may in their Judgment require Secrecy; and the Yeas and Nays of the Members of either House on any question shall, at the Desire of one fifth of those Present, be entered on the Journal.

Neither House, during the Session of Congress, shall, without the Consent of the other, adjourn for more than three days, not to any other Place than that in which the two Houses shall be sitting.

Section 6. The Senators and Representatives shall receive a Compensation for their Services, to be ascertained by Law, and paid out of the Treasury of the United States. They shall in all Cases, except Treason, Felony and Breach of the Peace, be privileged from Arrest during their Attendance at the Session of their respective Houses, and in going to and returning from the same; and for any Speech or Debate in either House, they shall not be questioned in any other place.

No Senator or Representative shall, during the Time for which he was elected, be appointed to any civil Office under the Authority of the United States, which shall have been created, or the Emoluments whereof shall have been encreased during such time; and no Person holding any Office under the United States, shall be a Member of either House during his Continuance in Office.

Section 7. All bills for raising Revenue shall originate in the house of Representatives; but the Senate may propose or concur with Amendments as on other Bills.

Every Bill which shall have passed the House of Representatives and the Senate, shall, before it become a Law, be presented to the President of the United States; If he approve he shall sign it, but if not he shall return it, with his Objections to that House in which it shall have originated, who shall enter the Objections at large on their Journal, and proceed to reconsider it. If after such

Reconsideration two thirds of that House shall agree to pass the Bill, it shall be sent, together with the Objections, to the other House, by which it shall likewise be reconsidered, and if approved by two thirds of that House, it shall become a Law. But in all such Cases the Votes of both Houses shall be determined by Yeas and Nays, and the Names of the Persons voting for and against the Bill shall be entered on the Journal of each House respectively. If any Bill shall not be returned by the President within ten Days (Sundays excepted) after it shall have been pre-sented to him, the Same shall be a Law, in like Manner as if he had signed it, unless the Congress by their Adjournment prevent its Return, in which Case it shall not be a Law.

Every Order, Resolution, or Vote to which the Concurrence of the Senate and House of Representatives may be necessary (except on a question of Adjournment) shall be presented to the President of the United States; and before the Same shall take Effect, shall be approved by him, or being disapproved by him, shall be repassed by two thirds of the Senate and House of Representatives, according to the Rules and Limitations prescribed in the Case of a Bill.

Section 8. The Congress shall have Power To lay and collect Taxes, Duties, Im-posts and Excises, to pay the Debts and provide for the common Defense and general Welfare of the United States; but all Duties, Imposts and Excises shall be uniform throughout the United States;

To borrow Money on the credit of the United States;

To regulate Commerce with foreign Nations, and among the several States, and with the Indian Tribes;

To establish an uniform Rule of Naturalization, and uniform Laws on the subject of Bankruptcies throughout the United States;

To coin Money, regulate the Value thereof, and of foreign Coin, and fix the Standard of Weights and Measures;

To provide for the Punishment of counterfeiting the Securities and current Coin of the United States;

To Establish Post Offices and post Roads;

To promote the Progress of Science and useful Arts, by securing for limited Times to Authors and Inventors the exclusive Right to their respective Writings and Discoveries;

To constitute Tribunals inferior to the Supreme Court;

To define and punish Piracies and Felonies committed on the high seas, and Offenses against the Law of Nations;

To declare War, grant Letters of Marque and Reprisal, and make Rules con-cerning Captures on Land and Water;

To raise and support Armies, but no Appropriation of Money to that Use shall be for a longer Term than two Years;

To provide and maintain a Navy;

To make Rules for the Government and Regulation of the land and naval Forces;

To provide for calling forth the Militia to execute the Laws of the Union, suppress Insurrections and repel Invasions;

To provide for organizing, arming, and disciplining, the Militia, and for governing such Part of them as may be employed in the Service of the United States, reserving to the States respectively, the Appointment of the Officers, and the Authority of training the Militia according to the discipline prescribed by Congress;

To exercise exclusive Legislation in all Cases whatsoever, over such District (not exceeding ten Miles square) as may, by Cession of particular States, and the Acceptance of Congress, become the Seat of the Government of the United States, and to exercise like Authority over all Places purchased by the Consent of the Legislature of the State in which the Same shall be, for the Erection of Forts, Magazines, Arsenals, dock-Yards, and other needful Buildings;—And

To make all Laws which shall be necessary and proper for carrying into Execution the foregoing Powers, and all other Powers vested by this Constitution in the Government of the United States, or in any Department or Officer thereof.

Section 9. The Migration or Importation of such Persons as any of the States now existing shall think proper to admit, shall not be prohibited by the Congress prior to the Year one thousand eight hundred and eight, but a Tax or duty may be imposed on such Importation, not exceeding ten dollars for each Person.

The Privilege of the Writ of Habeas Corpus shall not be suspended, unless when in Cases of Rebellion or Invasion the public Safety may require it.

No Bill of Attainder or ex post facto Law shall be passed.

No Capitation, or other direct, Tax shall be laid, unless in Proportion to the Census or Enumeration herein before directed to be taken.

No Tax or Duty shall be laid on Articles exported from any State.

No Preference shall be given by any Regulation of Commerce or Revenue to the Ports of one State over those of another: nor shall Vessels bound to, or from, one State, be obliged to enter, clear, or pay Duties in another.

No Money shall be drawn from the Treasury, but in Consequence of Appropriations made by Law; and a regular Statement and Account of the Receipts and Expenditures of all public Money shall be published from time to time.

No title of Nobility shall be granted by the United States: And no Person holding any Office of Profit or Trust under them, shall, without the Consent of the Congress, accept of any present, Emolument, Office, or Title, of any kind whatever, from any King, Prince, or foreign State.

Section 10. No State shall enter into any Treaty, Alliance, or Confederation; grant Letters of Marque and Reprisal; coin Money; emit Bills of Credit; make any Thing but gold and silver Coin a Tender in Payment of Debts; pass any Bill of Attainder, ex post facto Law, or Law impairing the Obligation of Contracts, or Grant any Title of Nobility.

No State shall, without the Consent of the Congress, lay any Imposts or Duties on Imports or Exports, except what may be absolutely necessary for exercising its inspection Laws: and the net Produce of all Duties and Imposts, laid by any State on Imports or Exports shall be for the Use of the Treasury of the United States; and all such Laws shall be subject to the Revision and Control of the Congress.

No State shall, without the Consent of Congress, lay any duty of Tonnage, keep Troops, or Ships of War in time of Peace, enter into any Agreement or Compact with another State, or with a foreign Power, or engage in War, unless actually invaded, or in such imminent Danger as will not admit of delay.

Article II

Section 1. The executive Power shall be vested in a President of the United States of America. He shall hold his Office during the Term of four Years, and, together with the Vice President, chosen for the same Term be elected, as follows:

Each State shall appoint, in such Manner as the Legislature thereof may direct, a Number of Electors, equal to the whole Number of Senators and Representatives to which the State may be entitled in the Congress but no Senator or Representative, or Person holding an Office of Trust or Profit under the United States, shall be appointed an Elector.

The Electors shall meet in their respective States, and vote by Ballot for two Persons, of whom one at least shall not be an Inhabitant of the same State with themselves. And they shall make a List of all the Persons voted for, and of the Number of Votes for each; which List they shall sign and certify, and transmit sealed to the Seat of the Government of the United States, directed to the President of the Senate. The President of the Senate shall, in the Presence of the Senate and House of Representatives, open all the Certificates, and the Votes shall then be counted. The Person having the greatest Number of Votes shall be the President, if such Number be a Majority of the whole Number of Electors appointed; and if there be more than one who have such Majority, and have an equal Number of Votes, then the House of Representatives shall immediately chuse by Ballot one of them for President; and if no Person have a Majority, then from the five highest on the List the said House shall in like Manner chuse the President. But in chusing the President, the Votes shall be taken by States, the Representation from each State having one Vote; A quorum for this Purpose shall consist of a Member or Members from two thirds of the States, and a Majority of all the States shall be necessary to a Choice. In every Case, after the Choice of the President, the Person having the greatest Number of Votes of the Electors shall be the Vice President. But if there should remain two or more who have equal votes, the Senate shall chuse from them by Ballot the Vice President.

The Congress may determine the Time of chusing the Electors, and the Day on which they shall give their Votes; which Day shall be the same throughout the United States.

No Person except a natural born Citizen, or a Citizen of the United States, at the time of the Adoption of this Constitution, shall be eligible to the Office of President; neither shall any Person be eligible to that Office who shall not have attained to the Age of thirty-five Years, and been fourteen years a Resident within the United States.

In Case of the Removal of the President from Office, or of his Death, Resignation, or Inability to discharge the Powers and Duties of the said Office, the Same shall devolve on the Vice President, and the Congress may by Law provide for the Case of Removal, Death, Resignation or Inability, both of the President and Vice President, declaring what Officer shall then act as President, and such Officer shall act accordingly, until the Disability be removed, or a President shall be elected.

The President shall, at stated Times, receive for his Services, a Compensation which shall neither be increased nor diminished during the Period for which he shall have been elected, and he shall not receive within that Period any other Emolument from the United States, or any of them.

Before he enters on the Execution of his Office, he shall take the following Oath or Affirmation:—''I do solemnly swear (or affirm) that I will faithfully execute the Office of President of the United States, and will to the best of my Ability, preserve, protect, and defend the Constitution of the United States.''

Section 2. The President shall be Commander in Chief of the Army and Navy of the United States, and of the Militia of the several States, when called into the actual service of the United States; he may require the Opinion, in writing, of the principal Officer in each of the Executive Departments, upon any Subject relating to the Duties of their respective Offices, and he shall have Power to grant Reprieves and Pardons for Offenses against the United States, except in Cases of Impeachment.

He shall have Power, by and with the Advice and Consent of the Senate, to make Treaties, provided two thirds of the Senators present concur; and he shall nominate, and by and with the Advice and Consent of the Senate, shall appoint Ambassadors, other public Ministers and Consuls, Judges of the supreme Court, and all other Officers of the United States, whose Appointments are not herein otherwise provided for, and which shall be established by Law: but the Congress may by Law vest the Appointment of such inferior Officers, as they think proper, in the President alone, in the Courts of Law, or in the Heads of Departments.

The President shall have Power to fill up all Vacancies that may happen during the Recess of the Senate, by granting Commissions which shall expire at the End of their next Session.

Section 3. He shall from time to time give to the Congress Information of the State of the Union, and recommend to their Consideration such Measures as he shall judge necessary and expedient; he may, on extraordinary Occasions, convene both Houses, or either of them, and in Case of Disagreement between them, with Respect to the Time of Adjournment, he may adjourn them to such Time as he shall think proper; he shall receive Ambassadors and other public Ministers, he shall take Care that the Laws be faithfully executed, and shall Commission all the Officers of the United States.

Section 4. The President, Vice President, and all civil Officers of the United States, shall be removed from Office on Impeachment for, and Conviction of Treason, Bribery, or other high Crimes and Misdemeanors.

Article III

Section 1. The judicial Power of the United States, shall be vested in one supreme Court and in such inferior Courts as the Congress may from time to time ordain and establish. The Judges, both of the supreme and inferior Courts, shall hold their Offices during good Behavior, and shall, at stated Times, receive for their Services, a Compensation, which shall not be diminished during their Continuance in Office.

Section 2. The judicial Power shall extend to all Cases, in Law and Equity, arising under this Constitution, the Laws of the United States, and Treaties made, or which shall be made, under their Authority;—to all Cases affecting Ambassadors, other public Ministers and Consuls;—to all Cases of admiralty and maritime Jurisdiction;—to Controversies to which the United States shall be a Party;—to Controversies between two or more States;—between a State and Citizens of another State;—between Citizens of different States;—between Citizens of the same State claiming Lands under Grants of different States, and between a State or the Citizens thereof, and foreign States, Citizens, or Subjects.

In all cases affecting Ambassadors, other public Ministers and Consuls, and those in which a State shall be a Party, the supreme Court shall have original Jurisdiction. In all the other Cases before mentioned, the supreme Court shall have appellate Jurisdiction, both as to Law and Fact, with such Exceptions, and under such Regulations as the Congress shall make.

The Trial of all Crimes, except in Cases of Impeachment, shall be by Jury; and such Trial shall be held in the State where the said Crimes shall have been committed; but when not committed within any State, the Trial shall be at such Place or Places as the Congress may by Law have directed.

Section 3. Treason against the United States, shall consist only in levying War against them, or in adhering to their Enemies, giving them Aid and Comfort. No person shall be convicted of Treason unless on the Testimony of two Witnesses to the same overt Act, or on Confession in open Court.

The Congress shall have Power to declare the Punishment of Treason, but no Attainder of Treason shall work Corruption of Blood, or Forfeiture except during the Life of the Person attained.

Article IV

Section 1. Full Faith and Credit shall be given in each State to the public Acts, Records, and judicial Proceedings of every other State. And the Congress may by general Laws prescribe the Manner in which such Acts, Records, and Proceedings shall be proved, and the Effect thereof.

Section 2. The Citizens of each State shall be entitled to all Privileges and Immunities of Citizens in the several States.

A person charged in any State with Treason, Felony, or other Crime, who shall flee from Justice, and be found in another State, shall on Demand of the executive Authority of the State from which he fled, be delivered up, to be removed to the State having Jurisdiction of the Crime.

No Person held to Service or Labour in one State, under the Laws thereof, escaping into another, shall, in Consequence of any Law or Regulation therein, be discharged from such Service or Labour, but shall be delivered up on Claim of the Party to whom such Service or Labour may be due.

Section 3. New States may be admitted by the Congress into this Union; but no new State shall be formed or erected within the Jurisdiction of any other State; nor any State be formed by the Junction of two or more States, or parts of States, without the Consent of the Legislatures of the States concerned as well as of the Congress.

The Congress shall have Power to dispose of and make all needful Rules and Regulations respecting the Territory or other Property belonging to the United States; and nothing in this Constitution shall be so construed as to Prejudice any Claims of the United States, or of any particular State.

Section 4. The United States shall guarantee to every State in this Union a Republican Form of Government, and shall protect each of them against Invasion; and on Application of the Legislature, or of the Executive (when the Legislature cannot be convened) against domestic Violence.

Article V

The Congress, whenever two thirds of both Houses shall deem it necessary, shall propose Amendments to this Constitution, or, on the Application of the Legislatures of two thirds of the several States, shall call a Convention for proposing Amendments, which, in either Case, shall be valid to all Intents and Purposes, as Part of this Constitution, when ratified by the Legislatures of three fourths of the several States, or by Conventions in three fourths thereof, as the one or the other Mode of Ratification may be proposed by the Congress; Provided that no Amendment which may be made prior to the Year One thousand eight hundred and eight shall in any Manner affect the first and fourth Clauses in the Ninth

Section of the first Article; and that no State, without its Consent, shall be deprived of its equal Suffrage in the Senate.

Article VI

All Debts contracted and Engagements entered into, before the Adoption of this Constitution, shall be as valid against the United States under this Constitution, as under the Confederation.

This Constitution, and the Laws of the United States which shall be made in Pursuance thereof; and all Treaties made, or which shall be made, under the Authority of the United States, shall be the supreme Law of the Land; and the Judges in every State shall be bound thereby, any Thing in the Constitution or Laws of any State to the Contrary notwithstanding.

The Senators and Representatives before mentioned, and the Members of the several State Legislatures, and all executive and judicial Officers, both of the United States and of the several States, shall be bound by Oath or Affirmation to support this Constitution; but no religious Test shall ever be required as a Qualification to any Office or public Trust under the United States.

Article VII

The Ratification of the Conventions of nine States shall be sufficient for the Establishment of this Constitution between the States so ratifying the Same.

Done in Convention by the Unanimous Consent of the States present the Seventeenth Day of September in the Year of our Lord one thousand seven hundred and eighty seven and of the Independence of the United States of America the twelfth. In witness whereof We have hereunto subscribed our Names.

Articles in addition to, and amendment of, the Constitution of the United States of America, proposed by Congress, and ratified by the several states, pursuant to the fifth article of the original Constitution.

Amendment I

[Ratification of the first ten amendments was completed December 15, 1791.]
Congress shall make no law respecting an establishment of religion, or prohibiting the free exercise thereof; or abridging the freedom of speech, or of the press; or the right of the people peaceably to assemble, and to petition the Government for a redress of grievances.

Amendment II

A well regulated Militia, being necessary to the security of a free State, the right of the people to keep and bear Arms, shall not be infringed.

Amendment III

No Soldier shall, in time of peace, be quartered in any house, without the consent of the Owner, nor in time of war, but in a manner to be prescribed by law.

Amendment IV

The right of the people to be secure in their persons, houses, papers, and effects, against unreasonable searches and seizures, shall not be violated, and no Warrants shall issue, but upon probable cause, supported by Oath or affirmation, and particularly describing the place to be searched, and the persons or things to be seized.

Amendment V

No person shall be held to answer for a capital, or other infamous crime, unless on a presentment or indictment of a Grand Jury, except in cases arising in the land or naval forces, or in the Militia, when in actual service in time of War or public danger; nor shall any person be subject for the same offence to be twice put in jeopardy of life or limb; nor shall be compelled in any capital crime case to be witness against himself, nor be deprived of life, liberty, or property, without due process of law; nor shall private property be taken for public use, without just compensation.

Amendment VI

In all criminal prosecutions, the accused shall enjoy the right to a speedy and public trial, by an impartial jury of the State and district wherein the crime shall have been committed, which district shall have been previously ascertained by law, and to be informed of the nature and cause of the accusation; to be confronted with the witness against him; to have compulsory process for obtaining witness in his favor, and to have the Assistance of Counsel for his defence.

Amendment VII

In Suits at common law, where the value in controversy shall exceed twenty dollars, the right of trial by jury shall be preserved, and no fact tried by jury, shall be otherwise re-examined in any Court of the United States, than according to the rules of the common law.

Amendment VIII

Excessive bail shall not be required, nor excessive fines imposed, nor cruel and unusual punishments inflicted.

Amendment IX

The enumeration in the Constitution, of certain rights, shall not be construed to deny or disparage others retained by the people.

Amendment X

The powers not delegated to the United States by the Constitution, nor prohibited by it to the States, are reserved to the States respectively, or to the people.

Amendment XI

[January 8, 1798]

The Judicial power of the United States shall not be construed to extend to any suit in law or equity, commenced or prosecuted against one of the United States by Citizens of another State, or by Citizens or subjects of any Foreign State.

Amendment XII

[September 25, 1804]

The Electors shall meet in their respective states and vote by ballot for President and Vice President, one of whom, at least, shall not be an inhabitant of the same state with themselves; they shall name in their ballots the person voted for as President, and in distinct ballots the person voted for as Vice President, and they shall make distinct lists of all persons voted for as President, and of all persons voted for as Vice President, and of the number of votes for each, which lists they shall sign and certify, and transmit sealed to the seat of the government of the United States, directed to the President of the Senate;—The President of the Senate shall, in the presence of Senate and House of Representatives, open all the certificates and the votes shall then be counted;—The person having the greatest number of votes for President, shall be the President, if such number be a majority of the whole number of Electors appointed; and if no person have such majority, then from the persons having the highest numbers not exeeding three on the list of those voted for as President, the House of Representatives shall choose immediately, by ballot, the President. But in choosing the President, the votes shall be taken by states, the representation from each state having one vote; a quorum for this purpose shall consist of a member or members from two-thirds of the states, and a majority of all the states shall be necessary to a choice. And if the House of Representatives shall not choose a President whenever the right of choice shall devolve upon them, before the fourth day of March next following, then the Vice President shall act as President, as in the case of the death or other constitutional disability of the President.—The person having the greatest number of votes as Vice President shall be the Vice President, if such number be a majority of the whole number of Electors appointed, and if no person have a majority, then from the two highest numbers on the list, the Senate shall choose the Vice President; a quorum for the purpose shall consist of two-thirds of the whole number of Senators, and a majority of the whole number shall be necessary to a choice. But no person constitutionally ineligible to the office of President shall be eligible to that of Vice President of the United States.

Amendment XIII

[December 18, 1865]

Section 1. Neither slavery nor involuntary servitude, except as a punishment for crime whereof the party shall have been duly convicted, shall exist within the United States, or any place subject to their jurisdiction.

Section 2. Congress shall have power to enforce this article by appropriate legislation.

Amendment XIV
[July 28, 1869]

Section 1. All persons born or naturalized in the United States, and subject to the jurisdiction thereof, are citizens of the United States and of the State wherein they reside. No State shall make or enforce any law which shall abridge the privileges or immunities of citizens of the United States; nor shall any State deprive any person of life, liberty, or property, without due process of law; nor deny to any person within its jurisdiction the equal protection of the laws.

Section 2. Representatives shall be apportioned among the several States according to their respective numbers, counting the whole number of persons in each State, excluding Indians not taxed. But when the right to vote at any election for the choice of electors for President and Vice President of the United States, Representatives in Congress, the Executive and Judicial officers of a State, or the members of the Legislature thereof, is denied to any of the male inhabitants of such State, being twenty-one years of age, and citizens of the United States, or in any way abridged, except for participation in rebellion, or other crime, the basis of representation therein shall be reduced in the proportion which the number of such male citizens shall bear to the whole number of male citizens twenty-one years of age in such State.

Section 3. No person shall be a Senator or Representative in Congress, or elector of President and Vice President, or hold any office, civil or military, under the United States, or under any State, who, having previously taken an oath, as a member of Congress, or as an officer of the United States, or as a member of any State legislature, or as an executive or judicial officer of any State, to support the Constitution of the United States, shall have engaged in insurrection or rebellion against the same, or given aid or comfort to the enemies thereof. But Congress may by a vote of two-thirds of each House, remove such disability.

Section 4. The validity of the public debt of the United States, authorized by law, including debts incurred for payment of pensions and bounties for services in suppressing insurrection or rebellion, shall not be questioned. But neither the United States nor any State shall assume or pay any debt or obligation incurred in aid of insurrection or rebellion against the United States, or any claim for the loss or emancipation of any slave; but all such debts, obligations, and claims shall be held illegal and void.

Section 5. The Congress shall have power to enforce, by appropriate legislation, the provisions of this article.

Amendment XV
[March 30, 1870]

Section 1. The right of citizens of the United States to vote shall not be denied or abridged by the United States or by any State on account of race, color, or previous condition of servitude.

Section 2. The Congress shall have the power to enforce this article by appropriate legislation.

Amendment XVI
[February 25, 1913]
The Congress shall have power to lay and collect taxes on incomes, from whatever source derived, without apportionment among the several States, and without regard to any census or enumeration.

Amendment XVII
[May 31, 1913]
The Senate of the United States shall be composed of two Senators from each State, elected by the people thereof, for six years; and each Senator shall have one vote. The electors in each State shall have the qualifications requisite for electors of the most numerous branch of the State legislatures.

When vacancies happen in the representation of any State in the Senate, the executive authority of such State shall issue writs of election to fill such vacancies: *Provided*, That the legislature of any State may empower the executive thereof to make temporary appointments until the people fill the vacancies by election as the legislature may direct.

This amendment shall not be so construed as to affect the election or term of any Senator chosen before it becomes valid as part of the Constitution.

Amendment XVIII
[January 29, 1919]

Section 1. After one year from the ratification of this article the manufacture, sale, or transportation of intoxicating liquors within, the importation thereof into, or the exportation thereof from the United States and all territory subject to the jurisdiction thereof for beverage purposes is hereby prohibited.

Section 2. The Congress and the several States shall have concurrent power to enforce this article by appropriate legislation.

Section 3. This article shall be inoperative unless it shall have been ratified as an amendment to the Constitution by the legislatures of the several States, as provided in the Constitution, within seven years from the date of the submission hereof to the States by the Congress.

Amendment XIX
[August 26, 1920]
The right of citizens of the United States to vote shall not be denied or abridged by the United States or by any State on account of sex.

Congress shall have power to enforce this article by appropriate legislation.

Amendment XX
[February 6, 1933]

Section 1. The terms of the President and Vice President shall end at noon on the 20th day of January, and the terms of Senators and Representatives at noon on the 3rd day of January, of the years in which such terms would have ended if this article had not been ratified; and the terms of their successors shall then begin.

Section 2. The Congress shall assemble at least once in every year, and such meeting shall begin at noon on the 3rd day of January, unless they shall by law appoint a different day.

Section 3. If, at the time fixed for the beginning of the term of the President, the President elect shall have died, the Vice President elect shall become President. If a President shall not have been chosen before the time fixed for the beginning of his term, or if the President elect shall have failed to qualify, then the Vice President elect shall act as President until a President shall have qualified; and the Congress may by law provide for the case wherein neither a President elect nor a Vice President elect shall have qualified, declaring who shall then act as President, or the manner in which one who is to act shall be selected, and such person shall act accordingly until a President or Vice President shall have qualified.

Section 4. The Congress may by law provide for the case of the death of any of the persons from whom the House of Representatives may choose a President whenever the right of choice shall devolve upon them, and for the case of the death of any of the persons from whom the Senate may choose a Vice President whenever the right of choice shall have devolved upon them.

Section 5. Sections 1 and 2 shall take effect on the 15th day of October following the ratification of this article.

Section 6. This article shall be inoperative unless it shall have been ratified as an amendment to the Constitution by the legislatures of three-fourths of the several States within seven years from the date of its submission.

Amendment XXI
[December 5, 1933]

Section 1. The eighteenth article of amendment to the Constitution of the United States is hereby repealed.

Section 2. The transportation or importation into any State, Territory, or possession of the United States for delivery or use therein of intoxicating liquors, in violation of the laws thereof, is hereby prohibited.

Section 3. This article shall be inoperative unless it shall have been ratified as an amendment to the Constitution by conventions in the several States, as provided in the Constitution, within seven years from the date of the submission hereof to the States by the Congress.

Amendment XXII
[February 26, 1951]

Section 1. No person shall be elected to the office of the President more than twice, and no person who has held the office of President, or acted as President, for more than two years of a term to which some other person was elected President shall be elected to the office of President more than once. But this Article shall not apply to any person holding the office of President when this Article was proposed by the Congress, and shall not prevent any person who may be holding the office of President, or acting as President, during the term within which this Article becomes operative from holding the office of President or acting as President during the remainder of such term.

Section 2. This article shall be inoperative unless it shall have been ratified as an amendment to the Constitution by the legislatures of three fourths of the several States within seven years from the date of its submission to the States by the Congress.

Amendment XXIII
[March 29, 1961]

Section 1. The District constituting the seat of Government of the United States shall appoint in such manner as the Congress may direct:
   A number of electors of President and Vice President equal to the whole

number of Senators and Representatives in Congress to which the District would be entitled if it were a State, but in no event more than the least populous State; they shall be in addition to those appointed by the States, but they shall be considered, for the purposes of the election of President and Vice President, to be electors appointed by a State; and they shall meet in the District and perform such duties as provided by the twelfth article of amendment.

Section 2. The Congress shall have power to enforce this article by appropriate legislation.

Amendment XXIV
[January 23, 1964]

Section 1. The right of citizens of the United States to vote in any primary or other election for President or Vice President, for electors for President or Vice President, or for Senator or Representative in Congress, shall not be denied or abridged by the United States or any state by reason of failure to pay any poll tax or other tax.

Section 2. The Congress shall have the power to enforce this article by appropriate legislation.

Amendment XXV
[February 19, 1967]

Section 1. In case of the removal of the President from office or of his death or resignation, the Vice President shall become President.

Section 2. Whenever there is a vacancy in the office of the Vice President, the President shall nominate a Vice President who shall take office upon confirmation by a majority vote of both Houses of Congress.

Section 3. Whenever the President transmits to the President pro tempore of the Senate and the Speaker of the House of Representatives his written declaration that he is unable to discharge the powers and duties of his office, and until he transmits to them a written declaration to the contrary, such powers and duties shall be discharged by the Vice President as Acting President.

Section 4. Whenever the Vice President and a majority of either the principal officers of the executive departments or of such other body as Congress may by law provide, transmit to the President pro tempore of the Senate and the Speaker of the House of Representatives their written declaration that the President is unable to discharge the powers and duties of his office, the Vice President shall immediately assume the powers and duties of the office as Acting President.

Thereafter, when the President transmits to the President pro tempore of the Senate and the Speaker of the House of Representatives his written declaration that no inability exists, he shall resume the powers and duties of his office unless the Vice President and a majority of either the principal officers of the executive departments or of such other body as Congress may by law provide, transmit within four days to the President pro tempore of the Senate and the Speaker of the House of Representatives their written declaration that the President is unable to discharge the powers and duties of his office. Thereupon Congress shall decide the issue, assembling within forty-eight hours for that purpose if not in session. If the Congress, within twenty-one days after receipt of the latter written declaration, or, if Congress is not in session, within twenty-one days after Congress is required to assemble, determines by two-thirds vote of both Houses that the President is unable to discharge the powers and duties of his office, the Vice President shall continue to discharge the same as Acting President; otherwise, the President shall resume the powers and duties of his office.

Amendment XXVI
[June 30, 1971]

Section 1. The right of citizens of the United States, who are eighteen years of age or older, to vote shall not be denied or abridged by the United States or any State on account of age.

Section 2. The Congress shall have the power to enforce this article by appropriate legislation.

Index

Price, John, 276
Primary elections, 161–162, 197
Production. *See* Commodity production
Profits
  in capitalist system, 82, 85, 87, 88–90
  and external diseconomies, 88
  function of, 82, 92n.3
  and managerial revolution, 124, 126
Progressives, 170, 330
Property, 76n.3, 82
  in Anglo-Saxon legal tradition, 53
  and black American, 103–104
  and capitalism, 81–85
  and Constitution, 53–57, 59, 66,
    76n.3, 78n.41, 180
  and human development, 85
  and income, 98–100, 107
  and law, 52–53
  and liberalism, 38–40, 44, 74
  and power, 99
  private/social, 342
  unequal ownership of, 99
Protestantism, and liberalism, 44
Protest movements, 204–213
  limited gains of, 213–215
Public interest movement, 331
Public opinion, molding, 166–167
Public policy, 180–183
Pure Food and Drug Act, 330

Quality of life, 95–98, 105

Reagan, Ronald, 181, 214, 225, 236,
    302
  and business, 156, 246, 296
  and Calvin Coolidge, 157n.8
  campaigns of, 163, 175–178, 178–179
  and Congress, 264
  as conservative, 16, 37
  impact of, 310
  and labor, 156, 213
  staff, 276
  style of, 243, 248n.5
Reagan administration
  and aid to cities, 202–203
  and antitrust laws, 294
  appointees, 278
  business leaders in, 138–141
  and Chile, 303
  Democratic support for, 180, 261
  deregulation by, 8–9, 10, 151,
    294–295, 331, 334n.21

and El Salvador, 264
and Freedom of Information Act, 71,
    263
fundamental changes by, 176
human rights record, 264, 312n.36
and inequality, 98, 100
and limited government, 41
and mergers, 127n.9
military budget, 299
poverty level and, 102–103
presidential advisors in, 277, 279
repression under, 71–72
and role of government, 310
social welfare cuts, 43, 289, 321, 322
staff, 277
tax law changes under, 100
war powers and, 235
welfare policy of, 321, 322, 333n.7
Recession, under capitalism, 87, 319
Reconstruction period, 196–197
"Red Raids," 67
"Red Squads," 70
Regan, Donald, 140, 276
Regan v. *Wald*, 72
Regressive tax, for Social Security, 325
Regulation of business. *See* Antitrust
    laws; Business regulation
Rent strikes, 212
Representative democracy, 24–26, 27,
    30, 317
Repression
  and capitalist disruption, 316–317
  by FBI, 77n.29
  through government harassment,
    70–72
  through legal system, 72–74
  patterning of, 67
  by private sector, 72
  violent, 69–70
Republican party, 164–165, 167–168,
    170, 175–176, 318
Responsible parties, and U.S. politics,
    180–181
Ricardo, David, 18, 44
Richardson, Elliot, 139, 249n.22, 279
Ridgeway, James, 176
Rivers and Harbors Commission, 272
Rivers and Harbors Congress, 292
Rockefeller, John D., 117, 290
Rogers, William P., 141, 275, 276, 302
Roosevelt, Franklin D., 168, 181, 225,
    235, 240–241, 299
  and business, 151